Oxford Socio-Legal Studies

Rules and Government

OXFORD SOCIO-LEGAL STUDIES

Oxford Socio-Legal Studies is a series of books exploring the role of law in society for both an academic and a wider readership. The series publishes theoretical and empirically-informed work, from the United Kingdom and elsewhere, by social scientists and lawyers which advances understanding of the social reality of law and legal processes.

RULES AND GOVERNMENT

ROBERT BALDWIN

Clarendon Press · Oxford

Oxford University Press, Great Clarendon Street, Oxford OX2 6DP
Oxford New York
Athens Auckland Bangkok Bogota Bombay
Buenos Aires Calcutta Cape Town Dar es Salaam
Delhi Florence Hong Kong Istanbul Karachi
Kuala Lumpur Madras Madrid Melbourne
Mexico City Nairobi Paris Singapore
Taipei Tokyo Toronto
and associated companies in
Berlin Ibadan

Oxford is a trade mark of Oxford University Press

Published in the United States
by Oxford University Press Inc., New York

First published 1995
First issued in paperback 1996

British Library Cataloguing in Publication Data
Data available

Library of Congress Cataloging in Publication Data
Baldwin, Robert, Dr.
Rules and government / Robert Baldwin.
p. cm.—(Oxford socio-legal studies)
1. Administrative procedure. 2. Police power.
I. Title. II. Series.
K3403.B34 1995 3429.066—dc20 [342.266] 94-45170
ISBN 0-19-825909-3
ISBN 0-19-826489-5 (Pbk.)

Printed in Great Britain
on acid-free paper by
Bookcraft (Bath) Ltd.

To Vanessa and the memory of
Ian Boothman Baldwin

Preface to Paperback Edition

In the two years since *Rules and Government* was written soft laws have neither diminished in governmental importance nor escaped attention from commentators. A number of decisions and publications have emerged and the attention of readers should be drawn to some of the most significant of these.

Of recent court decisions, mention should be made of those relating to pressure groups and their potential influence in rule-making processes (see pp. 73–4 *infra*). A newly flexible approach to standing has been demonstrated. Thus, in *R. v H.M. Inspectorate of Pollution, ex.p Greenpeace Ltd (No 2) [1994] 4 All ER 239*, Otton, J. declined to follow the *Rose Theatre* case (noted at page 73 *infra*) and decided that Greenpeace was entitled to challenge the Secretary of State's decision as to the discharge and disposal of radioactive waste at Sellafield. Stress was placed on Greenpeace's being well-qualified to make the application.

Certain individual members of Greenpeace, who lived in Cumbria, would have been directly affected by the proposed activity at Sellafield, but in a further liberalising court decision there was no set of individual members' interests to point to. In the Pergau Dam case, *R. v Secretary of State for Foreign Affairs, ex.p World Development Movement Ltd* [1995] 1 W.L.R. 386, the Divisional Court held that the WDM had sufficient interest to apply for judicial review, referring to the merits of the application; the importance of vindicating the rule of law; the importance of the issue raised; the likely absence of any other challenger; the nature of the breach of duty against which relief was sought; and the prominent role of the WDM in giving advice, guidance and assistance on these matters. There is thus growing evidence that the judges will relax the rules of standing to give pressure groups an increasing role as monitors of governmental rule and decision-making.

This approach accords with that of the Law Commission's 1994 report (Law.Com.No.226) and proposals therein that the courts, in considering standing in public interest challenges, should have regard to such factors as the importance of the legal point at issue; the chance of it being raised in other proceedings; the allocation of judicial resources; and the importance of presenting courts with the relevant conflicting points of view.

The courts have continued to scrutinise the use made of policy guidance (discussed pp. 105–6 *infra*). A recent celebrated instance involved the offering of franchises for passenger rail services and the implementation by the rail Franchising Director of the 'Objectives, Instructions and Guidance' that were issued to the Franchising Director in March 1994 by the Transport Secretary under section 5 of the Railways Act 1993. This guidance called for the minimum service levels (MSLs) stipulated in passenger rail franchises to be 'based on' former levels of British Rail provision.

In 1995, Save our Railways, a pressure group of rail unions and local authorities, successfully argued in the Court of Appeal that the Franchising Director had erred in law by setting MSLs on a number of franchises that departed substantially from those established by BR—in one instance fixing these 41 per cent below the levels of the existing BR timetable. (See *R. v Director of Passenger Rail Franchising ex part Save our Railways and Others*, Court of Appeal, 15.12.95). The effect of the Court of Appeal's ruling was to demand that the Franchising Director redraft the MSLs for the franchises at issue.

On the question of legitimate expectations, (discussed pp. 98–101 *infra*) note should be taken of the judgement in *R. v Ministry of Agriculture, Fisheries and Food ex part Hamble (Offshore) Fisheries Ltd* [1995] 2 All ER 714. Sedley, J. departed from the line taken by Laws, J. in *R. v Secretary of State for Transport ex parte Richmond-upon-Thames LBC* [1994] 1 All ER 577 and refused to accept the proposition that neither precedent nor principle went further than the enforcement of procedural expectations. Sedley, J. stated that *substantive* legitimate expectations were also worthy of protection, urging that it was difficult to see why it was less unfair to frustrate a legitimate expectation that something will or will not be done than to frustrate a legitimate expectation that one will be listened to.

The Court of Appeal has also continued to demonstrate a willingness to look at the substantive effects of regulations and to hold them ultra vires where their practical result in the undermining of statutory rights. A recent instance giving rise to much public debate was *R. v Secretary of State for Social Security ex parte Re B and Joint Council for the Welfare of Immigrants* (21.6.96). This case involved a challenge to the validity of the Social Security (Persons from Abroad) Miscellaneous Amendment Regulations 1996. These came into force on 5 February 1996 and had the effects of excluding from benefits two categories of asylum seekers: in country (as opposed to on-arrival) claimants; and all claimants pending appeal from an adverse determination of the Home Secretary. The Court of Appeal ruled that the Regulations were *ultra vires.* Simon Brown LJ regarded them as 'so uncompromisingly draconian in effect that they must indeed be held *ultra vires*'. He founded his decision on the basis that rights for asylum seekers conferred in the Asylum and Immigration Appeals Act 1993 were being overborne: 'Parliament cannot have intended a significant number of genuine asylum seekers to be impaled on the horns of so intolerable a dilemma, the need either to abandon their claims to refugee status or alternatively to maintain them as best they can but in a state of utter destitution. Primary legislation alone could in my judgement achieve that sorry state of affairs'.

The Government did, indeed, introduce primary legislation so as to reverse the effect of the Court of Appeal's decision. In the House of Lords on 1st July 1996 the Government was defeated on this issue when peers voted to change a key provision of the Asylum and Immigration Bill so as to give arriving asylum seekers three days grace instead of a single day in which to claim refugee status without losing eligibility to state benefits. On 15th July 1996, however, the House of Commons reversed that amendment so that asylum seekers will now have to lodge refugee applications on the day they arrive in Britain or else lose entitlements to welfare benefits.

Turning to the nature of rules and the connection between rule-type and regulation (see Chapters 5 and 6 *infra*), these are topics that have been discussed in a stimulating examination of the financial services sector, by Julia Black in '"Which Arrow?": Rule Type and Regulatory Policy' [1995] *Public Law* 94.

The use of economic appraisals in British regulation (see Chapter 7 *infra*) has recently been dealt with by the Deregulation Unit of the Cabinet Office in two 1996 publications entitled *Regulation in the Balance: A Guide to Regulatory Appraisal Incorporating Risk Assessment* and *Checking the Cost of Regulation: A Guide to Compliance Cost Assessment.* The first of these documents outlines how the Government has now moved beyond demanding compliance cost assessments (CCAs) for regulatory proposals that affect business towards requiring a 'Regulatory Appraisal' for all UK and EC regulatory proposals affecting business, charities and voluntary organisations. The Regulatory Appraisal goes further than the CCA by incorporating a structured assessment of the costs and benefits of regulatory options, by using risk assessments to place values on the potential benefits of regulatory options and by looking at costs, not merely to business (as formerly) but also to consumers and the Government. The movement, accordingly, is from simple CCA in the direction of cost-benefit analysis proper. On CCAs in practice see J. Froud, R. Boden, A. Ogus, and P. Stubbs, 'Toeing the Line: Compliance Cost Assessment in Britain' (1994) 4 *Policy and Politics* 24 and J. Froud and A. Ogus, '"Rational" Social Regulation and Compliance Cost Assessment' (1996) 74 *Pub. Admin.* 221.

Rules and their legitimation in the EU context are discussed in Chapter 8 *infra.* On the legitimation of supranational governance and legitimation through parliamentary processes see Markus Jachtenfuchs, 'Theoretical Perspectives on European Governance' (1995) 1 *European Law Journal* 115.

On the role of European independent agencies (discussed at pp. 267–8 *infra*) a useful review of issues is offered by Michelle Everson, 'Independent Agencies: Hierarchy Beaters?' (1995) 1 *European Law Journal* 180. For a study of a particular Euro-agency see John S. Gardner, 'The European Agency for the Evaluation of Medicines and European Regulation of Pharmaceuticals' (1996) 2 *European Law Journal* 48. On the general issue of implementing rules in the European Union—a central concern of Chapter 8 *infra*—reference should be made to Terence Daintith, 'European Community Law and the Redistribution of Regulatory Power in the United Kingdom' (1995) 1 *European Law Journal* 134 and to Terence Daintith (ed.), *Implementing EC Law in the United Kingdom* (Chichester, Wiley, 1995).

Finally, on the question of regulators and their accountability for rules, decisions or other actions, attention should be drawn to Cosmo Graham, *Is there a Crisis in Regulatory Accountability?* (Centre for the Study of Regulated Industries, 1995).

R.B.
August 1996

General Editor's Introduction

Oxford Socio-Legal Studies is already a well-established academic series of original works which examine the relationship of law and society from a variety of disciplinary perspectives. Its first three books appeared with Macmillan in 1979. In the next few years five more volumes were published under the Macmillan imprint before the series moved to Oxford University Press, where it was relaunched with four new research monographs. The University Press has now published a further twenty-two books in the series.

The appearance of three more works—Robert Baldwin's *Rules and Government*, Roger Cotterrell's book *Law's Community*, and *Wills, Inheritance and the Family* by Finch, Masson, Mason, Haynes, and Wallis—marks, however, a new beginning for this series. It will now have a wider institutional basis and will extend its range of academic interests. The existing Editorial Board has been enlarged by the addition of three further socio-legal scholars: Professor John Baldwin, Director of the Institute for Judicial Administration at the University of Birmingham, Professor William Felstiner of the University of California at Santa Barbara, and Professor Simon Roberts of the London School of Economics. With a newly-appointed International Advisory Board also in place, the series intends to be fully international in character.

A number of the existing Oxford Socio-Legal Studies have addressed governmental regulation in a variety of contexts. Robert Baldwin's new book *Rules and Government* is an important addition to the growing literature that addresses the problem of rules and regulation since its focus is not so much on the implementation of rules (nor, for that matter, on Parliamentary legislation) as on the idea of rules as a governmental tool, and particularly on the creation of different forms of regulatory regimes employing different forms of rule. The author's purpose is to weigh up the advantages and disadvantages of rules in an effort to encourage their more discerning use within government. The work is a product both of the author's longstanding theoretical interest in governmental rules and also their actual operation: indeed an important part of this book is drawn from empirical research Dr Baldwin conducted in the 1980s into the use of various forms of regulatory techniques, focusing on the work of the Factory Inspectorate in particular. His empirical analysis adds an important dimension to this book.

Dr Baldwin pursues his argument by dealing with the various types of rules employed by government, and the particular rationales for their adoption, then by assessing the familiar debate about the relationship of rules and discretion. The author also considers what he regards as 'government by circular', by which he means the tendency of government to eschew primary legislation in favour of rules classified as of a secondary or tertiary kind. Two important central chapters explore the actual use of legal rules, and the relationship of rule-type with effects observed in the regulation of occupational health and safety. The final chapters consider the validity of economic appraisals of costs and benefits in the context of a multi-valued view of rules, the European aspect of rule-making and rule-use, and alternatives to rules.

The new Oxford Socio-Legal Studies series will publish both theoretical and empirically-informed work which analyses law with the tools of social science, or explores law as a social phenomenon. The Editors are pleased that Robert Baldwin's book will be one of those to relaunch the series. It will be a significant contribution to a better understanding of governmental regulation, one that should be of interest not only to socio-legal scholars, but also to public lawyers and other students of governmental and public administration.

Keith Hawkins

Acknowledgements

This book is the result of an interest in governmental rules that has been sustained over a number of years. During that period I have worked with a series of co-authors to whom I owe a great debt. Many of the ideas that follow owe their origins to these colleagues and I express my particular gratitude to Christopher McCrudden, Keith Hawkins, Terence Daintith, and Cento Veljanovski.

My thanks also to erstwhile colleagues at the Centre for Socio-Legal Studies, Wolfson College, Oxford and former Director, Donald Harris for their support during my work in Oxford and since; to the Health and Safety Commission and Executive and the Factory Inspectorate for their assistance in my study of field enforcement. My particular thanks are offered to all the FI Inspectors who allowed me to accompany them on visits to premises.

Many academics and regulators have read drafts, suggested (or supplied) books, offered ideas, and pointed out errors—I am grateful to all who have assisted me in such ways and especially to Jill Anderson, Louise Ashon, Keir Ashton, Caroline Bradley, Inkeri Turkki, Erika Szyszczak, Daniel Bethlehem, Carol Harlow, Richard Rawlings, Joe Jacob, Damien Chalmers, Ross Cranston, Judith Freedman, Ken McGuire, Paul Fenn, Sir David Walker, and the anonymous OUP readers.

The draft manuscript was produced in the main by ball-point pen (some sections were scratched on a cave wall with a bone) and a huge debt of thanks accordingly is owed to Yanci Harper for her endless patience, good humour, and skill on the word processor. I express my gratitude also to Geraldine Tully and Pamela Hodges for their assistance to Yanci at various points, and to Stephen Rippington for his artwork.

Finally, for her support in all ways during the writing period—ranging from reading and commenting to suffering mental absences—I thank Vanessa Finch.

R.B.

Contents

Abbreviations xx

I. Rules and Governmental Processes

1. Introduction: Governing with Rules 3
2. Rule-types and Government 7
   1. The Dimensions of Rules 7
   2. The Uses of Rules 11
   3. Why Use Rules? 12
   Conclusions 15
3. Rules, Discretion, and Legitimacy 16
   I. The 'Rules versus Discretion' Approach to Process 16
      1. The Legal Paradigm 16
      2. The Legalistic Case for Rules 19
   II. Evaluating Governmental Processes 33
      1. The Search for Process Values 33
      2. Five Rationales for Legitimacy Claims 41
      3. The Nature of Legitimacy Claims 47
      4. Legitimacy and Democratic Theory 49
      Conclusions 57
4. Rules Made by Governments 59
   I. Secondary Legislation 60
      1. Justifications for Secondary Legislation 62
   II. Tertiary Rules 80
      1. Justifications for Tertiary Rules 85
      Conclusions 119

II. Regulating with Rules

5. Rules and Regulation 125
1. The Evolution of a Regulatory System: Health and Safety at Work 125
2. The Robens Report 126
3. Implementing Robens 128
4. Robens and Rules 129
5. The Design Appraised 133
6. The Robens Legacy and Agency Rule-making 139
Conclusions 140
6. Making Rules Work 142
I. Securing Compliance 143
1. Compliance-seeking and Rule-types 143
2. A 'Compliance-oriented' Approach to Rules 157
3. Compliance: Why Rule-makers Fail 159
II. Securing Results 174
1. Misformulation and Problems of Inclusiveness 175
2. The Problem of Creative Compliance 185
III. Guidelines for Rule-makers 189
1. Effectiveness and Other Values 189
Conclusions 191
7. Rules and Economic Appraisals 193
1. The Appraisal Strategy Developed 193
2. Appraisals Appraised 199
Conclusions 212

III. The European Dimension

8. Rules and the European Union 219
I. The Array of European Rules 219

1. Primary Rules 220
2. Secondary Rules 220
3. Tertiary Rules 226

II. Selecting Rules: Issues of Form and Design 230
1. Secondary Rules 231
2. Tertiary Rules 248

III. Enforcing Rules in the European Community 252
1. The Development of Health and Safety Regulation in Europe 254
2. Regulating Disparate Regimes 257
3. Assessing Evenness and Effectiveness: The Problem of Measurement 260
4. Improving the Evenness and Effectiveness of Implementation 263

IV. Assessing European Rules 271
1. The Legislative Mandate 271
2. Accountability and Control 273
3. Due Process 283
4. Expertise 285
5. Efficiency and Effectiveness 287

Conclusions 287

IV. Rules and Alternatives

9. Processes and Governmental Strategies 291

Conclusions 298

10. Conclusions 300

Appendix: Primary, Secondary and Tertiary Rules in Britain: Notes on Potential Legitimacy Claims 306

Bibliography 309

Index 325

Abbreviations

Ad.LR	Administrative Law Review
ALR	Arizona Law Review
BJCrim.	British Journal of Criminology
BJE	Bell Journal of Economics
BJSW	British Journal of Social Work
BTR	British Tax Review
BULR	Boston University Law Review
Cal.LR	California Law Review
Can.BR	Canadian Bar Review
CILJ	Cornell International Law Journal
CLJ	Cambridge Law Journal
CMLR	Common Market Law Review
Col.LR	Colombia Law Review
Crim.LR	Criminal Law Review
Duke LJ	Duke University Law Journal
ECLJ	European Community Law Journal
EJ	Economic Journal
ELR	European Law Review
G & O	Government and Opposition
GYIL	German Yearbook of International Law
Harv.LR	Harvard Law Review
IJCLLIR	International Journal of Comparative Labour Law and Industrial relations
IJSL	International Journal of Sociology of Law
IJSWFL	International Journal of Social Welfare and Family Law
Ind.LJ	Industrial Law Journal
JBL	Journal of Business Law
JCMS	Journal of Common Market Studies
JLE	Journal of Legal Education
JLS	Journal of Legal Studies
JLSoc.	Journal of Law and Society
JPE	Journal of Political Economy

JSPTL	Journal of the Society of Public Teachers of Law
JSWL	Journal of Social Work Law
LCP	Law and Contemporary Problems
LP	Law and Policy
LPQ	Law and Policy Quarterly
LQR	Law Quarterly Review
McGill LJ	McGill Law Journal
Mich.LR	Michigan Law Review
MLR	Modern Law Review
NLJ	New Law Journal
OJLS	Oxford Journal of Legal Studies
OSLJ	Ohio State Law Journal
PA	Parliamentary Affairs
Pub. Admin.	Public Administration
PAR	Public Administration Review
PL	Public Law
PP	Policy and Politics
Pol.Q.	Political Quarterly
PSJ	Policy Studies Journal
RJE	Rand Journal of Economics
Tex.LR	Texas Law Review
UCLALR	University of California Law Review
UPa.LR	University of Pennsylvania Law Review
Wis.LR	Wisconsin Law Review
Yale LJ	Yale Law Journal
YEL	Yearbook of European Law

PART I

Rules and Governmental Processes

1 Introduction: Governing with Rules

At first glance the world appears to be regulated by a host of different kinds of rule. The park by its by-laws, the city by its codes of practice, and the public corporation by its statute law. A second look, however, dispels the notion that all aspects of life are so tightly governed. Some activities are not covered by rules at all, large areas of action are unregulated, and in many fields the supposedly governing rules are bypassed, or compliance is so lacking that intended results are not achieved. Those engaged in government may proceed by means other than by the application or promulgation of rules. They may act executively or managerially, by means of decisions linked to inquiries, by consultations, mediations or arbitrations, or they may establish a variety of procedures for dealing with issues on a case-by-case basis. In some sectors, constraints on behaviour operate but not in the form of rules—thus other, perhaps political, cultural, or social systems of controlling, checking, and scrutinizing may take effect. Why different processes or controls are in operation is often not immediately explicable. 'What', one might therefore ask, 'can best be done according to rules?'

This book is concerned with rules as tools of government[1] and examines a number of central issues surrounding governmental

[1] Distinguishing governmental from non-governmental functions is of course, problematic. Here a function will be treated as governmental if it is such as to require justification by reference to democratically established institutions. That opinions may differ as to the proper province of government is no more clearly demonstrated than by the 'contracting state'—see I. Harden, *The Contracting State* (1992); J. Mayne, 'Public Power Outside Government' (1993) 64 Pol.Q. 327; N. Lewis, 'The Citizen's Charter and Next Steps: A New Way of Governing' (1993) Pol.Q. 316. On the public/private law distinction see e.g. J. Beatson, ' "Public and Private" in English Administrative Law' [1987] PL 34; P. Cane, 'Public Law and Private Law: A Study of the Analysis and Use of a Legal Concept', in J. Eekelaar and J. Bell (eds.), *Oxford Essays in Jurisprudence*, 3rd ser. (1987); Woolf LJ, 'Public Law, Private Law: Why the Divide? A Personal View' [1986] PL 220; I. Harden and N. Lewis, *The Noble Lie: The British Constitution and the Rule of Law* (1986); P. Birkinshaw, I. Harden, and N. Lewis, *Government by Moonlight: The Hybrid Parts of the State* (1990).

rule-use.[2] It does not focus on parliamentary (primary) legislation but on rules emanating from government—that is on the array of rules produced by the departments of state or other governmental agencies. The decision to focus on 'governmental' rather than parliamentary rules stems not merely from a concern to impose limits on this study but from a special interest in the problems of legitimating governmental rules—which differ from those associated with primary legislation.[3] It should be noted, nevertheless, that primary legislation is often an alternative to governmental rule-making, and that many points made in this book may be of relevance in assessing the role and use of primary rules.

Governmental rules may be divided into secondary and tertiary rules.[4] Secondary rules have legal force and are produced in exercise of a power to legislate that is conferred by an Act of Parliament. Tertiary rules do not create rights that are directly enforceable through civil or criminal proceedings, although they may produce indirect legal effects. They may, or may not, be produced in exercise of a statutory power. They are only of concern here if they emerge from official governmental sources and have written form—this distinguishes them from mere social conventions, or informal understandings and practices.

The purpose of this book is to examine the potential and

[2] I am thus not centrally concerned with such issues as the role of rules in guiding judicial decisions or the judicial interpretation of rules. On these matters see e.g. W. Twining and D. Miers, *How to Do Things With Rules*, 3rd edn. (1991); R. Dworkin, *Taking Rights Seriously* (1977); id., *A Matter of Principle* (1985); id., *Law's Empire* (1986); H. L. A. Hart, *The Concept of Law* (1961); D. J. Galligan, *Discretionary Powers* (1986); D. N. MacCormick, *Legal Reasoning and Legal Theory* (1978). For a philosophical analysis of rules see F. Schauer, *Playing By The Rules* (1991). From a public administration perspective see C. Hood, *Administrative Analysis: An Introduction to Rules, Enforcement and Organisations* (1986), and for a legal/anthropological treatment see J. L. Comaroff and S. Roberts, *Rules and Processes* (1981).

[3] For a checklist of issues of relevance in choosing between primary, secondary, and tertiary rules see the Appendix. On primary legislation see e.g. D. R. Miers and A. C. Page, *Legislation*, 2nd edn. (1990); M. Zander, *The Law-Making Process*, 4th edn. (1994); F. A. R. Bennion, *Statute Law*, 3rd edn. (1990); Hansard Society, *Making the Law Report of the Hansard Society Commission on the Legislative Process* (1992).

[4] Collectively secondary and tertiary rules have been called 'quasi-legislation'. The term 'Administrative Quasi-Legislation' was coined by R. E. Megarry (as he then was) in an article of that title (1944) 60 LQR 125: see G. Ganz, *Quasi-Legislation: Recent Developments in Secondary Legislation* (1987).

limitations of rules in order to contribute towards their more informed use within government. This, necessarily, involves considering how the 'appropriate' use of rules can be gauged.

The following chapter begins by reviewing the different kinds of rule that are encountered in government, their various qualities or 'dimensions' and the purposes to which rules may be put. The major reasons for selecting rules, or particular kinds of rule, will be outlined.

Some commentators, notably Kenneth Culp Davis,[5] have stressed that a key role for rules is the control of administrative discretion. Others have put the case for resorting to discretion in a less apprehensive manner and have suggested that the potential of rules for confining and structuring discretion can be exaggerated. The 'rules or discretion' debate is examined in Chapter 3, as are the problems of assessing governmental processes in terms of a choice between rules and discretion. Placing that debate in context demands an examination of the various problems involved in evaluating and choosing between different administrative processes. The notion of legitimacy in governmental processes is accordingly explored and it is contended that evaluating processes can be understood and carried out by making reference to a limited and identifiable set of criteria.

Chapter 4 focuses on the governmental tendency to rely not so much on primary legislation as on secondary and tertiary rules. The implications of 'government by circular' are explored and possible means of controlling the makers of less formal rules are canvassed. Judicial, administrative, and political controls over rule-making processes and the substance of rules are reviewed.

How rules are implemented and enforced is at least as important as their design and promulgation. Insufficient attention has often been paid, however, to the way that enforcers use and apply various rules, to the capacity of rules to influence enforcement activity or to the part that selection of rule-type plays in achieving results. Chapters 5 and 6 aim to

[5] K. C. Davis, *Discretionary Justice* (1971).

contribute on this front by looking at the actual enforcement of rules in a particular area—the regulation of workplace health and safety in Britain.

Chapter 5 describes how the problem of regulating workplace health and safety was seen in the 1970s and how a particular approach to rules was adopted by the committee responsible for designing the regulatory regime. The assumptions underlying that approach are examined.

Chapter 6 looks at the way rules are devised, negotiated, made, and enforced in practice. The different approaches of enforcement and of rule-making officials within the health and safety field are explored. This chapter also puts the case study in its broader context and investigates why rules often fail to work and why compliance is not always achieved in a satisfactory manner. It is argued that there are three fundamental problems facing those who employ rules, and potential responses to these problems are discussed. Finally, the chapter examines why achieving compliance may not secure desired results.

The feasibility of subjecting proposed regulatory rules to economic appraisals of their costs and benefits is the subject of Chapter 7. This discussion refers back to the analysis of Chapter 3 and asks whether the case for subjecting rules to economic appraisals can be reconciled with the view that governmental rules should aim to satisfy a number of values other than efficiency.

The European dimension to rule-making and rule-use is a matter of growing importance. Chapter 8 examines the particular difficulties that are encountered in designing and implementing governmental rules within the European Union—how (and whether), for instance, rules can be designed so as to produce consistent regulatory effects within the different legal, political, regulatory, and administrative regimes of the various Member States.

In Chapter 9 the alternatives to rules are outlined and in Chapter 10 conclusions are drawn on the choices facing rule-makers when choosing rule-types or when drafting rules.

2 Rule-types and Government

A wide variety of written rules is used within government. The list of different terms attaching to sets of rules is itself intimidating. Apart from primary legislation, a series of labels is encountered including: secondary legislation; delegated legislation; sub-delegated legislation; quasi-legislation; administrative rules; codes of practice; approved codes of practice; guidance; guidance notes; policy guidance; guidelines; circulars; framework documents; outline schemes, and statements of advice.

1. The Dimensions of Rules

A 'rule' may be defined as 'a general norm mandating or guiding conduct or action in a given type of situation'[1] and a legal rule has been said to be 'a legal precept attaching a definite detailed legal consequence to a definite detailed state of fact'.[2] The distinction between legal and non-legal rules is a problematic one and, as will be seen in Chapter 4, it is often difficult to tell what the legal consequences of a normative pronouncement are intended to be—or indeed actually are. My concern is with the array of rules that have a governmental role. Whether they are properly described as 'legal' or not is a less fruitful avenue of enquiry than is an assessment of the part they play in government. Here I bear in mind Loughlin's point: 'Public law should adopt as its principal focus the examination of the manner in which the normative structures of law can contribute to the tasks of guidance, control and evaluation in government.'[3]

Governmental rules possess a number of properties or dimensions.[4] Rule-makers, accordingly, have a number of

[1] W. Twining and D. Miers, *How to Do Things With Rules*, 3rd edn. (1991), 131.

[2] R. Pound, *Jurisprudence* (1959), ii. 124; see also G. Richardson, A. Ogus, and P. Burrows, *Policing Pollution* (1983), 21.

[3] M. Lougin, *Public Law and Political Theory* (1992), 264.

[4] On the varieties of rules see F. Schauer, *Playing By the Rules* (1991), ch. 1; Twining and Miers, *How to Do Things With Rules*, ch. 3.

variables to bear in mind when selecting rules and in assessing the appropriateness of rules for different purposes. Of special importance are the following rule dimensions:

- Legal form or status.
- Legal force or effect.
- Associated prescription or sanction.
- Specificity or precision.
- Accessibility and intelligibility.
- Scope or inclusiveness.

The *legal form* of an instrument refers to its mode of promulgation or formal legal status as for example: Statutory Instrument; by-law; Order in Council; code of practice; guidance note, or contract.[5] Such labels are indeed formal. As Gabriele Ganz has pointed out, the legal form of an instrument is quite a different thing from its legal force or effect: 'though one can distinguish formally between Acts, Statutory Instruments and other rule-making mechanisms, their legal effect can only be ascertained from statutory provisions and their judicial interpretation. There are degrees of legal force and these are not directly correlated to the procedure by which the provisions are made.'[6]

In formal terms, Statutory Instruments are readily identifiable since they are made with reference to the Statutory Instruments Act 1946. When Parliament delegates authority to legislate it does not, however, always stipulate that the relevant rules have to be set out in the form of a Statutory Instrument. Many Acts authorize ministers to make legislative rules but do not specify the form of promulgation, hence administrative rules such as circulars may possess legal force in spite of their lack of formal status as Statutory Instruments. In such cases the rules will derive their force not from their form but from a clear statutory delegation of authority. A mass of other informal rules, written and unwritten, infuses the governmental process and, apart from having practical significance, some of these may carry legal consequences as a result of judicial deci-

[5] For an extended discussion of government by contract and the nature of such contracts see I. Harden, *The Contracting State* (1992), esp. ch. 5.

[6] G. Ganz, *Quasi-Legislation* (1987), 6.

sions. As Harden has pointed out, many of the agreements now employed within 'the contracting state' take a legal form normally associated with private contracts but in reality fulfil public functions.[7] The legal form of a rule is only of limited help as an indication of its legal effect or governmental role.

Turning, then, to the *legal force or effect* of different rules, we again meet with impressive diversity. A rule may attach identifiable legal consequences to a precisely defined set of affairs—as is common, for example, with a provision in a criminal statute. On the other hand, the rule may merely offer guidelines on the interpretation of a statute or on the meaning of standards or duties incorporated in other legal rules. Thus a breach of the Highway Code does not constitute a criminal offence but in civil or criminal proceedings 'may be relied upon by any party to the proceedings as tending to establish or negative any liability . . .'.[8]

Similarly, the codes made under the Police and Criminal Evidence Act 1984 establish no direct civil or criminal liabilities but, if relevant, must be taken into account by courts if legal liability, as provided for under other rules, is at issue.[9]

A variation on the interpretative or evidentiary effect of rules is offered in the Health and Safety at Work Act 1974. Failure to comply with a code provision that is relevant to an offence established under the Act allows a court to take the offence as proved 'unless the court is satisfied that the requirement or prohibition was . . . complied with otherwise than by way of observance of the code'.[10]

Even informal rules may be given legal effects by the courts. Thus the judiciary, through application of the concepts of fairness and natural justice and by means of the notion of legitimate expectations, have indicated that those who publish rules or profess to follow them may not be free to depart from those rules without following certain procedures.[11]

[7] See Harden, *The Contracting State*, ch. 5.

[8] See e.g. The Road Traffic Act 1988, s. 38(7).

[9] See Police and Criminal Evidence Act 1984, s. 67.

[10] Health and Safety at Work Act 1974, s. 17(2), see also the Control of Pollution Act 1974, s. 72(6), and Ganz, *Quasi-Legislation*, 8–20.

[11] See R. Baldwin and D. Horne, 'Expectations in a Joyless Landscape' (1986) 49 MLR 685 and ch. 4 *infra*.

Closely related to the legal force or effect of a rule is another aspect: the *prescription or sanction* involved. In the civil law field a principal effect of rules is the allocation of rights and liabilities, but in the criminal and regulatory area two different approaches are taken. Rules based on the prescriptive model involve instruction plus some kind of sanction. This may be direct, as with criminal imprisonment and fines, or it may be indirect where, for example, an enforcement official is given a discretion to apply an administrative sanction or order, failure to comply with which may involve an offence.[12] In contrast, commendatory or enabling rules are used so as to organize, enable, or recommend a course of action. Failure to follow such advice will not necessarily involve direct or indirect legal liability. Thus the Health and Safety Executive uses Guidance Notes to advise on the attainment of hazard-reducing objectives and such notes deal with issues beyond the area of legal sanction.

Whatever the status, force, or sanction associated with a rule, it may possess a series of other dimensions reflecting its style of drafting. The first of these is the degree of *specificity or precision* with which it is formulated.[13] A rule on the safety of ladders may, for example, set down lists of figures, dimensions, strengths, and materials or it may use less precise terms, referring perhaps to 'reasonably strong and durable' types of ladder. Whether the rule-maker opts for one style of drafting or another may depend on a number of factors that will be returned to below in Chapter 6.

A further issue has to be considered by those designing rules—that is the *accessibility and intelligibility* of the rule.[14] Rules may be highly accessible in the physical sense (being, for example, widely available and inexpensive) or they may be costly and difficult to obtain. They may be readily intelligible in so far as they are phrased in concise everyday language or

[12] As e.g. with Improvement and Prohibition notices made under ss. 21 and 22 of the Health and Safety at Work Act 1974—see *infra*, ch. 6.

[13] See esp. C. S. Diver, 'The Optimal Precision of Administrative Rules' (1983) 93 Yale LJ 65; C. Hood, *Administrative Analysis* (1986). 36–42.

[14] See Hood, *Administrative Analysis*, 24–6 on 'knowability' and Diver, 'Optimal Precision', on accessibility.

they may be highly technical and couched in specialized jargon. The sheer length and lack of organization of a set of rules may present intelligibility problems for some of those using the rules or affected by them. Finally, rules or sets of rules vary in their *scope or inclusiveness*. Thus a statute or a code of practice may set out to govern merely the central aspects of an activity or it may attempt to control all facets, including matters of fine detail. It may apply only to take very worst examples of behaviour or, by incorporating very high standards may regulate a far broader range of activities and actors—again the rule-maker or designer is presented with strategic choices.

2. The Uses of Rules

Rules thus vary enormously according to legal form and effect, type of sanction or prescription and form of drafting. Governments also use rules in a wide variety of ways. We have already noted that certain rules (for example codes) can be used to supplement statutes by offering interpretative guidance or evidence as to the meaning of statutory standards. To instruct officials on substantive matters is another major role of governmental rules. The aim of such rules is usually to impose internal order so as to facilitate planning or to encourage consistency.[15]

Enabling rules also have a role in the organization and management of governmental activity. Thus, many rules have considerable impact by 'consisting of arrangements made by administrative bodies which affect the operation of the law between one subject and another'.[16] An example of such a managerial rule would be a departmental or agency policy statement on enforcement practice. Closely related are those rules that offer extra-statutory concessions. Thus the Commissioners for Inland Revenue will sometimes refine their application of the law by using such concessions (in exercise of what Ganz terms a 'dispensing power') and may rely on these

[15] See J. Bradshaw, 'From Discretion to Rules: The Experience of the Family Fund', in M. Alder and S. Asquith (eds.), *Discretion and Welfare* (1969).

[16] See R. E. Megarry, 'Administrative Quasi-Legislation' (1944) 60 LQR 125.

in arguing for a particular interpretation of a statute.[17] More dramatically, the rules of 'public' contracts can be used to allocate governmental functions to agencies, independent bodies and private concerns. Restructuring of the administration can thus be effected as with the 'Next Steps' programme and the marketization of public services seen in the 1980s.[18]

Governmental activity may, furthermore, be organized by setting down rules governing the procedures to be followed by the public and by officials. Thus, bodies engaged in the distribution of benefits or items of governmental largesse, or involved in disciplinary activity, commonly publish documents describing the procedures to be adopted by themselves or affected parties.

Particularly in the field of regulation, a significant governmental role of rules is the furtherance of various compliance-seeking strategies. Thus rules may be used so as to facilitate the prosecution of offenders in court or to educate individuals or to inform the public. Similarly, rules can be used to promote governmental aims more broadly—for example so as to encourage the taking of precautions to avoid energy wastage. Rules may serve as bases for negotiation (as, for example, between enforcing inspectors and potential hazard-creators) or as guidance and objectives for schemes of self-regulation. It will be seen in Chapter 6 that the kinds of rule that are appropriate for engaging in different tasks will vary.

3. Why Use Rules?

A number of supposed advantages have been associated with the use of rules.[19] These 'technical' rationales for rule-use may not prove convincing in all or many applications—as will

[17] See Ganz, *Quasi-Legislation*, 20–1.

[18] See N. Lewis, 'The Citizen's Charter and Next Steps: A New Way of Governing' (1993) Pol.Q. 316; C. Hood 'A Public Management for All Seasons' (1991) 69 PA 3; Prime Minister's Efficiency Unit, *Improving Management in Government: The Next Steps* (1988).

[19] For a useful review see e.g. C. E. Schneider, 'Discretion and Rules: A Lawyer's View' in K. Hawkins (ed.), *The Uses of Discretion* (1992). See also Schauer, *Playing By the Rules*, ch. 7; Hood, *Administrative Analysis*, 17–19; Twining and Miers, *How to do Things With Rules*, 159–71; J. L. Jowell, *Law and Bureaucracy* (1975), ch. 1.

become clear in this book—but they should be noted. According to a key rationale, rules allow accumulated experience and wisdom to be distilled and used efficiently. Cases can accordingly be decided in the light of that experience rather than on the spot—with reflective detachment rather than in the heat of the moment.[20] The effect of using rules is thus to place each decision in the broader context, allowing the longer view to be taken and incorporating more resources and evidence into the process of decision-making.[21] A second rationale is that rules supposedly encourage consistency, fairness, and equality of treatment across not simply persons, groups, organizations, or regions but also across time. Thus an application for a licence is often thought more likely to be treated in a manner both consistent with past practice and conducive to continuity of policy if a rule has been formulated and has been used to guide the relevant decisions. Third, rules are often considered useful in setting down the criteria that are appropriate in deciding a particular issue and in outlining relevant policies. They therefore serve a role in discouraging resort to irrelevant factors. This reduces the number of mistakes encountered in a decision- or policy-making process. An administrative advantage also ensues—rules not only mean that settled policies do not require reinvestigation in each case but they allow staff of relatively low training levels to process highly complex issues. Fourth, rules may be held to contribute to the perceived legitimacy of decisions by allowing those involved to cite the rule as a justification for action.

A fifth, oft-cited, reason for using rules lies in their perceived ability to limit the discretion of officials, thus reducing the danger that corruption or bias will enter into the decision-making process. The likelihood that the decision-maker will be 'captured' by affected parties may also be thought to be reduced

[20] Assuming, of course, that there is no interpretative behaviour involved in making sense of the rule or in deciding what it means, whether it applies, etc. On the problematic nature of such assumptions see K. Hawkins, 'The Use of Legal Discretion: Perspectives from Law and Social Science', in Hawkins (ed.), *The Uses of Discretion.*

[21] See J. Raz, *Practical Reason and Norms* (1975), 59, quoted in Twining and Miers, *How to Do Things With Rules*, 11.

by rule-use.[22] The process of drafting a rule allows a wide spectrum of opinion and expertise to be gathered and this may be said to bring a sixth advantage—that of producing a better, more effective rule. In political terms there is an associated benefit yielded in so far as the use of a rule allows greater public involvement than is usually provided for with the mere making of a decision. This might be termed a 'participatory benefit' to be valued in a liberal democracy. Whereas a decision may come to the notice of a small number of interested parties, a published rule will gain the attention of a broader spectrum of the population and is thus in a better position both to influence behaviour and provide a basis for comment.[23]

Governments may, with due propriety, seek to utilize all such 'technical' advantages of rules. There are, however, other reasons for using rules and these may be more closely related to the political interests of the government than to the public interest. Many of the supposed advantages of rules may, indeed, be seen to possess a darker side. Thus, governments may publish rules not so much in order to achieve results as to give the appearance of taking positive action. In reality, the rule may be inappropriate, ineffective, or poorly enforced. A rule may enhance legitimacy and consistency but it may also serve quite readily as a cover for unflinching policy beliefs or as a device that bureaucrats may use in deflecting individual or collective entreaties.[24] The rule may not so much offer consistency as a way to 'routinize' and rationalize decisions—its major result may be to limit the attention that is paid to the circumstances of the particular case. The overall effect of a rule may, indeed, be to make it more difficult than otherwise to challenge policies and thus to entrench rather than to throw light on those policies. Rules, in short, cannot be assumed to be either efficient or benign.

[22] On capture as excessive influence by the regulated over the regulator see P. J. Quirk, *Industry Influence in Federal Regulatory Agencies* (1981); for a review of different capture theories see B. M. Mitnick, *The Political Economy of Regulation* (1980) chs. 2 and 3; on rules and discretion see ch. 3 *infra*.

[23] See also D. J. Galligan, 'The Nature and Function of Policies within Discretionary Power' [1976] PL 332.

[24] See J. L. Jowell, *Law and Bureaucracy* (1975), 20–1.

Conclusions

Judging when it is appropriate to employ rules within government involves complex questions of design and strategy. Potential rule-users have at their disposal a host of different rule-types and they may seek to use rules for a variety of purposes and in association with a number of governmental strategies. Decisions have to be made concerning the case for a particular type of rule used in a particular way as against the case for alternative processes or alternative types of rule or modes of rule use. Such decisions in turn demand that the benchmarks for evaluating 'good' governmental processes be disclosed. A major concern of the chapters that follow is to identify such benchmarks and the conditions under which rules, of different types and employed in different ways, may enhance rather than detract from the quality of governmental processes.

3 Rules, Discretion, and Legitimacy

Rules have often been advocated as a means of controlling governmental discretions.[1] Indeed, when discussing how a governmental activity should be carried out there is a strong temptation (especially for lawyers) to ask: 'Should this activity be governed by rules or discretion?' Assessing governmental processes involves, however, far broader issues than are encompassed in the 'rules versus discretion' debate. The operation of government gives rise to a host of questions concerning the exercise of power and the acceptability of various means to control or facilitate the exercise of that power.

Using governmental rules is one way of controlling or executing governmental functions but it is by no means the only one. Alternative controls include accountability to variously constituted bodies; scrutiny, complaints, and inspection systems; arrangements to ensure openness (such as requirements to publish performance indicators and statistics) and schemes for giving effect to consumer's views. Alternative executive devices include arbitrations, managerial decisions, inquiries, adjudications, contracts, and negotiations.[2] The notion of discretion is, moreover, unduly narrow if seen only in the context of rules. As Keith Hawkins has pointed out, lawyers may see discretion as constrained only by legal rules but social scientists are likely to see discretion as shaped also by political, economic, social, and organizational forces outside the legal structure.[3] The relationship between rules and discretions, may, of course, often be so close as to constitute a blending. Discretion suffuses the interpretation and application of rules (as in the processes of defining the meaning, relevance, and scope of

[1] Notably by K. C. Davis in *Discretionary Justice* (1971).

[2] Primary legislation is a further option not to be overlooked. On the variety of governmental modes of control and execution see generally C. Hood, *The Tools of Government* (1983).

[3] K. Hawkins, 'The Use of Legal Discretion: Perspectives from Law and Social Science', in K. Hawkins (ed.), *The Uses of Discretion* (1992).

rules). Similarly the nature and quality of rules will often bear on the kind of discretion encountered.[4] This is not to imply that rules, rather than other factors or processes, are the primary influences on discretions and to make this point is quite consistent with holding that discretion can be seen in the context of processes and constraints other than rules.

In asking whether, when, and how rules may best contribute to good government, it is necessary to bear in mind the potential of controlling or enabling devices other than rules and to explore the array of values potentially served by different governmental processes. The alternatives to rules will be returned to in Chapter 9. The present chapter seeks, first, to make clear the limited set of values and vision of government that is reflected in the 'rules versus discretion' approach to processes and, second, to outline a basis for judging appropriateness in governmental processes—that is for assessing the legitimacy of those processes. I will argue that assessing the legitimacy of governmental processes involves asking whether they further certain identifiable values.

I. THE 'RULES VERSUS DISCRETION' APPROACH TO PROCESS

1. The Legal Paradigm

The stereotypical 'lawyers' view' of the world is one built on a particular set of approaches and values. It generally favours the regulation of human activity by means of clear, previously announced rules.[5] As Nicola Lacey has argued:

> Problems are typically seen as arising from ambiguities or 'gaps' in the rules, calling for clearer interpretation or further legislative or

[4] On different approaches to discretion see Hawkins, 'The Use of Legal Discretion', and Galligan, *Discretionary Powers* (1986), chs. 1 and 2.

[5] On discretion generally see Galligan, *Discretionary Powers*; Hawkins (ed.) *The Uses of Discretion*; Davis, *Discretionary Justice*; M. Shapiro 'Administrative Discretion: The Next Stage' (1983) 92 Yale LJ 1487; G. Bryner, *Bureaucratic Discretion* (1987); R. Dworkin, *Taking Rights Seriously* (1977); M. Adler and S. Asquith (eds.), *Discretion and Welfare* (1981).

quasi-legislative action. Disputes are seen as calling for resolution on the basis of the given rules and according to standards of due process. This approach is closely associated with the ideal of the 'rule of law' and hence with liberalism as a doctrine of political morality.[6]

The paradigm, of course, gives rise to difficulties in areas where governance by rules is inappropriate or cannot be arrived at, but a slowness to recognize the existence of such areas is an inescapable aspect of the paradigm. Owing much to Dicey's concept of the rule of law, the approach is eager to build processes around the courts and to protect individuals' procedural rights. The concept of collective rights, of public policy issues is alien.[7] A model of justice built on fairness to individuals looms sufficiently large to obscure such values as efficiency in the public interest, since it focuses on procedures and, instead of a concern for substantive results, there is, as Lacey notes: 'faith in the idea that openness, rationality, generality and predictability (values centrally located in the rule of law ideal) will conduce to fairness.'[8] It has been argued, notably by Jeffrey Jowell,[9] that in spite of its well-known deficiencies, the rule of law nevertheless provides 'a principle which requires feasible limits on official power'.[10] This argument is not, however, without dangers. If the notion of the rule of law is treated as useful in pointing to certain values that are relevant in assessing governmental processes, this is relatively unproblematic. Much remains, however, to be said about the other values to be served by such processes and how 'rule of law' values relate to these—hence Jowell comments: 'The scope of the Rule of Law is large, but not, however, large enough to serve as a principle upholding a number of other requirements of a democracy.'[11]

[6] N. Lacey, 'The Jurisprudence of Discretion: Escaping the Legal Paradigm' in Hawkins (ed.), *The Uses of Discretion*, 362.

[7] See J. W. P. B. McAuslan, 'Administrative Law, Collective Consumption and Judicial Policy' (1983) 46 MLR 1. On the 'traditional' view of public law and Dicey see P. Craig, 'Dicey: Unitary, Self-correcting Democracy and Public Law' (1990) 106 LQR 105.

[8] Lacey, 'The Jurisprudence of Discretion', 369.

[9] J. Jowell, 'The Rule of Law Today', in J. Jowell and D. Oliver (eds) *The Changing Constitution*, 3rd edn. (1994).

[10] Ibid. 78.

[11] Ibid. 76.

If, however, centrality is given to the notion of the rule of law so that it becomes a focal point or a principal bench-mark for assessing processes then it may well be countered that the 'rule of law' vision constitutes a view of the world through legalistic eyes and a distorting perspective.

To see the world as essentially governable by rules leads naturally to the 'rules versus discretion' approach; it moreover encourages an understating of the drawbacks of rules and an exaggeration of their virtues. Such a vision tends to evaluate administrative procedures according to standards designed to ensure a fair trial and it leads to a neglect of non-lawyerly ways of seeing and evaluating governmental processes.[12] As a result, lawyerly critiques of governmental modes of operation tend to produce calls for more rules, more trial-type processes—in short, more of the trimmings of formal justice. The failings of a particular governmental process may be fundamental and may require substantial rethinking of such matters as broad governmental strategy, schemes of accountability, scrutiny procedures, organizational frameworks, and goals. To respond according to the prescriptions implicit in the legal paradigm may not prove merely obfuscatory, but, as shall be seen below, counter-productive.

These points can be underscored in relation to rules by examining the 'legalistic' case for rule-making as put forward by Kenneth Culp Davis.

2. The Legalistic Case for Rules

In his highly influential book *Discretionary Justice*[13] Davis argued that the greatest need and hope for improving justice for individuals in the governmental and legal system lay in the area where decisions depended more upon discretion than upon

[12] Lacey, 'The Jurisprudence of Discretion', 372. On why aiming to control discretion is 'unacceptable' as a route to 'sound government' see C. J. Edley, *Administrative Law: Rethinking Judicial Control of Bureaucracy* (1990), 217–21.

[13] (1971) Illinois. See the critiques by Lacey, 'The Jurisprudence of Discretion', and R. Baldwin and K. Hawkins, 'Discretionary Justice: Davis Reconsidered' [1984] PL 570. I am grateful to Keith Hawkins for allowing me to deploy here a number of points that owe their origins to him.

rules and principles, and where formal hearings and judicial review were mostly irrelevant.[14] The goal, he said, should be to eliminate unnecessary discretionary power in government, not to eliminate all discretionary power.[15] To this end, he argued that three techniques might profitably be employed: confining discretion by fixing its boundaries with statutory or administrative standards; structuring discretion by using rules and policy statements to control the manner of its exercise; and checking its use by having one official monitor another 'as a protection against arbitrariness'.[16] The way forward was not to improve the use of statutory standards but lay in 'earlier and more elaborate administrative rule-making and in better structuring and checking of discretionary power'.[17]

Davis freely conceded the need for discretion in a governmental of laws and men. Indeed, he criticized the 'extravagant version of the rule of law'[18] that had no place for discretion: 'The answer is in broad terms that we should eliminate much unnecessary discretionary power . . . The goal is not the maximum degree of confining, structuring and checking; the goal is to find the optimum degree for each power in each set of circumstances.'[19]

In cases of doubt, however, Davis was not disposed in favour of discretion. He argued that 90 per cent of injustice in administration flowed from discretionary activity and that: 'In a government of men and laws, the portion that is a government of men, like a malignant cancer, often tends to stifle the portion that is a government of laws.'[20]

In spite of Davis's assertions about the indispensability of discretion for the individuation of justice, the use of such language portrayed discretion as a corrupting force, a nasty growth that eroded the basis of 'justice'[21] Thus Davis commented: 'Our governmental and legal systems are saturated with excessive discretionary power which needs to be confined, structured and checked.' His central concern was to do what could be done 'to minimise discretionary power'. As Judge

[14] Davis, *Discretionary Justice*, 216.
[15] Ibid. 217.
[16] Ibid. 142.
[17] Ibid. 219.
[18] Ibid. 28–44.
[19] Ibid. 3–4.
[20] Ibid. 25.
[21] Ibid. 27.

Henry Friendly put it: 'Discretionary justice thus begins to look suspiciously like non-discretionary justice.'[22]

Davis directed attention to the less rule-governed areas of government and he did much to encourage the growth of governmental rule-making. His prescriptions for the use of rules were, however, legalistic and it is necessary to bear in mind the limitations of Davis's thesis when analysing governmental rule use. Five main difficulties can be identified.

(i) Davis's concept of justice

Davis' yardstick for evaluating governmental procedures—that of 'justice'—is highly legalistic. We might ask why this should provide the basis for assessing the acceptability of governmental activities and processes. Davis, after all, focuses not on social justice or policy-making but states his concern to be: 'that portion of discretionary power which pertains to justice, and with that portion of justice which pertains to individual parties'.[23]

It is this concern with individualistic justice that slants his account and restricts its wider applicability. His focus is on decisions that are made by individuals rather than by organizations or groups and on discretion that affects private citizens and not, say, sectors of the population. Attention is directed to the exercise of discretion in the handling and disposal of cases rather than to the ways in which choices are made about policy. There emerges a concept of administrative justice that plays down policy considerations and makes it easy both to focus attention on those demands typically made of administrators by subscribers to the legal paradigm (fairness, openness, predictability, etc.) and to minimize the importance in public decision-making of such factors as efficiency, adaptability, and the furtherance of public rather than private interests.

Such narrowness overlooks the substantial policy-making discretions that legislatures often give to administrative officials in order to deal with the subtleties and uncertainties of individual

[22] H. J. Friendly, 'Judicial Control of Administrative Action' (1970) 23 JLE 63, 65.

[23] Davis, *Discretionary Justice*, 5–6; see A. W. Bradley, 'Research and Reform in Administrative Law' (1974) 13 JSPTL 35.

regulatory problems. Thus commentators have questioned an approach to administrative law that is preoccupied with individuals rather than policies addressing collective issues.[24]

It would thus be a mistake to think that any governmental procedure can be improved by adding ever more legalistic trimmings and accessories (the 'Escort XR3i' approach to processes). Davis's thesis, however, almost boils down to a simple plea for greater openness in government. Thus, in one article,[25] Davis reduced his whole position to the twelve-word slogan: 'As far as feasible—open standards, open findings, open reasons, open precedents.' This might be an attractive proposition on its face but it is too simple—as indeed is the notion that 'justice' is an agreed, unproblematic, apolitical benchmark. Within the same bureaucracy a number of different notions of justice may exist and there may be found within any group of parties affected by a decision-maker some very different conceptions of 'justice'. Thus, for example, when considering the decision of a body that distributes air transport licences, a large airline may consider that a 'just' system is one that is judicialized, rational, based on published rules, mindful of the *status quo*, and amenable to low-risk planning (one, incidentally, that constitutes a formidable barrier to new entrants to the industry). A newer, smaller, more aggressive operator who benefits from some disturbance of the *status quo* may consider a just regime to be one that is fast-reacting, not necessarily based on slowly-developing rules, open to innovation, and rewarding of enterprise.

(ii) Rules and the Pursuit of Justice

A legalistic approach to rules does not merely operate with narrow bench-marks for evaluating processes, it tends also to

[24] Patrick McAuslan has said: '[Administrative Law] has, even where collective agencies of grievance-handling have been created, concentrated overwhelmingly on refining, elaborating, extending and discussing remedies for individuals against the administration. The [administrative processes of collective consumption] have developed a multitude of agencies, processes and systems for deciding upon policies and allocating resources between the different programmes of collective consumption where the law is facilitative rather then regulatory . . .'. See P. McAuslan, 'Administrative Law, Collective Consumption and Judicial Policy' (1983) 46 MLR 1.

[25] K. C. Davis, 'An Approach to Legal Control of the Police' (1974) 52 Tex. LR 703.

exaggerate the potential of rules. A second major difficulty with the Davis thesis on rules is the view that to subject discretion to open rules, policy statements, and so on will generally push matters in the direction of 'justice'.[26] In fact, rules will often simply fail to work. As Albert J. Reiss Jr. has pointed out[27] rules may frequently be used by bureaucracies to circumvent the interests of individuals. Nor is it clear that 'unjust' or 'arbitrary' action necessarily occurs when discretion is unstructured by rules. Attempts to regulate with rules may in some circumstances lead to more, rather than less of the mischief to be avoided. An example is provided by Susan Long's analysis of US tax laws (a body of legislation whose detailed drafting Davis admired). Long found that the very complexity of such detailed provisions did not decrease but increased the agency's effective discretion: 'Varying fact patterns present in individual tax situations make determining the "correct" tax a matter of judgment on which opinions differ even among experts . . . Complexity itself adds to the potential for tax violations. Today . . . it is difficult to speak of a correct return.'[28]

It is thus not clear whether structuring with rules *will* reduce discretion at all. Administrators who can choose *which* rule to apply or who can make a new rule on the spot can hardly be taken to be strictly constrained by existing rules. For Davis the only course is to advocate 'the right mix of rule and discretion'[29] in relation to each individual action. He gives little help, however, in describing how the 'optimum' level of control over discretion may be recognized or arrived at. He repeats that the general objective should be to go 'as far as is feasible in making rules to confine and guide discretion in individual cases'[30] but states in a footnote: 'Unfortunately, how far is feasible, is a question that must be determined for each discretionary power in each particular context.'[31]

[26] Davis, *Discretionary Justice*, 226–7.

[27] Book Review of *Discretionary Justice* (1990) 68 Mich. LR 794.

[28] S. B. Long, 'Social Control: The Civil Law: The Case of Income Tax Enforcement', in H. L. Ross (ed.), *Law and Deviance* (1981), 206–7.

[29] K. C. Davis, 'An Approach to Legal Control of the Police' (1974) 52 Tex. LR 703, 706.

[30] Davis, *Discretionary Justice*, 221.

[31] Ibid.. 221 n. 15.

For rule-users, however, the issue of feasibility is central. How to decide what is and what is not feasible is the crucial question but on this point Davis's reader may feel stranded.

It may even be rash to assume that an activity involves such a degree of recurrence of factual considerations as to make it governable by rules at all. Daniel Gifford[32] has argued that what is wrong with the Davis thesis in the regulatory context is the idea that the needed narrowing of discretion will come from rules, standards, and precedents which gradually emerge as an agency acquires information through repetition of the decisional process itself.

Gifford contends that such an approach assumes that factual considerations recur. In real life, he suggests, many issues bear little in common with previous events. Thus, Davis's notion of agency decision-making differs from that of, say Sharfman,[33] historian of the Interstate Commerce Commission, who emphasizes not standards or rules in decisions but the non-repetitious caseload of the agency and its *ad hoc* or 'managerial' mode of decision-making. Gifford seems to be on firm ground in concluding that both the ability to develop standards or rules and their worth in controlling regulatory activity will be a function of, *inter alia*, the degree of recurrence of issues and the value of precedents in resolving cases under decision.

(iii) The Nature of Decision-making

A legalistic conception of decision-making underplays the complexity of decisions and tends to see the 'decision' as existing at a particular point in the administrative process, as an isolated event logically separable from its surroundings.[34] This conception in turn produces a particular rule-centred view about the control of discretionary powers. Decisions, in short, are seen as simple, discrete, and unproblematic as opposed to complex, subtle, and woven into a broader process.

[32] D. J. Gifford, 'Decisions, Decisional Referents and Administrative Justice' (1972) 37 LCP 3.

[33] I. L. Sharfman, *The Interstate Commerce Commission* (1931).

[34] On discretion in making legal decisions see (1986) 43/4, *Washington and Lee Law Review* and articles by K. Hawkins, D. R. Novack, E. Kimbrough, J. M. Thomas, and P. K. Manning; see also K. Hawkins and J. M. Thomas (eds.) *Making Regulatory Policy* (1989).

An examination of parole decision-making demonstrates the point. The 'decision' of a parole board is typically treated within the legalistic paradigm as a choice by an individual or panel based on 'factors' or 'criteria'.[35] This mechanistic analysis, however, little reflects decision-making as a continuing process, as a subtle and shifting affair that is the result of substantial human interpretative work. Such an approach pays too little attention to the problematic nature of the information upon which the decision is based, to the judgements involved in defining issues as relevant and to the ways in which cases or policies proceed through the organizational handling system. 'Facts of the case' are thus treated as some taken-for-granted reality rather than as the results of complex processes in which reality is socially constructed and reconstructed. In contrast with such a mechanical approach, 'decisions' can be seen as involving interpretations of reality, as reflecting the moral or ideological stances of various participants in a process, and as the products of a whole series of frameworks within which the decision-makers work: symbolic, socio-political, economic and organizational.

A product of the mechanical view of decisions is the idea that much discretionary behaviour tends to be 'arbitrary' or 'capricious'—it is then easy to assume that if a decision is not rule-governed it must be free from all constraints and explanations. It is necessary, however, to question how 'disparity' is assessed. Close investigation often reveals that a patterned, rational process is at work even in those kinds of decision (like parole or sentencing judgments) that are readily characterized by lawyers as exercises of 'unfettered' discretions. Some commentators have for this reason gone so far as to argue that aggregate patterns of 'discretionary' behaviour are usually so clear that discretion, in the sense of an individualized decision on the merits, is in fact a 'myth'.[36] What can at least be argued with conviction is that it is the narrow legalistic

[35] See K. Hawkins, 'On Legal Decisionmaking' (1989) 4 *Washington and Lee Law Review* (1989) 1161.

[36] See M. P. Baumgartner, 'The Myth of Discretion', in K. Hawkins (ed.), *The Uses of Discretion.*

conception of 'decision' upon which many accusations of capriciousness are founded and that it is this narrow conception that implies that the answer lies in structuring with rules.

A further consequence of the 'discrete' notion of decisions is the belief that, since discretionary power exists at a particular point in the legal or administrative process, it can be controlled effectively by attention at that one point. In fact, discretion often so permeates a process that such simple controls are rarely feasible.[37] To structure or confine discretion at one point without attention to the shaping of that discretion often leads to the phenomenon of displacement. Squeeze in one place and, like a tube of toothpaste, discretion will bulge at another. Thus sentencing and parole practice in California was revised in the mid-1970s following concern at the use of discretion by the Adult Authority (the State's administrative sentencing and parole board). The response was to remove all post-conviction discretion to fix or change prison terms. In addition, the legislature rejected a discretionary sentencing model in favour of determinate sentences fixed by statute. The result of such changes was not, however, to eliminate discretion but to displace it. Since convictions for particular offences were tied to defined sentences, and since pre-trial plea and conviction bargaining continued unabated, this meant that real authority to fix sentences of imprisonment was effectively transferred to prosecutors—unaccountable officials doing their work by (highly discretionary) bargaining in private. Thus, even in a case where confining or structuring is 'feasible', it may (within Davis's own terms) have adverse consequences.

(iv) Rules, Rights, and Protections

A further difficulty inherent in the legalistic approach lies in its assumption that making rules to foster openness and give rights to individuals will actually improve the position of those individuals. In practice, the introduction of lawyers and rights may not only fail to eradicate discretion but it may prejudice the very people that it is supposed to benefit. Thus it has been

[37] On the selective enforcement of even clear-cut rules see Jowell, 'The Rule of Law Today'.

argued that to legalize welfare decision-making may not benefit recipients if they have to go through the process of hiring and instructing lawyers and have to endure the vastly increased decision-making times that are likely to result.[38] On this point Davis himself argues that the way to improve welfare administration is not to increase emphasis on adjudicative rights but to improve informal procedures. The real point, however, is that administrative formalization of procedure can no more be assumed to improve the recipient's position than can resort to 'lawyers' ' law in the courts. If the key defect of legal rules in this field is, as Titmuss argued,[39] their slowness to respond to rapidly changing human needs and circumstances, it cannot be taken for granted that administrative rules will prove more responsive.

Procedural justice, moreover, cannot be taken as ensuring substantive justice. Procedures can be made more open to the point of inefficiency—thus two farmers may dispute shares in a fruit crop by an open, fair, and lengthy procedure while the fruit rots. Not only that, but procedural concessions may be used to disguise poor substantive rights.[40] Without proper regulation, rule-making procedures may lead to as much 'injustice' as adjudication—for example by allowing poorly trained staff to administer a complex scheme for the purposes of bureaucratic convenience,[41] or by excluding small or poorly organized groups from rule-making in favour of larger and more powerful groups.[42] Thus Jeffrey Jowell has pointed out that administrators under certain conditions use rules as 'shields' to allow decisions to be routinized, reasons for any findings to be produced with ease, and decision-makers to be both insulated from political pressures and lent authority for any particular exercise of power.[43]

Even within the legal paradigm there are circumstances in

[38] See R.M. Titmuss, 'Welfare "Rights" Law and Discretion' (1971) 42 Pol.Q. 113; J. L. Jowell *Law and Bureaucracy* (1975); cf. C. Reich, 'Individual Rights and Social Welfare: The Emerging Legal Issues' (1965) 74 Yale LJ 1245.

[39] R. M. Titmuss, 'Welfare "Rights" ', 124.

[40] See A. Adler and S. Asquith (eds.), *Discretion and Welfare*, 16–18 and 169–70.

[41] See T. Prosser 'The Politics of Discretion', in Alder and Asquith, ibid.

[42] See B. A. Hepple, book review of *Discretionary Justice* [1969] CLJ 313.

[43] Jowell, *Law and Bureaucracy*, 20–1.

which it may be 'better' for an administrative body to resist the temptation to make rules and, instead, to rely on adjudicative processes. Thus, where decisions are taken in conditions of rapid (perhaps economic) change, then to purport to decide on the basis of rules that are outdated may help no one. Policy-making by trial-type adjudication has a number of advantages over rule-making,[44] notably its flexibility and its ability to focus on those closely affected by the policy. Again, it cannot be assumed that a discretion limited by rules or standards is necessarily 'better' or more helpful to individuals than one that is less confined but more often reconsidered.

(v) The Feasibility of Structuring

Davis is happy dealing with rule-following bureaucrats (here the mechanistic model is at home) but he is less concerned with the problems of technocratic or expert decision-makers. As Reiss has commented: 'Bureaucracies are built on rules and on the notion that decisions must be made according to those rules and with relatively little choice is applying them. Professional decision-making is based on quite the opposite model—the necessity to exercise judgment when confronted with the individual case.'[45]

Davis's approach is thus attuned to the 'transmission-belt' model of administration in which statutory objectives are applied to particular facts in an unproblematic fashion, but this model is of diminishing relevance to systems of government that delegate ever-broader powers to agencies.[46] Thus Unger argues[47] that in the movement from the liberal to the welfare state, government assumes managerial responsibilities in areas where the complexity and variability of factors are too great to allow recourse to general rules. There is a rapid rise in the use of open-ended standards in legislation, administration, and

[44] See D. L. Shapiro, 'The Choice of Rule Making or Adjudication in the Development of Agency Policy' (1965) 78 Harv.LR 921.

[45] A. Reiss Jr., review of *Discretionary Justice* (1970) 69 Mich.LR 792.

[46] See R. B. Stewart, 'The Reformation of American Administrative Law' (1975) 88 Harv.LR 1067.

[47] R. M. Unger, *Law in Modern Society* (1976); T. Lowi, *The End of Liberalism* (1969), 133–41. See also C. Diver 'Policymaking Paradigms in Administrative Law' (1981) 95 Harv.LR. 393.

adjudication. This is accompanied by a movement from *formalistic* styles of reasoning (in which all legal choices can be deduced sufficiently from rules) to *purposive* reasoning, in which decisions on how to apply rules depend on judgements on how the purposes ascribed to rules may most effectively be achieved. A formal notion of justice, Unger points out, is persuasive in the realm of exchanges between individuals but is less so when dealing with issues of government and distribution.

Put in other terms, certain areas of activity may be ill suited to governance according to rules, because the issues are 'polycentric'[48] in nature. In polycentric (as opposed to yes/no, or binary) issues, many factors interact and shift the grounds of decision beneath the decision-maker's feet. In deciding these issues rational justifications offer less solid foundations than do balanced judgements. To attempt to control such decision-makers by use of rules may thus be to use the wrong tools for the job. The danger here may not be an under-structuring of discretion but an over-use of rules. Davis gives the impression that in general it is useful to increase structuring via administrative rules, but his approach contrasts with that of other commentators. Thus Eugene Bardach and Robert Kagan focus their attention on the tendency of US officials to regulate excessively by filling in the 'holes' in regulatory schemes with over-indulgent rule-making.[49]

Governments, moreover, may adopt modes of operation that are not highly conducive to the control of discretions by means of rules. Thus the last decade and a half has seen the rise of the 'new public management' in British government.[50] The

[48] M. Polanyi, *The Logic of Liberty* (1951); P. Weiler, 'Two Models of Judicial Decisionmaking (1968) 46 Can BR 406; L. Fuller, *The Morality of Law* (1964), 83; Jowell, *Law and Bureaucracy*, 151–5, 213–4.

[49] See E. Bardach and R. Kagan, *Going by The Book: The Problem of Regulatory Unreasonableness* (1982).

[50] See e.g. C. Hood, 'A Public Management for All Seasons' (1991) 69 Pub. Admin. 3; I. Harden, *The Contracting State* (1991); N. Lewis, 'The Citizen's Charter and Next Steps: A New Way of Governing' (1993) Pol.Q 316; G. Drewry; 'Mr Major's Charter: Empowering the Consumer' [1993] PL 248; M. Henkel, 'The New Evaluative State' (1991) 69 Pub. Admin. 121; A. Barron and C. Scott, 'The Citizens' Charter Programme' (1992) 55 MLR 526; J. McEldowney, 'Contract Compliance and Public Audit on Regulatory Strategies in the Public Sector', paper to Citizens' Charter Conference,

emergence of this approach reflected concerns in successive Conservative governments that administrative bureaucracies were expensive, inefficient, and unresponsive. The answer was seen to lie in a new philosophy placing emphasis on reducing the size of government; shifting away from public towards the private provision of services and pursuing effectiveness, as seen in terms of satisfying consumer demands. A series of measures was introduced. Against the background of a continuing privatization process, the Next Steps programme transferred a mass[51] of 'executive' functions from central departments to independent agencies which were to operate under framework documents but which were to enjoy the 'freedom to manage'.[52] Public services were to be provided by establishing internal markets (as is the National Health Service) so that purchasers of public services were separated from providers. Arrangements for compulsory competitive tendering were introduced (as in local authority construction work)[53] so as to increase the contracting-out of tasks to private enterprises. Competition was extended by providing for the market testing[54] of every function of government, central and local, NHS and nationalized industry, unless it was part of the 'core' business of the organization. The Citizens Charter was launched so as to emphasis the rights of individuals to choice and quality in services.[55]

The new public management is based on the notion of separating policy-making from service delivery. The nature of the service is treated as free from policy implications but a new emphasis is put on the effective delivery of the service by professional managers. The latter are accordingly accountable for

University of Warwick, 23 Sept. 1992; C. Scott, 'Rule Versus Discretion in the New Public Sector', paper to Citizens' Charter Conference, University of Warwick, 23 Sept. 1992; N. Lacey, 'Government as Manager, Citizen as Consumer: The Case of the Criminal Justice Act 1991' (1994) 57 MLR 534.

[51] In five years the transfers involved some 90 agencies and 350,000 staff—see J. Mayne, 'Public Power Outside Government' (1993) 64 Pol.Q. 327.

[52] See Prime Minister's Efficiency Unit, *Improving Management in Government: The Next Steps* (London 1988); id., *Making the Most of Next Steps* (London 1991).

[53] See Local Government Planning and Land Act 1980; Local Government Act 1988; Harden *The Contracting State,* 18.

[54] i.e. testing in-house public service bids against those from the private sector.

[55] See *The Citizens Charter: Raising the Standard* (Cm 1599, 1991).

producing results. A variety of contractual devices serves to distance the citizen from the policy-maker and the public are seen, not so much as participants in the policy-making process as consumers of services.[56] Accountability operates not at the level of policy-making (or service definition) but at the point of delivery—on market-derived principles. Thus Hood has noted the debt owed by the new public management: first, to 'reform doctrines built on ideas of contestability, user choice, transparency and close concentration on incentive structures . . . doctrines very different from traditional military– bureaucratic ideas of "good administration" '; second, to 'ideas of professional management expertise as portable, paramount over technical expertise, requiring high discretionary power to achieve results (free to manage).'[57]

Whatever the merits or demerits of the new public management,[58] it should be noted that the potential part to be played by rules may be quite different under such a system than in arrangements relying more heavily on public bureaucracies. Clearly rules will be required in order to establish, for example, the frameworks under which the Next Steps agencies are to operate,[59] but in any system built on 'expert', 'managerial' discretions which are exercised quite freely under 'contractual' frameworks and which are evaluated according to results (rather than questioned as to policies pursued) special attention has to be paid to control devices other than rules and which are attuned to a quasi-contractual context rather than the exercise of statutory discretions by a public bureaucracy. Thus, emphasis might be placed on audit mechanisms; systems of inspection and evaluation; performance targets and indicators; competition as a yardstick for effectiveness; quality controls; managerial incentives; complaints and redress mechanisms;

[56] On citizen as consumer see Barron and Scott, 'The Citizens' Charter Programme', 543–5 and Lacey, 'Government as Manager, Citizen as Consumer', 534–5, 553.

[57] See Hood, 'A Public Management for All Seasons', (1991) 69 Pub. Admin. 3, 5–6.

[58] A style of government that can be evaluated by the bench-marks offered in this chapter.

[59] As noted, the status of such rules may be problematic, see Harden, *The Contracting State*, ch. 5.

and the capital markets as sources of scrutiny and discipline.[60] To view the administrative process in legalistic terms is not helpful in assessing the place of either 'alternative' controls or of rules in such a context.

A final problem with the legalistic argument for rules stems from its tendency to overlook those practical and political realities that demand flexibility rather than a rule-bound consistency. Thus it might be argued that, for the sake of fairness and justice, all polluters should be treated equally. If, however, fixed standards are set and enforced on polluters in a mechanical way and without discretionary intervention, larger enterprises might be in a position to comply, but a number of smaller operators might well go out of business. The regulatory agency would then face a public outcry against oppressive regulation, lose esteem in the public eye, and be likely to pay the political price. In short, the mechanical approach would not be politically feasible. Other considerations, such as limitations on resources and time, also rule out non-discretionary enforcement. In practice, street-level enforcers of all kinds have to operate by negotiation and bluff.[61] Automatic resort to law would be extravagant in terms of resources, it would risk exposing the low penalties that accompany many regulatory offences, provoke damaging attacks by opponents where penalties were substantial, and possibly make enforcement enormously difficult for individual inspectors. A system based on a large measure of discretion might thus be preferable on a number of counts.

To summarize, the above analysis of Davis is not offered in order to deny the value of rules within government but to show, first, that in assessing the role of rules it is necessary to recognize values other than those implicit in the legal para-

[60] See Scott. 'Rule versus Discretion in the New Public Sector'.

[61] See Hawkins, *Environment and Enforcement* (1984) and Hawkins and Thomas (eds.), *Enforcing Regulation* (1984); Richardson *et al.*, *Policing Pollution*, chs. 5 and 6; B. Hutter, *The Reasonable Arm of the Law?* (1988), chs. 5 and 6. For an economic justification of compliance-seeking by negotiation see P. Fenn and C. G. Veljanovski, 'A Positive Economic Theory of Regulatory Enforcement' 98 EJ (1988) 1055; C. G. Veljanovski, 'The Economics of Regulatory Enforcement', in Hawkins and Thomas (eds.), *Enforcing Regulation*. See also S. Shavell, 'The Optimal Structure of Law Enforcement' (1993) Journal of Law and Economics 255.

digm and, second, that a narrowly legalistic approach can produce unrealistic expectations as to the practical potential of rules. Davis is open to criticism on a number of counts. His notion of justice is bound up with lawyers' values and so is question-begging. In many areas of government the application of rules is not feasible and it cannot be assumed that rules will protect individuals' interests. The Davis approach builds on a narrow view of governmental decision-making and offers prescriptions whose appropriateness to modern governmental processes may increasingly be questioned.

Above all, Davis offers no convincing means of justifying any particular method of carrying out government business in any particular context. This challenge was avoided by stating that what was 'feasible' had to be considered in each individual context and by operating with an unexplained bench-mark of 'justice.' The latter notion served only to invoke, in an imprecise manner, certain values implicit in the legal paradigm.

Earlier it was argued that the real test of a governmental process should be whether it furthers recognized and acceptable values. What, then, are those values if they are not (or at least are not exclusively) those encountered within the legal paradigm? In both making a case for certain values and suggesting a method of evaluating governmental processes it is useful to consider how approaches to evaluating procedures have developed in a number of key respects since Davis wrote *Discretionary Justice.*

II. EVALUATING GOVERNMENTAL PROCESSES

1. The Search for Process Values

Six years after *Discretionary Justice* was first published, Richard Stewart, in a celebrated article,[62] attacked the 'traditional' view of administrative law and examined the case for seeing such

[62] R. B. Stewart, 'The Reformation of American Administrative Law' (1975) 88 Harv.LR 1667.

law as a system for ensuring the representation of affected interests. His analysis deals with a series of different bases for judging the appropriateness of governmental procedures.

Stewart contrasted the 'interest-representation' model of administrative law, marked by its emphasis on ensuring the adequate representation of affected interests in decision-making, with the 'traditional' model and its focus on whether governmental intrusions into private liberty and property interests were authorized by the legislature.

The traditional view, according to Stewart, required of government a number of essentials, notably that coercive controls on individuals be authorized by the legislature; that the legislature must promulgate rules, or principles, to guide the exercise of delegated powers; that officials should apply legislative directives rationally; and that judicial review be available to ensure the above. In short, the traditional view saw the governmental official or agency as a mere 'transmission belt' for implementing legislative directives.

The debt such a view owes to the Diceyan notion of the rule of law is clear and it encounters similar problems in dealing with discretion. Vague, general, or ambiguous statutes create discretion and threaten the legitimacy of actions under the transmission-belt theory since the relevant statute does not dictate the decision or policy and, instead, the priorities of officials, who are unaccountable to the electorate, hold sway. Such statutes have proliferated on both sides of the Atlantic. The idea of objective goals for administrators had by the mid-1970s been discredited and Stewart wrote: 'Today the exercise of agency discretion is inevitably seen as the essentially legislative process of adjusting the competing claims of various private interests affected by agency policy.'[63]

It was, he argued, no longer possible to legitimate agency action by the transmission-belt theory. Nor was another model of legitimation still convincing. This was the 'expertise' model

[63] Stewart, 'The Reformation of American Administrative Law', 1683. For a defence of bureaucratic rationality and an important neo-Weberian endorsement of bureaucracy as 'the best hope for justice and rationality' see J. Mashaw, *Bureaucratic Justice* (1983); quotation from book review of Mashaw by L. Liebman and R. B. Stewart (1983) 96 Harv.LR 1952.

put forward in the 1930s by defenders of the New Deal and the practice whereby Congress delegated sweeping powers to a host of new agencies. Championed by James M. Landis,[64] proponents of the expertise model offered no apologies for the broad discretions operated by agencies and officials. They maintained that these discretions were necessary for successful planning and management. 'Expertise' was thus held out as a solution to the 'problem' of discretion since the application of specialized knowledge, skills, and experience was the means with which to effect agency goals. Administrators, according to this view, were not political but professional, and public administration was treated as objective in nature.

Faith in the expertise model waned, pointed out Stewart, as experience eroded the general belief in an objective public interest, in the disinterestedness of agencies and in their ability to achieve goals. The unravelling of the objective notion of the public interest made way for the pluralist interest-representation model. This model looked to the affirmative side of government, which has to do with the representation of interests during the development of policies, in contrast with the negative approach of the traditional model and its focus on the checking of governmental power. What was not possible, argued Stewart, was any revived application of the traditional model by means of closer legislative specification of policies (the 'non-delegation doctrine'). This was 'neither feasible nor desirable'[65] and could not realistically be demanded by the judges. Nor could administrative rules remove 'inevitable' discretions.[66] Stewart lodged a further objection to Davis's notion that judges should locate the optimum degree of structuring in each respect for each discretionary power, calling it 'unrealistic

[64] See J. M. Landis, *The Administrative Process* (1938).

[65] Stewart, 'The Reformation of American Administrative Law', 1695. A number of commentators have argued that the US Supreme Court should ensure that Congress does not unnecessarily delegate social policy discretion to administrators: e.g. J. Ely, *Democracy and Distrust* (1980), 131–4; J. Freedman, *Crisis and Legitimacy* (1978), 78–94; T. Lowi, *The End of Liberalism* (1969), 129–46, 297–9. On US courts and delegation see S. Breyer and R. Stewart, *Administrative Law and Regulatory Policy* 3rd edn. (1992), 66–91; E. L. Rubin, 'Law and Legislation in the Administrative State' (1989) 89 Col.LR 369, and P. L. Strauss 'Some Comments on Rubin' (1989) 89 Col.LR. 427.

[66] Stewart, 'The Reformation of American Administrative Law', 1712.

and unwise' given limitations on judicial experience and specialized knowledge.[67]

Did this mean that the notion of interest representation was left as the appropriate yardstick for assessing governmental procedures? In the end this was also said to fail as a general structure for legitimating agency action. The case for valuing the representation of interests in governmental decisions was based on a number of points: such representation would improve agency decisions; make then more responsive to the needs of various interests; give citizens a sense of involvement in government; and increase confidence in the fairness of government decisions. A number of objections, however, pointed to the limitations of the notion: unlimited provision for interest representation would lead to chaos and the stultification of government; the courts, if chosen as the arbiters of participatory rights, would be given too much control over access to decision-making and ultimately a power to control policy choices; whether judicial protections for participating rights were better than political or administrative measures was contentious; to formalize participatory rights would not only prove intolerably burdensome but would increase the expense of participation and thus would discriminate against participation by certain groups; limiting participatory rights in the interests of effective decision-making was a process that itself involved highly discretionary decisions, and whether participation would *influence* governmental decisions was also problematic.[68]

For Stewart, the unavoidable conclusion was that, although interest representation might have a useful role, it provided no comprehensive yardstick for assessing governmental procedures. Failing the prospect of interest representation maturing into a more convincing model, the real issue could be stated as how best to use different measures to control power. In response, the 'nominalist thesis' suggested that governmental tasks, functions and contexts be classified and then:

[67] Stewart, 'The Reformation of American Administrative Law', 1701.

[68] Ibid. 1803–5. See also P. P. Craig, *Public Law and Democracy in the United Kingdom and the United States of America* (1990), 128–36. On the practicalities of participation see J. L. Mashaw, *Bureaucratic Justice* (1983).

Such a classification . . . .might be parallelled by a similar classification of the various techniques for directing and controlling administrative power, including judicial review, procedural requirements, political controls, and partial obligation of agency functions. The two systems of classification might then be meshed to determine the most harmonious fit between the purposes and characteristics of particular agencies and various control techniques.[69]

Such an approach offers at first sight a number of useful rules of thumb for the designers of governmental processes but, again, it fails to provide any coherent basis for evaluating such processes. It does not, for example, tell us how to decide what indeed is 'the most harmonious fit' between powers and controls.[70]

In order to progress from this point it is necessary to come to grips with the problem of identifying the broad array of values that is to be served in the governmental process. This challenge has notably been taken up by Denis Galligan.

In his book, *Discretionary Powers*, Galligan looks at the role of ideas of legality in restraining and directing the exercise of discretion and argues that legal accountability is not 'self-contained and independent of political morality'.[71] He emphasizes that the law serves a number of purposes: 'It is not clear why we should expect there to be one central idea of what law is, or of the tasks it is meant to perform or of the values it is supposed to serve.'[72]

How, then, can one evaluate the acceptability of governmental processes involving the exercise of discretionary power? Galligan's view is that: 'there is no fundamental and irreducible ideal or principle, but rather . . . law and legal institutions are

[69] Stewart, 'The Reformation of American Administrative Law', 1810.

[70] Stewart does offer three 'bases' for administrative intervention in a later article. These are: securing rights; promoting efficiency; and protecting 'non-commodity values'. See R. Stewart, 'Regulation in a Liberal State: The Role of Non-Commodity Values' (1983) 92 Yale LJ 1357. For criticisms of Stewart's concept of 'non-commodity values' and of his claims to neutrality, see P. H. Schuck, 'Regulation, Non-Market Values and the Administrative State: A Comment on Professor Stewart' (1983) 92 Yale LJ 1602; G. E. Frug, 'Why Neutrality?' (1983) 92 Yale LJ 1591.

[71] D. J. Galligan, *Discretionary Powers*, 4.

[72] Ibid. 89. On 'discovering fundamental values' see Ely, *Democracy and Distrust*, ch. 3.

part of the political and social composition of a society and that they can be made instrumental in upholding values several and diverse. What those values are depends on the political theory and practice of a society.'[73] Thus, he argues that to separate law from political considerations gives an unduly narrow approach. The task is to identify the set of political values that is to serve as the basis for developing legal principles relevant to the control of discretion. At this point in his argument Galligan appears reluctant to argue for a particular set of values or an underlying theory of democracy. He says choice of values 'must depend on a certain degree of personal preference both as to the values selected and the importance of each'.[74] In a quest for further content, however, he adopts an eclectic approach:

reflection on the political theories that underlie modern, democratic, liberal societies would tend to suggest that the following have a position of importance and that each provides scope for the development of more specific legal principles. The four basic values suggested are: stability in legal relations, rationality in decision-making, fair procedures and, finally, a rather loose residual category of moral and political principles.[75]

Each item is explained. *Stability in legal relationships* is a value traditionally associated with the rule of law; *rationality in decision-making* is said to be a 'fundamental' value; and *fair procedures* to be central to the legal enterprise but to have a place within a wider political framework where 'the concept of participation is of undoubted importance'. It is, however, the residual category of *moral and political principles* that proves the most problematic. This set of principles is said to generate constraints on discretion and examples are of non-discrimination and 'general ideas of justice and equity'. There is, however, no unifying basis for such values (for example a rationale founded on respect for persons) and this is a conscious aspect of Galligan's eclecticism. All four of these values are nevertheless problematic since it is not clear whence they derive. Why, one might ask, are *these* values rather than any others important in any

[73] Galligan, *Discretionary Powers*, 89–90. [74] Ibid. 90. [75] Ibid.

system of good government? Why should these be the benchmarks? A further issue is whether different *systems* of government are based on the same set of values and whether there is a particular or 'core' model of liberal democracy being offered. (If so what is it like?)

These difficulties make the identification of good governmental processes a complex task. Galligan notes that a combination of procedure and substance is involved: 'Good government means more than good results in terms of one or other set of political goals, it depends partly on consideration of and compliance with a range of values and ideals in arriving at those results.'[76] He summarizes:

> I have suggested that there are certain values which are important in any system of good government, and that these may be the basis for creating a framework of legal principles, or principles of process, which constitute constraints on the exercise of discretionary authority. Such principles complement rather than compete with more direct methods of political accountability by contributing to the overall justifiability and legitimacy of discretionary decisions.[77]

The strength of Galligan's approach is that it recognizes that many issues arising in modern government are best resolved by institutions other than courts and according to strategies other than rules and adjudications; that the balance of political and legal accountability is itself an aspect 'of a wider sense of political accountability'. More problematically, though, a principle for selecting certain values is difficult to discern in Galligan's account and, as a result, there fails to emerge a convincing explanation of how justifications for particular governmental processes can be made and evaluated.

The seeds of an explanation do lie, however, in Galligan's notion that values play a role in justifying and legitimating particular governmental procedures. The legitimacy of an administrative process can thus be seen in terms of the persuasive power of the arguments made in its favour. Such an approach is consistent with the focus adopted by Christopher Hood and Michael Jackson in their book *Administrative*

[76] Ibid. 98. [77] Ibid. 99.

Argument[78] in which they concentrate not so much on the performance of processes but on the 'link between argument and acceptance'[79] As they put it: 'administrative argument is typically not a process of validation and disproof using hard data, but rather a process of persuasion.'[80]

The American administrative lawyer Jerry Mashaw adopted elements of such a strategy in *Bureaucratic Justice* in 1983. He contended: 'The justice of an administration system . . . means simply this: those qualities of a decision process that provide arguments for the acceptability of its decisions . . . These justificatory structures, once identified, should appear to be ubiquitous in the legal structure of public institutions and in ordinary experience.'[81] Mashaw suggests that there are three types of justice argument.[82] The *bureaucratic rationality* model of justice demands that decisions be accurate and efficient concrete realizations of the legislative will. The *professional treatment* model calls for the application of appropriate special skills and recognizes the incompleteness of facts, the singularity of contexts, and the intuitive nature of judgements. The *moral judgement* model requires fairness and independence in decision-making and promises a 'full and equal opportunity to obtain one's entitlements'.

How, though, do the models interact? Mashaw argues that they are 'distinct conceptual models' which are each coherent and attractive but, while not mutually exclusive, they are 'highly competitive'.[83] It follows that: 'the internal logic of any one of them tends to drive the characteristics of the others from the field as it works out in concrete situations.'[84]

A problem for Mashaw (and, indeed, for Hood and Jackson) is, however, the notion of acceptability. One might ask not only: 'What constitutes acceptable?' but also: 'Acceptable to

[78] C. Hood and M. Jackson, *Administrative Argument* (1991).
[79] Ibid. 200.
[80] Ibid. 26.
[81] Mashaw, *Bureaucratic Justice*, 24–5.
[82] Ibid., ch. 2, and also James O. Freedman, *Crisis and Legitimacy* (1978), 11. Freedman argues that the legitimacy of the administrative process may be supported by public recognition that administrative agencies are indispensable in the constitutional scheme of government; that they are accountable; that they are effective in meeting their statutory responsibilities; and that their decision-making is fair.
[83] Mashaw, *Bureaucratic Justice*, 23.
[84] Ibid.

whom?' On the latter point, it can be questioned whether the judges of a bureaucratic process are to be the consumers of services, the general public, the management of the agency, the front-line officials, the government, the media, or some other grouping. Without further theoretical underpinning it seems that Mashaw is exposed to many of the objections faced by the participatory model.

Mashaw concedes that his technique for developing the models is 'in part empirical and in part intuitive and analytic'.[85] It is the eclectic nature of this technique that is the root of many of the problems encountered in using his models. Thus a particular difficulty is the relationship between different models of justice. Mashaw argues that these are competitive but not that they are mutually exclusive. They are theoretically inconsistent, they contain internal tensions that reflect alternative justice perspectives, and they compete to achieve dominance as the accepted model. The notion is of three models or 'visions'[86] of justice each of which may serve to legitimate a particular process but which all exist in a stressed relationship. There is by no means 'a happy blending of justice models'.[87] Without clarification on the matter of 'acceptability' it is accordingly difficult to justify either the 'triumph'[88] of one model or the appropriateness of a particular mixing of models. One might protest that the offer of the different bench-marks for administration is of limited utility if one is not told which bench-marks are appropriate and when.

2. Five Rationales for Legitimacy Claims

An explanation can be offered, however, which explores the nature of legitimacy claims or attributions and employs the notion of a *discourse* of justification within which certain values operate. Such a notion holds that evaluations of procedures are, as a matter of practice, argued out with reference to

[85] Ibid. 17. For an attempt to derive some process values from the American liberal democratic tradition see J. Mashaw, 'Administrative Due Process: The Quest for a Dignitary Theory' (1981) 61 BULR 885.

[86] Ibid. 7.

[87] Ibid. 40.

[88] Ibid. 46.

certain recognized values. Language users, on this view, distinguish between claims that bureaucratic processes are justifiable or appropriate (let us call these 'legitimacy claims'[89]) and claims that processes are constitutionally correct, legal, or morally praiseworthy. When legitimacy claims are made, those involved can recognize both relevant and irrelevant arguments and can see that relevant arguments invoke certain understood values and only these. Thus different persons may employ different models of the optimal democracy but each is able to recognise the basis of the arguments as to legitimacy being made by the other. They may each place different emphasis on the furtherance of certain values but they share a common recognition that certain values are relevant.

When there is talk of this or that process being legitimate or illegitimate, in the sense that certain values are argued to be satisfied or left unsatisfied, reference is made to a limited set of values or justificatory arguments. Thus Gerald Frug argues that in justifying bureaucracy: 'we have adopted only a limited number of ways to reassure ourselves about these institutions.'[90]

These justifications are all problematic in some respects but, as will be argued, it is their *cumulative* force that justifies.[91] The types of claim can be outlined as follows:[92]

[89] On legitimacy see D. Beetham, *The Legitimation of Power* (1991); R. Barker, *Political Legitimacy and the State* (1990); id., 'Legitimacy, Obedience and the State', in C. Harlow (ed.), *Public Law and Politics* (1986); W. Connolly (ed.), *Legitimacy and the State* (1984); J. O. Freedman, *Crisis and Legitimacy* (1978); P. McAuslan and J. McEldowney (eds.), *Law, Legitimacy and the Constitution* (1985); J. Habermas, *Legitimation Crisis*, trans. T. McCarthy (1976).

[90] See G. E. Frug, 'The Ideology of Bureaucracy in American Law' (1984) 97 Harv.LR. 1277.

[91] On the 'deception' involved in combining rationales see Frug, 'The Ideology of Bureaucracy' 1378–9. For an argument that rationales should be used in an integrated fashion so that they cannot be teased apart see C. Edley *Administrative Law: Rethinking Judicial Control of Bureaucracy* (1990) ch. 7.

[92] See R. Baldwin and C. McCrudden, *Regulation and Public Law* (1987). In 'The Ideology of Bureaucracy' Frug offers four models of bureaucratic legitimacy: formalist; expertise; judicial review; and market/pluralist. The formalist, expertise, and market/pluralist models correspond to what are termed here the legislative mandate, expertise, and accountability rationales. Frug's judicial review model can be seen as a sub-category of the accountability rationale (judicial control being a particular species of accountability). The efficiency rationale discussed here may be subsumed to some extent under Frug's formalist heading, and the due process rationale, though not stressed by Frug, is reflected in his comments on judicial review and its role in controlling

(i) The Legislative Mandate Claim

This claim attributes value to achieving objectives that are set out in legislative form (it echoes Mashaw's 'bureaucratic rationality' model). Thus in Britain a support claim would point to the existence of an authorizing mandate from Parliament. The proponent of the claim is in effect stating: 'Support what is being done because that is what Parliament, the fountain of democratic authority, has ordered.'[93]

There are, of course, problems with this rationale as were pointed out by Stewart in his attack on the traditional model of administrative law.[94] The claim is weakened in so far as the legislature has provided administrators with broad discretions ('What *did* Parliament order?') Implementation of the mandate demands interpretation and, accordingly, legitimacy claims become problematic. Nor is it usually feasible for the legislature to overcome such problems by setting down precise standards and objectives. Parliament has neither the time nor the expertise to solve all problems in advance and, indeed, it may deliberately decline to do so and give, say a regulatory agency, a set of discretionary powers so as to allow it to make judgements on policies and implementing strategies.

(ii) The Accountability or Control Claim

Like the legislative mandate claim this model seeks justification in the assent of the people but, instead of relying on the people's voice as expressed in Parliament, it looks to more narrowly-defined groupings as conduits for the democratic voice.[95]

processes. Edley, *Administrative Law*, argues that three paradigms underpin prescriptions about administrative procedure: the adjudicatory fairness; the scientific (or expertise); and the political (interest-balancing/participatory) paradigms. See also James Freedman's analysis of justificatory rationales in *Crisis and Legitimacy*.

[93] Disputes may, of course, arise as to the need for any kind of public mandate—as for example when it is asserted that an action is purely of private concern. Where functions of an arguably public nature are contracted out to private bodies such disputes are likely to arise—see Harden, *The Contracting State*, ch. 8. On legal and bureaucratic authority see H. Gerth and C. W. Mills (eds.), *From Max Weber: Essays in Sociology* (1958); see Frug, 'The Ideology of Bureaucracy', 1207–300 (on the 'formalist' model).

[94] Stewart, 'The Reformation of American Administrative Law', 1671–87.

[95] See Freedman, *Crisis and Legitimacy*, ch. 5. See also Frug, 'The Ideology of Bureaucracy' on accountability through the political and market processes as well as by judicial scrutiny (pp. 1355–61 and 1334–9).

Thus, where a particular interpretation of the mandate is put into effect, the implementer(s) may claim that they are accountable for that interpretation to a representative body and that this oversight renders the chosen mode of implementation acceptable. Rights of participation and consultation are valued, as is openness.[96]

This claim is not unproblematic. Deciding to whom the bureaucrat is to be made accountable is controversial. In so far as a system of accountability or control is not exercised by Parliament or elected persons, it may be open to criticism as unrepresentative. Where control is exercised by means of certain institutions (e.g. courts) then the competence of those institutions in a specialist area may be called into question.

(iii) The Due Process Claim

This claim values the use of certain procedures which imply a respect for individuals and fairness or even-handedness in government. Support claims are based on the level of consideration that has been shown, not to the broad public will, but to the interests of those persons affected by the process, decision, policy, or action.[97]

As a complete claim this is again limited. There is no guarantee that maximizing the recognition of individuals' rights will deal with collective or social issues or will produce an efficient decision (it may lead to stagnation and indecision). The dictates of such a claim may not correspond with the legislative mandate and to pay heed to process rights beyond a certain point may not be consistent with the development and exercise of necessary expertise and judgement.

[96] On participation see Stewart, 'The Reformation of American Administrative Law'; Freedman, *Crisis and Legitimacy*, ch. 10; C. Pateman, *Participation and Democratic Theory* (1970); id., *The Problem of Political Obligation* (1985); N. Poulantzas, *State, Power, Socialism* (1980); C. B. Macpherson, *The Life and Times of Liberal Democracy* (1977); D. Held, *Models of Democracy* (1987), 254–64. But cf. the New Right theorists and their hostility to democratic as opposed to market-based processes within the minimalist state, and e.g. F. A. Hayek, *The Constitution of Liberty* (1960); R. Nozick, *Anarchy, State and Utopia* (1974), and the discussion in P. Dunleavy and B. O'Leary, *Theories of the State: The Politics of Liberal Democracy* (1987), ch. 3.

[97] On protecting individual interests as a first priority of administration and administrative law see e.g. J. Dickinson, *Administrative Justice and the Supremacy of Law in the United States* (1927). On rationales for due process see Craig, *Public Law and Democracy*, 137–9.

(iv) The Expertise Claim

Many governmental, and particularly regulatory, functions require that expert judgements be made and applied. In such cases the issues are often polycentric[98] and the decision- or policy-maker has to consider a number of competing options and values so as to form a balanced judgement on incomplete and shifting information. Where this is so, it is inappropriate to demand either that rules or guidelines be set out in advance so as to govern the matter or that, beyond a certain point, reasons and justifications can be given. The expertise claim urges that the expert will take the most appropriate action when given an area of freedom in which to operate and that his/her performance will improve over time.[99] As Mashaw put it in relation to his 'professional treatment' model: 'The basis for the legitimacy of professional treatment is that the professional is master of an arcane body of knowledge and supports his judgement by appealing to expertise. But whereas the bureaucrat displays his or her knowledge through instrumentally rational routines designed to render transparent the connection between concrete decisions and legislatively validated policy, the professional's art remains opaque to the lay man.'[100]

This comment points to the problems of making claims to expertise. Lay observers find it difficult to understand the bases for expert judgements and often impossible to assess the success with which the expertise has been applied. The patient who is not a surgeon tends not to know if the operation was as successful as it might have been. The observer may not know

[98] See references at n. 48 *supra*.

[99] For a defence of expertise see J. M. Landis, *The Administrative Process* (1938). See also Mashaw's 'professional treatment' model, Mashaw, *Bureaucratic Justice*, 26–9; Frug, 'The Ideology of Bureaucracy', 1318–22, 1331–4; Freedman, *Crisis and Legitimacy*, 44–57. A recent example of the rationale in operation occurred when Mr Neil Hamilton defended the regulation of accountants by their own professional bodies. The then Corporate Affairs Minister said: 'There is a possibility of conflict. But the great merit of self-regulation is that it uses experts.' *Financial Times*, 26 Nov. 1992.

[100] Mashaw, *Buraucratic Justice*, 28. The 'new public management' places a good deal of faith in the manager as expert. It is expertise that is held to justify the 'freedom to manage'; see C. Hood, 'A Public Management for All Seasons', 6; Harden, *The Contracting State*, 70.

what would have happened if alternative strategies had been adopted. It is, moreover, difficult for the expert to explain why *this* issue demands expert judgement. Attacks on the competence and independence of experts serve further to undermine claims. Such attacks are fostered by an instinctive distrust of those who claim to 'know best', who fail to give full reasons, or who pursue a specialist or arcane mode of analysis.[101] Where expert opinions conflict within a field or between disciplines, this again undermines legitimacy claims.

(v) The Efficiency Claim

Two kinds of claim can potentially be made on the basis of efficiency. First, that stated objectives are being achieved in an effective manner, and second, that economically efficient actions are being taken.[102] The first kind of claim can be considered a version of the legislative mandate claim and, accordingly, problems arise in so far as it is difficult to define the content of the given objectives. Even if objectives are clear, the absence of comparators usually makes it difficult to demonstrate that the most effective approach is being taken at any one time—what might have happened had another approach been adopted is often impossible to judge.

The second form of claim—that efficient results are produced—is highly contentious, indeed it is the most dubious form of claim discussed here. It is difficult to see efficiency as a value independent of distributional considerations and, unless there is legislative authority for taking 'efficient' action there is liable to be a degree of conflict between the dictates of efficiency and the distributional implications of a statute. An efficiency claim may have a role, however, in so far as support may be claimed according to a particular efficiency-based interpretation of a legislative mandate.

[101] Harold Macmillan expressed such distrust: 'We have not overthrown the divine right of kings to fall down before the divine right of experts.' See N. Beloff, *The General Says No* (1963), 59, quoted in P. Hennessey, *Whitehall* (1989) 159.

[102] On the role of economic appraisals in rule-making, see Ch. 7 *infra*. For a critique of efficiency as the measure of governmental success see Lacey, 'Government as Manager, Citizen as Consumer'.

3. The Nature of Legitimacy Claims

How are the above claims made and how can they be identified? The contention here is that there is a language of justification that invokes certain values. These values are recognized and given meaning according to a discourse of justification (or legitimacy) which attributes relevance to certain forms of argument in discussions of legitimacy and which distinguishes these from other forms of argument. Thus if I were to argue that the Director General of OFTEL should be supported because he wears elegant suits, this argument would be recognized by my listener as not bearing on the issue of legitimacy. Language-users are able to separate legitimacy claims from moral, legal, constitutional, or even aesthetic assertions.

Why the five rationales or values described? The answer is that these are the rationales that are employed and have currency: that an analysis of justificatory arguments will reveal a consistent resort to these rationales—at least in Britain and North America.[103]

What, then, is involved when a critic assesses the legitimacy of an institution or process? A distinction should be drawn at this point between assessing the legitimacy of a state or regime and assessing the legitimacy of an institution or process that operates within a regime or governmental system whose broad

[103] For similar comments on the extent of resort to such rationales see the works cited at n. 92 *supra*. It is noteworthy that in his account of the rise and fall of police legitimacy Robert Reiner points to a series of legitimating rationales under the headings: (1) bureaucratic organization; (2) the rule of law; (3) the strategy of minimal force; (4) non-partisanship; (5) the service role; (6) preventive policing; (7) police effectiveness; and (8) incorporation of the working class. The justifications Reiner refers to fit quite readily into the five rationales argued for in this chapter; see R. Reiner, *The Politics of the Police*, 2nd edn. (1992), ch. 2.

To take another example, a collection of justificatory arguments resulted from discussions on the BBC's future. See the White Paper *The Future of the BBC* (Cm. 2098, Nov. 1992) and the BBC's response: *Extending Choice: The BBC's Role in the New Broadcasting Age* (November 1992). A reading of these documents shows debate to centre on: the nature of the BBC's future role (i.e. its proper *mandate*); making the BBC *accountable*; the *fairness* with which different viewer interests are dealt and the fairness of different ways of funding the BBC; the *expertise* shown by the BBC in its 'original contribution' to broadcasting; and the *efficiency* displayed by the BBC in giving viewers value for money.

legitimacy is accepted.[104] This book is concerned with the second form of legitimacy assessment. A second distinction should also be drawn between normative *judgements* as to legitimacy and *descriptions* of legitimacy.[105] A judgement as to legitimacy involves the critic's making an assessment of the legitimacy that an institution or process deserves to be attributed when evaluated according to commonly recognized criteria. A description of legitimacy outlines the legitimacy that the public, or a section of it *in fact* accords to the institution or process.[106] If a description of legitimacy is offered then recognition will be given to legitimacy which is gained by mystification, or deception, of the public. If a judgement as to legitimacy is made, an opinion is offered on the *merits* of any legitimacy claims.[107] (The opinion is personal but the criteria for assessing merits are established impersonally). It is on the basis of such judgements that is appropriate to go about designing rules or evaluating governmental processes. In David Beetham's words: 'the social scientist, in concluding that a given power relationship is legitimate, is making a judgement, not delivering a report about people's beliefs in legitimacy.'[108]

Thus far my argument has sought to identify the benchmarks for legitimacy claims by referring to a language of legitimacy. Such an account may explain how people go about legitimacy claiming, but how can the critic make a judgement on legitimacy (as judged with reference to the five claims) without explaining how the different claims interact, without justifying a particular weighting of the claims?

In the first instance, it can be responded that when an argument is made in support of a process, act, or institution of government what matters is the collective justificatory power of

[104] See generally Barker, *Political Legitimacy and the State*, 20–7; Beetham, *The Legitimation of Power*. The foundations of a state's or regime's legitimacy may be explained in quite different terms and raise issues beyond the scope of this book.

[105] See Barker, *Political Legitimacy and the State*, 10–13, 47–9, 195.

[106] See M. Weber, *Economy and Society* (1968), 213; S. M Lipset, *Political Man* (1963), 77. For criticism see, *The Legitimation of Power*, ch. 1; J. Habermas, *Legitimation Crisis*, 100; Connolly, *Legitimacy and the State*, 12.

[107] On political argument as a concern with trade-off between different principles see B. Barry, *Political Argument* (reissue 1990), ch. 3 and p. 286.

[108] Beetham, *The Legitimation of Power*, 13.

the five forms of claim. A claim under one head may be weak but may be compensated for by a strong claim under another. Where strong claims can be made under all heads (a rare event) then a high level of legitimacy is assured; where only weak claims can be made under each heading then the power to justify will be low. Where a claim under one head can be improved by a reform that does not weaken claims under other heads then a convincing case for such a reform can be made. What, however, of the mass of cases in the middle? How can one say whether a trade-off between different kinds of claim is desirable?

4. Legitimacy and Democratic Theory

Surely, it could be argued, such trade-offs require reference to some theory of democracy? Without such a theory, it may be contended, it is impossible to choose between efficiency or accountability, fairness or expertise. Paul Craig argues: 'The very meaning to be given to concepts such as legitimacy and accountability will be affected by the meaning ascribed to. . . substantive and procedural rights, and will be coloured by the political theory which underlies the existence and content of such rights.'[109]

Subscribers to some political theories, contends Craig, may not merely differ regarding the weight they ascribe to certain values, they may refuse to attribute weight to some supposed values. Thus, speaking of the Thatcherite right, and those who favour market-based pluralism, Craig comments:

> Conservative policy is not based upon any communitarian philosophy . . . Any suggestion that central aspects of this policy, such as the regulation of privatized industry, should be legitimated by a conception of participatory rights which flows from a communitarian thesis would simply be rejected by those who do not expouse any such thesis.[110]

[109] See P. P. Craig, *Public Law and Democracy* (1990), 213.

[110] Ibid. 223. Craig's point may be an exaggeration—it follows from my argument that only an eccentric would refuse to acknowledge the relevance for legitimacy purposes of a 'recognized' value such as that contained in the right to participate; see *infra*.

One solution for problems of value selection and for setting down the bench-marks of legitimacy may be to grasp the nettle and make out the case for a particular model of democracy. Thus, 'ethical liberals',[111] as exemplified by John Rawls, [112] Ronald Dworkin,[113] and Bruce Ackerman,[114] seek to derive liberal conclusions about social justice from premisses concerning human nature. These premisses purport to remain neutral about the nature of the good in life but questions, of course, are begged in establishing such premisses. As Shiffrin argues:

> Ethical liberalism invokes neutrality (or variants of it) as a principle from which large and powerful political conclusions are to be drawn. Lurking behind this neutralility is a conception of what human beings ought to be like and how they ought to think. This underlying conception however . . . will not support general conclusions . . . the entire enterprise of drawing general political conclusions from sparse premises, rooted as it is in a rationalistic desire to transcend human differences, obscures the diversity of human beings.[115]

The problem of establishing an 'objective' or uncontentious basis upon which to erect normative principles in one that afflicts all theories of the state be these pluralist, New Right, élitist, Marxist, or neo-pluralist.[116] All have a particular view of human nature that is contestable and to this extent all fail to provide a secure means of resolving tensions between different legitimacy claims. Even if it is accepted that contestable cases may, nevertheless, possess force, the above approaches fail on another front—they do not explain the nature of arguments concerning legitimacy, nor does their own mode of argument seem to correspond with the way in which people debate issues of legitimacy. The essence of such debates is the making of appeals to a series of commonly recognized values rather than the positing of a particular model of democracy.

[111] See S. Shiffrin, 'Liberalism, Radicalism and Legal Scholarship' (1983) 30 UCLA Law Review 1103.

[112] J. Rawls, *A Theory of Justice* (1971).

[113] R. Dworkin, *Taking Rights Seriously* (1977).

[114] B. Ackerman, *Social Justice in The Liberal State* (1980). See also Mashaw, 'Administrative Due Process'.

[115] Shiffrin, 'Liberalism, Radicalism and Legal Scholarship', 1107. On liberalism and public law see Craig, *Public Law and Democracy*, chs. 8 and 9.

[116] See Dunleavy and O'Leary, *Theories of the State*, 338–43.

For some, the reality to come to terms with is that attempts to legitimate bureaucratic power are doomed to failure. Thus Gerald Frug[117] offers the approach of a democratic radical[118] and, speaking of the formalist, expertise, judicial review, and market/pluralist justifications for bureaucratic action, contends:

> all of these defences of bureaucratic power are no more than variations on a single story about the acceptability of bureaucratic organisation and . . . this story, far from building a convincing case for bureaucracy, is a mechanism of deception . . . we all engage in this kind of deceptive procedure when we comfort ourselves about bureaucratic power.[119]

Frug sets out to expose the deception and argues that the above four models of justification have been used to legitimate bureaucracy but they fail because they cannot reconcile the constraint of power according to objective premises with the subjective value of individuality. The contribution of critical theory, says Frug, is to make manifest the 'false consciousness through which people understand the world'[120] and to suggest alternative forms of organization. Frug thus offers the prospect of 'participatory democracy'. This would be no final 'solution' to social life but would seek to avoid new forms of domination and hierarchy and would offer processes 'by which people create for themselves the form of organised existence within which they live'.[121] He explains: 'The term participatory democracy does not describe a fixed series of limited possibilities of human organisation but the ideal under which the possibilities of joint transformation of social life are collected.'[122]

Frug's analysis, like that of his fellow democratic radical Unger, may offer a refreshing view of liberalism, it may point to the problematic nature of legitimating arguments, but the vision offered by participatory democracy is indeterminate. Such indeterminacy may help to fend off embarrassing questions concerning the nature of the alternative participatory arrangements envisaged but it is the ideal and hazy nature of

[117] Frug, 'The Ideology of Bureaucracy'.

[118] See also R. Unger, *Knowledge and Politics* (1975); id., *Law in Modern Society* (1976).

[119] Frug, 'The Ideology of Bureaucracy', 1278.

[120] Ibid. 1295.

[121] Ibid. 1296.

[122] Ibid.

the vision that undermines its force. As Shiffrin put it with reference to Unger:

> by departing from rationalism . . . democratic radicals flee to excessive romanticism. Recognising that political values cannot be legitimised by resort to abstract premises, they turn to democratic utopias where all will be equal and where individuality will be everywhere encouraged. This sunny view, however, cannot be sustained.[123]

In the absence of 'objective' foundations for assessing legitimacy and rejecting utopian visions, two final strategies should be considered. The first seeks to advance by borrowing the best from major theories and can be termed 'eclectic' liberalism. The second disentangles legitimacy claiming from the positing of a political theory or vision.

The model of electic liberalism that I will examine is that of Steven Shiffrin.[124] It is based on the premiss that human beings are diverse and complex, that they espouse values, perspectives, and outlooks of enormous variety. On this view, such diversities do not rule out the existence of 'important shared similarities'[125] but deductive 'proof' and monistic explanations concerning human nature and social reality are ruled out. Eclectic liberalism 'seeks to accommodate conflicting values in concrete contexts.. showing the impossibility of achieving all goals at once and advocating accommodation of values tailored to particular circumstances'.[126] It is a theory of balancing that addresses tensions and the potential for resolving these.

What though are the values recognized within this eclecticism? Here Shiffrin argues that eclectic liberalism offers more than a middle way between the rationalism of the ethical liberal and the romanticism of the democratic radical: 'it offers an alternative soundly based on the moral ideals that have made both those traditions attractive'.[127] The theory thus affirms free will, individual autonomy and choice, it assumes all have something to teach, it values diversity, it accepts 'most of the normative presuppositions of the ethical liberals . . . and the standard liberal commitments to civil rights, freedom of

[123] Shiffrin, 'Liberalism, Radicalism and Legal Scholarship', 1110.
[124] Ibid. [125] Ibid. 1194. [126] Ibid. 1211. [127] Ibid. 1192.

speech, due process, equality and economic redistribution'.[128] At the same time, eclectic liberalism (with an eye to democratic radicalism) emphasizes the social character of human nature. It recognizes the importance of rational discourse and the assessment of policies with reference to values that are in flux. The multi-principled basis for rights and the complex interaction of rights is acknowledged and eclectic liberalism stresses the need for institutional structures to be fashioned so as to protect rights. Such rights, however, are not guarded by absolute principles but values of importance are identifiable under the theory, which assesses issues of legitimacy with regard to the particular context.[129] The notion of equality is respected so that eclectic liberals support both political and civil liberties as well as entitlements to adequate food, housing, and necessities. Such liberals both respect dignity and permit redistributive taxation while they do not deny that those who work more should receive more. Eclectic liberalism seeks to promote community and participation without sacrificing individuality.

The difficulty posed by electic liberalism is that it takes on board not only the strengths of the ethical liberal and radical democratic approaches, but also their weaknesses. If ethical liberalism is underpinned by questionable premisses then the values borrowed from ethical liberalism are similarly tainted. If the social character of human nature is an aspect of the democratic radicals' romanticism, it is doubtful whether that romanticism is removed on endorsement by the eclectic liberal. If all values are deemed worthy of respect then eclectic liberalism means all things to all persons and 'anything goes'. It is not rendered immune from this attack by assertions that real life is very complicated and that in order to resolve conflicts of value it is necessary to analyse particular circumstances and constituencies.

A further criticism of eclectic liberalism is that its extreme liberality attributes legitimacy indiscriminately and uncritically. In assessing the legitimacy of bureaucratic action the eclectic

[128] Ibid. 1195. [129] Ibid. 1205.

liberal would give weight to an open-ended series of justificatory rationales. As Frug points out, however, important questions are begged at the stage of choosing which rationales to employ or to emphasize.[130] The effect of what Frug dubs such 'modest realism' is to abandon attempts to articulate justification and to accept the *status quo* with the words 'but everything is a tough policy choice, and every decision we make will have its faults. All we can do is the best we can'.[131]

Disentangling legitimacy claims from political theories may, however, offer more hope than seeking to shore up the former by making reference to the latter. Such an uncoupling bears in mind Niklas Luhmann's point that the complexity of social systems requires different levels of generalization to be distinguished: 'It is no longer possible to find a point for man's highest fulfilment that is equidistant from all values and is at the same time an ethical maxim for action. We have to think in a more differentiated manner—we have to separate the levels of values, norms and goals from one another.'[132]

A first step in the process of disentangling is to examine what normative political theories and legitimacy assessments do. The former, it can be argued, aim to make statements about the way that society or government ought to be organized and will commonly attempt to derive such statements from premisses allegedly immune from contention. To assess legitimacy can be seen, however, as engaging in a distinct activity that operates at a different level. It involves, as noted, making judgements as to the merits of legitimacy claims but constitutes what might be termed an intermediate discourse. It is intermediate because it allows a discussion of legitimacy to take place without *immediate* linkage to any particular vision of democracy.

To assert this does not imply that those individuals who are engaged in a discourse on the legitimacy of a governmental process will at heart possess no personal belief in a particular

[130] Frug, 'The Ideology of Bureaucracy', 1379. [131] Ibid. 1383.

[132] N. Luhmann, *The Differentiation of Society* (1982), 119. On the difference between moral, legal, political, and legitimacy assertions see also Mashaw, *Bureaucratic Justice*, 25.

balancing of rationales or values. An individual's own preferences or vision of the optimal society will suggest such a balancing. The point is that it is possible to converse on legitimacy with another individual (perhaps one of a very different political persuasion) by making reference to rationales or values that have unspecified weight or ranking but are nevertheless commonly recognized. It has to be acknowledged, that in theoretical terms this is a discourse within limits and that these limits may be reached (at which stage preferred political visions may be referred to). This does not mean, however, that justificatory discourse on legitimacy is not possible or useful. In practical terms such discourse is the general currency of debates concerning governmental processes.

How, on this view, should the critic or the designer of a governmental process judge the legitimacy of that process? First, he or she should assess the merits of the claims under the individual five headings while having an eye to cumulative claims. This will ensure that where action can be taken to improve a claim under one heading (e.g. to efficiency) the case for the action will be recognized as legitimacy maximizing where other claims are not prejudiced. Given the resource and informational constraints usual in government, such relatively uncontentious assessments will often be as far as it is feasible to pursue analysis. An approach that recognizes the five forms of justification avoids both the narrowness and the lack of realism associated with, for example, legalistic analyses. Moreover, it accords more fully with the breadth of justificatory argument employed and recognized by the public.[133]

Second, where it is necessary to consider a trade-off between two or more types of claim (e.g. a step that increases efficiency and diminishes accountability) the critic should recognize that, although choosing between different distributions of legitimacy claim does at root demand reference to some notion of the optimal model of state or democracy, it may make no sense to base such a choice on a purely personal vision. This is because the strength of a legitimacy claim made under one heading

[133] As Rodney Barker has noted, 'most people are neither political nor moral philosophers' (*Political Legitimacy and the State*, 10).

may be affected by the willingness of a variety of persons to attribute legitimacy under other headings. Thus, for instance, I might, because of my personal vision of democracy, be inclined to design or change a process so as to trade off lower accountability for greater efficiency. Without further thought, I might judge the process I propose as highly legitimate on that basis. In the real world, however, the greater efficiency I envisage may not be realizable because other persons may attack the process (or its operating institution) for lack of accountability, and such attacks may detract from the achievement of results.[134] Thus, if I set up a process in which (in the interests of efficiency) a regulator acts in an unaccountable fashion, objectors to that lack of accountability (e.g. the regulated industry or consumer groups) may be so hostile and uncooperative that hoped-for efficiency is not realized.

In judging a governmental process, therefore, it is appropriate to consider how the merits of some legitimacy claims (e.g. the efficiency and expertise claims in particular) stand to be affected by anticipated reactions to claims under other headings (notably under the accountability and due process heads). This is not to argue that what is legitimate is what seems legitimate to other people (or to people generally), it is to recognize that claims are made in the real world, that, even within the terms of a particular person's judgement as to legitimacy, it may be necessary to take on board the potential attributions of legitimacy of other persons.[135] The personal judgement has to be placed in the context of the anticipated reactions of others and a position of tempered idealism adopted. The implication is that the critic or designer of processes may be on unsure ground in seeking to argue for extreme trade-offs of legitimacy claims by making reference to a personal vision. Such a critic/designer should, accordingly, be wary of endorsing processes which score conspicuously badly on any of the five headings since those poor scores may tend to undermine the

[134] Since attacks from some quarters may be more detrimental to e.g. efficiency claims than others, the sources of potential attacks should also be considered.

[135] In Barry's terms ideal—regarding considerations are thus tempered by want-regarding factors—see Barry, *Political Argument*, ch. 3.

higher scores anticipated under other headings. (Non-extreme trade-offs may, of course, be more safely made on the basis of the personal vision.)

To summarize: governmental processes can be assessed by making judgements about the merits of legitimacy claims under the five headings. To criticize or design processes on this basis is not to assert that the chosen processes are the most morally or politically correct, it is to assert that they are the processes most meriting support according to recognized bench-marks. In most practical assessments of ligitimacy, immediate resort to a vision of democracy is not necessary, but where trade-offs of legitimacy claims have to be made such references are unavoidable. Even in the case of such references, however, the personal vision has to be tempered in so far as legitimacy assessing presupposes operation in the real world and such operation is in turn affected by the attributions of legitimacy of others.

Conclusions

Debates concerning governmental processes are unduly confined if conducted with reference solely to what might be called 'traditional legal values'. In order to break out of the straitjacket of the legal paradigm it is necessary to consider the wide range of values being served by governmental processes and it is necessary also to explore the nature of disputes concerning legitimacy. The notion of a discourse of legitimacy makes it possible to explain the role of five rationales for legitimacy claims. The same notion involves a degree of indeterminacy in so far as the weighting of rationales is flexible, but the five rationales can be identified and the values appealed to are not open-ended in nature.

The idea of a particular discourse of legitimacy also allows a distinction to be drawn between assessing legitimacy and the assertion of prescriptive political theories. It sees assessing legitimacy as an intermediate level of argument which has significance and offers practical guidance in a way that an immediate appeal to a normative theory of democracy does not. The nature of legitimacy assessing, furthermore, means that, where resort has to be made to a personal vision, that vision may have to be tempered in its application and attention paid to the dangers of conspicuously weak claims. Such an approach admittedly leaves legitimacy assessing as a contentious operation but there is no way to avoid this. Contentiousness, indeed, lies at the very heart of legitimacy claiming, which employs rationales of an intrinsically contestable nature. The notion of a discourse on legitimacy presupposes the identification of rationales rather than the ordering of rationales—thence derives its strength as well as its limitations. Bearing in mind such limitations, it is with reference to the five rationales identified in this chapter that the ensuing discussion of governmental rules will be conducted.

4 Rules Made by Governments

Parliamentary, or primary, legislation might be taken to be the most important category of rule-making. In some respects, however, such a supposition would be mistaken. The bulk of primary legislation is vastly exceeded by that of rules made by ministers, departments, and agencies. Thus, the Public General Acts on average cover 2,000 pages whereas Statutory Instruments (which do not include by-laws or many classes of administrative rule) average 6,000 pages.[1] Nor is the issue one of quantity alone. Increasingly the key functions of government are carried out by means of secondary and tertiary rules, which have experienced what Ganz has called 'an exponential growth'.[2] As Hayhurst and Wallington have put it: 'primary legislation has become a skeletal enabling framework conferring not just the functions of detailed implementation but the power to determine major policy questions on ministers.'[3]

This chapter looks at the governmental uses of secondary and tertiary rules and assesses these generic forms according to the bench-marks described in Chapter 3.[4] By secondary

[1] S. A. De Smith and R. Brazier, *Constitutional and Administrative Law*, 7th edn. (1994), 360. Even in the 1920s delegated legislation was said to 'dwarf' primary legislation. See C. T. Carr, *Delegated Legislation: Three Lectures* (1921), 2, quoted in M. Loughlin, *Public Law and Political Theory* (1992), 242.

[2] G. Ganz, *Quasi-Legislation: Recent Developments in Secondary Legislation* (1987).

[3] J. D. Hayhurst and P. Wallington, 'The Parliamentary Scrutiny of Delegated Legislation' [1988] PL 547, 551. In 1986 the Joint Committee on Statutory Instruments noted the increasing use of Statutory Instruments and their being employed not merely to implement the details of legislation but also to change policy: HC 31—xxxvii (1985–6), p. 2., quoted in A. W. Bradley and K. D. Ewing, *Constitutional and Administrative Law*, 11th edn. (1993), 625. For examples of statutes imposing heavy reliance on secondary legislation see the Social Security Act 1986; the Abolition of Domestic Rates (Scotland) Act 1987; the Legal Aid Act 1988; the Education Reform Act 1988; the Education (Student Loans) Act 1990; and the Child Support Act 1991, which contains over 100 regulation-making powers. See also the Hansard Society, *Making the Law: The Report of the Hansard Society Commission on the Legislative Process* (1992), 64–5 185–6.

[4] As indicated in Ch. 1, primary legislation is not within the scope of this volume, being considered in detail elsewhere (see e.g. D. Miers and A. Page, *Legislation*, 2nd edn. (1990) and references therein). On the choice between primary legislation and 'governmental' rules see *infra* pp. 62–3, pp. 85–121 and Appendix. Primary legislation as a device is susceptible of assessment according to the Ch. 3 bench-marks

legislation is meant 'every exercise of a power to legislate conferred by or under an Act of Parliament'.[5] The term 'tertiary rule' refers here to the wide array of governmental rules that are not directly enforceable through criminal or civil proceedings but which may nevertheless produce indirect legal effects. These rules include such items as codes of practice, guidance, guidance notes, guidelines, circulars, practice statements, codes of conduct, and administrative rules.

I. SECONDARY LEGISLATION[6]

The power to make law may be delegated by Parliament to a variety of bodies, ranging from ministers, central departments, and agencies to public corporations, local authorities, and private associations. Such powers may be put into effect with rules taking various forms, for example: Orders in Council, Statutory Instruments, regulations, rules, orders, schemes, warrants, and directives. Uniformity of promulgating procedures is ensured for Statutory Instruments by the Statutory Instruments Act 1946, but this Act does not cover all items of secondary legislation which, as we will see, may be the end product of various procedures.

Secondary legislation came into widespread use in the nineteenth century with the rise of collectivism and the realization that Parliament had to delegate powers to make detailed rules to the new central government departments.[7] By the time that the Donoughmore Committee came to consider ministerial powers in 1932[8] it was generally accepted (in spite of certain

and, it should be noted, the legislative mandate cannot be assumed to be unproblematic even in the case of primary legislation—see e.g. *Pepper* v. *Hart* [1993] 1 All ER 42; F. Bennion, *Statutory Interpretation* (1984), and W. Twining and D. Miers, *How to Do Things with Rules*, 3rd edn. (1991), 202–211.

[5] Report from the Joint Committee on Delegated Legislation (1971–72; HL 184, HC 475), para. 6; quoted in Miers and Page, *Legislation*, 104.

[6] See generally Miers and Page, *Legislation*, ch. 8.

[7] See C. Carr. *Delegated Legislation* (1921); C. K. Allen, *Law and Orders* (1945), ch. 2, and B. L. Jones, *Garner's Administrative Law*, 7th edn. (1989), 53–4.

[8] See Report of the Committee on Ministers Powers, Cmd 4060 (1932); R. Rawlings, 'Continuity and Evolution: From Donoughmore to Justice via Franks' in M. Citi (ed.), Il Controllo Guirisditionale dell' Arrivita Administrativa in Ingliterra (1982); W. A. Robson, 'The Committee on Ministers' Powers' (1932) 3 Pol.Q. 346.

well-known attacks[9]) that delegated legislation was inevitable given the nature of governmental tasks and the limitations of parliamentary time and expertise. The Donoughmore Committee itself accepted this inevitability, but recommended a number of safeguards against the possible abuse of such legislation and, *inter alia*, recommended: the systematization and rationalization of delegated legislation; a simplification of nomenclature; amendments to the relevant publication rules; extending the practice of departmental consultation; increasing the use of explanatory notes; and establishing a uniform procedure for laying regulations before Parliament. The Statutory Instruments Act 1946 set down procedures for Statutory Instruments (SIs) and Orders in Council but, in its non-application to other forms of delegated legislation, failed to effect the rationalization that Donoughmore had advocated. Classifying by originating procedure, the following varieties of secondary rule are encountered:

(i) *Orders in Council.* Many statutes confer important legislative powers on the Sovereign in Council—thus states of emergency are proclaimed by Orders in Council under the Emergency Powers Act 1920.

(ii) *Regulations, directives, and orders.* On matters thought less central in constitutional terms, Parliament commonly confers legislative power on the relevant member of the executive. Thus the minister heading a central department, or a public corporation, or an agency will be given powers to make rules of a legally binding nature and these may be issued under a variety of headings—for example as 'regulations', 'directives', 'orders', or 'rules'. These terms are used haphazardly and, as noted, the Statutory Instruments Act 1946 covers some but not all Orders in Council, regulations, directives, and orders.

(iii) *Special Procedure Orders.* These are orders made under the Statutory Orders (Special Procedure) Acts 1945 and 1965. An enabling Act may provide for such orders to be made by a local authority or statutory undertaking and

[9] e.g. Hewart, *The New Despotism* (1929).

submitted to the appropriate government department for approval. If approved by the Secretary of State, the order is then laid before Parliament and, if not annulled or amended by a resolution of either House by the end of a prescribed period, the order will come into effect.

(iv) *Local Authority Orders.* A statute may authorize a local authority to issue orders with legal force (e.g. in the field of compulsory purchases). These orders require ministerial confirmation before having effect and provision is made for the holding of local inquiries into objections before the minister considers approval.

(v) *By-laws.* Power to make by-laws is often conferred on local authorities, public corporations, and, less commonly, on certain independent non-governmental bodies such as the National Trust.

On the nomenclature of delegated legislation, the Donoughmore Committee, as noted, recommended rationalization and objected to indiscriminate use of terms such as 'regulation', 'rule', and 'order'. Thus it was proposed:

> The expression 'regulation' should be used to describe the instrument by which the power to make substantive law is exercised, and the expression 'rule' to describe the instrument by which the power to make law about procedure is exercised. The expression 'order' should be used to describe the instrument of the exercise of (*a*) executive power, (*b*) the power to take judicial and quasi-judicial decisions.[10]

Such rationalization is still awaited.

1 Justifications for Secondary Legislation

(i) Expertise and Efficiency

The case for employing delegated rather than primary legislation is now familiar to public lawyers.[11] First, it is argued that

[10] Donoughmore Report, 64.

[11] See e.g. Jones, *Garner's Administrative Law*, 54–7; D. Foulkes, *Administrative Law*, 7th edn. (1990), ch. 3; D. Pollard and D. Hughes, *Constitutional and Administrative Law* (1990), ch. 5; Bradley and Ewing, *Constitutional and Administrative Law*, 625–6 Hansard Society Report, 64–7.

Parliament has neither the time nor the personnel to legislate on matters of detail since it could not, as presently organized, consider and debate such issues. Instead, Parliament properly focuses on questions of broad principle and the establishing of frameworks upon which ministers or agencies can be authorized to base more precise provisions. Delegated legislation is, accordingly, said to serve a valuable purpose in keeping primary legislation as clear, simple, and short as possible and in assisting Parliament to focus on essential points, policies, and principles.[12] Second, the issue to be legislated upon may be too technical to be understood and debated properly in Parliament. It is better in such cases to allow ministers or agencies to employ or consult with experts and to produce considered rules. Third, particular constituencies may have to be consulted on matters of detail (e.g. trade associations, specialists, and unions) and this is more effectively done by the executive than by Parliament. Fourth, unforeseen circumstances may have to be anticipated or responded to quickly. Parliament cannot lay down a blueprint that provides for all eventualities and using delegated legislation allows plans for the future to be developed as events unfold (perhaps employing experimental strategies and adjusting these in a course of 'muddling through').[13] Delegated legislation also allows rapid responses to be made to crises and emergencies. Thus, in wartime, ministerially issued regulations can be provided for in order to maintain public order and safety. Fifth, secondary legislation offers a useful way to bring Acts of Parliament into force at the appropriate time or by stages.

In terms of the five bench-marks of Chapter 3, the case for delegated legislation is principally grounded on the expertise and efficiency rationales. As one parliamentary committee noted: 'Parliament and Government would grind to a halt if

[12] See Hansard Society Report, 65–6. The Hansard Society Commission was divided on whether the desirable balance of primary and delegated legislation had been arrived at but 'on balance' believed that the main advantages of making greater use of delegated legislation (subject to procedural reforms) outweighed the 'very real' disadvantages.

[13] On 'muddling through' see D. Braybooke and C. Lindblom, *A Strategy of Decision* (1963).

there were not built into our constitution an adequate system of executive legislation.'[14] The arguments for acceptability on the basis of the legislative mandate, accountability/control, and due process rationales are, however, more problematic.

(ii) Legislative Mandate

To assert that delegated legislation effects the will of Parliament in a rational manner involves a number of difficulties. For a start, the varieties of secondary legislation outlined above do not evidence a system marked by a high degree of rationality.

As for Parliament's will, in many instances it is not clear what Parliament desired in the first place—indeed Parliament's inability to form a view may have been a central reason for the initial delegation. There may, moreover, be a threat to the power of Parliament itself if a delegation is so wide that it is not easy to discern the limits that Parliament intends to impose on the delegated legislative power. There is difficulty also in the notion that Parliament can debate and decide upon matters of broad framework policy and can leave 'detail' to those given delegated legislative powers. This idea presupposes that it is possible to separate the framework from the detail. In fact this may prove to be impossible and the results may prove alarming. Thus Parliament may find itself debating issues that lack real content and then being asked to give (and giving) enormously wide legislative powers to Ministers. Parliament, accordingly, finds itself debating 'blind' and giving powers on trust to the executive.[15] Nor is this a recent phenomenon—in the 1970s when a number of regulatory bodies were created, MPs were more than once found protesting that they were debating Bills in a vacuum because the agencies were to operate on lines established by, then unpublished, codes or rules.[16] Where there is a so called 'Henry VIII clause' that enables a Minister to modify an Act of Parliament so far as is necessary

[14] First Special Report from the Joint Committee on Statutory Instruments, 1977–8, HC 169, para. 37, quoted in Foulkes, *Administrative Law*, 62.

[15] For a review of expressions of concern (*inter alia* from the Bar Council, Law Society, and National Consumers Council) see Hansard Society Report, 64.

[16] See R. Baldwin, *Regulating the Airlines* (1985), 265.

to bring it into operation, any claim to legitimacy on the legislative mandate rationale is patently weak.[17] Membership of the European Community tends to render claims under this rationale yet more problematic since delegated legislation may be used to implement Community requirements (e.g. in Directives) and there may be tensions between those requirements and mandates under domestic law or between Community styles of control and domestic modes of governing through law.[18]

(iii) Accountability/Control

Whether those exercising delegated legislative powers are adequately accountable and controlled is also questionable. Accountability to and through Parliament is possible but is limited in scope.[19] Ministers can be called to account by Parliament for the delegated legislation that they make but those chairing public corporations and agencies are not responsible to Parliament. Parliamentary scrutiny of ministerial legislation is also limited by the rules governing the publication of draft regulations, codes, etc. The relevant enabling Act may lay down a particular procedure for publication but there are no general rules on publication. The Rulės Publication Act 1893 introduced standard rules on primarily printing and publication, but this Act was repealed and replaced by the Statutory Instruments Act 1946 which sets down detailed procedures for Orders in Council and SIs. The 1946 Act lays down provisions on the making, printing, and publication of

[17] See e.g. Local Government Act 1972, s. 262, Health and Safety at Work etc. Act, ss. 15 and 80; Sex Discrimination Act 1975, s. 80(3). The Hansard Society Report of 1992 strongly recommended that 'Henry VIII' clauses should not be included in future Acts of Parliament (p. 67). When the Government launched the Deregulation and Contracting Out Bill on 19 Jan. 1994 much controversy attended the inclusion of 'Henry VIII' powers in clause one of the bill. These powers would allow ministers to quash delegated legislation ('red tape') without resorting to primary legislation. See comments on Second Reading at *HC Debs.*, vol. 237 cols. 169, 178, 199, 202 (8 Feb. 1994).

[18] For an examination of the way that Community requirements can affect domestic regulatory regimes see A. C. Neal, 'The European Framework Directive on the Health and Safety of Workers: Challenges for the United Kingdom' (1990) 6 IJCLLIR 80; R. Baldwin and T. C. Daintith (eds.), *Harmonization and Hazard* (1992).

[19] See Hayhurst and Wallington, 'The Parliamentary Scrutiny of Delegated Legislation' [1988] PL 547, and Hansard Society Report, 89–95.

Orders and Instruments but, again, there are no general provisions covering other forms of subordinate legislation apart from local authority by-laws to which special rules apply.[20]

The parent statute may also provide for parliamentary control of delegated legislation by demanding a variety of 'laying' procedures, notably:

- The Act may require 'bare laying'—an instrument merely being laid before Parliament after being made. Instruments are thus made then laid and come into operation on the date specified. An instrument cannot come into operation before laying if laying is stipulated.[21] Normally a parent Act will require the laying of delegated legislation before both Houses of Parliament but sometimes (as e.g. where taxation is involved) laying only before the House of Commons may be involved.
- Negative resolution procedure' may be indicated, according to which an instrument must be laid after being made but prior to coming into operation. When so laid any Member of either House may within forty days move a prayer for annulment[22] following which the Government may revoke the instrument by Order in Council.
- Affirmative resolution procedure requires that an instrument be made and laid but it cannot come into effect unless approved.
- Draft laying may be required for approval or for disapproval.

In addition to these four principal procedures there are other possibilities: there may be no laying requirement for a set of rules at all or it may be stated that an instrument made will expire at the end of a specified period unless approved by the relevant House(s) of Parliament.

The wide variety of laying procedures is not placed into any framework of clear principles governing the choice of different procedures. The Donoughmore Committee criticized the lack

[20] See Local Government Act 1972, ss. 235–8.

[21] 'Laying' means delivering a copy of the rules to the Votes and Proceedings Office of the House of Commons.

[22] See Statutory Instruments Act 1946, s. 5.

of such principles but governments have failed to introduce guidance on the topic.[23]

Laying procedures are thus unreliable as devices for triggering parliamentary scrutiny of delegated legislation. Not only that but the quality of such scrutiny is also questionable on a number of grounds.[24] Even when laying requirements apply, it may be a matter of chance whether any Member of Parliament (MP) notices any contentious provisions. The Houses of Parliament set up the Joint Committee on Statutory Instruments (the Joint Committee) in 1973 to scrutinize subordinate legislation, but this Committee's functions are limited. Its terms of reference require it to consider all Statutory Instruments laid, or laid in draft before either House together with schemes requiring approval by Statutory Instrument and all general Statutory Instruments not required to be laid. The Joint Committee then decides whether to draw the attention of either House to the instrument on a number of grounds, for example: if it imposes a tax; purports to exclude the courts; is retrospective; makes unusual use of the delegated power; or is defectively drafted. Each year the Committee considers over a thousand SIs, but it takes no direct action on these, merely drawing attention to points of concern. Time constraints mean that the Joint Committee's reports are rarely debated.

On the floor of the House of Commons no debate on an instrument will occur (except in cases requiring affirmative resolution) unless notice of a prayer against it is tabled. A prayer will be debated in the House, but only if time is provided (this depends mainly on Opposition pressure)—in 1990/1, a typical year, only twenty-five out of 114 tabled prayers were debated.[25] A debate may take place in standing committee but only if a Minister successfully moves the reference of it and such a motion can be blocked by twenty MPs. Instruments liable to

[23] See Donoughmore Report, 42, and Miers and Page, *Legislation*, 117.

[24] See J. Beatson, 'Legislative Control of Administrative Rule-making: Lessons from the British Experience?' (1979) 12 CILJ 199; M. Asimow, 'Delegated Legislation: United States and United Kingdom' (1983) 3 OJLS 253.

[25] See Hansard Society Report, 93–4, for further figures, expressions of concern, and a recommendation that Ministers and Whips ensure that enough committees are established and sufficient time made available to allow prayers to be properly debated.

affirmative resolution can also be referred to standing committee but are subject to the same limitations. Such debates, moreover, are restricted in time (being limited to one and a half hours in the Commons) and Parliament cannot amend an instrument—it can only approve or reject it.[26] No procedure, moreover, ensures that the Joint Committee's views are considered before action on an instrument is taken. It has been argued that scrutinizing delegated legislation is not one of Parliament's priorities or one of the functions most sought after by MPs, and that, as a result, the task is not carried out as effectively as it might be.[27] Hayhurst and Wallington conclude their review of scrutiny procedures:

> the inescapable judgement on the standing committee procedure is that it serves no real purpose in the scrutiny of Statutory Instruments . . . The declining availability of Parliamentary time to debate delegated legislation, the increase in decisions taken before the [Joint] Committee's report is published and the unwillingness of either the Commons or (more surprisingly) the Lords to allow legal points to use up prime battle time, all compound the process . . . The securing of additional facilities for scrutiny is of limited value unless there are indicators that the process of scrutiny will assume a higher priority.[28]

The work of the Joint Committee itself is, moreover, concerned with means not ends, with technicalities rather than merits, and this weakens the Committee's scope for review. Party politics may also militate against Commons consideration of the kinds of point made by the Joint Committee. As instruments attract more party controversy, technical or procedural points receive less attention, and debate tends to centre on the merits of the proposed measures. Points raised by the Joint Committee will, at best, be used as ammunition by the Opposition.[29]

The Committee itself has also expressed concern at the executive's propensity to bypass Parliament by omitting details

[26] See Hayhurst and Wallington, 'Parliamentary Scrutiny of Delegated Legislation', 356.

[27] See Beatson, 'Legislative Control'.

[28] Hayhurst and Wallington, 'Parliamentary Scrutiny of Delegated Legislation', 574.

[29] Ibid.

from instruments and, instead, conferring broad discretions on ministers or making references to other documents. Thus it has stated that delegated legislation should be detailed, specific, and self-explanatory and should not depend on ministerial discretions unless the enabling statute expressly provides for this.

A further questionable practice is that of legislating by reference—the process whereby an instrument of delegated legislation refers to another publication. The official publication *Statutory Instruments Practice* states that references must be made to specific, dated items only, otherwise: 'if the authors of the publication alter it, the effect of the instrument will be altered, which will constitute unauthorised sub-delegation.'[30] Where an instrument has to be laid then it may be argued that the other document referred to should also be laid.[31]

Such is the weakness of the Joint Committee's position that the House of Commons has on occasion approved instruments at a time when the initiating department has been aware of Committee doubts about the *vires* of the order. In the case referred to, the Committee reported its doubts to the House, the department withdrew the order, and a replacement had to be brought to the House for approval. The Committee concluded that 'a farce' had been made of its appointment.[32] In a proportion of instances the House has considered instruments before the Joint Committee has published its reports. In the period 1973–83, twenty-one out of sixty-four debates in standing committees preceded the issue of the report and in the Commons Chamber itself, ten out of forty-two reported instruments were debated before the issue of the report.[33] The Government has yet to amend the rules to comply with a number of suggestions that have been made for improving scrutiny procedures—for example by providing that affirmative

[30] Quoted Foulkes, *Administrative Law*, 89.

[31] See *R* v. *Secretary of State for Social Services, ex parte Camden LBC* [1987] 1 All ER 560; A. I. L. Campbell, 'Statutory Instruments: Laying and Legislating by Reference' [1987] PL 328.

[32] First Special Report from the Joint Committee on Statutory Instruments 1977–8, HL 51, para. 21.

[33] See Hayhurst and Wallington, 'Parliamentary Scrutiny of Delegated Legislation', 565.

and negative resolutions should not precede Joint Committee consideration.[34]

The merits of SIs can, since 1973, be considered by a House of Commons Standing Committee on Statutory Instruments—or Merits Committee. A Minister may move that an instrument or draft be referred to a Merits Committee. Such a committee may discuss the instrument for up to 90 minutes, but the merits cannot be voted upon. The Committee can nevertheless disapprove of an instrument by refusing to agree to a motion that it has 'considered the instrument'[35] and the Government may well take views expressed in committee into account. No debate, however, can take place on the floor of the House in relation to such an instrument and the Select Committee on Procedure criticized this aspect of procedure in 1978.

It is clear that the task of the Joint Committee has become increasingly difficult as the drift from primary to secondary legislation has accelerated. Thus the Committee reported in 1986 that the volume, scope, and complexity of SIs had increased in the previous five years:

> Instead of simply implementing the 'nuts and bolts' of Government policy, Statutory Instruments have increasingly been used to change policy, sometimes in ways that were not envisaged when the enabling primary legislation was passed . . . we accept that this trend is not one which it will necessarily be easy to reverse.[36]

Some steps have been taken to review and improve Parliament's control over delegated legislation. The Government has moved to establish a Delegated Powers Scrutiny Committee in the House of Lords with the function of examining the appropriateness of employing delegated legislation.[37]

[34] See Foulkes, *Administrative Law*, 90–1; see also St John Bates 'Scrutiny of the Administration', in Ryle and Richards (eds.), *The Commons under Scrutiny* (1988).

[35] See Standing Committees, vol. iv, 1977–8, 6th Standing Committee 31 Jan. 1978 and 943 HC Official Report, 5th ser., col. 256; Foulkes *Administrative Law*, 91.

[36] See Foulkes, *Administrative Law*, 92.

[37] The Select Committee of the House of Lords on the Committee Work of the House (the 'Jellicoe Committee', HL 35–1 of 1991–2) recommended the establishment of a Delegated Powers Scrutiny Committee with a first task of devising ground rules on what should be dealt with in primary legislation and what might be left to dele-

Further measures could, however, be taken to improve Parliament's position in relation to delegated legislation. Thus the Hansard Society[38] has argued that such legislation should be treated 'as seriously as primary legislation' and has recommended, *inter alia*, that:

- Departmentally related select committees might review Statutory Instruments in their fields when they are laid before Parliament, and report on those that raise matters of public importance.
- All Statutory Instruments requiring affirmative resolutions, and all prayers for the annulment of other Statutory Instruments, should automatically be referred to standing committees for debate[39].
- Standing committees on Statutory Instruments should be able to question ministers on the purpose, meaning, and effect of the instrument.
- Debates on Statutory Instruments in standing committees should be held on a motion approving, rejecting, or expressing opinions on the instrument.
- MPs should be able to suggest amendments to Statutory Instruments without actually amending the instrument and, accordingly, amendments to a motion on an instrument should be allowed either recommending non approval of the instrument or approval subject to amendments being made to the instrument itself.
- There should be no time limits on debates on Statutory Instruments in standing committees.

gated legislation. The Hansard Society Report, para. 406, welcomed this development and the Government set up the committee on an experimental basis; see HL Debs., vol. 540, col. 91 (10 Nov. 1992).

[38] Hansard Society Report, 89–95; see also Annex A (p. 149) for a suggested procedure for debating SIs in the Commons.

[39] An echo of the Select Committee on Sittings of the House,—the Jopling Committee—see HC 20–I of 1991–2. One innovation was prompted by the Deregulation and Contracting Out Bill and its contentious use of Henry VIII orders—the Government was prepared to set up two new committees to scrutinize regulation-abolishing orders in both Houses of Parliament before such orders are put to the vote. At Second Reading Michael Heseltine, President of the Board of Trade, called this 'a special and exceptional form of parliamentary scrutiny'. (HC Debs., vol. 237, col. 151 (8 Feb. 1994)).

Until steps along these lines are taken, justifying the use of delegated legislation on the basis of its effective control by Parliament will remain problematic. Such legislation may be necessary on efficiency grounds, but the constraints of parliamentary time, expertise, and procedure mean that claims under the accountability/control heading carry limited conviction. Where delegated legislation owes its origins to policies emerging from the European Union (as where that legislation implements a Directive) the claim that parliamentary control operates may be yet weaker still since key policy decisions may be *faits accomplis* at the stage of domestic parliamentary scrutiny.

It might be argued that the courts are effective in controlling the use of delegated legislation. They can declare items of delegated legislation to be void because correct procedures of a mandatory nature have not been followed or on the ground that they are substantively *ultra vires* the parent statute.[40] Thus, if the parent statute imposes a duty to consult, then failure to do so may lead the court to declare the delegated legislation *ultra vires*.[41] Similarly, if it is shown that an item of delegated legislation is being used for purposes other than those envisaged by the parent Act or unreasonably, it will be declared void.[42] It should be noted, however, that the courts have shown themselves unwilling to declare items of delegated legislation invalid on the grounds of their substantive unreasonableness where political judgements are at issue and the House of Commons has approved the instrument.[43]

Judicial reviews of secondary rules have, moreover, to be instituted by litigants and a series of factors militates against court scrutiny. Individuals face the considerable costs of court action with shrinking legal aid and no contingency fee system.

[40] See e.g. *Commissioner of Customs and Excise* v. *Cure and Deeley Ltd.* [1962] 1 QB 340. *Cinnamond* v. *British Airports Authority* [1980] 2 All ER 368.

[41] See e.g. *Agricultural, Horticultural and Forestry Industry Training Board* v. *Aylesbury Mushroom Ltd.* [1972] 1 All ER 280; *Lee* v. *Secretary of State for Education and Science* (1967) 66 LGR 211.

[42] See *Attorney-General for Canada* v. *Hallett and Carey Ltd* [1952] AC 206; *Kruse* v. *Johnson* [1898] 2 QB 91.

[43] *Nottinghamshire County Council* v. *Secretary of State for the Environment* [1986] AC 240; [1986] 1 All ER 199.

Well-established rules governing access to court have long made it difficult for pressure-groups to contest governmental rules.[44] Traditionally a party who wished to apply for judicial review has had to demonstrate standing (*locus standi*) in the form of a particular interest over and above that of the general public.[45] The law has been attuned to the protection of private interests and the function of representing the public interest has been given to the Attorney-General, who has automatic standing to initiate or intervene in litigation but who may not be strongly inclined to challenge the secondary rules produced by cabinet colleagues.[46]

Since 1977, however, and the reform of judicial review procedure, some movement has been made in the direction of allowing representative actions by pressure-groups. The post-reform test for standing is one of 'sufficient interest' and, in the leading case of *R* v. *Inland Revenue Commissioners ex parte National Federation of Self-Employed and Small Business Ltd.*,[47] the House of Lords allowed an interest group to challenge a tax amnesty granted to certain part-time workers in the newspaper industry. That interest group was, nevertheless, seen as an aggregate of individual members' interests[48] in contrast to the position in *R* v. *Secretary of State for Social Services ex parte Child Poverty Action Group and Greater London Council*[49]where a further step was taken and CPAG was allowed standing to represent unidentified supplementary benefits claimants.

[44] See C. Harlow and R. Rawlings, *Pressure Through Law* (1992), esp. chs. 3 and 7; The Law Commission, Consultation Paper No. 126, *Administrative Law: Judicial Review and Statutory Appeals* (1993), 55–65; P. Cane, 'Statutes, Standing and Representation' [1990] PL 307; Harry Woolf, 'A Possible Programme for Reform' [1992] PL 221.

[45] *Gregory* v. *Camden LBC* [1966] 1 WLR 899.

[46] *Gouriet* v. *Union of Post Office Workers* [1977] 3 WLR 300; Harlow and Rawlings, *Pressure Through Law*, 145.

[47] [1982] AC 617.

[48] See also *Royal College of Nursing of the UK* v. *DHSS* [1981] 1 All ER 545, 551b–h (Woolf J) [1981] AC 800 (concerning advice to nurses on the lawfulness of carrying out abortions), but in *R* v. *Secretary of State for The Environment ex parte Rose Theatre Trust Co.* [1990] 1 QB 504 a group of experts and local residents formed to assert an interest in the Rose Theatre site were said not to have created an interest if the individuals had not themselves possessed interests. See Cane, 'Statutes, Standing and Representation'.

[49] *The Times*, 16 Aug. 1985; *R* v. *Secretary of State for Social Services ex parte Child Poverty Action Group* (1988) [1990] 2 QB 540.

Does this mean that pressure-group action through the courts may now operate as an effective control over rule-making? It does not. The door of standing has opened to some extent but it is not clear how readily the judges will confer representative status (particularly where the general public interest is concerned) and certain judges are clearly more committed to a 'public interest' ethos of administrative law than others.[50] The courts have yet to develop clear rules to classify types of allowable representative applicant and their interests, to establish priorities between different group applicants, and to define the nature of any subsequent rights of initiation and intervention in court proceedings.[51] Until such developments occur,[52] it is difficult to portray the courts as rigorous scrutineers of secondary (or, indeed, tertiary) rules. Parliamentary control over governmental rule-making may be weak, but judicial scrutiny cannot be said to make good this shortcoming.

(iv) Due Process

Under the due process rationale, it may be claimed that delegated legislation is legitimated by the processes of consultation. Again, however, this practice, although widespread, is not closely regulated. Under the Rules Publication Act 1893, forty days' notice had to be given of proposals to make rules of a permanent nature, but the Statutory Instruments Act 1946 repealed this provision. There is now no general requirement of notice for delegated legislation and the public may have little opportunity to become apprised of proposed SIs. Particular Acts of Parliament may, however, call for publication and notice or for consultation, either generally or with stipulated organizations or individuals. A number of Acts leave

[50] Harlow and Rawlings, *Pressure through Law*, 300–9. On the danger that a public interest ethos may lead to litigiousness and increases in costs, and will impede negotiated settlement of regulatory problems, see R. B. Stewart, 'The Discontents of Legalism: Interest Group Relations in Administrative Regulation' (1985) Wis.LR 685.

[51] See P. Bryden, 'Public Interest Intervention in the Courts', 66 Can.BR 490, discussed by Harlow and Rawlings, *Pressure through Law*, 313–14. For a review of reform options see Law Commission, *Administrative Law*, 62–5.

[52] Instituted perhaps by legislation referring to factors other than the applicant's link with the subject matter as considerations in determining if an application is in the public interest; see Law Commission, *Administrative Law*, para 9.21.

it to ministers to consult with such associations and bodies as appear to them to be affected by the provisions being promulgated.[53]

The common law does not, in the absence of a legislative requirement to consult, impose a general obligation for the rule-maker to hear the comments of affected parties.[54] An exception occurs, however, when a legitimate expectation of consultation arises. The courts will recognize such an expectation where a public body has established a past practice of consulting on a matter,[55] where it has given an undertaking to consult, or where it has established a rule which is relied upon by an individual or group and which it proposes to change or to depart from.[56]

As a matter of practice, government departments and agencies do engage in extensive consultative procedures before promulgating items of delegated legislation, but there is still room for contention as to who should be consulted; how extensive consultation should be for a particular class or item of delegated legislation; who should bear the costs of the consultation process; and how much delay should be imposed on rule-making for the sake of consultation. For consultative procedures to legitimate there must, moreover, be an effective process of communication between rule-maker and affected parties. Where, accordingly, the rules owe their origins to European Community policies and actors, the distance between the rule-maker and affected party detracts markedly from legitimation.

As to means of increasing legitimation through consultation, particular statutes that delegate rule-making powers could tailor rule-making procedures according to context and might

[53] e.g. Industrial Training Act 1964, SI (4); see *Agricultural Horticultural and Forestry Industry Training Board* v. *Aylesbury Mushrooms Ltd* [1972] 1 All ER 280.

[54] *Bates* v. *Lord Hailsham* [1972] 1 WLR 1373. On the adequacy of consultation see *R* v. *Birmingham City Council, ex parte Dredger and Paget* [1993] COD 340; *R* v. *Brent London Borough Council, ex parte Gunning* (1985) 84 LGR 168 and on the significance of the *Open Government* White Paper of 1993 see *infra* pp. 118–19.

[55] *Council of Civil Service Unions* v. *Minister for the Civil Service* [1985] AC 374; [1984] 3 All ER 935.

[56] *Attorney-General of Hong Kong* v. *Ng Yuen Shiu* [1983] 2 WLR 735; see R. Baldwin and D. Horne, 'Expectations in a Joyless Landscape' (1986) 49 MLR 685, and *infra*, pp. 91–100, on expectations. On pressure-groups and legislative processes see J. J. Richardson and A. G. Jordan, *Governing under Pressure* (1979) ch. 6.

provide, for example, for the giving of notice of rule-making; the publication of draft proposals; the granting of opportunities to comment on such proposals; processes for reviewing, cross-examining on, or discussing such comments; and the giving of reasons for particular choices of rule.[57] The anticipatory powers of legislators are, however, limited by such factors as resources, expertise, and the adequacy of information, and it may, therefore, be realistic to expect such tailoring of procedures to be feasible only with regard to a minority of rule-making powers.

Steps might be taken to create general duties of consultation and disclosure. Thus, in the case of secondary legislation something akin to 'notice and comment' procedure, as set out under section 553 of the US Administrative Procedure Act 1946, might be provided for.[58] Basic rule-making procedure might thus involve:

- Giving notice of the proposed rule-making in a national register.
- Granting an opportunity to interested persons to comment in writing on the proposals (with an option on the rule-maker's part to conduct such oral hearings as seem appropriate).
- The issuance, with the promulgated rules, of a statement as to their basis and purpose.
- A period of post-promulgation delay before the rules are effective.

Adopting such procedures would enhance not only due process claims but would also improve accountability claims—especially

[57] Thus in relation to the contracts between purchases and providers of public services, legislators might impose a general duty to publish and hear comments—see Harden, *The Contracting State*, 74 and N. Lewis, *How to Reinvent British Government* (1993), 16: 'if in future increasing divisions of responsibilities between purchasers and providers are established then it is vital that the purchaser receives legitimacy from the community.'

[58] On the US Administrative Procedure Act and notice and comment procedure under section 553 see S. Breyer and R. Stewart, *Administrative Law and Regulatory Policy*, 3rd edn. (1992), 536–648; G. Bryner, *Bureaucratic Discretion* (1987), ch. 2; I. Harden and N. Lewis. *The Noble Lie*, 235–7. 275–7; 302–5; R. W. Hamilton, 'Procedures for the Adoption of Rules of General Applicability: The Need for Procedural Innovation in Administrative Rulemaking' (1972) 60 Col.LR 1976.

if the term 'interested persons' was to be interpreted broadly so as to recognize the concerns of pressure and public interest groups as well as the interests of individuals directly affected by proposed rules. It would fall to the courts to monitor compliance with such procedural legislation and judges might be encouraged to bear in mind the twin rationales underlying such provisions.[59]

To impose statutory procedural requirements on rule-makers is, however, a fraught enterprise—as commentators on the US Administrative Procedure Act 1946 (APA) have made clear.[60] Notice and comment procedures as described would not involve the expense, and delay, of formal or 'on the record' rule-making procedures employing trial-type hearings[61] but a series of problems has to be confronted. First, which rules are to be covered by notice and comment procedures? The APA provides many exceptions to the basic notice and comment requirements. These exceptions include rules relating to military and foreign affairs, agency management or personnel, public property, loans, grants, benefits, or contracts. Nor do the requirements apply to interpretative rules, general statements of policy, or rules of agency organization, procedure, or practice; or when the agency, for good cause, finds that notice and comment procedure is impracticable, unnecessary, or contrary to the public interest.

Notice and comment procedures under the APA have been held to apply to rules that carry the force of law and bind, but not to other rules, to rules issued under powers delegated by Congress but not others—in short, to secondary but not to tertiary rules.[62] Here I advocate that secondary, but not tertiary,

[59] For further discussion of the problems involved with statutory rulemaking procedures see infra pp. 112–13. On regulating interest representation as a rationale for judicial action see Stewart, 'The Reformation of American Administrative Law'.

[60] See e.g. R. W. Hamilton, 'Procedures for the Adoption of Rules of General Applicability: The Need for Procedural Innovation in Administrative Rulemaking' (1972) 60 Cal.LR 1976; G. Bryner, *Bureaucratic Discretion* (1987), ch. 2; Breyer and Stewart, *Administrative Law*, ch. 6; T. O. McGarity, 'Some Thoughts on Deossifying the Rulemaking Process' (1992) 41 Duke LJ 1385. For arguments in favour of a British APA see Harden and Lewis *The Noble Lie*, 235–7, 274–7, 302–5; but cf. J. Beatson, 'A British View of *Vermont Yankee*' (1980) 55 Tulane LR 435.

[61] See ss. 556 and 557 of the APA 1946.

[62] See *Batterton* v. *Marshall* 648 F. 2s 694 (DC Clf. 1980); *Community Nutrition Inst.* v.

rules should be covered by notice and comment procedures. Thus rules exercising delegated legislative power (power to make rules directly enforceable in the courts) should be subject to such procedures but rules that are not directly legally binding should not. This, as has been pointed out,[63] is a difficult distinction to draw and one liable to give rise to litigation. It is perhaps best approached by looking at the envisaged legal effect of the rules (whether Parliament has intended there to be an exercise of legislative power) rather than by analysing the practical impact of the rule.[64]

Second, problems arise as to the kinds of activity covered by the requirement—what constitutes an exercise of legislative rule-making as opposed to an adjudication may, as has been found in the USA, prove to be a thorny issue.[65] A third difficulty arises from the propensity of administrators to avoid designated procedures. It is often not difficult to dress up a legislative rule-making as either an adjudication or a managerial decision and bureaucrats may be liable to proceed by means of non-rule-making devices and back-door methods when presented with notice and comment requirements.[66]

In many circumstances even modest demands to give notice of rules and to hear comments on draft rules may prove impracticable, unnecessary, or contrary to the public interest—perhaps because the expense and delay involved is disproportionate to the effect of the rule. A fourth problem to be faced is, accordingly, that of drafting exemptions to cater for such circumstances (particularly concerning the promulgation of minor rules). Such drafting also has to be done in a manner that avoids a fifth difficulty—that of imposing undue expense on rule-makers and of encouraging legalism and defensiveness

Young 818 F. 2d 943 (DC Cir. 1987); *Air Transport Association of America* v. *Dept of Transport* 900 F. 2d 369 (DC Cir. 1990) vocated 111 S. Ct. 944 (1991); Breyer and Stewart, *Administrative Law*, ch. 6, sect. B.

[63] See M. Asimow, 'Nonlegislative Rulemaking and Regulatory Reform' (1985) Duke LJ 381. On British judicial responses to this problem see *infra* pp. 86–91.

[64] See Asimow, 'Nonlegislative Rulemaking', 389–402.

[65] See Bryner, *Bureaucratic Discretion*, 22, Breyer and Stewart, *Administrative Law*, 524–34; McGarity, 'Thoughts on Deossifying', 1393.

[66] McGarity, 'Thoughts on Deossifying'.

in the agencies of government.[67] Statutory procedural requirements offer pegs upon which the opponents of governmental rules may hang challenges to the validity of those rules. Avoiding such challenges is likely to consume the resources and budgets of administrators and, unless care is taken in drafting and applying such requirements, legalism, defensiveness, and a watering-down of governmental vigour may result.[68]

A sixth problem is that, in spite of exemptions, a general increase in the length, formality, and complexity of rules may result from participatory requirements—as objections are resolved by undue compromises and qualifications.[69] In so far as rules have to be processed through rigorous consultations, they are more likely to contain fudges and to leave tensions to be resolved at the enforcement stage[70]—to defer rather than to solve problems.

Seventh, and finally, statutory procedural requirements, may not produce equal and fair participation on the ground. The fundamental bias of such processes in favour of well-resourced, well-organized interests is not likely to be overcome automatically by such a statute and further steps may also need to be taken to make access a real possibility for some groups and interests.[71]

The challenge facing the judges, in ruling on the applicability of notice and comment requirements to individual instances, would be to seek to achieve gains under the accountability and due process headings whilst avoiding the efficiency losses associated with legalism, bureaucratic defensiveness, and the over-inclusive application of notice and comment requirements. In scrutinizing, the judges might be

[67] See e.g. McGarity, 'Thoughts on Deossifying'; on the costs of interest representation, see Stewart, 'The Discontents of Legalism' and 'The Reformation of American Administrative Law', 1770–6.

[68] See Hamilton, 'Procedures for the Adoption of Rules', 1312–13; McGarity, 'Thoughts on Deossifying', and Harlow and Rawlings, *Law and Administreation* (1984), 155–7.

[69] See C. McCrudden, 'Codes in a Cold Climate: Administrative Rulemaking by the Commission for Racial Equality' (1988) 51 MLR 409.

[70] See *infra*, Ch. 6.

[71] See Stewart, 'The Reformation of American Administrative Law', 1776–7.

particularly concerned to see that rule-makers have been open about their proposed rules, that they have given proper attention to opposing arguments, that they have taken all relevant factors into account, and that the rule produced can be justified. To this end British judges might draw lessons from the US courts and their development of the 'hard look' review.[72] This approach assesses whether the rule-maker has properly considered all relevant factors and made a reasoned choice. It requires rule-makers to record the factual and analytical bases for their decisions, to explain their reasoning, and to give 'adequate consideration' to the evidence and analysis submitted by private parties.[73] Hard look review thus imposes pressure on rule-makers to grant reasonable access to the policy-making process and to justify the rules produced. It is possible to push such procedural requirements too far,[74] but where major interests or economic or social issues are involved it seems not unreasonable to demand that rule-makers adopt processes from which *it can be seen* that relevant factors, interests, and arguments have been given proper attention—standard *Wednesbury*[75] testing, after all, demands that all relevant considerations be taken into account.

II. TERTIARY RULES

In the case of secondary legislation, the power to legislate is conferred by an Act of Parliament. This offers some assistance in identifying the resulting instrument and in assessing its legal force. Such help is usually absent in the case of tertiary rules, where there may be statutory authorization, though not to make directly enforceable rules but where, more often, any sources of legislative authorization are unclear or lacking. Such

[72] See Breyer and Stewart, *Administrative Law*, 363–394; Harden and Lewis, *The Noble Lie*, 275–8.

[73] See Breyer and Stewart, *Administrative Law*, 363–94.

[74] See *Vermont Yankee Nuclear Power Corp.* v. *Natural Resources Defence Council* 435 US 519 (1978) and Beatson, 'A British View of *Vermont Yankee*'.

[75] *Associated Provincial Picture Houses Ltd.* v. *Wednesbury Corporation* [1948] 1 KB 223; *Bromley LBC* v. *Greater London Council* [1983] 1 AC 768.

rules may not be directly enforceable but they may produce indirect legal effects. The tendency of governments to resort to informal or tertiary rules instead of primary or secondary rules is again marked and increasing.[76] The Joint Committee expressed concern as long ago as 1977:

> Circulars can be very useful to the general public and to the administration. But the Committee hope that Parliament will condemn subordinate legislation by Departmental Circular when Parliament has itself passed a parent Act which requires such legislation to be by statutory instrument.[77]

As with secondary legislation, tertiary rules present problems of classification which, if done according to function, has to make reference to no less than eight varieties of administrative rule[78]:

(i) *Procedural Rules.* Most governmental bodies issue rules describing the procedures to be adopted in making applications to them or in performing certain functions. Thus the Prison Rules lay down disciplinary procedures for prisoners[79] and the codes made under the Police and Criminal Evidence Act 1984 (PACE) lay down practices to be adopted, for example in dealing with suspects and arrested persons.[80] A recurring issue is whether such rules are mandatory or directory.

(ii) *Interpretative Guides.* This heading covers all official statements of departmental or agency policy that are offered as explanations of how statutory rules will be applied and which lay down criteria to be followed, standards to be enforced, or considerations to be taken into account.[81]

[76] See generally R. Baldwin and J. Houghton, 'Circular Arguments: The Status and Legitimacy of Administrative Rules', [1986] PL 239; Ganz, *Quasi-Legislation*; Asimow, 'Nonlegislative Rulemaking'.

[77] First Special Report from the Joint Committee on Statutory Instruments 1977–8, HL 51, para. 12.

[78] For a more detailed review see Baldwin and Houghton, 'Circular Arguments'.

[79] Prison Act 1952, s. 47.

[80] Police and Criminal Evidence Act 1984, s. 66.

[81] Guidance as to relevant considerations may go too far, however, for example where a minister issues policy guidance to a body and the effect of this is to undermine the statutory criteria laid down for that body. See *R* v. *Secretary of State for the Environment, ex parte Lancashire CC*, *The Times*, 3 Feb. 1994, where such guidance was held unlawful. See also *Laker Airways Ltd.* v. *Department of Trade* [1977] QB 643.

(iii) *Instructions to Officials*. These rules are aimed not so much at persons outside a bureaucracy but at officials within the bureaucracy. The aim is usually to impose order and to encourage consistency or facilitate planning. Well-established examples are Home Office Circulars to Chief Constables and Prison Department Circulars. A more recent and highly significant instance of this kind of rule is the framework document that is used to set out the aims and objectives of a Next Steps agency and to make clear the relationship of that agency to the 'parent' department of government.[82] As Harden has pointed out, the precise nature of such framework documents has not been made clear but the governmental view has been that Minsters and the chief executives of such agencies are in a quasi-contractual position?[83]

(iv) *Prescriptive Rules*. Regulatory bodies may desire to do more than describe their policies—they may want to instruct regulated parties on actions to be taken. This is often done by prescriptive rules which urge a course of action on the understanding that a sanction exists at law (in primary or delegated legislation) or administratively (e.g. through non-allocation of a licence). A common posture for such a prescriptive rule is that of a 'guide to compliance' with other legislation.

(v) *Evidential Rules*. Closely related to the prescriptive rule and the interpretative guide is the evidential rule which offers advice to courts on the meaning of other legal rules. A well-known example is the Highway Code.

[82] On Next Steps agencies see G. Drewry, 'Forward from FMI: "The Next Steps"' [1988] PL 505; R. Baldwin, '"The Next Steps": Ministerial Responsibility and Government by Agency' (1988) 51 MLR 622; N. Lewis, 'The Citizen's Charter and Next Steps: A New Way of Governing? (1993) Pol.Q. 316. Proposals giving rise to the Next Steps agencies arose from the Ibbs Report, more formally cited as: K. Jenkins *et al.*, 'Improving Management in Government: The Next Steps' (1988); see also 'Making the Most of Next Steps' (1991) and 'Next Steps Agencies in Government Review 1993' (1993).

[83] See I. Harden, *The Contracting State* (1992), 27, and also ch. 3 where it is argued that contracts in the NHS internal market and in competitive tendering for local authority services possess a public dimension.

Breach of this is not an offence in itself but it may be taken into account in judging civil or criminal liability.[84]

In the health and safety and employment fields a number of codes offer 'practical guidance' but also have an evidential role. Thus the Employment Act 1980 stated that any provisions of the Secretary of State's Code of Practice on Picketing (1980) might be taken into account in proceedings before a court or tribunal and the Employment Protection Act 1975 made the industrial relations codes issued by the Advisory, Conciliation, and Arbitration Service (ACAS) admissible and relevant in determining issues (these provisions were later echoed in the Trade Union and Labour Relations (Consolidation) Act 1992). As for codes under the Police and Criminal Evidence Act 1984, breaches of these do not involve police officers in civil or criminal liability but such breaches have disciplinary consequences and the courts have a duty to consider the terms of codes where they are relevant to questions before them—as for example may be the case when the admissibility of confession evidence is at issue.[85]

(vi) *Commendatory Rules.* Whereas prescriptive rules call for action against a background of potential legal sanctions, commendatory rules simply recommend a course of behaviour without reference to direct or indirect legal liability. Examples are the guidance notes issued by the Health and Safety Commission (HSC). Unlike the HSC's regulations and Approved Codes of Practice, guidance notes merely advise on how to achieve certain safety objectives—they are based on a facilitative rather than a sanctioning principle.

(vii) *Voluntary Codes.* Self-regulatory codes often operate in the shadow of government. Organizations frequently employ these to stave off government regulation and, in spite of

[84] See Road Traffic Act 1988, s. 38(7). On the evidential role of rules see *infra* pp. 103–6.

[85] See PACE 1984 ss. 67(11), 76, and 78. For a detailed review of PACE codes and the exclusion of evidence see M. Zander, *The Police and Criminal Evidence Act 1984*, 2nd edn. (1990), 186–207.

their non-governmental origins, they may carry considerable force. Breach of such codes and expulsion from a professional or trade association may have severe consequences. Instances of such codes are to be found in many industries, such as advertising and house-building. A particularly noteworthy example of the voluntary code is the City Code on Takeovers and Mergers. This code is administered by the Panel on Takeovers and Mergers and, in spite of both the voluntary nature of the code and the non-statutory basis of the Panel's powers, the courts have shown themselves willing to review the Panel's application of the code. The rationale for such scrutinizing is that the Panel, in applying rules of such a wide-ranging and important nature, is performing a public duty.[86]

Governmental approval may be given to voluntary codes. Thus section 124(3) of the Fair Trading Act 1973 imposed a duty on the Director General of Fair Trading to encourage trade associations to prepare codes of practice for guidance in promoting consumer interests.

A special kind of voluntary code is the 'Citizen's Charter' document,[87] for example the Patient's Charter or the (Rail) Passengers' Charter.[88] Such documents set out the standards of service that users can expect, but are of no formal legal effect. They can be characterized as customer guarantees, as voluntary clarifications of standards aspired to, rather than as provision setting down legally enforceable rights. As Gavin Drewry has said of the Citizen's Charter, '[it] comprises an amorphous *mélange* of aims and exhortations'.[89]

(viii) *Rules of Practice.* Some rules have considerable effects

[86] See *R* v. *Panel on Takeovers and Mergers ex parte Datafin plc* [1987] QB 815; [1987] 1 All ER 564 CA.

[87] See e.g. HM Treasury, *The Citizen's Charter*, Cm 1599 (1991); *The Citizen's Charter: First Report*, Cm 2101 (1992). See also A. Barron and C. Scott, 'The Citizen's Charter Programme' (1992) 55 MLR 526; Lewis, 'The Citizen's Charter'; G. Drewry, 'Mr Major's Charter: Empowering the Customer' [1993] PL 248.

[88] Twenty-eight charters were published in the first eighteen months of the programme; see Drewry, 'Mr Major's Charter', 253.

[89] Ibid. 253.

without being directly normative or exhortatory. These are rules laying down arrangements made by governmental bodies for the operation of the law. Examples are the extra-statutory concessions made by the Commissioners for Inland Revenue.[90] The courts have been uncertain in their responses to such concessions, on the one hand deeming them 'conducive to great justice',[91] on the other talking of 'the word of the minister outweighing the law of the land'.[92] In *R* v. *Preston* in 1984 Lawton LJ referred to the IRC's decision to cancel a tax advantage as a 'managerial discretion' only reviewable for abuse of power.[93]

1. Justifications for Tertiary Rules

(i) Expertise and Efficiency

As with secondary rules, many of the arguments in favour of tertiary rules can be classified as claims under the expertise and efficiency headings. Thus administrative rules are said to possess a number of advantages over discretions and primary or secondary rules in so far as they can be used: swiftly and inexpensively to routinize the exercise of complex discretions; to encourage consistency; to allow staff to operate at levels of specialization or complexity that are high considering their training; to allow collective experience and expertise to be distilled and applied. Tertiary rules are, additionally, said to yield a flexibility that primary and secondary legislation does not offer;[94] to allow the use of non-technical language which encourages speedy drafting together with high levels of comprehensibility to affected and lay parties;[95] and to allow rules

[90] See D. W. Williams, 'Extra-Statutory Concessions' (1979) 3 BTR 137.

[91] *IRC* v. *Korner* [1979] 1 All ER 679, 686, 45 TC 287 (HL) (Lord Upjohn).

[92] *R* v. *Commissioner of Customs and Excise ex parte Cooke and Stevenson* [1970] 1 All ER 1068, 1072 (Lord Parker CJ).

[93] *R* v. *Inland Revenue Commissioner ex parte Preston*, *The Times*, 16 Aug. 1984.

[94] See Baldwin and Houghton, 'Circular Arguments', 19–20; for a comparison with primary and secondary rules in note form see Appendix *infra*.

[95] See Ganz, *Quasi-Legislation*, 96. Michael Zander notes that the codes of practice produced under the Police and Criminal Evidence Act 1984 were issued as codes, rather than Statutory Instruments because, *inter alia*, of a perceived need to create a

to be couched in persuasive or voluntarist terms rather than the language of commands. Tertiary rules thus encourage compromises to be effected between different political, economic, social, or industrial interests[96] and can deal with broad policy matters in a way that strictly legal language cannot. Finally, such rules allow rules to be introduced into areas where legislation is either inappropriate or of dubious political feasibility.

The discussion conducted in Chapter 3 indicates that the force of such claims should not be accepted unquestioningly. Thus it cannot be assumed without further thought that rule-making always reduces discretions, that routinizing decisions is beneficial or that it is always possible to produce rules that are simple, intelligible, and flexible. In spite of this broad caveat, however, it is clear that modern governments do find tertiary rules enormously useful, if not indispensable, in a wide range of circumstances. Can such rules, however, be supported according to the legislative mandate, accountability/control, and due process rationales?

(ii) Legislative Mandate and the Legal Force of Tertiary Rules

On whether tertiary rules, in spite of their haphazard form, may be legitimated on the basis that they implement legislative mandates, there are considerable uncertainties. With secondary legislation the substance of the mandate is often questionable and this is all the more so in relation to the less formal and more random tertiary rules where the existence of a mandate is liable to be dubious. There is often, moreover, a level of doubt concerning the legal force that flows from tertiary rules.[97] Judges may or may not attribute such force and the

comprehensive set of guidelines for custody officers. This required that summaries of statutory provisions be combined with other forms of guidance—a linkage thought possible in a code but not a Statutory Instrument: see Zander, *Police and Criminal Evidence Act*, 151.

[96] Ganz, *Quasi-Legislation*, 106.

[97] Where contracts are used to effect governmental purposes there may be considerable uncertainty as to the governmental or public nature of such rules and whether they create expectations, see Harden, *The Contracting State*, esp. pp. 44–5. On the use of non-legislative, or interpretative, rules to achieve binding effects in the USA, see R. A. Anthony, 'Interpretative Rules, Policy Statements, Guidances, Manuals and the Like: Should Federal Agencies Use them to Bind the Public?' (1992) 41 Duke LJ 1463.

principles governing the judicial stance are complex. Thus a first factor of relevance is the nature of the legal mandate (if any) for such rules. Tertiary rule-making may be envisaged in some way by a statute or it may not and what the statute *does* envisage is often unclear. Judges, for their part, tend to attribute legal effects more readily in so far as rules have received some parliamentary or executive sanction. The point can be made by contrasting a well-known condemnation of a Home Office circular with an endorsement of the Immigration Rules. In *Patchett* v. *Leathem*,[98] Streatfield J said of the Home Office circular:

Whereas ordinary legislation, by passing through both Houses of Parliament or, at least lying on the table of both houses, is thus twice blessed, this type of so called legislation is at least four times cursed. First it has seen neither House of Parliament; second, it is unpublished and is unacceptable even to those whose valuable rights of property may be affected, thirdly it is a jumble of provisions, legislative, administrative, or directive in character . . . and, fourthly, it is expressed not in the precise language of an Act of Parliament or an Order in Council but in the more colloquial language of correspondence which is not always susceptible of the ordinary canons of construction.

The Immigration Rules, on the other hand, were found by Roskill LJ to be based on solid foundations in *R* v. *Chief Immigration Officer Heathrow Airport ex parte Bibi*[99]:

If one looks at section 3(2) which empowers the Secretary of State to make these rules, one finds that he shall lay before Parliament statements of the rules . . . These rules are just as much delegated legislation as any other form of rule-making which is empowered by Parliament. Furthermore, rules are subject to a negative resolution and it is unheard of that something which is no more than an administrative circular . . . should be subject to negative resolutions of both Houses of Parliament. These rules are . . . just as much a part of the laws of England as the 1971 Act itself.[100]

[98] (1949) 65 Tex.LR 69, 70.

[99] [1976] 1 WLR 979.

[100] See also *R* v. *McCoy* [1990] Crim.LR 338 and *Nottinghamshire CC* v. *Secretary of State for the Environment* [1986] 1 All ER 199 (HL).

The courts thus look for indications from Parliament that certain rules are to have legal effects. As well as looking at the processes by which the rules have emerged, the judges will assess the terms of the parent statute to see if effects are stipulated. The position is, however, often uncertain. Many rules are fully tertiary with no trace of delegation about them and when there is an express provision it often fails to make anything more than the vaguest of statements concerning effects.[101] Not only that, but where, as in the Counter-Inflation Act 1973,[102] a broad enabling provision authorized different kinds of rule to be made (e.g. to establish particular duties or to offer 'practical guidance') it might be difficult to relate the individual rule to a precise authorizing power. The courts will thus look to the nature of any delegation or any statement as to legal effect, but if the Act is silent on these matters they will look at the nature of the rule itself.

A second major consideration for the judiciary is the degree of precision of the rule. The judges tend to treat clear and precise language as evidence of authority to make rules that are to be given legal effect by the courts. Similarly, they will be disinclined to attribute legal effects to rules that appear to be non-justiciable. For example, in the case of *Payne* v. *Lord Harris*,[103] Lord Denning considered the status of the Local Review Committee (LRC) Rules 1967, made under the Criminal Justice Act 1967, section 59(6). That section stated that the Secretary of State could 'by rules make provision for the establishment and constitution' of LRCs which would review the cases of prisoners who are or will become eligible for release. Lord Denning MR commented:

> It seems to me that the statute and rules together form a comprehensive code. They set out the procedure in such detail that there is nothing more needed to supplement it . . . They set out the occasions when the prisoner is entitled to make representations and when he is to be informed of reasons.[104]

[101] See Counter-Inflation Act 1973, s. 2; Employment Protection Act 1975, s. 6; Education Act 1962 s. 2; Prison Act 1952, s. 47; Immigration Act 1971, s. 3(2).

[102] Counter-Inflation Act 1973, s. 2.

[103] [1981] 1 WLR 754.

[104] Ibid. 359.

Thus, in spite of his reluctance to give mandatory effect to the Prison Rules (discussed *infra*), Lord Denning was inclined to give effect to the LRC rules which were said to give shape to Parole Board procedure and to confer rights. Shaw LJ added: 'The duties so imposed [on the LRC] confer corresponding rights on the prisoner concerned: he is entitled to complain if those duties are not observed and to insist that they should be duly carried out . . .'.[105]

The rule-maker, of course, may control the kind of language used in rules and the judicial attraction to precise rules is important. If a code or set of rules is meant to create legal effects then precise language can be used. If, on the other hand, rule-makers fear that courts will attribute rights to affected parties and will review bureaucratic decisions, then it may pay to employ rules that are imprecise and so likely to be deemed 'managerial' and 'non-justiciable'.

The legal force attributed to a rule tends to vary according both to the strength of the mandate and to the precision of the rule's formulation. Imprecise language as criticized in *Patchett* v. *Leathem*,[106] however, will not *necessarily* mean that a circular is deemed to have no force—in that case the circular was deemed *intra vires* and had to be complied with in order to make the requisition of Mr Patchett's house legal. Attention should also be paid to both the language of the set of rules as a whole and the nature and form of a particular rule. Within each code or set of rules there may be a wide variety of rule-types. Some may be substantially prescriptive, some facilitative, some procedural, and some may set standards. Confusion, as a result, may ensue if whole sets of tertiary rules are talked of as if all rules within the set are of the same status and effect. A brief review of cases on the Immigration Rules shows what happens when insufficient attention is paid to the mandate, the precision of the language and the legal effect at issue.

In the *Bibi* case, as we saw, Roskill LJ treated the Immigration Rules as if they were the law of the land. The question was whether the Rules could contain a restriction not contained in

[105] Ibid. [106] (1949) 65 Tex.LR 69.

the Act (namely that the immigrant should possess an entry clearance certificate). Roskill LJ found that the rules were 'delegated legislation' and so indicated that the restriction applied. It is arguable that his Lordship failed to tease apart three issues: (i) whether there was a valid delegation of power; (ii) whether this delegation authorized the making of a certain kind of rule (e.g. a procedural or a substantive rule); (iii) whether the type of rule authorized was sufficiently precise to determine legal rights on a particular issue. Roskill LJ conflated these issues so that satisfaction of (i) was deemed also to include (ii) and (iii).

A year after *Bibi*, Lord Denning took a different view when an individual sought to rely on the Immigration Rules. In the *Hosenball*[107] case, a journalist, who was about to be deported, argued that non-compliance with a rule of the Immigration Rules for Control after Entry involved a breach of natural justice. Lord Denning, however, thought that Roskill LJ had gone too far in referring to the Immigration Rules as rules of delegated legislation. Geoffrey Lane LJ agreed with Lord Denning, and referred to the rules as 'a practical guide for immigration officers . . . little more than explanatory notes in the Act itself'.

The divergence of judicial approaches seen in *Bibi* and *Hosenball* suggests that tertiary rules may be particularly useful for administrators. The courts appear to be reluctant to construe such rules in a manner that creates due process rights for individuals but, where *intra vires*, will concede their status as legitimate foundations for the exercise of discretionary power.

Other immigration cases offer further contrasts. In *R* v. *Secretary of State for the Home Development ex parte Ram*,[108] failure to comply with the Immigration Rules did not render entry illegal, but in the *Kharrazi*[109] case Lord Denning said that an officer who had not interpreted the rules properly had 'misdirected himself in point of law'.

At this stage a number of points should be noted. First, rules may have very different roles in relation to different legal

[107] *R* v. *Secretary of State for Home Affairs ex parte Hosenball* [1977] 1 WLR 766.
[108] [1979] 1 WLR 148 DC.
[109] *R* v. *Chief Immigration Officer, Gatwick Airport, ex parte Kharrazi* [1980] 1 WLR 1396, 1402.

issues and they may possess force only in limited aspects. Second, it could be argued (as by Allen[110]) that courts tend to adopt an expedient approach to quasi-legislation, deeming it to be 'administrative' where flexibility is required and tending to favour the administration. Challenges to the legality of such rules can accordingly be deflected with some ease by attributing informal status to them and thereby removing the obligation on the rule-maker to justify his/her action by statutory authority. Thus, objections to the guidelines on jury vetting have been unsuccessful because those guidelines were said to constitute 'advice', rather than directions having the force of law.[111] Third, courts will tend to favour the rule-makers for another reason—a rule may more easily be said to provide grounds for the reasonable exercise of discretion than breach of such a guideline can be shown to vitiate the use of a power. Finally, other things being equal, courts tend to attribute legal consequences to a rule where there is a traceable delegation and where scrutiny procedures are provided.

The uncertainties described clearly make it difficult to justify tertiary rules on the basis that they effect Parliament's will in a predictable and rational way. In looking at the particular legal effects that tertiary rules can have there are further uncertainties. Thus when tertiary rules are employed and their legal implications are examined, four particular questions tend to arise, singly or in combination: whether the reasonableness or *vires* of a decision is to be judged by the standards set out in an informal rule; whether, having set down a policy, a body has a duty to adhere to it; whether procedural rules have special legal effects; and whether evidential rules have predictable effects.

Reasonableness, *Vires*, and Expectations

From the rule-maker's point of view it is important to know whether one will be bound by the rule being made. The

[110] C. K. Allen, *Law and Orders*, 3rd edn. (1965), 187, quoted in C. Harlow and R. Rawlings, *Law and Administration* (1984), 29.

[111] See *R* v. *Sheffield Crown Court ex parte Brownlow* [1980] QB 530, and *R* v. *Mason* [1981] QB 881, CA.

judges have in notable instances answered this question in the affirmative, even in the case of rules with the weakest of claims to any delegated authority from Parliament. Thus under the doctrine of legitimate expectations[112] a public body that promulgates guidelines or rules may be bound to apply these rules correctly and failure to do so may provide a basis for challenging a decision or rule. Thus in *R* v. *Secretary of State for the Home Department, ex parte Khan*[113] the Home Office had issued a circular letter giving guidance on immigration for adoption which was departed from at a later date. Parker LJ stated that the Secretary of State was at liberty to change the policy, but a new policy could 'only be implemented after the recipient of such a letter had been given a full opportunity to make representations, and only after full and serious consideration whether there was some overriding public interest which justified a departure from the procedures stated in the letter.'[114] Dunn LJ added: 'Although the circular letter did not create an estoppel, the Home Secretary set out therein for the benefit of applicants the matters to be taken into consideration, and thus reached his decision upon a consideration which, on his own showing, was irrelevant. In so doing he misdirected himself according to his own criteria and acted unreasonably.'[115]

There is, moreover, some evidence that informal rules may prove binding even where legitimate expectations are implied rather than express. This was so in *Niarchos (London) Ltd.* v. *Secretary of State for the Environment.*[116] Occupiers applied for planning permission to continue to use some houses as offices. The local planning authority refused permission and the Secretary of State confirmed this decision on appeal because the policy of the development plan for the area was to encourage residential use.

The High Court quashed the Secretary of State's decision on

[112] See e.g. R. Baldwin and D. Horne, *Expectations in a Joyless Landscape* (1986) 49 MLR 685; P. P. Craig, Legitimate Expectation: A Conceptual Analysis (1992) 108 LQR 79; G. Ganz, 'Legitimate Expectation' in C. Harlow (ed.), *Public Law and Politics* (1986); P. Elias, 'Legitimate Expectation and Judicial Review' in J. Jowell and D. Oliver (eds.), *New Directions in Judicial Review* (1988).

[113] [1985] 1 All ER 40.

[114] Ibid. 48.

[115] Ibid. 52.

[116] (1977) 35 P & CR 259.

the grounds that he should have asked himself whether the premises could reasonably be adapted for residential use, not whether an exception to policy was merited. He had, therefore, misdirected himself as to the provisions of the development plan and acted in excess of his powers. Sir Douglas Frank, QC, said: 'When he expresses himself to be deciding a case under a stated policy, it must follow that if he decides the case other than in accordance with that policy he misdirects himself.'[117]

The *Niarchos* decision was endorsed on this point (though not on others) in *Bell and Colville Ltd.* v. *Secretary of State for the Environment and Guildford BC*[118] where Forbes J agreed that 'where the Secretary of State decided a case by applying a policy, he had to get the policy right'.[119]

If we now turn to the Prison Rules, the importance of looking at rules individually becomes clear. Unfortunately, these rules (promulgated by Statutory Instrument and subject to negative resolution procedure) have hovered between secondary and tertiary status and have produced a case law hardly more coherent than that relating to the Immigration Rules.[120] The early decisions are marked by statements that the Prison Rules confer no enforceable rights on prisoners,[121] that no question of breaches of statutory duty may arise from internal directions[122] to staff, and that the Rules are regulatory and not mandatory.[123] In 1981, however, it was accepted that a breach of the Rules was relevant in establishing the unlawfulness of detention and that there was an 'arguable case' that a contravention conferred a right of action for breach of statutory duty.[124]

That the judges might, in some circumstances, review the construction of the Rules was made clear in *R* v. *Deputy Governor of Camphill Prison, ex parte King.*[125] Here it was accepted

[117] Ibid. 264. [118] JPEL 823. [119] Ibid. 826.

[120] See G. Zellick, 'The Prison Rules and the Courts' [1981] Crim.LR 602, and 'The Prison Rules and the Courts: A Postscript' [1982] Crim. L.R. 589. See also M. Loughlin and P. M. Quinn, 'Prisons, Rules and Courts' (1993) 56 MLR 497.

[121] e.g. *Arbon* v. *Anderson* [1943] KB 252.

[122] *Hinds* v. *Home Office, The Times*, 17 Jan. 1962.

[123] *Becker* v. *Home Office* [1972] 2 QB 407, 418.

[124] *Williams* v. *Home Office (No 2)* [1981] 1 All ER 1211.

[125] [1984] 3 All ER 897. In *Leech v. Parkhurst Prison Deputy Governor* [1988] 1 AC 533 the House of Lords went on to assert jurisdiction over governors' disciplinary decisions.

that a Deputy Governor had misconstrued rule 47(7) by deeming a disciplinary offence to have been committed by the mere presence of a hypodermic needle in a cell, without proof of any degree of prisoner's control. Although the Court of Appeal was not concerned to supervise a governor's management of a prison, Lawton LJ did indicate that if the Secretary of State rejected a well-founded petition alleging misconstruction of the rules, the courts might review the matter.

Here again the courts have responded in a confused fashion to informal rules. One way to have avoided such troubles might have been to have considered the details of particular prison rules and to have asked both whether they were *intended* to be enforceable (by whom and for what purpose) and whether, in terms of their clarity, precision, and justiciability, they were *capable* of enforcement. Such an approach has been suggested by Graham Zellick[126] and it is instructive to note both his categories of rule and (paraphrasing) his conclusions on their enforceability. He deals with five classes of prison rule:

- *Rules setting general policy objectives* (e.g. concerning the purposes of training and treatment). It is 'inconceivable' that departure from these would be amenable to judicial supervision.
- *Rules of a discretionary nature* (e.g. remission). Judicial control would avail for improper exercise of a statutory discretion.
- *Rules of general protection* (e.g. food to be wholesome). Their imprecision is indicative that it was at no time intended to entrust their enforcement to the courts.
- *Rules as to institutional structure and administrative functions* (e.g. Boards of Visitors to meet monthly). Courts would be inclined to view failure to meet these rules as a matter for the Secretary of State to deal with. In the last resort, the courts might supervise, but only after previous complaint to the Home Secretary.
- *Rules of specific individual protection* (e.g. disciplinary offences and penalties). These are so concrete and precise in nature that it is inconceivable that any latitude should be left to the authorities in their implementation. The courts would supervise.

[126] See Zellick articles at n. 120 *supra*.

Failure to draw such distinctions, and to mix authorities as if a case on the first kind of rule determined an issue on the last kind, only leads to confusion. The law is unfortunately replete with such confusion.

Another difficulty in assessing the binding force of rules has been judicial resort to fictions. In the field of criminal injuries compensation the courts have ignored the non-statutory nature of a body of rules. The Criminal Injuries Compensation Scheme was set up in 1964 as an act of prerogative power, and principles were published describing the basis upon which compensation would be awarded.[127] The judicial response to such rules was expressed in the case of *R* v. *CICB ex parte Lain.*[128] A police officer's widow was made an award but contested the validity of particular deductions in terms of certain paragraphs of the CICB scheme. The CICB responded that it was free from court supervision and that since it did not act under statute, its determinations did not give rise to enforceable rights but merely to the opportunity to receive bounty.

In the Divisional Court the provisions of the scheme were interpreted as if of full statutory force. Diplock LJ said: 'The Scheme not only constituted and defined the authority of the Board to make such payments but, as published to applicants, was a lawful proclamation stating the conditions required to be satisfied . . . The Scheme defines and limits the Board's authority.'[129]

Similarly, in *R* v. *CICB, ex parte Ince*[130] the Court of Appeal was prepared to give legislative effect to non-statutory rules. Here there was a choice to be made: should the courts use quasi-legislation as the basis for the strict application of jurisdictional tests or should they restrict themselves to asking

[127] Provisions to place the criminal injuries compensation scheme on a statutory basis were set out in the Criminal Justice Act 1988, Part VII, but have not been brought into effect at the time of publication—see *R v. Secretary of State for the Home Department, ex parte Fire Brigades Union and Others*, *The Times* 10 Nov. 1994.

[128] [1967] 2 QB 864.

[129] [1967] 2 QB 864, 888. More recently in *R* v. *CICB, ex parte Thompitone*, and *R* v. *CICB, ex parte Crowe*, *The Times*, 5 Oct. 1984, the Court of Appeal asserted that CICB decisions could be reviewed on grounds of unreasonableness or 'if the Board misconstrued its mandate'. See Barnes LJ in *R* v. *Port of London Authority, ex parte Kynock Ltd.* [1919] 1 KB 176.

[130] [1967] 1 WLR 1334.

whether there were grounds on which a reasonable or fair body might have come to such a decision?

The more liberal test would have allowed public bodies to indicate 'matters to be taken into consideration' without being held to have made a precise, binding, or exhaustive statement. Examples of such an approach came from the planning and housing fields. In *Enfield London Borough Council* v. *Secretary of State for the Environment*[131] Melford-Stevenson J[132] commented that a duty 'to have regard to' a plan did not mean 'slavishly adhere to'.[133] There was nothing in the *Enfield* case, he said, to imply that the Minister had failed to have regard to all material considerations.

Enfield may, of course, be reconciled with such cases as *Niarchos* and *Khan* as involving no representation so as to create expectations. Similarly, there were no expectations in *Bristol District Council* v. *Clark*,[134] where a local authority was alleged to have failed to consider departmental circulars. The Court of Appeal was reluctant to interfere. Scarman LJ commented: 'I do not think it possible to rely on those circulars as imposing any direct statutory duty upon a housing authority: but I think they are a good indication as to the purposes to be served by the Housing Acts and as to what are relevant matters within the language of Lord Greene MR in the *Wednesbury* case . . . to be taken into account by a local authority.'[135] Planning and housing codes would thus appear not to be mandatory in the absence of any indication that they will be relied upon, but they do have a role in defining what constitutes reasonable action.

To summarize, it is possible to obtain judicial review on the basis on non-compliance with self-imposed rules. The decisions considered point to the following conditions for intervention:

- the creation of legitimate expectations (as in *Khan*) so as to render departure from announced decisional referents unfair or unreasonable; or

[131] (1974) 233 EG 53.
[132] Citing the Scottish case, *Simpson* v. *Edinburgh Corporation* (1960) SC 313.
[133] See e.g. *British Oxygen Co. Ltd.* v. *Minister of Technology* [1971] AC 610.
[134] [1975] 1 WLR 1443, 74 LGR 3, CA.
[135] Ibid. 1451.

- the existence of implied expectations, where, although a decision-maker does not expressly undertake to follow certain rules, it would be unreasonable not to expect existing rules to be followed (e.g. the CICB cases and *Niarchos*); or
- where the decision-maker has not merely made an exception to a policy or to set criteria in recognition of a special case but has either:
  (*a*) taken another, previously unmentioned, factor into account and, by so doing, unfairly changed the basis for decision-making, or
  (*b*) adhered to existing standards or criteria but misapplied them.

There are a number of serious problems in applying reasonableness tests to tertiary rules, as was pointed out in *Schofield* (*supra*), but the courts have gone some way down this road. Even when circulars impose no direct duties, it seems (from Scarman LJ in *Bristol D.C* v. *Clark*) that they have a secondary role as guides to relevant factors in *Wednesbury* testing. The next step in developing the law will be where reasonableness is judged by self-imposed standards in the absence of implied or express expectations. *Niarchos* moved in this direction but stopped short. The decision-maker's mistake there was professing to be deciding on one matter (the development plan) and misinterpreting it. Another planning case went as far, if not further. This was *J.A. Pye (Oxford) Estates Ltd.* v. *West Oxfordshire District Council and the Secretary of State for the Environment*[136] where it was said that improper weight had been attached to one circular and another relevant circular had been ignored. The judge, David Widdicombe, QC, said that 'the Secretary of State must take his decision in the light of the relevant considerations in existence at the time of the decision, and if a relevant new circular came into existence before the decision, it was a material factor of which account must be taken . . . the circular was a material factor, it was left out of account and the decision therefore had to be quashed'.[137]

Such a case might be treated as one of implied expectations.

[136] [1982] JPEL 557. [137] Ibid. 579.

Other readings are, however, possible. First, that since there was a duty to hear fairly and to give reasons, no intelligible and adequate reasons could be given by a decision-maker who erred in applying a policy. The second, and more plausible, ground for decision, was that *Wednesbury* reasonableness testing demands that an authority must have regard to 'relevant circumstances' and that relevant departmental circulars are just such circumstances. To ignore such circulars or apply them mistakenly would thus involve unreasonableness—independently of the creation of expectations on the part of the applicant. Such a view is consistent with the dicta (quoted above) of Scarman LJ in *Bristol DC* v. *Clark.*[138]

It remains to be seen whether the argument, thus seeded, will come to fruition, so that failures with respect to unpublished administrative rules will give rise to judicial review. There is one good reason why this development should take place. If judicial review were to be triggered only by publication then the judges could be excluded by non-publication of rules. This hardly offers an incentive to open government or encourages Ministers and officials to indulge in open structuring of their discretionary powers.

The Duty to Adhere to a Rule

Not only may the adoption of a rule or policy bind the rule-maker according to the standards of reasonableness, or *vires*: natural justice and fairness may mean that the stated policy must not be departed from or changed without certain procedures being followed. The two arguments were fused in the *Khan* case, described above, when Parker LJ said that a new policy could only be implemented after recipients of the letter at issue had 'been given a full opportunity to make representations'.[139]

[138] [1975] 1 WLR 1443, 74 LGR 3, CA. See also *R* v. *Buckinghamshire County Council, ex parte The Government of Turville Church of England Voluntary Aided Combined School* QBD, (unreported CO/318/83), 27 Apr. 1983. That a planning authority, having considered the advice of a circular, is free to override it was made clear in *R* v. *London Borough of Camden ex parte Comyn Ching and Co.* (unreported), for an account, see (1983) 133 NLJ 1075).

[139] *R* v. *Secretary of State for the Home Department, ex parte Asif Mahmood Khan* [1985] 1 All ER 40, 49. Under recent French legislation, directives and circulars may be invoked in proceedings against the administration: Art. 1, decreed 28 Nov. 1983.

The pioneering decision in this area was *R* v. *Liverpool Corporation, ex parte Liverpool Taxi Fleet Operators Association.*[140] Liverpool Corporation had for years limited the number of taxi cab licences to 300 and had assured taxi-owners that they would not change this policy without listening to their representations. The Corporation had then brought forward a resolution to increase the number of taxi-cabs without affording a hearing.

In the Court of Appeal, Lord Denning MR said that if the Corporation were going to change the numbers, they had a duty to hear the Association because its members were greatly affected. As for the undertaking to adhere to the *status quo*, 'they ought not to depart from it except after the most serious consideration and hearing what the other party has to say: and then only if they are satisfied that the overriding public interest requires it'.

The basis of the requirement was fairness, rather than a general duty to consult when making rules—which the judges have not imposed.[141] In *HTV* v. *Price Commission*[142] the Commission was challenged when it decided to depart from the terms of its published Price Code. Lord Denning said: 'they should not depart from it in any case where they have, by their conduct, led the manufacturer or trader to believe that he can safely act on that interpretation of the Code . . . and he does so act on it.' Scarman LJ added: 'It is a code which directly affects the rights of commercial and industrial enterprises. It is not really surprising that a Code must be implemented fairly and that the courts have power to redress that fairness . . .'.[143]

As Lord Fraser put it in *Attorney-General of Hong Kong* v. *Ng Yuen Shiu*: 'when a public authority has promised to follow a certain procedure, it is in the interests of good administration that it should act fairly and should implement its promise, so

[140] [1972] 2 QB 299. See J. M. Evans, 'The Duty to Act Fairly' (1973) 36 MLR 93.
[141] *Bates* v. *Lord Hailsham* [1972] 2 All ER 1019 see discussion *supra* pp. 74–80.
[142] [1976] ICR 170.
[143] Ibid. 189.

long as implementation does not interfere with its statutory duty.'[144]

Fairness, moreover, may now demand that, even where there is no promise or practice of consultation, a policy adhered to over a period of time should (in some circumstances) not be changed without giving those affected a right to be heard—though it also appears that if a public authority does grant a proper hearing it will be free to judge the merits of any policy change rather than be bound to retain existing policy or be second-guessed on the merits of such a change by the courts.[145]

Expectations meriting protection are less likely to be found where a body is engaged in large-scale non-recurring policy decisions than where it deals with a series of similar decisions. Thus, in the *Enfield* planning case (*supra*), the High Court could find no implied representation that the Secretary of State would not depart from the original development plan and accordingly held that he had an unfettered discretion to look to the merits of the case.

To summarize, a body may be bound to adhere to a stated policy or to hear representations before changing a policy, even if that policy is set out informally, but only under certain conditions, namely:

[144] [1983] 2 AC 629, 638. On procedural rights attaching to expectations see also: *Council of Civil Service Unions and Others* v. *Minister for the Civil Service* [1985] AC 374; R v. *Secretary of State for the Home Dept., ex parte Ruddock* [1987] 2 All ER 518; *R* v. *Secretary of State for Transport, ex parte Richmond upon Thames LBC* [1994] 1 All ER 577. For a case in which the legitimate expectations argument failed to take root see *In re Findlay* [1985] 1 AC 318. Rights of standing may also result from expectations under rules: see *O'Reilly* v. *Mackman* [1983] 2 AC 237; [1982] 3 All ER 1124.

[145] See *R* v. *Secretary of State for Transport, ex parte Richmond upon Thames LBC* [1994] 1 All ER 577, but also Popplewell J in *R* v. *Devon County Council, ex parte Baker* [1993] COD 253; *R* v. *Birmingham City Council, ex parte Dredger and Paget* [1993] COD 340; and P. P. Craig, *Administrative Law*, 3rd edn. (1994), 256–9. The *Richmond* case and *In re Findlay* [1985] 1 AC 318 are unsympathetic to the notion that legitimate expectations create substantive rather than procedural rights. As for the circumstances in which expectations might be recognized in the absence of a promise or practice of consultation, Laws J in the *Richmond* case alluded to the 'important distinction' between the situation where a class of persons have specific expectations for the determination of their individual cases and instances where the policy at issue is of a general nature and does not involve the resolution of any individual claims of right or status [1994] 1 All ER 577, 596.

- if there has been created an expectation by express undertaking—as in *Liverpool Taxis*;
- if past practice has produced such an expectation—as in the *HTV* case.
- if a policy has been followed and, in the circumstances, it would be unfair to change the policy without giving those affected a right to be heard—as in the *Richmond* case.

Do 'contracts' between public bodies and service providers create legitimate expectations of either a substantive or a procedural nature? (Examples might include Next Steps framework documents; contracts for health services with public or private providers; agreements with private enterprises after contracting-out has taken place). The law, again, is uncertain. It has been argued [146] that the courts have in the past refused to give public law remedies in respect of contractual relationships;[147] that the judges might be reluctant to apply the principle of legitimate expectations where this would infringe the doctrine of privity; and that there is doubt as to the applicability of public law remedies against private bodies. Harden is perhaps right to conclude that the courts *might* develop the doctrine of legitimate expectations into a Citizen's Charter for those public services that are provided by contract, but that seems unlikely.

Procedural Rules

Although the judges have been ready to treat tertiary rules as effective in defining substantive powers, they are less inclined to treat such rules as binding on procedural matters. Thus, in *Hosenball* (*supra*), all three judges in the Court of Appeal agreed that the Immigration Rules did not have such force as to create legal rights of due process. It would seem, in the case of the Prison Rules, that any remedy depends not on breach of those rules but on breach of the principles of natural justice directly. In *R* v. *Board of Visitors of Hull Prison, ex parte St Germain*,[148] Megaw LJ cautioned:

[146] Harden, *The Contracting State*, 44–5.
[147] See *R* v. *IBA ex parte Rank Organisation*, *The Times*, 14 Mar. 1986.
[148] [1979] 1 QB 425, 450–1.

It is certainly not any breach of any procedural rule which would justify or require interference by the courts. Such interference, in my judgement, would only be required, and would only be justified if there were some failure to act fairly . . . and such unfairness could reasonably be regarded as having caused a substantial, as distinct from a trivial or merely technical injustice.

Can procedural rules ever be mandatory? Yes, but only if they satisfy the test of precision. This was the case in *Payne* v. *Lord Harris*, discussed above,[149] which concerned the LRC Rules 1967 of which Lord Denning said: 'They set out the procedure *in such detail that there is nothing more needed to supplement it.*'

Why, then, was such force given to the LRC Rules by Lord Denning and not, say, to the Prison or Immigration Rules? The LRC Rules are Statutory Instruments like the Prison Rules but unlike the Immigration Rules. The LRC and Prison Rules are subject to negative resolution procedure[150] and the Immigration Rules to a variant of this.[151] The real difference, therefore, would appear to be one of form. Whereas the Immigration and Prison Rules are each a hotchpotch of different kinds of rule—some prescriptive, some advisory, some expressing discretionary powers—the LRC Rules are a precise and comprehensive set of provisions prescribing procedures. As in European Community law, therefore, it counts that they are provisions eminently capable of direct effectiveness.[152] Their precision makes them justiciable and, it could be argued, creates expectations that they will be followed.

There are many examples of powers to make regulations governing procedure which are promulgated by Statutory Instrument. These, on the basis of *Payne*, may be said to owe their force to a mixture of precision and parliamentary authority. Many other procedural codes, however, have lesser credentials and we can say of them:

[149] [1981] 1 WLR 754; see discussion *supra* p. 88. For the creation of procedural rights via expectations, see cases cited at n. 144 *supra*.

[150] On negative resolution procedure see *supra* n. 19.

[151] See Criminal Justice Act 1967, ss. 66(4) and 100, and Immigration Act 1971, s. 3(2).

[152] On precision and the direct effect of European Community Directives see Case 41/74; *Van Duyn* v. *Home Office* (No. 2) [1974] ECR 1337.

- they are in the main directory rather than mandatory;
- the same rules may be directory on procedural matters and mandatory on issues of substance;
- an expectation may be a precondition of bindingness;
- procedural rules may affect a court's assessment of the nature of a body's decision-making functions and so may bear on the remedies available; and
- to administrators and officials, procedural codes are useful in reassuring client groups and commentators without leading to real liabilities at law or to the creation of effective remedies for their breach.

The Evidential Role of Rules

Tertiary rules may lack direct force but may nevertheless be taken into account in determining issues. In the case of the codes made under PACE the evidential role of the rules is expressly stated in the statute.[153] A breach of, say, Code C on Detention Treatment and Questioning of Persons by Police Officers must, if it appears relevant, be considered by a judge in deciding whether to exclude evidence on statutory grounds. Such a breach may, but will not inevitably, lead to exclusion.[154] Statutes do not always, however, make clear the evidential role of rules, nor is this necessary in order for legal consequences to follow. In *Powell* v. *Phillips*,[155] it was stated that a breach of the Highway Code might be relied on as tending to establish civil liability on the part of the person in breach but a breach created no presumption of negligence calling for an explanation, still less a presumption of such negligence as made a real contribution to causing an accident or injury. It was merely one of the circumstances on which one party was entitled to rely in establishing the negligence of the

[153] PACE, s. 67(11) states that code provisions are admissible in evidence and if any code provision appears to a court to be relevant to any question arising 'it shall be taken into account in determining that question'.

[154] See e.g. *R.* v. *Canale* [1990] 2 All ER 187. Zander, *Police and Criminal Evidence Act*, 150–75 and 186–207 offers a sustained discussion of the PACE codes and subsequent case law on their significance in assessing the admissibility of evidence.

[155] [1973] RTR 19; [1972] 3 All E.R. 864, CA.

other.[156] With the onus-reversing code of the health and safety type,[157] it follows, however, that such provisions do not either require or ensure exclusive conformity with a particular standard.

In the 1984/5 mining dispute, the picketing code proved highly contentious.[158] The code required pickets and organizers 'to ensure that in general the number of pickets does not exceed six at any entrance to a workplace; frequently a smaller number will be appropriate'.[159] This rule had a bearing on civil liability for nuisance and also on certain criminal offences such as obstruction. The code was not 'law' as such but it operated very like law. Indeed, the Department of Employment's *Working Paper on Picketing*[160] stated that the code was aimed to produce 'a more consistent interpretation of the law by the police and the magistrates' courts'.[161]

Although the picketing code was subject to the affirmative resolution procedure, it is arguable that it has been over-extended in application by the courts and by enforcement officials. Roy Lewis refers to 'a species of unconstitutional legislation'[162] and, on juxtaposing the code and statute, the ambition of the former is quite dramatic. The Trade Union and Labour Relations Act 1974 defined in broad terms a right to picket—nothing was said of the lawfulness or otherwise of the pickets' activities—and the picketing code filled the gaps with a gloss on the law. The Act said: 'It shall be lawful . . . to attend at or near a place where another person works or carries on business or any other place.'[163] The code read: 'But

[156] [1972] 3 All E.R. 864, CA per Stephenson J; see also Road Traffic Act 1988, s. 38.

[157] Health and Safety at Work Act 1974, s. 17. See C. D. Drake and F. B Wright, *The Law of Health and Safety at Work: A New Approach* (1982), 117–18.

[158] e.g. Roy Lewis, 'Codes of Practice on Picketing and Closed Shop Agreements and Arrangements' (1981) 44 MLR 198.

[159] Department of Employment, *Code of Practice of Picketing* (1980), para. 13 (the Code was revised in 1992 and authority to issue Codes was repeated in s. 203 of the Trade Union and Labour Relations (Consolidation) Act 1992).

[160] Department of Employment, *Working Paper on Picketing* (1979), para. 13.

[161] See Lewis, 'Codes of Practice on Picketing', 200.

[162] Ibid. 201.

[163] Trade Union and Labour Relations Act 1974, s. 15. For correspondence between the terms of the picketing code and an injunction, see *Thomas* v. *National Union of Mineworkers (South Wales)* [1985] IRLR 136. See also *British Airports Authority* v. *Ashton* [1983] 3 All ER 6.

not at an entrance to or exit from any place of work which is not his own, even if those who are employed there are employed by the same employer or covered by the same collective bargaining arrangements.' The code was used as a method of offering instructions to the judiciary and of redefining the law in a sensitive and politically contentious area.

Codes of practice may be invalidated by the courts if they are found to be beyond the powers given by Parliament,[164] but tertiary rules are usually made without reference to any mandate and where some delegation is involved this is often vague in nature. Where the status of the rules is vague it is difficult to mount a legal challenge. The problem in attacking, say, the code on picketing, would lie in demonstrating that it was more than 'practical guidance' available for evidential purposes. The real difficulty lies in the judicial tendency to treat evidential codes with a respect that they perhaps do not deserve. The promoters of tertiary rules tend to be on favourable ground for two reasons. If the courts deem a code to be 'advisory only', they will be unwilling to review discretionary action that takes it into account. If, on the other hand, a code is accredited with considerable weight by a judge, then that same judge is unlikely to view the code with an overcritical eye. Thus, the ACAS *Code on Disciplinary Practice and Procedure in Employment* (a classic example of the procedural/evidential code) was applied in *Earl* v. *Slater and Wheeler Ltd.*[165] Sir John Donaldson, in looking at this unfair dismissal case, allowed the Code a pre-eminent role in defining current procedure. He said:

Section 1 of the 1971 Act contains the guiding principles which both the industrial tribunals and this court are required to apply . . . The

[164] See *Laker Airways* v. *Department of Trade* [1977] QB 643; *R* v. *Secretary of State for the Environment ex parte Lancashire CC*, The *Times*, 3 Feb. 1994 (policy guidance to Local Government Commission held to be unlawful as government's hoped-for result laid down in relation to an LGC review of boundary changes, and this undermined the relevant statutory criteria governing the review). If Parliament has authorised a particular statutory regime to be brought into force by ministerial order and a minister, by the prerogative, issues tertiary rules to create a radically different scheme, this will be unlawful according to the Court of Appeal—see *R v. Secretary of State for the Home Dept., ex parte Fire Brigades Union, The Times*, 10 Nov. 1994.

[165] [1973] 1 All ER 135.

principle requires orderly procedures . . . the Code of Practice is far more relevant. Accordingly, the appellant is fully entitled to rely on para. 132 of the Code which provides that the disciplinary procedure shall give the employee the opportunity to state his case.

Evidential codes are increasingly used by administrators and this is understandable. Codes allow ministers to regulate extensively without having to go through anything more than positive resolution procedure and both courts and enforcers often pay as much attention to codes as if they were law. For such reasons, Patrick Elias made the following comment on the *Code of Practice on the Closed Shop* and its guidance on disciplinary action by unions:

Leaving aside the highly contentious ideological assumptions lying behind the code . . . it is constitutionally unacceptable that provisions of this kind should be in a code rather than the body of the law. It comes close to government directing the tribunal to reach a particular decision and then disowning responsibility for it.[166]

To conclude on tertiary rules and claims under the legal mandate rationale, there are significant problems on this front, notably:

- the haphazard variety of and difficulty of classifying such rules and their uncertain legal credentials;
- the vagueness of the mandate involved;
- the legal freedom enjoyed by judges in attributing legal effects to such rules;
- the lack of consistency in judicial principles governing the effects of tertiary rules;
- the silence of statutes on contentious issues together with the use of tertiary rules to govern such issues;
- the variety of legal effects that may flow from one set of rules;
- the existence of tensions and conflicts between statutes and tertiary rules; and
- the usurping by the executive of functions traditionally conceived of as legislative and judicial.

[166] P. Elias, 'Closing in the Closed Shop' (1980) 9 Ind.LJ 201, 211.

(iii) Accountability/ Control

Can tertiary rules be justified according to the accountability/ control rationale? This, in fact, may be their weakest suit. Legislative controls are lacking because the Statutory Instruments Act 1946 applies only to Orders in Council, to ministerial rule-making powers stated in a statute to be exercisable by Statutory Instrument and to rules made under a statute covered by the Rules Publication Act 1893. It does not apply to the mass of tertiary rule-making. Parliamentary control by scrutiny procedures is also lacking and hardly seems feasible across the board given a lack of parliamentary time so acute that even the present system of scrutinizing Statutory Instruments is overloaded and unsatisfactory.[167] Massively to increase such a workload would be to indulge in little more than a presentational exercise. One may point, furthermore, to other deficiencies of the existing system: the *de facto* executive control of the legislature; the lack of information about the substance of a rule in advance of parliamentary scrutiny; the restrictions on debate; and the low priority that Members of Parliament give to technical or substantive scrutiny. These problems would all be aggravated if informal rules were brought into the system. Nor does it seem realistic to expect that procedural reforms in Parliament (e.g. the allocation of more time and advance notice) would readily be forthcoming or could make the system work effectively.

A further reason why it is difficult to subject such rules to formal parliamentary scrutiny lies in the nature of their emergence. Often a department or agency will commence operations by taking decisions (e.g. in licensing) on the basis of statutory provisions alone. If cases recur and principles are established, the agency may begin to develop rules, principles, and standards to guide applications. It may 'structure' discretion in Davis's terms[168] and soon it may issue policy statements and various kinds of rule, as it proves possible to set these down. To subject each of these nascent rules to

[167] See Beatson, 'Legislative Control', 222.
[168] K. C. Davis, *Discretionary Justice*, ch. 4.

parliamentary scrutiny would create problems of selection between rules at different evolutionary stages. At which point would scrutiny be applied? Such scrutinizing would swamp Parliament with work, deprive such rules of their flexibility and act as a disincentive to bodies that desire to structure discretion with open policy statements.

Parliament might attempt to control rule-makers by laying down standards. Thus, in the United States the non-delegation doctrine means that Congress cannot delegate part of its legislative power 'except under the limitations of a prescribed standard'.[169] Rule-making authority thus has to be given for a designated purpose and there can be no allocation of open-ended legislative power.

There are a number of problems encountered in using statutory standards to control tertiary rule-making. Such a strategy has no purchase on rules that are made without pretence of delegation and, even where statutory authority is desired or claimed, there are limits to the extent that legislators can devise in advance a suitable set of standards. Precise standards are required in order to control rule-makers but precision may not only be beyond the legislators' anticipatory powers, it may conflict with the agencies' needs for flexibility and autonomy. In the United States necessity has meant that many of the great regulatory agencies have to exercise powers according to standards of enormous breadth such as 'public interest . . . public convenience and necessity' (the Federal Communications Commission). Without such breadth, the agencies could not cope with economic change or apply their expertise.

Although only so much can be accomplished by setting down the limits of rule-making in advance, many statutes are unnecessarily vague on rule-making issues and could offer more precise guidance in the following respects:

- They could set out the purposes of anticipated rule-making and any considerations to be taken into account.

[169] *United States* v. *Chicago M. St. P. and P. R.R.*, 282 US 311, 324 (1931); *Schechter Poultry Corporation* v. *United States*, 295 US 495 (1935). See also Schwartz and Wade, *Legal Control of Government* (1972), ch. 4; on the limits of the non-delegation doctrine see Stewart, 'The Reformation of American Administrative Law', 1695; S. Breyer and R. B. Stewart, *Administrative Law*, 66–91.

- They could state whether an envisaged code or rule is binding, on whom and for which purposes (indicating, for instance, whether a code is purely procedural or of mixed effect).
- They could state the effects of a breach of the rule, indicating, for example, whether a rule is evidential in relation to statutory offences, whether it is relevant to criminal or civil liability, and whether breach constitutes an offence in itself.
- They could stipulate disclosure and consultative requirements, in relation to particular sectors and issues.

Even if all of the above suggestions were implemented, a massive body of administratively-issued rules of various kinds would still emerge in a form unrelated to statutory powers. Justifying tertiary rules by pointing to legislative controls over the rule-maker is always, therefore, likely to be problematic unless new legislative requirements are to be introduced to create broad duties to consult—the arguments for which are discussed in the following section.

Judicial scrutiny of tertiary rules is not encouraged by the problems of standing that were noted in discussing secondary rules,[170] nor does the frequently encountered lack of legislative clarity concerning the purposes, effects, and force of tertiary rules make for strong judicial controls over such rules. The courts, are, as indicated above, involved in ruling on the legal force and effects of tertiary rules, notably, in assessing the legitimacy of expectations that such rules will be applied when decisions are taken. What the courts have not done is shown consistency or resolution in controlling tertiary rules or in developing the law so as to improve consultative and disclosure arrangements concerning such rules. (On the case for which see the following section.) Until the courts take such steps they can be seen as doing little to legitimate tertiary rules.

Governments may, of course, increase claims to legitimacy through accountability by demonstrating (and delivering on) a commitment to openness and disclosure. Freedom of information legislation would thus contribute to such claims. The

[170] See *supra* p. 73.

Local Government (Access to Information) Act 1985 represents a movement in this direction, but a development of such statutory provision to cover central government activities would more significantly enhance many rule-makers' claims to be broadly accountable.[171] At a non-legislative level, the White Paper on open government of July 1993[172] may be seen as an expression of commitment to openness. A central theme of the White Paper is 'handling information in a way which promotes informed policy-making and debate and efficient service delivery'.[173] The breadth of exemptions from that commitment is, however, considerable[174] and it remains to be seen whether the follow-up Code of Practice on Access to Government Information (published by the Cabinet Office in June 1994) will produce more accountable policy-making in practice.

Another opportunity for rendering governmental rule-making more open can be seen in the greater involvement of the private sector in the provision of public services.[175] Thus, the processes of privatization, franchising, and 'government by contract' have considerable potential to enhance accountability in so far as the licences, franchises, and contracts employed might be discussed by say, enterprises, regulators, departments, consumers, and the public against a background of disclosed information and clearly stated targets and performance standards. Such processes as licensing, franchising, and contracting also, however, have a potential to conceal—particularly when seen in private rather than public law terms and where notions of commercial confidentiality and privity of contract are emphasized. As commentators have noted, therefore, it is particularly important that the public and governmental aspects of

[171] See Birkinshaw, Harden, and Lewis, *Government by Moonlight*, 250–1. On openness in government see P. Birkinshaw, *Freedom of Information* (1988), ch. 5.

[172] Chancellor of the Duchy of Lancaster, *Open Government* Cmd 2290 (1993).

[173] Ibid., para. 1.7.

[174] Ibid., part II; for discussion see *infra* pp. 118–19.

[175] See C. Graham and T. Prosser, 'Rolling Back the Frontiers? The Privatisation of State Enterprises' in Graham and Prosser (eds.), *Waiving the Rules: The Constitution Under Thatcherism* (1988); N. Lewis, 'Regulating Non-Governmental Bodies: Privatisation, Accountability and the Public–Private Divide', in J. Jowell and D. Oliver (eds.), *The Changing Constitution*, 2nd edn. (1989); N. Lewis, *How to Reinvent British Government* (1993).

such processes are not lost sight of.[176] The need to legitimate does not disappear with the involvement of the private sector or the use of contracts within government—it increases.

In discussing the accountability of types of rule, it should not be forgotten that rules are made by different institutions, *inter alia*, by departments, regulatory agencies, executive agencies, and authorized private bodies. These institutions may operate under very different frameworks of accountability, and although it is not the purpose of the chapter to focus on institutional accountability[177] as opposed to the particular problems involved in legitimating rule-making, it should be noted that taking steps to improve institutional accountability will clearly enhance claims that can be made on behalf of rules produced by those institutions. (Deficiencies in institutional accountability will, similarly, undermine such claims.) Attention might, accordingly, be given[178] to potential improvements in the accountability of governmental organizations, and such measures as: reforms of oversight, audit and scrutiny bodies within government;[179] adapting the ombudsman system to the 'contracting state'; opening up the 'contracting state' so that policy-making is visible; developing public interest litigation; increasing the public accountability of those private bodies that exercise governmental functions; developing the select committee system so as to monitor regulatory activity more fully;[180] and publicly assisting pressure- and consumer groups who seek to comment on emerging rules.

(iv) Due Process

The essence of a claim under the due process rationale is that affected parties' interests have been respected. In relation to

[176] See I. Harden, *The Contracting State* (1992); N. Lewis, *How to Reinvent British Government*, and id., 'The Citizens Charter and Next Steps: A New Way of Governing' (1993) Pol.Q. 316.

[177] On which see e.g. Harden and Lewis, *The Noble Lie*.

[178] See e.g. Lewis, *How to Reinvent British Government*.

[179] On the National Audit Office as a vehicle for accountability see J. McEldowney, 'The National Audit Office and Privatisation' (1991) MLR 933.

[180] On the accountability of regulatory agencies and calls for a Regulated Industries Select Committee, see Baldwin and McCrudden, *Regulation iand Public Law*, 39, and C. Veljanovski, *The Future of Industry Regulation in the UK: A Report of an Independent Inquiry* (1993).

rule-making this involves a claim adequately to have consulted and considered comments and so to have acted fairly. As noted above, however, there is no general obligation for tertiary rule-makers to consult on or disclose the contents of tertiary rules and there is no statutory process laid down for issuing such rules. Justifications on the due process basis are accordingly liable to be weak unless effective voluntary arrangements to consult are in place. Nor should it be forgotten that membership of the European Community affects tertiary rules and their openness to participation. Promulgating a tertiary rule is unlikely to constitute a clear fulfilment of the obligation to implement a Directive that Article 189 EC imposes on a Member State.[181] Tertiary rules may, however, be used as components in legislative packages which are prompted by Directives—indeed, the policies driving many domestic regulatory regimes now flow in large part from Community sources.[182] Where such use occurs, there tends to be a distancing of the 'real' rule-makers from those persons in the Member States who are affected by the ensuing rules. Such distancing can only weaken claims that effective participation takes place.

Should a broadly framed statutory duty to consult be introduced? As indicated above, 'notice and comment' procedures are perhaps appropriate in the case of secondary rules but not in relation to tertiary rules. Asimow has argued[183] that 'to open all non-legislative rules to advance public participation would have a devastatingly negative effect on the administrative process'. His reasoning has force: few non-legislative rules have the practical significance of most legislative rules—the vast majority of non-legislative rules are insignificant or of internal bureaucratic relevance only—an invitation to comment would thus be wasteful as in most cases it would produce

[181] Unless the rule is of binding force, certain and clear: see Case 102/79, *Commission* v. *Kingdom of Belgium* [1988] ECR 1473. Mere administrative practices will not suffice to implement, but certain provisions of collective agreements may: see Case 91/81 *Commission* v. *Italian Republic* (1982) ECR 2133, and, generally, G. Gaja, P. Hay and R. Rotunda, 'Legal Techniques for Integration' in M. Cappelletti *et al.*, *Integration Through Law* (1986), i, bk 2.

[182] See *infra*. p. 256.

[183] Asimow, 'Non-legislative Rulemaking', 426.

no response; to demand notice and comment would impose huge costs on the administration and would delay rule-making; in addition, formalizing procedures would discourage the promulgation of helpful guidance and policy statements through the imposition of costs and creating fear of legal challenges. In short, gains in due process and accountability would be purchased at too high a price in efficiency. The public would, accordingly, lose more than it would gain from mandatory non-legislative rule-making procedures.

There may, moreover, be more attractive means of stimulating greater access to tertiary rule-making processes than by controlling procedures in the stage before a rule is made. One proposal is to impose a duty on rule-makers to publish tertiary rules and to hear and comment on responses made in a fixed period *after* the rule is promulgated.[184] Such a post-adoption procedure is attractive for a number of reasons:[185]

- It would not delay the introduction of the typical rule.
- Most rules would elicit no comments and so the rule-maker would not have to bear the costs of responding.
- A requirement of post-adoption procedure would in practice lead rule-makers to give advanced notice and hear comments in the case of important rules likely to provoke substantial comments.
- Post-adoption processes would usefully point to shortcomings in rules and prompt revisions.
- A record of post-adoption comments and responses would assist the courts when reviewing tertiary rules.
- Post-adoption commenting would enhance the public legitimacy of rules.

Post-adoption comment processes would not guarantee access to and influence within the rule-making processes. Problems would also be encountered in defining which particular rules have to be disclosed (and which classes of rule would be exempt) but, as indicated, such processes would encourage

[184] Administrative Conference of the United States 1 CFR 305–76–5 (1984) discussed Asimow, 'Non-legislative Rulemaking', 421–5. (The periods suggested for comments and responses are 30 and 60 days respectively.)

[185] See Asimow, 'Non-legislative Rulemaking', 421–5.

pre-adoption access in important cases and would impose far lower costs than pre-adoption notice and comment requirements. This is a proposal worth pursuing and it is consistent with possible developments in judicial approaches to rule disclosure.

Turning, then, to the judges, could they develop the common law so as to increase participation and accountability in rule-making? Two proposals for judicially developed rules should, be considered.

(*a*) *A rule on unfair non-disclosure.* This rule would impose a duty to publish a rule where it is in operation. ('Publish' here may simply mean 'make available to the affected party'.) The implication of this duty would be that where body *X* makes a decision in the case of person *Y* and does so in application of a rule or policy, then *Y* should be able to challenge that decision where the policy affects rights or interests, where the rule or the policy is unreasonably not disclosed and where this operates to his or her prejudice.

The proposed duty is founded, therefore, on the concept of fairness. Davis puts the argument thus:

> As soon as discretion gives way to rules, the rules should be available to affected parties. Precedents and rules provide a beneficial structuring of discretion, but not if they are kept secret, for the administrator then can ignore a precedent or violate a rule, engaging in discrimination and favouritism without detection. . . . . Secret law, whether in the form of precedents or in the form of rules, has no place in any decent system of justice.[186]

Although Scott LJ said in *Blackpool Corporation* v. *Locker*[187] that there was no duty either by statute or at common law to publish sub-delegated legislation, he did consider it 'vital to the whole English theory of the liberty of the subject' that those affected by sub-delegated legislation should be able to ascertain its existence and nature. Indeed, the seeds of such an approach are to be found in the law. It is the duty of 'everyone who decides anything to act in good faith and listen fairly to both

[186] Davis, *Discretionary Justice*, 110 [187] [1948] 1 KB 349.

sides'.[188] The right to a fair hearing also involves a person's right to know the case against him or her. Lord Denning has said: 'He must know what evidence has been given and what statements have been made affecting him and then he must be given a fair opportunity to correct or contradict them.'[189]

In a series of cases,[190] decisions have been overturned where relevant reports have not been made known, where there were secret grounds for decision, or where previous decisions or resolutions were followed without disclosure. In a number of licensing cases also, a duty to disclose policies has been indicated. In *R* v. *Torquay Licensing Justices, ex parte Brockman*,[191] Lord Goddard CJ said: 'It would seem clear that if the justices have decided upon a policy to guide them in considering applications it is only fair that they should make it public so that applicants may know what to expect.' Similarly, in *R* v. *Holborn Licensing justices, ex parte Stratford Catering Co. Ltd.*,[192] Salter J said that it was 'both right and convenient' that 'standards of practice' should be stated publicly by licensing justices.

The same principles, it seems, apply to bodies such as the Criminal Injuries Compensation Board. In *R* v. *CICB, ex parte Ince*[193] Megaw LJ said:

> I think that justice and paragraph 22 of the Scheme alike require that if the Board in any particular case are minded to be guided by

[188] Lord Loreburn in *Board of Education* v. *Rice* [1911] AC 179.

[189] *Kanda* v. *Government of Malaya* [1962] AC 322. More recently the House of Lords has endorsed this approach (citing *Kanda*) in calling for the disclosure of reasons. In *Doody* v. *Secretary of State for the Home Department* [1993] 3 All ER 92, a prisoner had a right to make representations to the Home Secretary concerning release on licence and the House of Lords stated that fairness demanded disclosure in advance to the prisoner of the corpus of material upon which the release decision would be based (a corpus that included the trial judge's advice on the penal element of the sentence and the reasoning behind this). Lord Mustill noted the modern judicial tendency to call for greater openness in administrative decision-making and argued that without disclosure there was a danger that facts, opinions, and *policies* might wrongly go unanswered (pp. 107, 109). See also *R* v. *Parole Board ex parte Wilson* [1992] 2 All ER 576 CA (disclosure to prisoner of Parole Board reports on forthcoming review) and A. W. Bradley, 'Tell Us Why', *Solicitors Journal*, 4 Feb. 1994.

[190] *Kanda* v. *Government of Malaya*; *R* v. *Westminster Assessment Committee, ex parte Grosvenor House; Park Lane* v. *Mahmud* [1967] 1 AC 13; *R* v. *Criminal Injuries Compensation Board, ex parte Ince* [1973] 1 WLR 1334.

[191] [1951] 2 KB 748, 788.

[192] 42 T.LR 778, 781.

[193] [1973] 1 WLR 1334, 1345.

any principle laid down in any pre-existing minute of the Board, the applicant must be informed of the existence and terms of that minute, so that he can, if he wishes, make his submissions with regard thereto.

In similar vein Henry Molot has contended:

An individual denied adequate knowledge of the policy or rule that a tribunal intends to apply to his case can no more respond to the situation or allegations against him than the person who complains of ex parte representations or that materials and evidence on which the tribunal might base its decision, and to which he has had no access, have not been disclosed to him before the hearing.[194]

Disclosure of a relevant policy, moreover, seems part and parcel of exercising a discretion reasonably. Lord Reid said in the *British Oxygen* case:

There may be cases where an officer or authority ought to listen to a substantial argument reasonably presented urging a change of policy. What the authority must not do is to refuse to listen at all. But a Ministry or large authority may have had to deal already with a multitude of similar applications and then they will almost certainly have evolved a policy so precise that it could well be called a rule. There can be no objection to that, provided the authority is always willing to listen to anyone with something new to say.[195]

Viscount Dilhorne added: 'It was both reasonable and right that the Board should make known to those interested the policy it was going to follow.'

It is hard to see how one might show willingness 'to listen to anyone with something new to say' without disclosing a relevant policy for comment. Similarly, the duty to consult, where one exists, demands that those consulted 'must know what is proposed before they can be expected to give their views.'[196] A rule of unfair non-disclosure thus appears necessary to avoid undermining the rules on fettering and on exercising a discretion properly.

[194] H. Molot, 'The Self-Created Rule of Policy and Other Ways of Exercising Administrative Discretion' (1972) 18 McGill LJ 310.

[195] *British Oxygen Co.* v. *Board of Trade* [1971] AC 610, 625.

[196] *Port Louis Corporation* v. *Attorney-General of Mauritius* [1965] AC 1111 (PC).

This is not, of course, to say that an oral hearing is required every time a policy is disclosed. The kind of opportunity to comment on or challenge the policy should depend on what is reasonable, fair, and practicable in the circumstances. This is a kind of issue familiar in administrative law[197] and would hardly involve new difficulties.

The primary questions the judge might ask would be:

- Was there applied here a rule (in the broadest sense) that might reasonably have been disclosed and did its non-disclosure prejudice the applicant?
- Would disclosure have been reasonable given:
  (*a*) the rule's degree of relevance to the issue and its determination?
  (*b*) the degree of weight given to the rule in the decision or action at issue?

(*b*) *A Duty to Develop Rules?* The courts might go further and compel authorities not only to make known any rules that they apply but to structure their discretion by formulating rules where this is practicable. Otherwise, it could be said, an authority might avoid accusations of unfair non-disclosure by not developing rules that might be challenged—in other words, by pursuit of unstructured, *ad hoc* decision-making.

K. C. Davis, again, has advocated this reform in the United States.[198] His object is to 'protect against unguided discretionary power . . . whenever meaningful guides are feasible'. Where, therefore, legislators have failed to provide standards, the administrators should be required by the courts to supply standards, principles, and rules.[199] The case for this second new rule seems, however, weaker than that for the first. An authority's failure to structure is not the same thing as its committing acts of injustice.[200] Nor does traditional British emphasis on considering of the merits of a case (as opposed to

[197] See e.g. *R* v. *Gaming Board, ex parte Benaim and Khaida* [1970] 2 QB 417; *Ceylon University* v. *Fernando* [1960] 1 WLR 233; *British Oxygen Co.* v. *Board of Trade* [1971] AC 610; *Doody* v. *Secretary of State for the Home Department* [1993] 3 All ER 92, 109.

[198] See Davis, *Discretionary Justice*, 57–9. On judicial requirements that agencies narrow their discretions by adopting rules, see Breyer and Stewart, *Administrative Law*, 396–410.

[199] Ibid. 59.

[200] See Baldwin and Hawkins, 'Discretionary Justice'.

rule-making and structuring) seem particularly welcoming to such a rule.

The evidential and informational difficulties in enforcing compulsory rule-making would be huge. In order to say that a body should have structured a discretion, the court would have to be able to assess the ability of the agency to formulate and state a rule with precision and clarity. To do this properly would involve detailed analysis, often in a complex and specialist regulatory area.[201] This is not something which the courts are manifestly competent or willing to undertake. (Where a policy is deliberately suppressed, the courts would have scope for action under the proposed unfair non-disclosure rule.) The case for the 'duty to develop' rule does not, therefore, seem convincing in its present form.

An alternative to new legislation or judicially developed rules on legislation is voluntary governmental action. Promises of disclosure were contained in the White Paper on Open Government of July 1993[202] but will these serve to legitimate tertiary rules according to a due process rationale? The White Paper and its 1994 Code of Practice on Access to Government Information commit departments and public bodies 'to publish the facts and analysis of the facts which the Government considers relevant and important in framing major policy proposals and decisions'.[203] It should be noted, however, first, that the Code is not intended to be legally binding. Second, such disclosure will normally occur 'when policies and decisions are announced'[204] rather than beforehand and so constitutes a form of *ex post facto* accountability rather than access to policy-making. Third, that exempt from such commitments to disclosure are internal opinions, items of advice, recommendations, consultations and deliberations, projections and assumptions relating to internal policy analysis, analyses of alternative policy options, information on rejected options, and 'confidential'

[201] See Breyer and Stewart, *Administrative Law*, 389, and Stewart, 'The Reformation of American Administrative Law' (1975) 88 *Harv.LR* 1667, 1698–702.

[202] Chancellor of the Duchy of Lancaster, *Open Government* Cm 2290 (1993).

[203] See Cabinet Office, *Code of Practice on Access to Government Information* (1994), para. 3(i).

[204] Ibid.

communications between departments, public bodies, and regulatory bodies.[205] Fourth, that open government, per the White Paper, is largely thought of in Citizen's Charter terms—as openness concerning the meeting of performance targets rather than as a means of allowing access to policy-making processes. The Code of Practice can perhaps be welcomed as an exhortation to broad public accountability. It might be a mistake, however, to view it as strongly legitimating on a due process basis or as a substitute for more rigorous provisions on access.

Conclusions

Governmental rule-making is a hugely extensive activity but we have seen that, in the case of secondary legislation and tertiary rules, it is difficult to make clear-cut claims of justification other than on the bases of expertise and efficiency. Secondary legislation often lacks clear parliamentary authorization as to its content; the systems of accountability and control that regulate it are in many respects necessarily weak and in some respects more than necessarily weak; and the procedures associated with the promulgation of such legislation are not marked by their advancing the participatory interests of affected parties.

In the case of tertiary rules, these difficulties are all the more severe. Tertiary rules may have a positive role to play in defining and clarifying statutory mandates and may bring expertise and efficiency gains, but the relationship between the substance of the rules and any legislative mandate is very often unclear; tertiary rules constitute a confusingly haphazard mass; the legal effects of such rules are uncertain (particularly in the 'contracting state'); and such rules allow judges too much leeway in choosing whether to give effect to them. The accountability claims of those making tertiary rules also seem weak. Accountability to and control by Parliament is poor because scrutiny processes are weak and because tertiary rules are

[205] Ibid., part II, para. 2.

employed as a means of bypassing Parliament on problematic or contentious issues. Accountability to the courts is made difficult because tertiary rules are often couched in language that is vague and not susceptible to court adjudication.

As with secondary legislation, it is difficult to make strong claims on behalf of tertiary rules on the basis of their realizing the participatory aspirations of affected parties, and European Union membership may not ease participation.[206] The irregular forms of publication and consultation that have been adopted scarcely strengthen the case for resort to tertiary rules and the uncertainties surrounding the legal effects of tertiary rules further serve to undermine participatory processes—it is difficult to express opinions concerning provisions when their potential legal effects are not known.

The implication of the above points is not that secondary and tertiary rules have no place in government. They clearly cannot be avoided—although some matters might be covered by 'higher-level' rules than are presently employed. A first conclusion to draw is that since justificatory claims tend to be weak, all possible should be done to improve claims under the various headings where undue losses under other headings would not be occasioned. I have suggested some areas of potential improvement. Thus, for example, the status and legal effects of secondary and tertiary rules could be made more clear in primary legislation. Accountability and control claims could be improved by reforms as proposed, for example, by the Joint Committee, the Hansard Society, and others. Consultation and publication requirements could be rationalized, new legislation might be introduced to improve participation in secondary rule-making, and the judges might develop more consistent approaches to tertiary rules. Rules demanding disclosure of tertiary rules might, as indicated, be developed by the judges.

A second conclusion is that expectations concerning the jus-

[206] In some respects Community membership can be seen as an opportunity for participation that can and should be grasped—see C. Harlow, 'A Community of Interests: Making the Most of European Law' (1992) 55 MLR 331 (discussed *infra* pp. 276–7), but participation at Community level may tend to focus on legislative levels higher than those that tertiary rules occupy.

tificatory claims of secondary and tertiary rules should not be pitched at levels that are unrealistically high. The operation of government now demands extensive rule-making and the efficiency offered by rules may to some extent have to be traded off against lower levels of, for example, accountability. To be excessively ambitious in attempts to improve justificatory claims may not merely lead to efficiency losses but may produce a weakening of the very claims sought to be strengthened—as may occur, for example, when highly legalistic procedures are introduced. 'Legal' solutions to justificatory problems have, indeed, to be weighed carefully against others, against, for example, the option of political reforms.

Finally, since secondary and tertiary rules find their main justification in the effectiveness of their contribution to government, all possible steps should be taken to ensure that the rules chosen do produce results effectively. To this end they must be rules with the appropriate dimensions and they must be rules that can be applied effectively on the ground. These issues of design and enforcement are major concerns throughout the rest of this book.

PART II

Regulating with Rules

5 Rules and Regulation

This and the following chapter consider how governmental rules can be designed and enforced, particularly in the sphere of regulation. The focus is on experience in regulating workplace health and safety but more general lessons will be drawn from the case study described. This chapter amounts to a description of how mistakes in rule design can occur. It looks at the evolution of the present system of regulating health and safety at work and notes especially the development of a particular approach to governmental rules. An assessment of that approach is offered. Chapter 6 examines the enforcement of health and safety regulation on the ground and considers the importance of rule-design in enforcement. It asks why it is that rules often fail to work, how effective rules can be designed, what it is that impedes the making of effective rules, and how securing compliance is linked to producing desired results. Finally, I consider how values other than efficiency can be reflected in designing rules.

1. The Evolution of a Regulatory System: Health and Safety at Work

The roots of the British system of health and safety regulation are to be found in the factories legislation of the Industrial Revolution.[1] It was the Factories Amendment Act of 1844 that first provided minimum safety standards, required the fencing of dangerous machinery, and provided for the compensation of accident victims. A series of factories statutes eventually led to a major work of consolidation in the Factories Act 1961. By this time the rules governing the area were highly fragmented

[1] See N. Gunningham, *Safeguarding the Worker* (1984), ch. 4; P. Bartrip and P. Fenn, 'The Administration of Safety: The Enforcement Policy of the Early Factory Inspectorate 1844–1864' (1980) 58 Pub. Admin. A 87; W. G. Carson, 'The Conventionalisation of Early Factory Crime' (1979) 7 IJSL 37–69.

and complex. The mass of detailed regulations and subordinate legislation that had been made under former statutes continued in force after 1961 and was supplemented with regulations made under the 1961 Act. Such legislation imposed highly specific duties on employers and saw worker participation as solely a matter of workplace discipline.[2] It was, moreover, restricted to factories as defined by statute. Certain other premises were covered by separate legislative schemes (for example coal mines and railway premises), but many more occupations went unregulated.

During the 1960s the industrial accident rate increased and widespread demands for statutory reform were made.[3] The relevant legislation was still rooted in the factories model, being fragmented and affording little involvement to the workforce. In 1966 a Labour government was re-elected and the Trades Union Congress (TUC) began to press for workers' committees to be given a statutory role to play in safety matters. The response came in 1970 when Barbara Castle, then Secretary of State for Employment and Productivity, asked Lord Robens to head an investigating committee. The report that followed in 1972[4] provided the foundations upon which the present regulatory system is built.

2. The Robens Report

Three core issues dominated the findings and recommendations of the Robens Report. These concerned legal rules, governmental institutions, and regulatory philosophy. A first finding was that the law existing at 1970 constituted a haphazard mass that was complex, difficult to amend, and out of date. Robens had encountered a system in which nine different groups of statutes were separately administered by five central government departments through seven separate inspector-

[2] See S. Dawson *et al.*, *Safety at Work: The Limits of Self-Regulation* (1988), 9, and L. Howells, 'Worker Participation in Safety' (1974) 3 Ind.LJ 87, 89.

[3] See Dawson, *Safety at Work*, ch. 1.

[4] *Safety and Health at Work*, Report of the Committee 1970–2 Cmnd 5034 (1972) (The Robens Report).

ates.[5] There was said to be too much law with, apart from the statutes, over 500 subordinate Statutory Instruments. Such laws were said to have become counter-productive in regulatory terms. They had an 'all-pervading psychological effect'[6] that conditioned people to think of health and safety at work as a matter of detailed rules imposed by external agencies. Robens considered that the system he investigated encouraged rather too much reliance on state regulation and rather too little on personal responsibility and voluntary, self-generating effort. The Report commented: 'This imbalance must be redressed. A start could be made by reducing the sheer weight of the legislation.'[7]

Apathy was found to be the greatest single contributing factor to accidents at work and Robens stated that this attitude would prevail so long as people thought that safety could be ensured by ever more inspectors and legal regulations. What was said to be needed was a new tack in which 'the primary responsibility for doing something about the present levels of occupational accidents and disease lies with those who create the risks and those who work with them'.[8]

On institutional arrangements, Robens found that there were various enforcement authorities which overlapped in their jurisdictions and that this caused confusion. It was clear that a coherent method of organization had to satisfy four major requirements: control had to be given to a self-contained organization clearly responsible for the area; it had to have day-to-day autonomy; it had to be organized in a manner consistent with responsible and accountable management; and, finally, those involved in the area, employers, workers, local authorities, and so on, had to be fully involved in managing the new institution.

As for the overall regulatory strategy, there was put forward a new 'Robens philosophy' based on two assumptions. First, that the primary function of health and safety law was to establish a framework within which self-regulation could flourish and industry itself could take responsibility for health and safety

[5] Ibid., para. 28. [6] Ibid. [7] Ibid. [8] Ibid.

matters. Second, that there should be workforce involvement so that health and safety should be the responsibility not only of employers and senior management but also of employees.

Incorporated in the second assumption was the view that there was no substantial conflict of interest between workers and employers on health and safety issues. As *Robens* put it: 'there is a greater natural identity of interest between "the two sides" in relation to health and safety problems than in most other matters.'[9]

3. Implementing Robens

On all three fronts action followed. The Health and Safety at Work etc Act 1974 (HSWA) was framed by a Conservative government, but enacted by an incoming Labour administration. Institutional change came in the shape of two linked agencies which were set up to regulate in the field: the Health and Safety Commission (HSC) and the Health and Safety Executive (HSE). The HSC consists of a Chair, appointed by the Secretary of State, plus three nominees from the CBI and TUC and two nominees from the local authorities (the latter to represent the public interest). It is thus a tripartite body and is responsible for setting objectives, allocating resources, making policies, and reviewing priorities. The HSE is a three-person statutory body headed by a Director General and responsible for enforcing health and safety legislation—including putting into effect the directions of the HSC. Robens had advocated a unified inspectorate to cover all spheres of activity,[10] but separate inspectorates were retained and to date these deal with factories, agriculture and quarries, railways, mines, nuclear installations, and offshore safety.

Other organizational changes affected the Robens philosophy of self-regulation combined with worker representation. The union role under the HSWA was to be played through the innovatory system of safety representatives and safety committees. The Act provided that organized trade unions be

[9] *Safety and Health at Work*, Report of the Committee 1970–2 Cmnd 5034 (1972), 21.
[10] Ibid. 63.

given the right to appoint safety representatives from amongst the employees and the employer was obliged to consult those individuals.[11] Safety representatives were empowered to call for the creation of a safety committee whose functions were principally to investigate complaints, potential hazards, dangerous occurrences, and accidents; to make relevant representations on these matters to employers; and to inspect the workplace. As well as through the tripartite structure of the HSC and the major committees in the system, the consensual and self-regulating approach was reflected in other requirements. Within firms, health and safety objectives had to be set out in a written statement of health and safety policies.

4. Robens and Rules

For the purposes of this book, however, the most noteworthy changes instituted by Robens were those relating to rules and their enforcement. A key finding, as we have seen, was that regulation was being hindered by the nature of the rules being enforced, which were inappropriately detailed and presumed a system of regulation based on external commands. Robens wanted to 'reduce the negative influence of an excessively regulatory approach'[12] and suggested that the basic function of state inspection should be the provision of advice and assistance towards better safety standards. Prosecution was not to be the first priority: 'any idea that standards generally should be rigorously enforced through the extensive use of legal sanctions is one that runs counter to our general philosophy.'[13]

Robens wanted to move away from fragmented and complex statutory rules towards a mixture of statutory regulations and voluntary codes, a combination that clearly stated principles, was intelligible and was 'constructive rather than prohibitory'.[14] Moreover, Robens stated: 'We recommend that in future no statutory regulation should be made before detailed consideration has been given to whether the objectives might

[11] HSWA, s. 2(4).
[12] Robens Report, para. 254.
[13] Ibid., para. 255.
[14] Ibid., ch. 5, p. 40.

adequately be met by a non-statutory code of practice or standard.'[15]

The movement being advocated clearly involved placing increased reliance on rules that were subject to very little parliamentary control but the Robens Report was aware of this and considered the development to be necessary. Full scrutiny of all health and safety rules was in any case not practicable, and ministers, it was said, would be responsible for the rules that they had made.

Alongside this revised approach to rules went the new approach to enforcement. As noted, prosecution was not envisaged as a method of first resort: instead of detailed and regular external inspections, reliance would be placed on a system of self-regulation, complemented by occasional monitoring by government agencies. There was also to be greater use of administrative sanctions rather than the application of criminal penalties through the courts. Thus Robens recommended that inspectors should have the power to issue improvement and prohibition notices which could be delivered on the spot and would order employers respectively to remedy specified faults within a stated time or (in more urgent cases) to discontinue the use of specified plant or machinery pending compliance with the relevant rules.

Such a preference for administrative, rather than criminal, sanctioning reflected Robens's views on the role of the criminal law in regulatory matters. Thus Robens argued:

> the traditional concepts of the criminal law are not readily applicable to the majority of infringements which arise under this type of legislation. Relatively few offences are clear-cut, few arise from reckless indifference to the possibility of causing injury, few can be laid without disqualification at the door of a particular individual. The typical infringement arises rather through carelessness, oversight, lack of knowledge or means; inadequate supervision or sheer inefficiency. In such circumstances the process of prosecution and punishment is largely an irrelevancy.[16]

[15] Robens Report, para. 142. [16] Ibid., para. 261.

The voluntarist approach was thus deeply rooted and the HSWA reflected this. It set out a framework of legal duties and provided a hierarchy of rule forms. Robens's preference for 'lower-order' rules took legislative shape in section 1(2) of the HSWA, which instructed the HSC and HSE progressively to replace existing statutory provisions with a new system of regulations and approved codes. The Act itself attempted to establish a broad regulatory consistency through the establishment of a single standard of care—that of 'reasonable practicability'. This standard ran through sections 2–9 of the Act which imposed general duties on the various parties involved. Thus HSWA, section 2, placed duties on employers, to ensure *inter alia* and within the limits of reasonable practicability, a safe and healthy workplace,[17] to prepare a written statement of health and safety policy, and to consult with employees' safety representatives. The Act thus enshrined the common law right to a safe system of work in statute. It became clear in the courts that 'reasonably practicable' was a narrower term than 'physically possible' and allowed the employer to balance the quantum of risk against the costs in terms of money, time, or trouble of prevention.[18]

Regulations constituted the next layer in the hierarchy of rules. Section 15 of the Act gave the Secretary of State powers to make regulations for any of the general purposes of the Act and (notably in the light of Chapter 4 above) the Secretary of State was thus empowered not only to repeal or modify existing statutory provisions but to exclude or modify the general duties of sections 2–9. The regulations were meant to provide the main means of replacing outdated statutory provisions and represented a powerful form of delegated legislation. Regulations under the HSWA carry the full force of law and, whereas breach of a general HSWA duty may result in criminal but not civil liability, breach of a regulation may give rise to both forms of liability.

The Approved Code of Practice (ACOP) was the next level

[17] On the development of the HSWA, see Dawson, *Safety at Work*, ch. 1.

[18] See *Edwards* v. *National Coal Board* [1949] 1 KB 704; [1949] 1 All ER 143; *Marshall* v. *Gotham & Co.* [1954] AC 360.

of rule introduced by the Act and attempted to reap the benefits of flexibility and informality while at the same time operating with some legal force. The ACOP was established under section 17 in order to provide 'practical guidance' in relation to the requirements of either regulations or the Act itself. Failure to comply with a code provision does not render a person automatically liable in civil or criminal proceedings. If, however, it is shown that there has been a failure to observe a code on a matter relevant to the contravention of a requirement or prohibition, that matter is taken as proved unless it can be shown that compliance has been achieved other than by observing the code.

Whereas regulations are subject to approval by the Secretary of State, ACOPs are approved by the HSC which does, however, have to obtain the Secretary of State's consent beforehand and must consult appropriate government departments and other interested parties. ACOPs were seen by the government as useful in a number of respects: they could be used to spell out technical matters in detail; they could specify alternative ways of carrying out a required action; they could provide a flexible approach to compliance; they could be updated readily in the light of technological developments or operational experience; they provided a way to involve both sides of industry; and they supplemented regulations without determining a particular mode of compliance.

During the HSWA's passage through Parliament the accountability of those making ACOPs was raised. ACOPs were given some legal force by the HSWA, but they were not made by Parliament or by a person immediately responsible to Parliament. At the time the HSWA was passed, the government's thinking centred on two points. In view of the anticipated volume of ACOPs and the need to have them approved quickly, it was not practicable for all of them to be laid before Parliament. On the other hand, some form of accountability that went beyond the HSC's overall answerability to ministers was considered to be necessary. The requirement of the Secretary of State's consent was a compromise—one that was adhered to in spite of Opposition arguments that an expert body should be fully responsible for the codes and should be able to issue them without the delay inherent in seeking consent. (This dispute evidenced notably explicit trading-off between the accountability, efficiency, and expertise rationales.)

The final level of rule in health and safety matters is the guidance note. This may be developed by the HSC or by industry itself. The guidance note has no formal legal significance but is aimed at assisting employers and others to comply with the law.

Within three years of the passing of the HSWA, the HSE's management board had agreed a general approach to rule-types. *Regulations* would be used to set out specific aims, principles, objectives of control, or numerical standards which were important enough to be mandatory. They would generally be wide in application and would apply across the board to some risk or subject. ACOPs would set out the preferred methods for meeting the mandatory requirements of regulations. Only exceptionally would a code be linked directly to a statutory duty (which, it was anticipated, would be too general in most cases). Guidance would constitute authoritative advice of an explanatory or descriptive nature and might frequently be process- or industry-specific in scope.

5. The Design Appraised

The Robens Committee produced a blueprint for a highly consensual approach to regulation and this in turn resulted in a particular vision of governmental rules.[19] Central to Robens's consensualism was the notion of a 'natural identity of interest' between the 'two sides' of industry on health and safety matters. This notion, however, may have represented wishful thinking rather than a properly considered analysis. Others have condemned the idea. Patrick Kinnersly commented: 'Identity of interest is a dangerous myth which

[19] The institutional structure developed by Robens is not central to the focus here: see, however, R. Baldwin, 'Health and Safety At Work: Consensus and Self-Regulation', in R. Baldwin and C. McCrudden, *Regulation and Public Law* (1987).

dovetails with the fiction that most accidents are caused by carelessness and can therefore be eliminated if everyone "pulls together".'[20]

Robens use of inverted commas in referring to the 'two sides' of industry implied that there were not two sides at all. Nichols and Armstrong drew attention in 1973 to Robens's 'home-spun psychology that placed naïve trust in the goodwill of men like themselves—notably administrators rather than those involved in business'.[21]

In economic terms the notion of an identity of interest is highly suspect. In *some* circumstances it may be the case that the employer possesses incentives to avoid accidents just as the worker does. Thus in a chemicals or explosives factory where an accident might not merely injure or kill workers but is likely to demolish the plant, there is something close to an identity of interest. In many instances, however, there is no identity of interest: the accident imposes costs on the worker but does not damage machinery, slow the production process down, or impose other direct costs on the employer. Liability rules may compel the employer to bear costs but, even so, he or she may still have an incentive not to spend money on hazard avoidance up to the socially efficient level.[22] Suppose employer E runs a woodworking factory with machinery that cuts off ten workers' fingers annually. Assuming that the value of a finger is £1,000 (and that the accident does not damage the machine or slow the production process) the allocatively efficient level of spending on hazard-reducing guards would be up to £10,000 per annum (above that sum it is, in economic terms, more efficient to let accidents happen and compensate victims). Will E feel obliged to spend up to £10,000? In the real world E will not, because the operation of liability rules is such that E is not likely to have to pay out £10,000 to injured parties. Assuming

[20] P. Kinnersly, *The Hazards of Work: How to Fight Them* (1973), 10.

[21] T. Nichols and P. Armstrong, *Safety or Profits: Industrial Accidents and the Conventional Wisdom* (1973).

[22] In terms of allocative efficiency it is desirable from society's point of view that the employer spends money on hazard avoidance up to the point where the costs of avoidance exceed the costs of the accidents that avoidance will prevent: see e.g. S. Breyer, *Regulation and its Reform* (1982), 175.

that the courts would award £1,000 to each injured party, E might correctly anticipate that the injured parties will accept compensation in a lesser sum. They will do so if E makes an offer that realistically reflects the costs and uncertainties of pursuing a claim. The injured parties would have a number of hurdles to overcome in attempting to recover compensation: the costs of legal advice and lost time would be incurred with no certainty of recovering these; there could well be evidential problems in proving the required case or necessary lack of care; the relevant law might be vague and causation would have to be proved (for example that the injury was not occasioned by the employee's own negligence or some cause unrelated to the employment). E will also know that some victims may not pursue claims for other reasons—they may move house, emigrate, die, or simply lack the energy or resolve to pursue the matter.

Taking all of the above factors into account, it may well be the case that E would consider purchasing a guard system if it cost £2,000 per annum but not if it cost £8,000 or £10,000—at those prices it is economically rational to let accidents happen rather than guard against them. The example demonstrates why state regulation may be necessary in order to achieve what is, from society's point of view, the economically efficient level of spending on hazard avoidance.[23]

This is all the more so when managements are involved in highly competitive industries and place profits and productivity above safety. Gunningham quotes a commentator on the activities of the Chrysler Corporation: 'It was just a question of the Corporation deciding which is cheaper, to take some injuries, take some deaths, pay Workmen's Compensation or spend a lot of money and make it safe.'[24]

[23] A system of punitive damage awards might be used to create the appropriate level of incentive to spend on hazard avoidance, but the courts would face severe informational problems in putting such a system into effect. Ethically, of course, it may be preferable to prevent accidents rather than compensate victims—see T. O. McGarity and S. Shapiro, *Workers at Risk* (1993), 194. On liability rules and their limits see e.g. S. Shavell, 'Liability for Harm Versus Regulation of Safety' (1984) 13 *JLS* 357; 'A Model for the Optimal Use of Liability and Safety Regulation' (1984) 15 *RJE* 271.

[24] N. Gunningham, *Safeguarding the Worker* (1984), 270.

When health as opposed to safety hazards are at issue, the conflict with profit becomes even more problematic. Safety hazards tend to involve highly visible and immediate accidents and costs. Health hazards, in contrast, produce symptoms after a considerable period of time. They accordingly have low visibility; they do not involve immediate halts to production or costly damage; the causal relationship between the illness and the employment may be especially difficult to establish and damages are far from easy to obtain. For such reasons, employers will incline to continue with the given mode of production rather than spend money to avoid health hazards to workers.[25]

In a competitive environment a firm will, of course, be obliged to consider the level of its costs relative to those of its competitors. In such an environment a firm is likely to spend on hazard avoidance where its interests concur with those of the employees but otherwise even the well-disposed employer cannot afford to invest in health and safety unless *all* employers are compelled to do so. This implies that a policy of voluntarist self-regulation is likely to produce a high incidence of diseases and deaths.[26]

In economic terms, therefore, Robens's notion of an identity of interest is ill founded. It may be, however, that Robens spoke of the identity of interest in a social or moral sense as if assuring the reader that '*nobody* really wants accidents to happen'. The problem is that Robens failed to pay regard to the variety of employers to be encountered in the real world. Some employers may genuinely wish to avoid imposing risks on their workers and may be disposed to take energetic action to avoid or reduce hazards. Others, however, may have less feeling for the welfare of their employees or, even if favourably disposed, may lack the resolve or application necessary to turn these feelings into action. Even assuming that those at the top of an organization are disposed, as a matter of policy, to com-

[25] See Gunningham, *Safeguarding the Worker*, 271.

[26] Ibid. 272–3. The Chief Inspector of Factories reported in November 1991 that in Britain more than 27 million days a year are lost from work-related injuries and sickness with two people on average killed per day and 3,500 injured: *Independent*, 21 Nov. 1991.

ply with health and safety rules, such inclinations to comply may not be channelled effectively down to the relevant staff at the shop floor level. Some employers, moreover, may be concerned principally with levels of production and be oblivious to safety measures. Nichols and Armstrong stress:

The Robens Report was largely written by administrators, the kind of people for whom, maybe, the thought comes hard that the real safety and health problem is to protect workers against the inherent unnatural excesses of a society dominated by the market; a society in which some men are paid to squeeze as much production as possible out of others.[27]

Lacking empirical evidence on the nature of employers, Robens's assumption of an identity of interest thus appears highly suspect.

Similarly, Robens's finding that accidents are the result of apathy has been challenged and alleged to be 'disastrously' wrong.[28] Critics have explained accidents to be largely caused by dangerous systems of work used in pursuit of high production levels[29] and have linked the apathy explanation to Robens's 'common interest' assumption:

there is no surer way of reaching such a conclusion [that accidents are caused by apathy] than to begin by assuming a common interest between employer and employee—indeed what else *could* be responsible for accidents, given common interests and the apparent intentions of all concerned? . . . Not only does it look suspect theoretically—it is markedly lacking in evidence to back it up.[30]

Gunningham has argued that the 'conventional wisdom' that accidents are caused by apathetic workers is a myth unsupported by the evidence—which indicates that only a third or less of accidents are caused by 'unsafe acts' (person failure) as opposed to 'unsafe conditions' (e.g. machine failure).[31] He argues, moreover, that although unsafe acts do undoubtedly contribute towards some accidents, 'there is much evidence that inexperience, inadequate language comprehension, insufficient training and information, production

[27] Nichols and Armstrong, *Safety or Profits*, 30. [28] Ibid. 21. [29] Ibid.
[30] Ibid. 10. [31] Gunningham, *Safeguarding the Worker*, 268.

pressures, fatigue, stress and monotony are among the most common explanations of worker error rather than apathy'.[32] The Robens approach is accordingly alleged by Gunningham to be misconceived. It relies on making workers more self-conscious, but fails to appreciate that more might be achieved by controlling working conditions, particularly if it really is the case, as has been suggested in one major analysis, that nearly all accidents are the result of unsafe systems of work.[33] (As will be seen in Chapter 6, such disputes may have considerable implications for designers and users of rules.)

A further assumption made by Robens has also been called into question.[34] This is found in paragraph 231 of the Report, where the Committee states its disinclination to make any specific recommendation about the size of the new inspectorate it advocates: 'We have framed our views in the context of the resources currently available . . . without the complication of any significant increase in numbers.' As Woolf has pointed out[35] this assumption placed out of reach any fundamental review of the problem and led Robens towards the same trap into which Chief Inspectors, starved of resources, had fallen: 'It has been the habit of successive Chief Inspectors to defend their record by claiming that the way in which they have been forced, by lack of resources, to work is the most effective way they could work whatever resources they had.'[36]

The assumption on resources tied Robens's hands on issues of law and rule-use. Woolf puts the point thus:

> Having decided against seeking an increase in resources, the Robens Committee was faced with a choice between unenforceable law or law which, as a matter of declared policy, was not to be enforced. It has opted for the latter . . . it recognised the reality that as a society we have never enforced the laws we enact for the safety and health of workers and that we have no intention of starting to do so now.[37]

[32] Ibid. 268; see also N. A. Ashford, *Crisis in the Workplace: Occupational Disease and Injury* (1976); J. M. Stettmen and S. M. Daum, *Work is Dangerous to Your Health* (1973).

[33] Gunningham, *Safeguarding the Worker*, 267; see also Powell *et al.*, *2,000 Accidents*, National Institute of Industrial Psychology (UK), Report 21 (1971); J. Surry, *Industrial Accident Research: A Human Engineering Appraisal* (1969).

[34] See A. D. Woolf, 'Robens Report: The Wrong Approach?' (1973) 2 Ind.LJ 88.

[35] Ibid. [36] Ibid. 92. [37] Ibid. 95.

6. The Robens Legacy and Agency Rule-making

How, then, is the Robens approach, with its questionable underpinnings, reflected in the HSC's and HSE's rule-making processes? A first product is the tripartite procedure which infuses nearly all levels of HSC and HSE policy and rule-making. The HSC is tripartite in composition and so are the HSC and HSE advisory committees and working parties that are set up on a standing or *ad hoc* basis and which have an important role in developing and co-ordinating policy proposals on particular topics or industries.

Tripartism is said to be useful in producing an 'agreed' approach to regulatory issues and it provides channels for consultation. There are limits, however, to the representativeness of such processes and tripartism can provoke the accusation that large or well-organized firms and groups are well represented in policy-making in contrast with smaller, less well organized firms. This, it could be argued, leads to a regulatory bias in which officials tend to see those to be regulated as better-informed, organized, and disposed than is the common reality. This does not mean that HSC and HSE consultations are worthless, but it does suggest that such a tripartite process produces distortions and has a limited role to play in providing relevant information to those affected by a new rule or policy (or in providing the HSC or HSE with convincing due process claims). It leads to accountability only in so far as it gives a voice to certain 'involved' parties and is quite weak in representing the interests of non-unionized or poorly organized members of the general public who must rely on the local authority representatives to put forward their views in HSC and HSE policy-making.

A further aspect of tripartism is its providing a degree of resistance to regulatory rules of a radical nature. Since the consensual approach is built on attaining agreement, parties who oppose a rule or policy may exercise something akin to a veto. Where the solution to a regulatory problem demands an innovative or rigorous approach this may be less forthcoming from a system run on tripartite lines than from, say, a

Morrisonian agency in which consultation occurs but in which the members of the board are not appointed to represent defined sectors of industry or society.[38]

Conclusions

Robens's consensual approach resulted in a distorted view of rules and enforcement—almost a starry-eyed one. The Committee, we have noted, wanted to see not only a movement away from primary legislation towards secondary and tertiary rules, but the use of rules that were clear, intelligible, and constructive. Robens placed a high degree of faith in self-motivation as an alternative to criminal prohibition—a faith that we have seen commentators criticize and that, at the time, was too much for some parliamentarians to swallow. Thus Nichols and Armstrong recount how in May 1973 in the House of Commons 'a justifiably enraged Labour backbencher' called Neil Kinnock scorned the reasoning of the Robens Report and its offering the solution that: 'If we have less law, we shall have more safety.'[39] Not only did Robens assume that employers would have the goodwill and energy to read, understand, and apply the rules but it was also assumed that clarity and intelligibility in rules was indeed feasible. As will be seen in Chapter 6 this may in itself have been a highly optimistic vision.

In another respect, however, Robens's ill-founded strategy was due not so much to romanticism as realism. Thus we have seen that in making no case for increased inspectorate resources the Committee left itself little alternative but to place faith in self-motivation as opposed to external regulation.

In sum, then, a good deal can be learned about governmental rule-making from the Robens experience. It demonstrates quite vividly how a mistaken analysis of regulatory problems can produce quite unrealistic approaches to rules and to

[38] On Morrisonian agencies see H. Morrison, *Socialisation and Transport* (1933); also Baldwin and McCrudden, *Regulation and Public Law*, 16.

[39] N. Kinnock, HC Debs., vol. 857 col. 69 (21 May 1973), quoted in Nichols and Armstrong, *Safety or Profits*, 3.

expectations of rules. It indicates the importance of understanding the motivations of those affected by rules. It shows how those designing regulatory systems can quite easily make ill-founded assumptions about the potential of certain forms of rule-making process. It suggests that agencies set up with regulatory remits that are based on a particular philosophy may, for resource, structural, and legal reasons, find it very difficult to reshape the established regulatory regime into something more effective. Finally, it indicates how even simple assumptions on resources can dictate strategies on rule-making and enforcement. How rules can be made to work against such a background is the issue for consideration in the next chapter.

6 Making Rules Work

Making rules work involves more than producing rules that are conducive to compliance. If the rules are not designed properly then even perfect enforcement and compliance with the terms of the rules may not lead to the results that are desired by legislators or those regulating in the public interest (e.g. safe factories, clean rivers). Misformulation may mean that the wrong standards of performance are induced. The wrong kinds of behaviour may be targeted by misformulated rules so that either socially valuable activity is deterred or mischiefs that ought to be caught by the rules may escape them. Some rules may even be sidestepped and avoided without being broken. Effective rule-use demands both that compliance is produced and that compliance is linked to desired results.

This chapter looks at the importance of rules and rule designs in producing desired results. It starts by examining in Section I the issue of compliance and pursues further our scrutiny of health and safety rules. The relationship between rules and enforcement strategies is analysed and a series of questions is asked: Why do rules often fail to produce compliance? How can rules conducive to compliance be designed? What is it that impedes the making of rules conducive to compliance?[1] In Section II the relationship between compliance and desired results is then explored and questions of rule design are considered. Finally, Section III deals with the relevance of values other than effectiveness.

[1] The first section of this chapter is based on information gained from field observations, interviews, and analysis of records and secondary sources. This work was conducted as a member of the Regulation Group at the Centre for Socio-Legal Studies, Oxford. For a more detailed account, on which the chapter partly draws, see R. Baldwin, 'Why Rules Don't Work' (1990) 53 MLR 321. On accounts of compliance-seeking see the exchange of views in F. Pearce and S. Tombs, 'Ideology, Hegemony and Empiricism' (1990) 30 BJCrim. 423, and K. Hawkins, 'Compliance Strategy, Prosecution Policy and Aunt Sally' (1990) 30 BJCrim. 444; see also K. Hawkins and J. Thomas (eds.), *Enforcing Regulation* (1984).

I. SECURING COMPLIANCE

1. Compliance-seeking and Rule-types

Securing compliance with health and safety rules in Britain is the responsibility of the HSE and Local Authorities[2] rather than the police (who do not themselves possess the enforcement powers set out in the HSWA). Our focus here rests on the HSE whose regulatory tasks are daunting. HSE officials inspect work activities; provide advice to employers, workers, and the public; investigate accidents and ill health; consider complaints; and enforce relevant health and safety legislation. There are, as noted, a series of inspectorates of the HSE which deal *inter alia* with factories, agriculture and quarries, railways, mines, nuclear installations, and offshore safety. The largest of these is the Factory Inspectorate (FI) which operates with 650–700 field inspectors (overall the HSE employs around 4,500 staff at 1994 figures[3]). This chapter focuses on FI enforcement, but two caveats should be entered. First, it should be remembered that the different inspectorates of the HSE operate in quite different regulatory environments. Second, it would be rash to assume that all of the HSE inspectorates, with their different traditions, possess a common philosophy. They do not.[4] The prosecution policies and enforcement strategies of the FI contrast with, for example,

[2] Local Authority enforcement officials (increasingly known as Environmental Health Officers (EHOs)) are responsible for enforcement in 1.2 million premises ranging from hotels and shops to warehouses and offices: see HSC, *Local Authorities Report on Health and Safety in Service Industries* (1993) and Health and Safety (Enforcing Authority) Regulations 1989. On the regulation of occupational health and safety see J. Mendeloff, *Regulating Safety* (1979); N. Gunningham, *Safeguarding the Worker* (1984); J. Braithwaite and P. Grabosky, *Occupational Health and Safety Enforcement in Australia* (1985); G. K. Wilson, *The Politics of Safety and Health* (1985); B. Creighton and N. Gunningham (eds.), *The Industrial Relations of Occupational Health and Safety* (1985); C. Noble, *Liberalism at Work* (1986); E. Tucker, *Administering Danger in the Workplace* (1990); S. Dawson *et al.*, *Safety at Work: The Limits of Self-Regulation* (1988); T. O. McGarity and S. A. Shapiro, *Workers at Risk: The Failed Promise of the Occupational Safety and Health Administration* (1993); B. M. Hutter, 'Regulating Employers and Employees: Health and Safety in the Workplace' (1993) 20 *JLSoc.* 452.

[3] HSC, *Annual Report 1993/94*.

[4] See C. D. Drake and F. B. Wright, *Law of Health and Safety: A New Approach* (1983), 24.

those of the Nuclear Installations Inspectorate (which relies on licensing regimes under the Nuclear Installations Act 1965) and the Mines Inspectorate, which, for example, makes relatively scarce use of prosecutions.

The FI has to deal with around half a million establishments, and inspections of premises are relatively rare. Thus the HSE has in the past conceded: 'Only a handful of workplaces will be visited by an inspector as often as three of four times a year—once a year is relatively frequent and many workplaces will not see an inspector for several years.'[5] In the case of a medium-sized factory with unexceptional levels of hazard it would be quite normal to have four- or five-year gaps between visits. The frequency of inspection visits is governed by a number of factors: the present standards of health and safety in those premises; the nature of the worst problem that might arise; management's ability and attitudes; and the possibility of changes in standards or hazards between visits.[6] As well as routine visits, the FI engages in a number of campaigns to respond to particularly acute or contentious risks. Thus they have carried out 'pre-emptive inspection programmes' to target hazards from such sources as noise, asbestos, and the conveyance of dangerous substances by road.[7] Other 'planned special visits' have again concentrated on specific hazards and the FI periodically conducts initiatives to focus on key areas.

Factory inspectors (hereafter 'inspectors') are given a battery of powers with which to perform their functions. Section 20 of the HSWA allows them to enter premises (with police and equipment if necessary) to examine and investigate; to direct premises to be left undisturbed until examined; to measure and record; to take samples; to order dismantling or testing; to take possession of articles; to require answers and information; and to inspect, copy, and order the production of documents.

As was seen in Chapter 5, the HSE has a hierarchy of rule-types to hand: the general statutory duties of sections 2–9 HSWA; the regulations made under section 15 HSWA; the

[5] HSE, *Director General's Report 1979–80*, 16.
[6] See HSC, *Plan of Work 1981–2*, 9.
[7] Interview, 1985, HM Chief Inspector of Factories.

Approved Codes of Practice (ACOPs) provided for in sections 16 and 17 HSWA; and the guidance notes and leaflets produced without direct reference to HSWA. A rule-making package or initiative is usually set in motion by an HSE head office policy branch or by one of the HSE's tripartite advisory committees or working parties. A first step for a policy branch is to draft a submission to be put to the HSC through the HSE to seek authority for detailed work. HSE economists map out potential costs and benefits at this stage. When approval is given, the regulation, ACOP, or guidance is drafted and informal consultations with both sides of industry are undertaken. Formal approval for the draft rules to go to consultation is then sought from HSC. At this stage, the HSE 'goes public' with press notices. Comments are then invited, *inter alia*, from industry, government departments, and HSE enforcement officials. These are collected and assessed, the drafts are revised and are resubmitted to the HSC for approval. A period of around 160 weeks is allowed by HSE planners for the production of a set of regulations or an ACOP.

The task of the enforcing inspectorate is to secure compliance with the HSWA and the rules—which are often combined in packages comprising different rule-types with rules of various dimensions. These packages may deal with hazards in a particular industry or, more commonly, with a particular type of hazard. A series of packages may thus apply to each employer, and in seeking compliance with such rules, field inspectors utilize a number of enforcement techniques.

Inspectors enjoy a considerable degree of discretion in organizing their work in spite of being subject to a variety of rules themselves. The focus here, however, lies not on the extent to which the chosen strategies of enforcement (however these are selected) are structured by rules but on how those strategies are helped or hindered by the kinds of written rule employed.[8] (I will argue below that choices of strategy tend to be made independently of the available rule-type even though implementation of the selected strategy is often affected by rule-type). My

[8] This analysis takes the severity of the sanction as constant.

primary objective is not to explain why certain strategies are used, but I do offer a classification of enforcement strategies that is based on interviews and on observing inspectors' visits to a wide variety of premises.[9] The following major strategies were found to be used singly or, more usually, in combination.

(i) Prosecutions and Notices

Prosecutions are comparatively rarely used by the FI.[10] In 1993/94 the joint figure for the FI, Agriculture and Quarries Inspectorates was 1,771 informations laid and 1,488 convictions secured.[11] These figures reflect the resource implications of prosecutions—inspectors prepare and present most prosecutions themselves and cases are said by field inspectors to take an average of three person-days each. Penalties are also seen by inspectors to be too low to act as effective deterrents (the average fine in 1993/94 was £2,735[12]) and this factor acts to discourage prosecution. Those heading the HSE, moreover, accord with the Robens Report's recommendations in not seeing prosecution as a first-choice method of enforcement. Thus in 1990 the HSE Director General, John Rimington, reported

[9] On compliance-seeking strategies see K. Hawkins, *Environment and Enforcement: Regulation and the Social Definition of Pollution* (1984), P. Grabosky and J. Braithwaite, *Of Manners Gentle: Enforcement Strategies of Australian Business Regulatory Agencies* (1988); B. Hutter, *The Reasonable Arm of The Law* (1988); K. Hawkins and B. Hutter, 'The Response of Business to Social Regulation in England and Wales: an Enforcement Perspective' (1993) 15 *LP* 199. For seven case studies see M. L. Freidland (ed.), *Securing Compliance* (1990). On the array of enforcement options see C. Hood, *Administrative Analysis* (1986), 51–60. Hood (pp. 74–81) also looks at the enforceability of rules. For an economic perspective on enforcement strategies see S. Shavell, 'The Optimal Structure of Law Enforcement' (1993) Journal of Law and Economics 256.

[10] See K. Hawkins, 'The Prosecution Process' (1987), unpublished MS on file at Centre for Socio-Legal Studies, Oxford; id., 'Rule and Discretion in Comparative Perspective: The Case of Social Regulation' (1989) 50 OSLJ; id., 'FATCATS and Prosecution in a Regulatory Agency' (1989) 3 LP 370; C. Veljanovski, 'Regulatory Enforcement: An Economic Study of the British Factory Inspectorate' (1983) 5 LPQ 75. On prosecutorial versus 'compliance' approaches compare Pearce and Tombs, 'Ideology, Hegemony and Empiricism' with Hawkins, 'Compliance Strategy'; and see S. Kelman, *Regulating America, Regulating Sweden: A Comparative Study of Occupational Safety and Health Policy* (1981); D. Vogel, *National Styles of Regulation: Environmental Policy in Great Britain and the United States* (1986); R. Kagan, 'Understanding Regulatory Enforcement' (1989) 11 LP 89. Pearce and Tombs, 'Ideology, Hegemony and Empiricism', 426 state that only 0.005% of factory inspector visits result in prosecution.

[11] HSC, *Annual Report 1993/94.*

[12] Discounting one fine of £250,000, one of £150,000 and one of £100,000 (HSC Annual Report 1993/94, Table 24).

that legal proceedings took up 10 per cent of inspectors' time which, he said, represented 'a subtraction from our primary effort of assisting and advising the generality of well-conducted companies and of determining good practice'.[13] Rather greater resort is made to Improvement and Prohibition Notices (of which the FI, Agriculture and Quarries inspectorates together issued 10,457 in 1993/94[14]).

When prosecution is the chosen strategy, does the type of rule that has been breached affect the difficulty of securing compliance? An argument made by some inspectors is that 'control is the first thought' and that, given the existence of a major hazard, they will prosecute irrespective of, say, the specificity of the relevant legal rule. The majority of inspectors, nevertheless, do see a difference between prosecuting under 'old-fashioned' rules involving absolute duties and under newer, broader-based rules incorporating reasonableness tests. The post-HSWA 1974 rules differ from their predecessors in offering wider coverage through the general duties imposed by the Act, but many inspectors see it to be more time-consuming and more difficult to prosecute under these less specific rules. One experienced inspector expressed the prevalent view:

> Prosecution is very infrequent. Prosecutions under precise regulations are thought by inspectors to be less likely to be defended. If a widely drawn general duty or reasonably practicable test is involved, an occupier will be more likely to argue their case—they may not be more likely to win but there is more scope for debate. It's time-consuming so it does make the inspector think twice.

Considered purely from the point of view of formal legal action, specific and 'absolute' rules thus appear attractive to inspectors.[15] The main disadvantage of such rules is seen as lack of breadth. Less specific forms of rule using reasonableness tests give broader coverage (greater inclusiveness) as well as greater across the board consistency of formal standards, but their utility decreases as enforcement in any particular area depends on prosecutions.

[13] HSC/E *Annual Report 1989/90*, viii.

[14] HSC Annual Report 1993/94.

[15] See E. Bardach and R. A. Kagan, *Going By The Book: The Problem of Regulatory Unreasonableness* (1982), 35–37.

(ii) Persuasion/Negotiation[16]

This strategy is used when inspectors seek to have a hazard remedied and attempt to overcome a degree of resistance. They often do this by making reference to the employer's self-interest, to morality, or to the law. Inspectors adopt a variety of approaches to persuasion and negotiation. These approaches are mainly determined by the inspector's assessment of the employer and the type of hazard at issue. Four broad categories of employer and three varieties of hazard appear to be used by inspectors as bases for action.[17].

The first category is that of the *well-intentioned and well-informed employer*. This occupier is generally a large business employing its own safety staff. It is usually seen as well disposed to comply but not necessarily wholly efficient in putting its good intentions into unprompted effect.[18] Negotiations with such occupiers are usually unproblematic and persuasion is hardly ever necessary. One senior inspector described such inspection as 'professional talking to professional'. On finding a fault, the inspector often merely points a finger at the offending shaft or unguarded drill and the firm's safety adviser notes down the problem for attention. The rules are seldom referred to at all. This does not mean that such rules play no role (actions may have taken place in the shadow of rules), merely that matters are in the main unsaid and uncontested. Thus, concluding a visit to one such employer, the inspector commented:

I will write to him setting down the relevant points but I won't quote chapter and verse. He knows the law roughly and knows I wouldn't ask for things I couldn't back up. There's no point in getting heavy.

[16] For detailed studies of negotiated compliance-seeking see K. Hawkins, *Environment and Enforcement*, chs. 6–10; Hutter, *The Reasonable Arm*, chs. 5 and 6; and J. Braithwaite, *To Punish or Persuade* (1985) ch. 4.

[17] On employer types see R. Kagan and J. Scholz, 'The "Criminology of the Corporation" and Regulatory Enforcement Strategies', in K. Hawkins and J. M. Thomas (eds.), *Enforcing Regulation* (1984), who focus on three types of corporation: political citizens, the organizationally incompetent, and amoral calculators. (On the latter see *infra* at II. 2). See also Hood, *Administrative Analysis*, 58–60; Braithwaite, *To Punish or Persuade*, 98–100.

[18] On self-enforcement see Hood, *Administrative Analysis*, 81–84; Dawson *et al.*, *Safety at Work*, chs. 7 and 10.

He's so far done what he said he'd do. With small operators you would have to let them know a bit more that you have the power to compel action.

The *well-intentioned and ill-informed employer* is (in the absence of serious hazards and accidents) generally treated sympathetically by the inspector and is commonly a small or medium-sized firm. Hazard-reducing actions and a timetable for implementation are usually agreed and undertakings given. In the case of such employers, inspectors often combine negotiation with advice, education or information-giving. On such premises inspectors are disinclined, as one put it, to 'get all legalistic'.

The *ill-intentioned and ill-informed employer* tends to be deemed so because of his/her attitude and/or record and, once more, is usually a small or medium-sized firm. Faced with such an employer, inspectors are inclined to reveal more readily the legal powers that reinforce their negotiating stance. References may be made to the Act and legalistic terms dropped in conversation.

The *problematic employer*[19] is usually itinerant or ephemeral in nature. This employer might vary in intention or degree of knowledge but is seen as inherently difficult to deal with. In the construction industry, persuasion is more direct and negotiations tougher not merely because of the high risks involved but because of the lack of a continuing relationship between employer (or worker) and inspector. Threats are thus used openly. ('I will threaten prosecution for not wearing ear defenders. I like to see the visit having an impact on them.') Examples of problematic employers in a low risk industry are to be found in the 'rag trade' where inspectors waste little time on persuasion/negotiation. Given their short-lived relationship with such firms, inspectors often order action by force of personality alone rather than by reference to rules or laws.

Turning to risks, *minor hazards*, as has been noted, tend to

[19] At this point the reader might have expected a discussion of the *ill-intentioned and well-informed* employer as the model that completes the set. This kind of employer was not encountered during the course of the research but the ill-intentioned, well-informed regulatee (the amoral calculator) is commonly met in other regulatory sectors (see Kagan and Scholz, *The Criminology of the Corporation*) and is considered below (II. 2) in discussing the problem of 'creative compliance'.

prompt a less legalistic, less confrontational approach on the part of inspectors. Thus, in the case of, say, a small manufacturer of leather goods, the inspector commonly issues orders, gives lectures, and offers verbal summaries and leaflets. Such inspections are rarely seen as meriting a follow-up letter. *Serious or major hazards*, as encountered in the construction industry, frequently result in direct threats of notices or prosecutions. A third category of risk is the *problematic hazard*. The difficulty here might lie in measuring the hazard (e.g. the level of exposure to a potentially harmful substance), in defining the hazard or in deciding whether there is a safer way to do the job that can reasonably be demanded. In relation to such hazards there is often a genuine process of persuasion and negotiation. With a well-intentioned occupier the inspector often 'puts heads together' and tries to produce a solution or compromise. With 'bad' or 'problematic' employers the inspector usually negotiates but reserves the option of more serious sanctioning.

How then does choice of rule-type affect the efficiency of persuasive/negotiatory strategies? Some inspectors say that since the threat of prosecution underpins all negotiations, the most easily prosecuted rules are also the ones most easily negotiated. ('At the end of the day you have to be able to make it stick.') Other inspectors' comments, and research observations, however, indicate a more complex picture. Rules tailored to prosecution may (if there are huge numbers of precise rules) be difficult for employers to absorb and the ignorance thus created may hinder negotiation and compliance. Prosecution and the state of the law may, furthermore, hardly enter the picture. An experienced inspector reflected the more pragmatic, less prosecutorial stance: 'As you get older you fly by the seat of your pants. Most of them don't know the law so you just tell them it's wrong.' This inspector was talking about ill-informed, relatively well-intentioned occupiers rather than informed, specialist occupiers. Another inspector explained the difference:

> The small occupier doesn't think about how easy or hard it would be for you to prosecute. They still think that the inspector can shut them down overnight. You can bluff very effectively and not be challenged. It's like the police, you are seen as an official with swingeing

power. It's different with medium- or above sized firms who know more. Small operators will do what a leaflet says and not question its status. They would never distinguish it from the law. Only larger ones appreciate the distinction.[20]

Precise legal standards or rules thus might not be necessary in order to enforce without argument—provided an inspector is on the spot and the occupier is well intentioned. Given a well-intentioned, ill-informed employer, an inspector may well rely on general statutory duties and blur the distinction between legal compliance and sensible behaviour.

The place of rules in persuasion/negotiation and the optimal type of rule thus differs according to type of employer and risk.[21] In the case of the *well-intentioned and well-informed employer*, the rules are used by inspectors to keep that firm informed and to provide an agreed agenda for discussions and promptings. One can accordingly infer from enforcement practice a need for rules to be accessible to the firm as well as to the inspector. Rules have to be in a form that corresponds to the firm's capacity to absorb them. With *well-intentioned*, *ill-informed employers,* similar considerations apply but these occupiers are usually smaller and less able to inform themselves. A greater effort has to be made by the inspectorate to inform them but such efforts are thought likely to pay dividends in facilitating persuasion/negotiation as well as in improving voluntary compliance. The *ill-intentioned*, *ill-informed*, *employer* offers a contrast, however. Given ill-intention, the rules themselves are unlikely to produce voluntary compliance and persuasion may have to be backed with threats of formal action. This situation implies a need for rules that are addressed principally to inspectors, that are specific and attuned to effective formal legal action. Such rules would enhance persuasion/negotiation by casting a strong legal shadow and by offering assurances of consistent treatment between employers.

In the case of *problematic employers* (as in the construction

[20] On bluffing and the small versus the sophisticated trader see E. Bardach and R. Kagan, *Going by The Book* (1982); D. McBarnet and C. Whelan, 'The Elusive Spirit of the Law: Formalism and the Struggle for Legal Control' (1991) 54 MLR 848, 872.

[21] See Kagan and Scholz, *The Criminology of the Corporation.*

and clothing industries), there is seen to be an acute need to identify such employers and to have at the ready sets of rules that are consistent with fast-operating forms of negotiation. Where such employers are in the main ill-informed and liable to remain so, this indicates, particularly in the case of major hazards, a need for rules that are aimed at inspectors and can be prosecuted easily. In low-risk areas, highly accessible rules attuned to advice and information are indicated. Enforcement practice suggests less of a need for rules that presuppose longer-term relationships with inspectors or less immediate negotiating styles.

Returning to risks, where these are *minor*, rules tend to play a smaller role in influencing negotiations. Inspectors are especially inclined, if involved with the well-intentioned, to deal with problems rather than focus on legal issues. Conversely, in the case of *major hazards* inspectors are more inclined to demand strict compliance and rule-type comes more to the fore. With *problematic hazards*, rules affect persuasion/negotiation in so far as they create or solve problems of measurement and of defining the hazard. Where the difficulty is more technical ('Can this manufacturing process be set up in a safer way?') enforcement depends more on the *ad hoc* discretion and experience of the inspector than on rule-type.

To conclude, the rules do play a role, but one that varies. Where different enforcement strategies are applied to different categories of employer or risk, different kinds of rules are seen as appropriate and are used in a variety of ways. Inspectors, moreover, often point to a mismatch between type of rule and their chosen enforcement strategy.

(iii) Advice

Advising takes place when inspectors give occupiers instructions on an 'instant' basis with little intention of taking follow-up action. Advice work, in its pure form, involves a minimal level of persuasion. The inspector in such cases does not see the necessity of expending further resources on securing compliance. Advice thus tends to be used in areas where compliance is considered unproblematic, where risks are low or where it is thought that formal legal enforcement is not feasible. Even problematic occupiers doing high-risk jobs may, however, be given advice. (Thus an inspector was observed to inform steel erectors of a new ratchet shackle that could be used to hoist girders more safely.) Advice can avoid the issue of formal enforcement quite effectively, particularly given an amenable occupier. Advice giving of this 'instant' kind can accordingly be operated without explicit reference to rules. Written material is seen, however, to serve a useful ancillary role as an explanatory device—as when one inspector gave out a leaflet, *Small Clothing Factories*, while warning about the dangers of poor wiring. Where advising is the chosen regulatory strategy, enforcers look for brief and simple rules—not those focusing on prosecutability and, as a result, tending to be precise, detailed, and lengthy. They look for informal leaflets rather than ACOPs or regulations, but do not always find them.

(iv) Education

This is the strategy in which an inspector seeks to improve a particular occupier's thinking about health and safety or 'adopts' an individual or firm and, by taking a continuing interest, attempts to improve health and safety performance.[22] Inspectors differ considerably in their attitudes towards education. Some focus on securing compliance on a limited number of precise points, but others are more ambitious and seek to reorientate the occupier's general approach to health and safety. Thus on an observed visit to a small scrap metal yard, an inspector was asked by the company director if he would write a letter setting out the various points at issue. The inspector responded by asking the director to write back to him and said: 'I want you to do the thinking rather than me just lay down the rules.' The value of the educative approach is seen by a number of inspectors to lie in its long-term effect and in its application to circumstances that might or might not be covered by the rules. (In this respect the inspectors are

[22] See Bardach and Kagan, *Going by the Book*, 143–50 on 'the inspector as consultant'.

perhaps looking beyond compliance-seeking towards desired results.) As one inspector put it: 'You try to educate to get round the problem of the general law. Take 30 m.p.h. That may be safe on a dry day but dangerous in the wet or fog. You try to get the person in a state of mind to look at cases where he should more than satisfy the standard.' A more intensive form of education might be termed 'pupillage', where an inspector adopts a firm for special coaching. Often this proves to be a medium-sized operator who is relatively ill-informed and ill-intentioned, with a poor safety record and involved in an activity giving rise to not inconsiderable hazards. Usually these operators are seen not to be hopeless cases but to be 'problems' that are sufficiently serious (but solvable) to justify considerable input of resources.

As regards the role of various forms of rule in compliance-seeking, the educative strategy is somewhat exceptional. When occupiers are led to 'think for themselves' the strategy operates largely independently of the rules. Rules are only used in an ancillary manner as when a leaflet usefully summarizes a process or procedure. When the pupillage system is operated, the rules similarly take a back seat in favour of a continuing, personal, and more direct system of supervision and explanation. The occupier does not so much read rules as listen to the inspector and learn to think for him or herself. The conclusion to draw is that written rules play a relatively background role in relation to this strategy and, where they do have a role, this lies in informing the inspector rather than instructing the occupier.

(v) Promoting and Informing

These are strategies used when inspectors want to prevent hazards from arising by raising health and safety awareness on a general basis. They often want to do this independently of prosecuting a particular case. They are concerned that in using promotional material occupiers should be given accessible and practical advice. A view heard repeatedly is that the ACOPs, which are supposed to offer practical advice, have tended over the years to operate increasingly like regulations and are not practical enough. One inspector put the point thus:

It doesn't make much difference if they merely read the stuff. They have to realize the dangers. The nearest we get to useful handouts is the guidance note. It's still too far from reality—it deals with one thing in all its applications. It's better to say 'This is the problem with particular premises, e.g. garages'.[23]

On one visit to a medium-sized printing works, an inspector pointed out that the nature of the rules was affecting compliance, commenting: 'A lot of these smaller firms have had problems with the packaging and labelling regulations. It's a full-time job understanding them.' Another highly experienced inspector expressed the widely held view that policy-makers have a narrow approach to promotional activity: 'I always think that when policy-makers draft their leaflets they think of ICI or BL or Wimpeys or Laings, big people. They don't seem to know about the little man out there. They may say they do but they have no conception.'

The rules not only have to be in the right form, they have to be delivered to likely compliers and non-compliers. Distribution is seen by inspectors as a significant problem. The well-intentioned employer is thought likely to be fairly well-informed anyway and many inspectors doubt whether ill-intentioned or ill-informed employers read much promotional material 'unless there is an inspector there telling them to read it'. Does choice of rule make a difference? Inspectors clearly believe that inaccessible and complex rules are not conducive to the effective promotion of health and safety. They also believe that appropriately drafted rules can affect consciousness and that more can be done to produce accessible rules. That is not to say that it is *always* seen as possible to reduce complex sets of regulations to simple promotional rules. A chemicals inspector noted that the package of rules on classification and labelling involved regulations, five ACOPs, approved lists, and guidance notes and made up a pile of documents ten inches high. He pointed out: 'Even a well-intentioned firm has a problem digesting this. They haven't got the resources or time,

[23] For a more detailed analysis of employers' responses to and knowledge of regulatory rules, see H. Genn, 'Great Expectations: The Robens Legacy and Employer Self-Regulation', Centre for Socio-Legal Studies, Oxford, mimeo (1987).

nor can you produce simple guidance on a package this large and this technical.' In summary: when inspectors choose promotion rather than prosecution they look for (but again do not always find) rules that take the form that is appropriate given the persons being asked to comply. It is not, however, always possible to produce rules that are accessible to the affected parties.

The evidence in this field indicates that choice of rule-type does bear on (or is at least perceived by enforcers as bearing on) the efficacy of various enforcement strategies. It also shows that the role of the rules and the nature of the optimal rule differ according to a number of variables, notably the favoured enforcement strategy, the type of regulatee, and the type of hazard. The precise extent to which choice of rule-type affects compliance-seeking is difficult to quantify. Such quantification would have to be undertaken in relation to a large number of particular offences, it would have to deal with differences of hazard and employer-type, and it would have to anticipate enforcement by a wide variety of possible enforcement strategies. That task would involve a high level of speculation and is not attempted here. My argument is simpler: having presented evidence that choice of rule-type does bear on the efficacy of compliance-seeking, I will describe in the next section what a 'compliance-oriented' approach to the design of rules might look like. In doing so I will contend that the approach adopted by HSE rule-makers is not one calculated efficiently to match rule-types to the requirements of enforcers or potential compliers. (Many of the inspectors' comments discussed in this and the following two sections support this contention.) What impedes the making of effective rules will then be discussed.

An objection to the above reasoning should at this stage be anticipated. It might be argued that inspectors' views on 'correct' enforcement strategies must be unreliable since those views will themselves be influenced by the pattern of rule-types available in an area. The response to this point is that, save in exceptional cases, inspectors choose enforcement strategies largely independently of the rule-types (if prosecution is called for they will usually prosecute even if the rule-type makes this difficult). This strategic decision is determined by an assessment of the type of employer and hazard involved rather than the type of rule that is applicable. In some marginal cases the rule-type available may tip the balance but, since inspectors deal with a host of hazards, they have a wide knowledge of different rule-types and different strategies in operation and they are in a good position to judge, on the basis of that experience, which strategy will work on whom and where. There are of course different kinds of inspector, some 'conciliatory', some 'hard-line', but even inspectors at different ends of this spectrum tend to agree on strategies in the vast majority of cases. Bearing these points in mind, it is accepted in this analysis that inspectors are generally correct in assessing the appropriateness of a strategy to a particular employer and hazard.

2. A 'Compliance-Oriented' Approach to Rules

The above analysis indicates that in order to secure compliance efficiently, regulators need to target their enforcement strategies and choices of rules in a co-ordinated fashion. This approach calls for answers to the following questions:[24]

- What are the key hazards?
- Who creates these hazards?
- Which enforcement strategies will best influence the hazard creators?
- Which rule-types best complement those strategies?

Thus, suppose large numbers of workers were found to be dying of asbestos-related cancers. The key hazards might be identified as arising out of certain kinds of asbestos production process using certain types of asbestos. The kinds of employer engaged in such hazard creation would then be analysed, their dispositions and informational levels considered. (Are they mainly well-intentioned but ill-informed? Are they of mixed

[24] It will be noted that the set of questions listed here assumes that rules serve a *controlling* function. Where rules are used for *enabling* then the first three questions should be redrafted to read: What are the relevant policy objectives? Who has to be influenced to achieve these objectives? Which strategies will best influence such persons to act appropriately?

types?) From such analyses, conclusions could be drawn as to the kinds of pressure and sanctioning required to produce compliance. (What proportion simply need the relevant information on how to comply? What proportion require the threat of prosecution?) The kinds of rule best attuned to securing compliance could then be identified.

In a non-health and safety field, for example river pollution, a similar strategy could be adopted by analysing the nature of the pollutant, the kind of industrial activity and operator causing the pollution, the kind of pressure or sanction required (be this information, negotiation, prosecution, or another strategy), and the rule-type or types that will complement such compliance-seeking. It should be noted that where such analyses reveal substantial groups of mischief-creating regulatees that are of varying characteristics, this may point to the need for a number of different rule-types to be employed concurrently. Where resources do not permit such a variety of rules to be developed, a compliance-oriented approach will guide as to the first choice type of rule.[25] The approach will help to avoid misapplication of resources through, for example, spending too much time using rules that seek merely to inform the ill intentioned and ill-informed or applying over-complicated, inaccessible rules to the well intentioned but ill informed.

The FI does some targeting of enforcement priorities, but not generally of the kind advocated here. It has a computerized 'ratings' system to trace problem occupiers, but this does not directly identify particularly problematic types of hazard.

[25] Ayres and Braithwaite, *Responsive Regulation*, argue for 'responsive regulation' and the use of a pyramid of enforcement strategies (ranging from persuasion to criminal penalties and licence revocations) to be applied progressively to regulatees, commencing with appeals to the social responsibility of the regulatee. (See also Braithwaite, *To Punish or Persuade*, 142–8). The present analysis assumes that resources are finite and that it is not possible to draft rules to complement all potential regulatory strategies—that targeting is necessary. An analysis of regulatees also indicates that a progressive approach may work for some regulatees but not for others—that targeting may prove to be more effective than an unvaryingly progressive approach. Rule-makers, it follows, may be well advised to anticipate optimal enforcement strategies and prioritize these rather than cater for all potential strategies. It might be responded that in an ideal world rule-makers *would* be resourced in a way that allowed them to promulgate sets of rules to complement all potential regulatory strategies. The use of multiple formulations of rules might, nevertheless, produce problems of rule handling and accessibility.

Accident investigations give some information on hazards, but these necessarily occur on a sporadic basis. 'Planned special visits' by inspectors are used to collect data on suspected problem areas, but these only cover a limited number of areas. These methods may give a profile of hazard creators on selected topics, but they are less useful in indicating the extent to which occupiers in a particular industry will respond to different enforcement strategies—for example to threats of prosecution or to information-giving.

The most useful information on this issue (and, consequently, on appropriate rule-types) is that held by those inspectors who are familiar with an industry, its hazards, its different occupiers, their sizes, capabilities, traditions, cultures. This points to the potential of the National Industry Group (NIG) as an influence on policy-making. The NIG is the group of inspectors that specializes in a particular hazard or industry and there are twenty-three such groups within the FI. At present the NIGs play a limited role in the HSE rule-making process and they are not equipped with secretariats that would encourage a greater role. As will be seen in the following section, field inspectors are, in any event, sceptical of the weight given to the enforcement point of view by HSE policy branch rule-makers.

3. Compliance: Why Rule-makers Fail

Those who are reasonably well-disposed to comply with rules tend not to follow them because they do not know about them, or because they cannot or will not process the information necessary for compliance. In the case of those who are not well-disposed to comply, rules also tend to fail because the necessary enforcement strategy (or sanction) has not been applied. This last failing may be a product of resources (e.g. lack of enforcement staff or funding) or it may result from the use of unsuitable rules (e.g. rules that are low in intelligibility or difficult to use in court). Targeting, as described in the section above, seems to offer a way forward. If it is to be advocated as a practical proposition, however, it is necessary also to understand *why* administrators may be slow to adopt what seems on its face to be an almost common-sense approach to rule-making.[26] To this end it helps to examine those points where the approaches of enforcers and rule-makers diverge. This throws light on the difficulties faced by the administrator who makes rules. Accordingly, it is useful to review policy-making in three areas where major new packages of rules were introduced in the eighties.

In the lead, asbestos, and ionizing radiations fields, five main issues emerged as the foci of contention between rule-makers and enforcers. The following analysis is based on interviews with rule-makers and enforcers as well as on an examination of the extensive documentation held by both the FI and HSE on rule-making in the three areas.

(*a*) *Standards based on Reasonableness.* One school of thought within the FI favours regulation by specific rules and absolute duties and doubts the general enforceability of the type of package that HSE policy-makers tend to prefer—which is based on general principles and on rules that call upon occupiers to take such actions as are 'reasonably practicable' (rules that demand technically practicable safety measures to be taken but only in cases where the cost is not unreasonable on a balance of costs and benefits). Thus, in relation to the radiations package, FI inspectors argued that to move from numerically defined safety limits to the less precise requirements of 'reasonably practicable' performance would 'preclude general enforcement' of the rules, since field enforcers would have to balance risks against costs at every workplace and medical evidence would be required in each individual case. Similar points were made about the asbestos package.

(*b*) *Ease of Prosecution.* In the rule-making processes of the HSC and HSE, various assumptions are made about the ease with which rules can be enforced through prosecution. The HSE policy background paper on the lead package compared prosecutions under general statutory requirements (of reasonable practicability) and under rules based on practicability tests

[26] On the 'widening gap between what is known about policy-making and how policy is actually made' see Y. Dror, *Public Policymaking Re-examined* (1973), ch. 1.

(i.e. of technical feasibility) in the existing lead regulations. It concluded that both sorts of provision had been used successfully and a later policy paper argued that enforcement had been equally effective under both 'practicable' and 'reasonably practicable' formulations. Many of the field enforcers, however, favoured the use of 'practicable' duties because they believed in the particular value of such duties in facilitating prosecution.

(*c*) *The Size and Intelligibility of Packages.* The Robens Committee argued for clear, principled and intelligible rules.[27] In practice, however, the HSC and HSE find it difficult to produce accessible packages of rules. Thus in 1982 the FI produced a paper that summarized Area Directors' responses to the policy-makers' lead package:

> A repeated criticism of the package is the sheer volume of verbiage and the time needed to assimilate it . . . there is concern that packages comprising regulations, ACOPs and possibly guidance notes provide a daunting volume of material for employers and inspectors alike . . . Given the consultation time required before changes to ACOPs can be effected, imprecision in the wording and sheer bulk of the package will achieve not what Robens proposed but its antithesis.[28]

On the asbestos package, the combined views of FI rule-makers and field consultant group inspectors were that the rules were 'difficult to understand other than by seasoned professionals'. The radiations package was described by some inspectors as 'indigestible'. The inspectors' union, the Institution of Professional Civil Servants (IPCS) argued that vagueness was 'inherent to the four-tier presentation of HSWA, regulations, ACOPs and guidance notes'.[29] Most of the new packages, the IPCS said, were not easy to read, to understand or to act upon, they were costly to buy and costly (in resources) to read. This would lead, it was argued, to more infringements 'engendered quite genuinely by ignorance'.[30]

[27] See the Robens Report, ch. 5.

[28] On employers' difficulties with complex rules see H. Genn, 'Great Expectations'.

[29] Institution of Professional Civil Servants, HM Inspectors of Factories Branch, *A Critical Response to the HSC Consultative Document: The Ionising Radiations Regulations 198–* (1983), para. 3.

[30] Ibid., para. 11.

(*d*) *'Across the Board Regulation'.* HSE policy-makers tend to aim for consistency of standards wherever a problem occurs—whether, for example, the radiation hazard is encountered in a large hospital or at a small construction site. They seek to put Robens into effect by establishing broad principles of control. This approach, it is thought, ensures greater uniformity of treatment across industries, rules out variations between sectors of the same industry, cures omissions, and avoids repetitions. Field enforcers, however, see difficulties in applying one set of rules across very different areas. Thus the group of inspectors specializing in the construction industry was echoed by a number of FI Area Directors in arguing that the asbestos package did not cater adequately for transient sites or the construction industry. The CBI contended that the package 'fails to take into account many of the fundamental differences in working methods between manufacturing industry on the one hand, and installation, maintenance, repair and removal activities on the other'. The radiations package provoked similar comments. IPCS pointed to the price that was paid for producing rules of broad applicability. There were great disparities between radiation in hospital operating theatres and construction site radiography of pipelines. The draft regulations, said IPCS, sought to bridge such disparities by stipulating requirements 'where necessary', or which were 'reasonable' or 'adequate'. This led to vagueness, to further elaboration in an ACOP, and, in turn, to yet further explanation in guidance notes. The FI group specializing in radiation hazards agreed that the penalty for across the board legislation was increased difficulty of enforcement.

(*e*) *Self-Regulation and Self-Assessment.* A temptation for rule-makers is to see self-regulation as a means of making modest inspectorate resources go further.[31] Thus the lead package that was introduced in 1980 demanded that under stated conditions employers should conduct assessments in order to determine

[31] For a discussion of 'enforced self-regulation' in which those regulated devise the rules and government agencies enforce the rules see Ayres and Braithwaite *Responsive Regulation*, and Braithwaite, 'Enforced Self-Regulation: A New Strategy for Corporate Crime Control' (1980) 28 Public Policy 257.

the nature and degree of exposure to lead of their employees. This was deemed to be consistent with the self-help philosophy of the 1974 Act. Enforcers, however, soon had doubts about employers' willingness and competence to put the rules on assessments into effect. By 1982, FI Area Directors were reporting that industry was carrying out far fewer assessments than had been envisaged. Smaller companies had few persons competent in such exercises and were 'relying on inspectors' which was costly in terms of FI resources. In 1983 the Leeds Area of the FI conducted local research and found that only 53 per cent of employers had carried out the self-assessment that was the cornerstone of the lead regulations, that one in five of the assessments that had been conducted was found to be unsatisfactory, and that the majority of employers thought that they did not have the time to study the rules or their implications, typically they awaited the inspector's visit and oral instructions. Other areas reported that 'very few' employers were capable of adequate assessments. When the asbestos package was under consultation, some FI areas argued that experience with the lead regulations showed that, especially on construction sites, employers rarely made an adequate assessment but either guessed at hazard levels or adopted the levels established by the ACOP. There was no alternative, it was suggested, to actual measurement by inspectors. At discussions of the tripartite Asbestos Industry Working Group, all members of the group had reservations about the assessment procedure and considered that, as proposed, it was too complex and imprecise. In spite of such comments, the HSE adhered to its position on assessments and has more recently adopted a self-assessment procedure as a main element of its package on the control of substances hazardous to health (COSHH).[32]

These differences of approach between policy-makers and enforcers are a notable feature of HSC and HSE rule-making. On the one hand the FI inspectors stress enforceability, accessibility, and intelligibility, the need to be able to prosecute as a

[32] On employers' widespread failure to implement COSHH and failures to conduct assessments see C. Purnell, 'The Impact of the COSHH Regulations on the Working Environment' (1992) 1 International Journal of Regulatory Law and Policy 205.

last resort, and the resource implications of particular packages. On the other, the rule-makers set a high premium on consistency of standards and an 'across the board' approach to regulation. Rule-makers seem to many field inspectors of all ranks to place less emphasis on the practicalities of enforcement. The rule-makers, it appears, are slow to adopt a 'targeted' approach to rules, one that analyses and co-ordinates non-compliance, enforcement strategies, and choices of rule.

Why do rule-makers underperform in this manner? Why does their approach differ from the inspectors in the respects outlined above? Work in the field of policy analysis suggests a number of answers to these questions, answers that may be relevant not only to those regulating health and safety at work but to rule-makers in general.[33] The main arguments can be collected together under three headings.

(i) The 'Top-Down' Approach

Policy-makers, it has been maintained, tend to have a 'policy-centred' rather than 'action-centred' approach to life.[34] They tend to assume that policy is made at the centre or top and implemented lower down at the periphery or bottom of the organization.[35] This approach plays down the problematic nature of implementation and implies that regulatory difficulties can be overcome by top level policy changes. It draws, moreover, an unrealistic distinction between policy-making and implementation.[36] Policy is made and then 'handed down' for implementation. As Barrett and Fudge have put it: 'The stages

[33] For a useful review of approaches to policy analysis see C. Ham and M. Hill, *The Policy Process in the Modern Capitalist State* (1984).

[34] See S. Barrett and C. Fudge (eds.), *Policy and Action* (1981), 13.

[35] See R. Levitt, *Implementing Public Policy* (1980), 18–19.

[36] For criticism of the policy-making/implementation distinction see Barrett and Fudge, *Policy and Action*, parts 1 and 3; P. Knoepfel and H. Weidner, 'Formulation and Implementation of Air Quality Control Programmes' (1982) 10 PP 85; Ham and Hill, *Policy Process*, 101–8; M. Hill, 'The Policy–Implementation Distinction: A Quest for Rational Control?', in Barrett and Fudge, *Policy and Action*, ch. 9. On implementation generally see A. Dunsire, *Implementation in a Bureaucracy* (1979); Ham and Hill, *op.cit.*; Barrett and Fudge (eds.); J. Pressman and A. Wildavsky, *Implementation* (1973); R. Kagan, *Regulatory Justice: Implementing a Wage-Price Freeze* (1978); G. Richardson, A. Ogus and P. Burrows, *Policing Pollution*; J. L Jowell, 'Implementation and Enforcement of Law' in L. Lipson and S. Wheeler (eds.), *Law and the Social Sciences* (1986).

of implementation tend to be associated automatically with a hierarchical "chain of command" and this association has no doubt had an influence on the way in which the process of policy implementation is perceived by practitioners and researchers alike, and hence the tendency to take it for granted as an automatic follow-on from policy decisions'.[37] Weberian notions of rational bureaucracy and hierarchical organization and management are 'embedded in the conventional wisdom of public organizations'[38] and encourage the notion of unproblematic implementation. In so far as implementation is treated as unproblematic this leads policy-makers to minimize the policy-making role of enforcers. 'Superiors' may not want to be presented with knowledge about events in the field and information and feedback systems, as a result, may be highly inefficient.[39] These arguments suggest why policy-makers may be slow to delve into the problems of implementation even where they consider a comprehensively rational approach to be feasible. Policy-makers might not, moreover, think exhaustive reviews of options, goals, and strategies an efficient way to operate. Within the academic community there are certainly disparate views on the limits of rationality in policy-making—as the rationalist versus incrementalist debate indicates.[40] Policy-makers may indeed be able to point to valid reasons for leaving a good deal of discretion in enforcers' hands[41]—for example to allow conflicts to be resolved, information to be collected, local expertise or knowledge to be applied, negotiations

[37] Barrett and Fudge, *Policy and Action* 9.

[38] Barrett and Fudge, *Policy and Action* 9; see M. Weber, *Essays in Sociology* (H. H. Gerth and C. W. Mills (eds.)) (1946) ch. 8; for a review of the case against Weber see M. Albrow, *Bureaucracy* (1970) 54–66.

[39] See D. S. Van Meter and C. E. Van Horn, 'The Policy Implementation Process: A Conceptual Framework' *Administration and Society* (February 1975) 445, 456; A. Downs, *Inside Bureaucracy* (1967) ch. 12; HL Weekly, *Organisational Intelligence* (1967).

[40] For a review of the debate see G. Smith and D. May, 'The Artificial Debate between Rationalist and Incrementalist Models of Decision Making', 8, *Policy and Politics*, (1980) 147. See also C. E. Lindblom, 'The Science of Muddling Through', *Public Administration Review*, (1964) 24; D. Braybrooke and C. E. Lindblom, *A Strategy of Decision* (1963).

[41] On the case for discretion see *supra*, Ch. 3; Hawkins *Environment and Enforcement*; R. Baldwin and K. Hawkins, 'Discretionary Justice: Davis Reconsidered' [1984] PL 570.

and compromises to be effected, policies adjusted, and impacts to be assessed.[42] The case for discretion may in these circumstances serve as a convenient reason for leaving implementation issues out of the policy-making process—if problems are difficult to anticipate it may be thought best not to become involved but to let the implementers muddle through in the field. The danger is that problems that might be analysed and resolved come to be perceived as 'inevitable' by policy-makers and are left out of account.

It might be expected that even those administrators who reject the comprehensively rational approach might, in Simon's terms 'satisfice' or proceed incrementally, testing policies and rules so that even poorly chosen or framed rules evolve towards the efficient formulation.[43] As Colin Diver has pointed out, however, such a process demands, first, that information on the rules' defective operation is effectively communicated to the administrator and, second, that rule-makers will take remedial steps.[44] In practice, he points out, there may be problems on both fronts. Information may not flow, *inter alia*, because certain factions may benefit from the rules' defects (e.g. incumbent licensees may have an interest in preserving the complex rules that form protective barriers to entry by potential competitors). As for the willingness and ability of rule-makers effectively to revise rules, Diver dubs this a 'quaintly heroic' assumption,[45] arguing that selecting the best form for a given rule:

> would seem to require qualities beyond the reach of many administrators: a selfless concern for the public good, consistent goals, comprehensive vision, and accurate foresight. Real policy-makers, by contrast, are ordinary mortals burdened with incomplete knowledge, imperfect vision and selfish desires.[46]'

Looking to the HSE, there are some indications of a 'top-down' approach: major policies are devised by specialist

[42] See Ham and Hill, *Policy Process*, 106.

[43] H. Simon, *Administrative Behaviour*, 3rd edn. (1976), 79.

[44] C.S. Diver, 'The Optimal Precision of Administrative Rules' (1983) 93 Yale LJ 65.

[45] Ibid. 101.

[46] Ibid. 97–8.

policy-making branches at the 'top' of the organization; inspectors play a relatively small part in policy-making and specialist enforcement groups are not equipped for a more prominent role; applying rules across the board is given a high priority in spite of comments on enforceability (as is the policy of self-assessment); packages of rules are devised without co-ordinating rule-types and enforcement strategies; and the system of collecting data on enforcement does not encourage the targeting of rules. The case for giving inspectors a large degree of discretion in enforcement might be invoked in defence of HSE policy-makers but, in order to make this case strongly, the agency would have to be able to identify those hazards or industries where attention to rule-types would be wasted and those where co-ordination of rule-types and enforcement strategies would pay dividends. Without conducting the analysis necessary for targeting, the agency is in no such position. The message for the HSE or any other rule-making body is clear. To adopt a 'top-down' approach is unrealistic, it fails to give due regard to enforcement difficulties and diminishes the role of the enforcer. Such an approach may, however, be the one of least resistance.

(ii) The Problem of Process

Rule-makers often fail to produce the kinds of rule that are consistent with effective implementation because they misjudge the costs attached to the process of negotiating rules into existence.[47] Rules may commence life as short, clear statements but they tend to become less accessible and more fudged as powerful interests are accommodated and political flak is side-stepped.[48] There is, as Peter Self has indicated,[49] a tension between participation and effectiveness but rule-makers may be slow to see that the politics of participation impinge upon

[47] On policy/rule-making as a process of negotiation see Barrett and Fudge, *Policy and Action*, ch. 1, 257–64; Ham and Hill, *Policy Process*, 103–8; A. Strauss, *Negotiations* (1978); A. Dunsire, *Control in a Bureaucracy* (1978), ch. 4.

[48] See Ham and Hill, *Policy Process*, ch. 9; P. Knoepfel and H. Weidner, 'Air Quality Control Programmes'; N. Gunningham, *Pollution, Social Interest and the Law* (1974); C. McCrudden 'Codes in a Cold Climate: Administrative Rule-making by the Commission for Racial Equality' (1988) 51 MLR 409.

[49] P. Self, *Administrative Theories and Politics*, 2nd edn. (1978), 278.

administrative effectiveness. As Barrett and Fudge point out: 'The desire to separate "politics" and "administration", whilst in many ways discredited at an intellectual level, still forms part of the conventional wisdom among professionals and administrators in the public service.'[50] Pressman and Wildavsky emphasize the degree of co-operation that is required for successful implementation and argue that the price for co-operation may be very high: 'Since other actors cannot be coerced, their consent must be obtained. Bargaining must take place to reconcile the differences, with the result that the policy may be modified, even to the point of compromising its original purpose.'[51]

The process of producing rules can change both the form and the substance of many rules. Disputants in rule-making processes, however, argue almost exclusively about points of substance rather than form. Thus for example, they will debate the particular level of contamination to be made illegal rather than the type of rule specifying the level. The resulting tendency is for issues of enforcement and of rule choice to take a back seat.

In HSE rule-making there is again evidence that lends weight to these warnings. HSE policy-makers are by no means unaware of the difficulties attending rule-making but rules do tend to become far less accessible as rule-making progresses. A recurring criticism of HSE rules, from inspectors as well as employers, is that they are too complicated. Codes of practice, for example, are said not always to offer simple, practical advice but frequently to operate more like detailed regulations. This is usually the product of negotiations and compromises. Both the CBI and the inspectors' union, the IPCS, have made the point that packages of rules that attempt to deal with a hazard in all its locations tend to become unmanageably complex as the special circumstances of more and more industries are taken into account. Problems associated with the form and

[50] Barrett and Fudge, *Policy and Action*, 9; see also A. Dunsire, *Implementation in a Bureaucracy* (1978), ch. 1.

[51] J. Pressman and A. Wildavsky, *Implementation*, 134. See also C. Hood, *The Limits of Administration* (1976), 9. For an account of negotiating a British code of practice see McCrudden, 'Codes in a Cold Climate'.

type of rule being produced are, moreover, not given the same attention in rule-making negotiations as points of substance. HSC and HSE policy files reveal an almost exclusive concern with the levels and standards to be enforced rather than rule-types or questions of enforceability.

The message for rule-makers here is that a more realistic approach to rule choice can be adopted, that it is a mistake to assume that a rule will emerge with the same degree of rigour and in the same form as the first draft. If the policy-maker is considering operating by, say, informal leaflet, code of practice, regulation, or some combination of these then the way in which a code of practice tends to 'turn into a regulation' during the rule-making process should be borne in mind. Trade-offs should be made in the real, not the ideal, world.

(iii) Political Constraints

Policy-making problems are commonly the product of either the internal politics of an organization or the political position of the organization as a whole.[52] Within an organization a division of functions can lead to a narrowness of perspective. Michael Hill has argued that:

> the policy–implementation distinction will tend to be more clearly drawn when, at some point in the chain, one of the parties asserts a right to prescribe goals for those at subsequent points in the chain . . . where one party regards itself as having a legitimate right to lay down 'policy' for others and where it has powers to do so.[53]

Different groups within an organization may see regulatory problems differently and may seek to further the values and norms of that group rather than those of another group or of the organization as a whole.[54] To understand events, it is said, 'the pattern of ideologies' operating on a process must be examined.[55] Indeed, the different ideologies and ways of

[52] See C. Hood, *The Limits of Administration*, chs. 1 and 11; M. Hill, 'The Policy—Implementation Distinction', 212–22.

[53] Hill, 'The Policy–Implementaiton Distinction', 212.

[54] See Barrett and Fudge, *Policy and Action*, 264–76; J. Edwards and R. Batley, *The Politics of Positive Discrimination* (1978); P. Selznick, *TVA and the Grass Roots* (1949).

[55] W. I. Jenkins, *Policy Analysis: A Political and Organisational Perspective* (1978), 40. See also K. Young, ' "Values" in the Policy Process' (1977) 5 PP 1.

attributing meaning of not just groups but of individuals and professions also should be considered.[56] Eugene Bardach employs the metaphor of a 'game' in which groups struggle for control over the administrative process. This metaphor, he says: 'directs us to look at the players, what they regard as the stakes, their strategies and tactics, their resources for playing, the rules of play . . . the nature of the communications (or lack of them) among the players and the degree of uncertainty surrounding the possible outcomes.'[57]

Rule-makers may fail to give enforcers what the latter want because the two groups construct reality differently, want different things and compete for control.

Within an organization, groups may even compete on costs. To some rule-makers, enforcement costs may be external and in extreme cases rule-makers may elect to draft rules that minimize initial rule-making expenditure but which export high enforcement costs to another group.[58] An approach to rule-making that involves targeting will tend to increase initial rule-making costs (though making subsequent enforcement easier). Where different types of regulatee are revealed in targeting analyses this may imply, as indicated above, the need to match such disparity with differing rule-types. The need to produce multiple sets of 'tailored' rules will substantially increase rule-making costs. This, in itself may be a strong reason why rule-makers tend to adopt an across the board rather than a targeted approach to rule-making.

The political position of the organization as a whole may affect rule-makers as much as the internal politics. The political support available to a regulatory body is never beyond question[59] and, if this results in a defensive approach to regulation, a bias towards relatively uncontentious regulatory strategies may result at the 'top' of an organization. Rule-makers, accordingly, may write rules for a pattern of strategies that the

[56] K. Young and L. Mills, *Public Policy Research: A Review of Qualitative Methods* (1980), chs. 8 and 9. On goal diversity in bureaucracies see A. Downs, *Inside Bureaucracy* (1967), ch. 18. See also C. Ham, *Policy-Making in the NHS* (1981), 271.

[57] E. Bardach, *The Implementation Game* (1977), 56.

[58] See Diver, 'Optimal Precision', 103 and *infra* p. 182.

[59] See R. Baldwin and C. McCrudden, *Regulation and Public Law* (1987), 54.

enforcers would not endorse. Matters, indeed, may be worse: the agency may be saddled with a regulatory scheme that is flawed in design.[60] It may have been decided at Whitehall level to opt for a particular style of regulation and this may not be appropriate to the task. Such design faults can result from inadequacies *inter alia* in governmental regulatory philosophy; in the approaches of ministerial departments; in the deliberations of committees and commissions; or in the parliamentary process.[61] Even at the post-legislative stage, court decisions and governmental constraints can apply distorting pressures to regulatory regimes.[62] When, for any of these reasons, rule-makers are required to implement schemes of regulation that are deficient they will necessarily produce rules that are flawed.

A number of commentators have listed the prerequisites for effective agency implementation.[63] Van Meter and Van Horn[64] point to the need for adequacy in staff competence, hierarchical control, resources (political and other), vitality, communication and co-ordination. Sabatier and Mazmanian[65] look to soundness of theory (strategy for achieving ends), clarity of statutory objectives, managerial skill, political support, and the absence of conflicting public policies or undermining socio-economic conditions. Where such prerequisites are not present, rule-makers will perform imperfectly.[66] Thus, in so far

[60] On explaining the US Occupational Safety and Health Administration's failings in terms of flaws in the agency's mandate see McGarity and Shapiro, *Workers at Risk*, 26 and part V.

[61] See C. McCrudden, 'The Northern Ireland Fair Employment White Paper: A Critical Assessment' (1988) 17 ILJ 162. On flaws in the Robens philosophy see *supra* Ch. 5. For a sustained argument that there is a disjuncture between US regulatory philosophy on workplace health and safety and the needs of effective regulation see Noble, *Liberalism at Work*.

[62] See C. McCrudden, 'The Commission for Racial Equality: Formal Investigations in the Shadow of Judicial Review' in R. Baldwin and C. McCrudden, *Regulation and Public Law*; see also Commission for Racial Equality, *Second Review of the Race Relations Act 1976* (1992).

[63] See e.g. Van Meter and Van Horn, 'The Policy Implementation Process'; P. Sabatier and D. Mazmanian, 'The Conditions of Effective Implementation: A Guide to Accomplishing Policy Objectives' (1979) Policy Analysis 481; C. Hood, *The Limits of Administration*, ch. 1.

[64] Ibid.

[65] *Supra*, n. 63.

[66] See McCrudden, 'Codes in a Cold Climate'; L. Dickens, 'The Advisory Conciliation and Arbitration Service', in Baldwin and McCrudden, *Regulation and Public Law*.

as, say, financial resources do not allow for adequate research work, rule-makers will operate in the dark. If inadequate resources are devoted to enforcement then rule-makers are liable to make assumptions about enforcement capabilities that bear little relation to reality.

In the case of the HSE, there are policy-makers who assume the task of making 'rules for others'. The section above indicated how rule-makers and enforcers do place different values on different aspects of rules, the former stressing consistency across the board and consensualism, the latter focusing on accessibility and enforceability. Different constraints operate on the different groups—the rule-makers are, for example, far more aware than enforcers of the way that compliance with the legislation of the European Community inhibits domestic rule-making. The rule-makers see it as their function to keep overall control of the system, and enforcers in turn strive to 'get the job done' in their own way.

The HSE has not found its most enthusiastic source of support in a Conservative government. The agency's inclination to keep a low profile is understandable but has arguably led to a bias in favour of safety rather than health controls, and the HSE's limited research on health issues has reflected this bias.[67] The agency has, to some extent, been saddled with a philosophy of consensualism, based on the Robens Report, that is sustained by the present government's commitment to a light regulatory touch, and which many academics and enforcers consider unrealistic.[68] Rule-makers, as a result, place a faith in voluntarism (e.g. schemes of self-assessment of hazards) that would not be echoed by most enforcers. As for resources, it can be argued (as was noted in Chapter 5) that Robens was faced with very limited inspectorate resources, did not contest these resource levels, and so did not design rigorous enforcement into the regulatory system. The HSE, moreover, suffered badly from cuts in the eighties.[69] Inspectors

[67] See R. Baldwin, 'Health and Safety at Work: Consensus and Self-Regulation', in Baldwin andMcCrudden, *Regulation and Public Law.*

[68] See e.g. N. Gunningham, *Safeguarding the Worker* (1984), 266–74, and ch. 5 *supra.*

[69] Notably in the six years 1980–6, when the number of inspectors employed by the HSE fell from 1,444 to 1,231: HSE, *Annual Report 1986–7.*

argue that some kinds of rule might be effective with more staff to apply them but are otherwise a waste of time. Senior HSE staff have been reluctant publicly to protest about the efficiency losses caused by staff reductions. In so far as these efficiency losses are understated this fosters unrealistic assumptions about enforcement on the part of rule-makers.

What is the lesson for the HSE and other rule-makers? Politics will not, in the real world, disappear but rule-makers can compensate for anticipated biases. Openness about the politics of rule-making would allow issues to be anticipated or responded to rather than ignored. The following steps might encourage the production of rules more conducive to compliance:

- avoidance of organizational divisions and arrangements that encourage the pursuit of group rather than organizational ends;
- facilitation of access by all major groups and perspectives to the rule-making process;
- discussion of 'group' objectives and perspectives during rule-making;
- exposure of resource, legal and other limitations that affect rule-makers detrimentally;[70]
- rejection of the fudged rule as a cover for lack of resources or weak political support;
- a willingness to expose unrealistic assumptions in the 'founding philosophy' of the scheme of regulation.

In summary, then, rules do not produce compliance when those willing to comply do not know what compliance involves and when those less willing or able to comply are not informed or stimulated in the appropriate manner. Finding the right rule for the job does make a difference to regulation. Effective rule-use demands that those who design rules take into account the enforcement strategies that will have to be used to achieve compliance. Targeting is necessary and centres on the four questions already noted:

[70] See e.g. the Commission for Racial Equality, *Second Review of the Race Relations Act 1976* (1992) produced by the CRE in pursuance of its duty under s. 43(1)(c) of that Act.

- What are the key hazards?
- Who creates these hazards?
- Which enforcement strategies will best influence the mischief-makers/hazard-creators?
- Which rule-types best complement those strategies?

It is one thing to know what an approach to effective rule-use might look like, another to understand how to put that approach into effect. There are a number of reasons why rule-makers tend to give inadequate consideration to enforcement: they are prone to a mistaken attachment to the 'top-down' approach to rules and policies; they commonly underestimate the problems associated with rule-making processes, and they are invariably subject to a variety of disruptive political pressures. These factors apply as much to rule-makers in other fields as to HSE staff. Awareness of such dangers can, however, help rule-makers to avoid them. Closer attention to enforcement can be given by the rule-maker who is conscious of the limits of the 'top-down' approach, who is realistic about the rule-making process, and who is reluctant to respond to political pressure with a fudged rule. Rule-makers, in short, tend to fail in a major respect when they do not look to the means of securing compliance.

II SECURING RESULTS

As already indicated, successful rule-use demands that rules can be applied so as to produce the right results. It is clear from Chapter 3 that talk of 'right' results raises issues concerning the nature of the rule-maker's mandate, but our present concern lies with the further difficulty of achieving correspondence between compliance and desired ends. Even assuming an unproblematic mandate and efficient compliance-seeking, rules may fail for two main reasons. First, they may be misformulated so that the wrong aspects or levels of performance are demanded or they prove over- or under-inclusive (that is they deter desirable, or fail to deter undesirable, behaviour). Second, they may be prone to avoidance.

1. Misformulation and Problems of Inclusiveness

Many regulatory rule-makers face twofold difficulties in formulating rules that incorporate standards of performance or behaviour. A first problem is the *kind* of standard to be employed, a second is the *level* of performance to be prescribed. What kind of standard to use is an issue of some concern in the water pollution field where three kinds of formulation can be distinguished.[71] *Emission standards* relate to the amount or concentration of a pollutant which may be discharged from a particular point. The problem in employing such standards lies in relating them to water quality objectives and in calculating the cumulative consequences of such discharges for the watercourse. (A problem of linking considerations of compliance with results.) The strength of emission standards is that proof of contravention and enforcement is easier than is the case with other forms of standard. *Ambient standards*[72] look to the maximum pollutant concentration permitted in the environment at a given place. The advantage of employing ambient standards is that they focus directly on results and the aggregate effects of pollution on the watercourse. *Specification (or design) standards* control the processes that give rise to mischiefs—for example by demanding that industrial activities conform to specifications on, for example, plant construction, equipment to be used or modes of operation. Such standards may allow regulators to lead industry towards better practices but their use implies considerable regulatory interference with industry and a lowering of incentives both to minimize the harmful effects of processes and to research into new, more efficient methods of abatement.

[71] See G. Richardson, A. I. Ogus, and P. Burrows, *Policing Pollution* (1983), 35–8; W. Howarth, 'Poisonous, Noxious or Polluting: Contrasting Approaches to Environmental Regulation' (1993) 56 MLR 171. On problems of standard-setting more generally see A. I. Ogus, *Regulation: Legal Form and Economic Theory* (1994) chs. 8, 9, and S. Breyer, *Regulation and Its Reform* (1982), ch. 5; for a discussion of standard types of US health and safety regulation see McGarity and Shapiro *Workers at Risk*, 200–9, and for a comparison of public and private sector standard-setting see R. E. Cheit, *Setting Safety Standards: Regulation in the Public and Private Sectors* (1990).

[72] 'Receptor' standards look to the perceptible harm that an individual discharger causes to the environment and this can be seen as a form of individualized ambient standard.

Choosing the right kind of standard or rule involves *inter alia* considering, in the relevant context, the trade-off between targeting results directly (which ambient standards do) and giving priority to efficient enforcement (which emission and specification standards do).[73] Having stated, above, that securing compliance does not guarantee results, it can now be suggested that a concern to specify the right results should not blind the rule-maker to considerations of efficient compliance-seeking.

Turning to the *level* of performance demanded by a rule, regulators are sometimes called upon by statute to control a mischief in a manner allowing a degree of discretion.[74] The rule-maker is thus frequently faced with the problem of deciding what is an acceptable level of pollution or concentration of hazardous material. In doing so a series of difficulties is encountered. If the socially efficient level of, say, pollution is the objective, the regulator will aim to minimise the sum of the costs of abatement (e.g. the costs of fitting filters and of slowing down the production process) plus the costs that the pollution imposes on others. Calculating the general standard that will minimize such costs is a highly complex task.[75] The costs of the damage occasioned by any particular level of discharge or lowering of water quality will vary from place to place (from trout stream to industrial drain), they will depend on the profile of the community affected by the discharge and may vary over time. Similarly, the costs of abatement will differ from polluter to polluter and will do so quite independently of variations in damage costs. Such costs may depend, *inter alia*, on the size of a firm, the nature of the production process, the product being manufactured, and the profitability of the enterprise as a whole. The socially efficient level of pollution is thus likely to be different for each polluter. Fixing one standard across the board is accordingly a fraught process and, in attempting this

[73] See Breyer *Regulation and its Reform*, 103–5 on standards that 'aim directly at the evil' versus standards that aim at 'surrogates' (e.g. emission levels).

[74] Statutes commonly call upon regulators to balance a number of vaguely stated objectives or to limit mischiefs to 'reasonable' levels.

[75] See Richardson, Ogus, and Burrows, *Policing Pollution*, 48–54; Ogus, *Regulation*, ch. 8; Breyer, *Regulation and its Reform*, chs. 4 and 5. Policy considerations may, of course, demand that certain rights be protected and so a socially inefficient level of pollution is aimed at. This is unlikely to simplify the regulator's task, however.

task, the rule-maker is likely to face considerable informational difficulties and costs. It should not be forgotten, furthermore, that the level of performance demanded by a rule may, like the kind of standard employed, affect compliance-seeking activity. As levels of allowable mischief are lowered, the costs of measurement, monitoring, and enforcement are likely to rise. Trade-offs again may have to be made between optimal performance levels and the dictates of efficient compliance-seeking.

Ill-formulated rules may, as indicated, also fail due to errors of inclusiveness—because they discourage desirable activity (through over-inclusiveness)[76] or they fail to rule out undesirable activity (through under-inclusiveness). In tackling this inclusiveness problem it is important to distinguish 'rule-level' inclusiveness from 'site-level' inclusiveness.[77] The rules may, as written, be over- or under-inclusive, but the rules as applied on the ground may have modified effects. How compliance-seeking affects inclusiveness has thus to be borne in mind as do the effects on compliance-seeking of attempts to optimize inclusiveness at the rule-making stage. Failure to link these issues can lead to a lack of realism about rules. This can be seen by examining the analysis of two well-known commentators in the law and economics field.

Isaac Ehrlich and Richard Posner have offered 'An Economic Analysis of Legal Rule-making',[78] aiming to spell out the costs and benefits associated with different choices along the continuum between highly specific and highly general rules. Their objective is to explain how to make the optimal choice and maximize the excess of benefits over costs. They argue, *inter alia*, that increased precision or detail in rules discourages undesirable conduct and encourages desirable conduct by increasing the probability of punishing undesirable activity. The more detailed the rule, the higher the probability that the activity will be correctly defined as illegal and the

[76] On the tendency to over-inclusiveness in US regulation see Bardach and Kagan, *Going by the Book*, ch. 3. On inclusiveness generally see F. Schauer, *Playing by the Rules* (1992), 31–4.

[77] Bardach and Kagan, *Going by the Book*, 7.

[78] Ibid.

higher the probability of conviction. Higher precision is thus said to reduce problems of over- and under-inclusiveness: it improves deterrence and avoids the 'chilling' of socially advantageous conduct.[79] It, moreover, increases the return on resources devoted to prosecution since convictions are more predictable, and as a result, settlements out of court are more likely where rules are precise.

An eye to compliance-seeking realities shows that a number of factors are insufficiently attended to in Ehrlich and Posner's analysis. First, their assumption is that prosecution is the prominent method in compliance-seeking. As we have seen, however, compliance-seekers have at their disposal a number of alternatives to prosecution (e.g. persuading, advising, and promoting) and it cannot be taken for granted that the kind of precise rule that complements a prosecution strategy will be the best kind of rule to use in association with other techniques. Second, their analysis focuses on the question of precision, whereas in practice there are a number of other dimensions to rules, such as legal form, force, prescription/sanction, or accessibility, which may have a bearing on benefits and costs. Third, they take insufficient account of compliance-seeking in the face of variations in kinds of employer, industry, and mischiefs. Thus, the contention that increasing precision adds to the likelihood of apprehension, conviction, and the imposition of a penalty is problematic because (even assuming prosecution is the appropriate mode of enforcement) excessive detail can increase the costs of rule application and so may reduce the likelihood that penalties will be imposed. The rules may become lengthy and cumbersome, and handling them may require expert knowledge and high levels of resources. Many regulators, moreover, believe imprecision to be a better deterrent than precision where actual penalties are modest.[80] When prosecution is not the enforcement strategy involved, highly detailed rules may reduce levels of both com-

[79] For an efficiency-based model of 'regulatory reasonableness' see ibid. 6–7.

[80] Diver, 'Optimal Precision', 78; N. Abrams, 'Internal Policy: Guiding the Exercise of Prosecutorial Discretion' (1971) 19 UCLA LR 1, 29; McBarnet and Whelan, 'The Elusive Spirit of the Law'.

pliance and effectiveness because even the self-motivated, self-regulating individual will not find the rule sufficiently accessible. Ehrlich and Posner state that increased precision improves success in discouraging undesirable activities and in encouraging desirable ones, but this will only be the case if it is also assumed that problems of accessibility and compliance-seeking are overcome. In practice, highly detailed rules may indeed 'chill' desirable conduct (even if they are not, on their face, over-inclusive) if they are so extensive or intricate that the costs of dealing with such rules deter potential entrants to a field.

A more sophisticated approach to the problem of inclusiveness in the drafting of rules is that of Colin Diver who accepts that: 'The degree of precision appropriate to any particular rule depends on a series of variables peculiar to the rule's author, enforcer and addressee. As a consequence, generalizations about optimal rule precision are inherently suspect.'[81]

Diver, nevertheless, does seek to 'draw some general inferences' on the optimal precision of rules and he does attend to the different dimensions of rules and to issues of compliance. He focuses on three different qualities of rules: their *transparency* (that is their formulation in words with well-defined and universally accepted meanings within the relevant community); their *accessibility* (the ease with which the intended audience can apply the rule to concrete situations without excessive difficulty or effort); and, their *congruence* with underlying policy objectives (whether the substantive content of the message communicated produces the desired behaviour).[82] It is, thus, *congruence* which in Diver's terminology takes in the issue of inclusiveness.

In order to exemplify the choices facing rule-makers, Diver supposes the need for a rule to compel pilots to retire when the social cost of allowing them to continue flying (measured as the probability of their causing accidents multiplied by the consequences of such accidents) exceeds the social benefits of not having to replace them. He offers three formulations for such a rule:

[81] Diver, 'Optimal Precision', 76. [82] Ibid. 67.

Model I: No person may pilot a commercial aeroplane after their sixtieth birthday.

Model II: No person may pilot a commercial aeroplane if they pose an unreasonable risk of an accident.

Model III: No person may pilot a commercial aeroplane if they fall within one of the following categories. (There follow tables displaying combinations of values for numerous variables, including years and levels of experience, hours of air time logged, age, height, weight, blood pressure, heart-rate, eyesight, and other vital signs, that would disqualify a pilot from further eligibility to fly aircraft.)

Model I is the most transparent and accessible but scores badly on congruence (for example some pilots over 60 may present lower risks than some under 60). Model III scores well on congruence but low on transparency and questionably on accessibility. On the latter point, Diver points out that it is difficult to say whether Model II or III is easier to apply. Model II is high on transparency (it is shorter and more memorable than Model III) but it poses problems of accessibility and congruence. It involves a single test but that test is more vague than the explicit criteria of Model III. Model III is precise but its length may make it difficult to apply. It follows from Diver's own argument, and from the discussion of HSE rule-making above, that a choice between Model II or III would have to be resolved by an analysis of the mischief involved, the rule's addressees and the enforcer's compliance-seeking strategies. Clearly such a balancing of variables places considerable demands on rule-makers and a good deal will depend on particular conditions. Nevertheless, Diver offers some general guidance by identifying circumstances in which a particularly high premium may be placed on one aspect of a rule. He makes, *inter alia*, the following points:[83]

(i) Where the costs of over or under-inclusiveness are high (for example when the death penalty might be applied to the 'wrong' individual as a result of an over-inclusive rule on murder), rational rule-makers will favour precise and intricate formulations of the rule. In contrast, where

[83] Diver, 'Optimal Precision', 74–8.

misapplication of the rule assumes only small social significance (e.g. in a case involving motor vehicle licensing) it may be rational to opt for a more transparent rule along the lines of Model I.

(ii) Where the costs of applying rules and of monitoring enforcement officials loom large, for instance because a large volume of issues is involved, it may be rational to reduce litigation costs by using 'bright-line rules', such as Model I. Similarly where large, decentralized enforcement staffs are used (as in occupational safety and health regulation) highly transparent rules may be called for.

(iii) Where the costs of making the rule are high—as in a collegial rule-making body such as a legislature or a multimember independent agency where there are large numbers of participants and the representation of highly divergent interests—rule-makers will tend to opt for vague rules on the lines of Model II since these minimize the range of agreement required and hence keep down the costs of promulgation.[84]

(iv) Where rules are addressed to officials themselves and establish priorities for the allocation of resources (e.g. by laying down prosecution policies) a high level of concern for accuracy or congruity is to be expected. Simple transparent rules may thus be avoided (as tending to misallocate resources) in favour of detailed, precise guidance.

(v) Rules imposing criminal sanctions, particularly severe sanctions, will tend to call for relatively precise formulations, compared to rules allocating civil liability.

Diver's analysis is narrower than the 'compliance-oriented' approach discussed above. It does not fully take on board such dimensions of rules as form, force, and type of sanction, but it does suggest a useful approach to inclusiveness and precision. It is important, nevertheless, to explore further *why* problems of inclusiveness may occur and how such problems may be dealt with during the compliance-seeking process.

At the rule-making stage, problems of inclusiveness may not

[84] See Ch. 8 *infra* on rule-making within the EU and the movement towards a more flexible approach, particularly in relation to market-completing provisions.

be dealt with adequately for many of the reasons that were discussed in looking at failure to address the issue of compliance. A number of points of special relevance to inclusiveness ought, however, to be noted.

Under-inclusiveness tends to result from a failure to identify and deal with mischiefs. This may stem from statutory inadequacies,[85] from lack of information, or from paucity of resourcing and, at the rule-making and policy levels, regulators tend to deal with this by pressing for greater governmental commitment on such fronts.

Over-inclusiveness at the rule-making stage is a problem that has been most notably discussed by the American political scientists Eugene Bardach and Robert Kagan[86] who have expressed concern at the extent to which US regulators have tended to over-regulate with over-inclusive rules. Why does this happen? Bardach and Kagan give a number of reasons.[87] First, the informational costs of designing rules of optimal inclusiveness are considerable. In order to design such rules regulators not only require information on the technological and economic conditions surrounding mischief abatement in all its contexts, but they will have to negotiate with industry for such information. The tendency for rule-makers is to avoid such difficulties by writing over-inclusive rules that externalize costs on to those who are regulated or on to enforcement officials who may have to employ their budgets and resources to deal with problems of inclusiveness.

The second reason is related. Presented with evidence of a mischief at a particular location, regulators (as already noted in Section I) tend to opt for an across the board solution: 'They are petitioned to prevent "that kind of thing" from happening again by reforming the system that created it. They thus transform individual acts of malfeasance into social problems requiring society-wide solutions.'[88]

[85] In Britain the CRE has more than once noted the shortcomings of its parent legislation—see CRE, *Second Review of the Race Relations Act 1976* (1992).

[86] Bardach and Kagan, *Going by the Book*.

[87] Ibid. 66–77, 186, 193; see also C. Veljanovski, 'The Economics of Regulatory Enforcement' in Hawkins and Thomas (eds.), *Enforcing Regulation*, ch. 8, esp. 173–85.

[88] Bardach and Kagan, *Going by the Book*, 67.

The results of such processes are rules that exert controls over (and impose costs on) good as well as bad regulatees. A third cause of over-inclusion is said to be pressure from various sources to have the rule of law evident in regulation rather that the rule of man. Thus politicians and regulated parties may press for regulatory discretions to be reduced in favour of impartiality, objectivity, and equal treatment under laws. In so far as rule-makers are influenced by such pressures they are induced to trade off lower effectiveness in favour of higher levels of accountability and due process.

Regulators have almost invariably to court political and public support for their rule-making activities. This gives rise to a fourth reason for failing to respond fully to issues of inclusiveness. Regulators often wish to produce rules to deal with a mischief before public concern dies down—while the memory of the disaster is still fresh. Responding to the resultant tight timescales may mean that rule-makers have insufficient opportunities to target their rules in a refined manner and have to opt for the broad-brush approach with over-inclusive rules.

A final posited cause of over-inclusiveness arises out of the 'regulatory ratchet'[89]—a syndrome whereby the undergrowth of regulation tends ever to thicken. Regulatory rules tend to grow rather than recede, argue Bardach and Kagan, because pruning is 'uncommon, dilatory and exceptional'[90]—economics of scale in rule-writing mean that revisions of regulations are infrequent; work on new rules drives out attention to old ones; for the agency the costs of over-inclusive old rules are an externality; and, in political terms, a relaxation of regulation may be seen as evidence of capture, weakness, or selling out.

Given that there is force in some of the above points, what can regulatory rule-makers do in response?[91] At the rule-making stage one course is for regulators to attempt to make more discriminating rules and (as indicated in relation to compliance-seeking in Section I) to target these more accurately. It has to be borne in mind, though, that such endeavours will increase rule-making costs; they will make heavy informational

[89] Ibid., ch. 7. [90] Ibid. 193.

[91] See Veljanovski, 'Economics of Regulatory Enforcement', 174–5.

demands; and if tailoring rules produces a greater number of more detailed rules, such complexity will affect compliance-seeking activity detrimentally and may escalate enforcement costs.

An alternative response is to write rules that devolve discretion down to enforcers so that issues of inclusiveness are dealt with by selective enforcement. Thus, health and safety inspectors can be asked to enforce rules which impose duties on employers to take actions 'so far as is reasonably practicable'.[92] Such a strategy invites inspectors to balance avoidance costs and benefits in particular situations.[93] It keeps costs low for rule-makers but raises questions. First, in relying on high levels of enforcer discretion it is open to objection by those who fear discrimination and capture and who desire accountability through legal mechanisms. Second, it may be asked whether enforcers will, in fact, act selectively in seeking compliance. Much depends on regulatory styles and traditions[94] and, at least in relation to health and safety matters, differences of approach have been noted on both sides of the Atlantic. Bardach and Kagan[95] suggest that field inspectors in the United States will tend to adopt a literal, legalistic, and inflexible approach to enforcement as a result of pressures exerted from within their bureaucracies but also resulting from scrutiny by courts and congressional committees and the activities of critics ready to accuse agencies of capture.

On the other hand, a contrast has been drawn between such 'penalty' systems of enforcing regulatory rules and 'compliance' systems,[96] as encountered in British health and safety regulation. In the latter sector, it has been argued,[97] field enforcers routinely behave in a highly discretionary, non-legalistic, and selective manner. They soften over-inclusive

[92] As per ss. 2–9 HSWA.

[93] See Bardach and Kagan, *Going by the Book*, ch. 5 on the 'Good Inspector'.

[94] On which see e.g. Vogel, *National Styles of Regulation*; Kelman, *Regulating America*.

[95] *Going by the Book*, 71–7.

[96] See A. Reiss and A. Biderman, *Data Sources on White-Collar Law Breaking* (1980).

[97] See Hawkins, *Environment and Enforcement*; B. Hutter, *The Reasonable Arm of the Law*; Vogel *National Styles of Regulation*; Kogan and Scholz, 'Criminology of the Corporation'; W. G. Carson 'Some Sociological Aspects of Strict Liability and the Enforcement of Factory Legislation' (1970) 33 MLR 396–412.

rules by negotiating compromises and occasionally deal with under-inclusion by a process of bluffing so as to achieve results where the rules are lacking.[98]

To summarize, problems of inclusiveness are, like issues of standard-type and level of standard, not matters that can be dealt with without reference to the processes that are used for seeking compliance. Rules can be designed in ways that deal with such issues but a number of genuine tensions cannot be escaped—as, for example, between optimizing inclusiveness and enhancing compliance-seeking. In any particular governmental or regulatory environment the means chosen to resolve such difficulties will be influenced *inter alia* by the resources and information available, the regulatory staffs employed and the levels of political support enjoyed by regulators. As was seen in looking at inclusiveness and the role of field-level discretion, familiar trade-offs may have to be made between considerations of accountability and effectiveness.

2. The Problem of Creative Compliance

In addition to the difficulties described above, rule-makers are faced with the possibility that their rules may prove ineffective because they are avoided. This has been dubbed the problem of 'creative compliance'[99]—the process whereby regulatees escape from regulation by wholly legal means. Doreen McBarnet thus argues:

> What regulation studies have underplayed is the extent to which the regulated do not violate but merely avoid the law. Responses to law are not just a matter of breaking it (crime) and obeying it (compliance). It is also possible to use legal techniques to achieve non-

[98] K. Hawkins, 'Bargain and Bluff: Compliance Strategy and Deference in the Enforcement of Regulation' (1983) 5 LPQ 35–73.

[99] See D. McBarnet and C. Whelan, 'The Elusive Spirit of the Law: Formalism and the Struggle for Legal Control' (1991) 54 MLR 848; D. McBarnet 'Law and Capital: The Role of Legal Form and Legal Actors' (1984) 12 IJSL 233; McBarnet, 'Law Policy and Legal Avoidance' (1988) JLSoc. 113; McBarnet, 'It's Not What You Do but the Way that You Do It: Tax Evasion, Tax Avoidance and the Boundaries of Deviance', in Downes (ed.), *Unravelling Criminal Justice* (1991); McBarnet and Whelan, 'Beyond Control: Law, Management and Corporate Governance', in McCaherty, Picciotto, and Scott (eds.), *Corporate Control and Accountability* (1992).

compliance with the intent of the law without technically violating its content. The law is not broken but it is nonetheless entirely ineffective in achieving its aims.[100]

The main proponents of creative compliance are the ill-intentioned, well-informed regulatees—those who devote resources to avoiding the intent of the law. This was the group conspicuously omitted from consideration when looking above at FI compliance-seeking by negotiation. The reason for this exception was the scarcity, in the health and safety sector, of employers cynical enough to spend time and money informing themselves of health and safety rules only in order to devise ways of circumventing those rules.[101] In other areas, such as taxation, however, whole industries are devoted to the avoidance of legal constraints. The struggle to control creative compliers has been described graphically by Doreen McBarnet and Christopher Whelan in dealing with tax and accounting rules. The two authors argue that formalism has often been presented as the dominant approach to legal control. This implies the use of clearly-defined, highly administrable and specific rules with an emphasis on uniformity, consistency, literalism, and predictability. Such detailed rules, however, 'contribute to the defeat of legal policy'[102] since regulatees can manipulate approaches, transactions, relationships, or legal forms to avoid the bounds of the legal rules. The formalistic approach with its 'cookbook' or code of specific and rigid rules can thus fail to control even if the letter of the rule successfully accords with the spirit in which the rule was framed.[103]

[100] D. McBarnet, 'Law, Policy and Legal Avoidance' (1988) JLS 113, 114. To give a simple example of creative compliance: suppose a law on Sunday trading limits the hours that a store larger than a given size may open. A store greater than that size might divide itself into a series of smaller units and (if this ruse is not anticipated) may be able to trade free from the time constraint. It thus avoids the intent of the law without breaking the law.

[101] On amoral calculators see Kagan and Scholz, 'Criminology of the Corporation'; on their prevalence see Bardach and Kagan, *Going by the Book*, 65.

[102] McBarnet and Whelan, 'Elusive Spirit', 849. See also Braithwaite, *To Punish or Persuade*, 102, who notes the process in which regulatees defy the spirit of rules by exploiting loopholes, regulators respond with more specific rules to cover the loopholes, and rule-making proceeds by accretion, eventually leading to a loss of coherence in the package of rules. Such a process, argues Braithwaite, is encouraged by 'nitpicking punitive enforcement of specific rules'.

[103] Formalistic or precise rules may be prone to avoidance but not all precise rules are narrow or necessarily easily avoided. Thus a rule such as Diver's Model I rule,

There is, however, an alternative 'anti-formalistic' approach to rules which rejects narrow legalism in favour of 'more flexible, open-textured and policy-oriented' rules.[104] This looks to the *substance* rather than to the form of transactions and to the purposes and 'spirit' of regulation rather than the letter of the rule or law. It favours a broad approach to rules, the formulation of 'catch-all' provisions which are left undefined or vague so as to prevent literal avoidance and it accepts that regulation must, like practice, evolve.

Anti-formalism may be useful in countering creative compliance, but a number of pressures oppose the adoption of such an approach and produce a 'drift' towards formalism. A first basis for attacking anti-formalism invokes the due process or fairness rationale. It involves the criticism that anti-formalism is anti-rule of law. Thus it is commonly asserted that the citizen has a right to know precisely what the law is rather than be exposed to the uncertainties and discretions of anti-formalist regulation. The Law Society's Revenue Law Committee has criticized anti-formalist taxation rules as 'unconstitutional'[105] and the accountancy and legal professions have lobbied strongly against such revenue rules while calling for more certainty and predicability. Vague or broad rules are said, furthermore, to be too lacking in specifics to be susceptible of implementation and to be so imprecise and over-inclusive as to prejudice innocent parties.[106]

which prohibits persons from piloting commercial aeroplanes after their sixtieth birthday is precise and difficult for the ageing pilot to escape. Where a rule makes tax liability contingent on precise arrangements, there is greater potential for avoidance. An important issue is thus the rule's breadth and the regulatee's flexibility in the face of the rule and other constraints.

[104] For a discussion of 'goal-oriented legislation' and of the need to legislate with implementation in mind see E. L. Rubin, 'Law and Legislation in the Administrative State' (1989) 89 Col.LR 369.

[105] McBarnet and Whelan, 'Elusive Spirit', 857.

[106] Similar points have been made in the financial services sector. Thus, in 1988 David Walker, then Chairman of the Securities and Investments Board (SIB), described his programme of moving from detailed rules to broader principles in financial services regulation. He noted that some in the sector had doubted whether the programme could be sustained because, they said, 'practitioners need the security of detailed rules'. See D. Walker, speech to the Foreign Banks Association, 29 Nov. 1988. On rule-use in financial services regulation, see A. M. Whittaker, 'Legal Technique in City Regulation' (1990) *Current Legal Problems* 35.

Experience in the tax and accountancy fields already reveals a retreat from broad, open, flexible laws in the face of such pressures and a move to tighter, narrower rules. The process of applying broad rules also produces a drift to formalism in so far as regulators subject broad rules to clarifications, guidelines, and explanatory notes; the courts narrow the rules with judicial expositions of their content; barristers give private opinions on transactions, and professionals adopt interpretations, seek approvals, or obtain informal rulings from regulators. The dynamics of application thus lead strongly towards formalism.

Is formalism, therefore, inevitable in regulatory rule-making? This would be an exaggerated view—creative compliance may be accompanied by pressures to formalize but this is not the only means of responding to rules. Regulatees may, for various reasons, prefer to negotiate on the basis of vague laws rather than opt for the formalistic solution: they may be wary of the costs of complying with large bodies of detailed rules and, indeed, may lack the expertise and resources to challenge the anti-formalist strategy. An area where formalism is arguably inevitable is that studied by McBarnet and Whelan who conclude their 1991 article:

> our analysis suggests that in the context of finance, anti-formalism is unlikely to survive as more than rhetoric or theory . . . where the stakes are high, where there is strong motivation to circumvent legal control and where there are the resources to achieve this, we would expect law to be avoided and control to be resisted.[107]

The health and safety sector offers a contrast. It is marked by a relative scarcity of regulatees who are both ill-intentioned and well-informed, who have the commitment, expertise, and resources to circumvent regulation in a methodical way. Not only that, but there is evidence of anti-formalism in sustained operation. The HSWA 1974 does contain broad general duties for the employer, for example, a duty 'to ensure, so far as is reasonably practicable, the health , safety and welfare at work

[107] McBarnet and Whelan, 'Elusive Spirit', 873. The movement of the SIB away from formalism in the years 1988–90 might thus be seen by McBarnet and Whelan as an attempt at regulatory reform that is liable to be overhauled in time as various pressures to formalize are brought to bear.

of all his employees.'[108] These broad duties are central to the regulatory system and the rules produced by the HSE frequently incorporate broad reasonableness tests. The effect of these is to allow the inspector generally to look to the substance of the workplace activity and to counter 'technical' circumventions of the law. The use of general duties and more formalistic rules in combination allows inspectors to have two sweeps at the potential escapee from the regulatory net—if the specific rule is avoided the general duty may be brought into play.

Creative compliance is nevertheless a problem to a greater or lesser extent in most regulatory systems. The severity of that problem depends on such factors as the nature of those regulated; the balance of power, information, and resources between controllers and controlled; the ease with which regulatees can reorganize their affairs so as to avoid the rules and the potential gains to be derived from circumventing the rules as compared to the costs of avoidance.

What is the implication of creative compliance for the compliance-oriented approach to rule-making outlined in this chapter? It is that the astute rule-maker will aim to devise rules that complement optimal compliance-seeking strategies but will do so bearing in mind the liability of the selected rule to circumvention. The compliance-oriented approach calls for analyses of those who are responsible for the relevant mischief and such analyses will inform judgements concerning potential rule avoidance.

III. GUIDELINES FOR RULE-MAKERS

1. Effectiveness and Other Values

It was argued in Chapter 3 that effectiveness is only one of the values that can be invoked in making a justificatory claim for a rule or set of rules. Assuming that effective action satisfies the

[108] HSWA, s. 2(1); the general duties are contained in HSWA, ss. 2–9.

dictates of the legislative mandate in so far as desired substantive ends are secured, there are still other values and claims to be considered. Should these values and claims be given attention alongside the effective securing of results when designing rules?

Diver is at least unequivocal on this point. He sets out to devise a normative principle for comparing formulations of rules but argues that invocation of 'moral values like fairness, equity or community' offers little promise because the trade-offs that would have to be considered occur along each and every dimension of the rule. He suggests, therefore, that the only solution is to reduce conflicting values to a common denominator, that of social utility, so that one can estimate the social costs and benefits flowing from each formulation and select the one with the greatest net social benefit.

Diver's argument here, however, is not wholly convincing. If social utility is defined in terms of money, then values such as accountability and fairness are left out of account. If social utility is given a broader meaning, it is necessary, in order to describe that meaning, to incorporate references to, and explanations of, those very values (e.g. fairness, equity, or community) whose invocation Diver asserts to be so problematic.

A more persuasive approach is to confront more directly the complexity of the task and to recognize that as well as making the kind of efficiency-based calculation outlined by Diver, reference does have to be made to the propensity of a rule to realize other values such as those implied by the accountability, due process, and expertise rationales.

General guidelines on such issues can also be developed. Claims under the accountability/control rationale can be strengthened by designing rules that are amenable to scrutiny by observers. The procedures normally adopted for making administrative rules and the organizational contexts of such rule-making do not normally lead to high levels of accountability. Observers also tend to be thin on the ground, so scrutiny usually only operates through schemes of internal checking, ministerial approvals systems, user/consumer-group monitoring, or by general public debate. A rule, nevertheless, that can be understood by lay persons, and which is transparent and non-technical, will tend to enhance claims to openness and accountability.

Claims that due process interests are recognized in rules and rule-making processes are similarly important.[109] As Galligan has stressed: 'It is not only final outcomes that matter, but also the processes whereby those outcomes are reached.'[110]

Rule design can again enhance or detract from such claims. Thus strong claims will tend to accompany rules that are formulated in a manner consistent with consultation and that are intelligible and accessible to affected parties. Rules that are highly technical, enormously long, difficult to obtain, or expensive to process will not enhance due process claims.

Finally, the expertise justification demands that rules are designed in a manner that reflects the agency or department's expertise and allows specialist judgements to be implemented. A tension clearly exists between potential claims under this heading and the requirements of the legal mandate, accountability, and due process rationales. The kind of rule format that maximizes scope for expertise may incorporate freedom from statutorily defined mandates and so may weaken claims on that basis; it may be expressed in technical terms and so reduce accountability; similarly, a rule aimed to encourage the application of expertise may not be highly intelligible or accessible and may not be amenable to broad consultation.

Conclusions

It is possible to offer a number of points of guidance for rule-makers, but the daunting nature of the rule-maker's task has to be recognized. Rule design does affect the efficiency with which enforcers can secure compliance with regulatory rules, and issues of design have to be faced across all the various dimensions of rules. Those devising rules have to look to

[109] See Diver, 'Optimal Precision', 71; Tribe, 'Structural Due Process' (1975) 10 Harv.LR 269; R. B. Saphire, 'Specifying Due Process Values: Towards a More Responsive Approach to Procedural Protection' (1978) 127 UPa.LR 111.

[110] Galligan, *Discretionary Powers*, 98.

anticipated regulatory strategies if compliance-seeking is to be enhanced and a 'compliance-oriented' approach to rule-making suggests that hazards and hazard-creators should be analysed before choices of enforcement strategy and rule design are made.

On why rule-makers fail to design rules conducive to compliance, there is evidence that the 'top-down' approach creates difficulties, that problems of process tend to be insufficiently understood, and that political pressures (internal and external) often prove disruptive. An awareness of these problems may produce rules more conducive to effective compliance-seeking, but compliance does not ensure effectiveness in the sense of securing the right results. As seen in Section II, rule-makers are faced with further issues: of selecting the kinds of rules and standards that will best yield desired results; of setting the levels of standards that will best produce such results; of achieving optimal levels of inclusiveness, and of avoiding 'creative compliance'.

To design effective rules is not, however, enough and an array of values other than efficiency has to be served if rule-makers are convincingly to claim justification for their designs. To this end attention should also be paid to the dictates of claims made with reference to the accountability, due process, and expertise rationales.

Is such an approach unrealistic? It clearly is if treated as an invitation to pursue an exhaustive, comprehensively rational, approach to all rule-making issues. That, however, is not the suggestion. What is proposed here is that, within the bounds of feasibility established by expertise, resources, and time, rule-makers should adopt the general compliance-oriented approach described and apply it with the kind of analysis and detailed attention that proves possible in the particular circumstances. On some occasions broad judgements will have to be made (and guidelines for such instances have been suggested) on others, the issues may be considered in greater depth. Any approach to rule-making may be applied with different degrees of rigour. It may as well be one that aims to prove worthy of support on all relevant fronts.

7 Rules and Economic Appraisals

Is there a case for using assessments of costs and benefits to appraise not the drafting of a rule but the broad justification for introducing a rule? Is there, moreover, a governmental role for such assessments in spite of arguments for satisfying values other than efficiency?

This chapter considers developments in the cost-benefit and compliance-cost testing of rules in the USA and in Britain. It reviews the theoretical and practical issues raised and assesses the possible contribution of economic appraisals to questions of rule choice.

1. The Appraisal Strategy Developed

(i) Experience in the United States of America

In the United States there was, by 1980, a broad current of dissatisfaction with the nature and practice of regulatory rule-making.[1] Numerous critics had argued that regulators were operating beyond the constraints of political control and were irrationally imposing burdens on industry. It was argued that companies were carrying a dead weight of regulation on their backs and that there was a need for reform in the shape of 'regulatory relief'[2] or else a change from rule-oriented or 'command and control' outlooks to those allowing greater managerial freedom within broad governmentally specified goals.[3] The criticisms and prescriptions were diverse. As McGarity put it:

By the beginning of the 1980s the regulatory reform movement had achieved a high profile, but it did not carry a unifying theme. To

[1] See T. O. McGarity, *Reinventing Rationality: The Role of Regulatory Analysis in the Federal Bureaucracy* (1991).

[2] G. Eads and M. Fix, 'Regulatory Policy', in J. Palmer and I. Jawhill (eds.), *The Reagan Experiment* (1982).

[3] On 'less restrictive' alternatives to 'classical' regulation see S. Breyer *Regulation and Its Reform* (1982) and A I. Ogus, *Regulation: Legal Form and Economic Theory* (1994), ch. 11.

some, regulatory reform meant regulatory relief; to others it meant bureaucratic accountability; to still others, it means rational analysis.[4]

The unifying theme was to come with President Reagan's imposing on regulators a requirement that they justify their rules by appraisals of costs and benefits.

Such employment of cost-benefit analysis (CBA) testing was not wholly new to US federal regulation.[5] In 1969 the National Environmental Policy Act had required that agencies prepare an Environmental Impact Statement (EIS) for every legislative proposal significantly affecting the quality of the environment. The EIS was required to describe such matters as environmental impacts, adverse effects, alternatives, and resource commitments. During President Nixon's period of office, the Environmental Protection Agency (EPA) and the Occupational Safety and Health Administration (OSHA) were required to submit proposed regulations to a 'Quality of Life' review with a summary of costs and review of alternatives. President Ford, in turn, expanded the review process by promulgating Executive Order 11821 which demanded that an Inflation Impact Statement (IIS) accompany all major federal proposals for legislation, rules, and regulations. To implement the new programme Ford set up a Council on Wage and Price Stability (CWPS). The CWPS was mainly concerned to act as a watchdog over the inflationary activities of government, but the programme was also intended to encourage government agencies to consider the costs and benefits of their proposals. CWPS economists would thus review proposed regulations and submit analyses to scrutiny as part of an internal review procedure.[6] President Carter sustained the initiative with his 'Improving Government Regulation' programme,[7] under which executive agencies were required to publish six-monthly agendas of forthcoming regulations and to prepare impact

[4] McGarity, *Reinventing Rationality*, 4.

[5] See G. R. Baldwin and C. G. Veljanovski, 'Regulation by Cost-Benefit Analysis' (1984) 62 Pub. Admin. 51. On scientific and economic analysis in rule-making generally see G. Bryner, *Bureaucratic Discretion* (1987), ch. 3; McGarity, *Reinventing Rationality*.

[6] See J. Miller and B. Yandle, *Benefit-Cost Analysis of Social Regulation* (1979); L. J. White, *Reforming Regulation-Process and Problems* (1981).

[7] Executive Order 12044; Eads and Fix, 'Regulating Policy', 54.

analyses of, and economic justifications for, regulations likely to have major economic consequences. The programme demanded that regulations were cost-effective, minimized burdens on industry, and were to be liable to review and elimination when no longer efficient.

President Reagan's significant step was to take this trend to its logical extreme by issuing Executive Order 12291 in early 1981. This required executive agencies to submit all major regulations to CBA and to put forward for presidential approval only those with a surplus of benefits. Under President Carter's programme, impact analysis had not involved CBA testing and the onus of proof lay not on the promulgating agency but on the President's reviewers, who had to show that a proposal was *not* cost-effective. The Reagan approach made CBAs obligatory and placed the burden of proof on the proponent of the regulation.

The stated objectives of Order 12291 were: to reduce the burden of regulation; to increase agency accountability; to provide for more effective presidential oversight of the regulatory process; and to ensure better-reasoned justifications for regulating. Agencies were ordered to pursue objectives maximizing net social benefits and achieving these at least cost. Rule-makers were to consider three key factors in setting their priorities: the state of the national economy; the condition of the regulated industries; and other contemplated regulatory actions. CBA testing was, however, only to apply to 'major rules' with effects on the economy of $100m. or more, or which involved either a major increase in costs or prices or a significantly adverse effect on competition, employment, investment, productivity, innovation, or international competitiveness.

The prescribed analysis became the Regulatory Impact Analysis (RIA), with agencies required to prepare a Preliminary Regulatory Impact Analysis (PRIA) for final major rules.

The RIA had to contain not only a description of the costs and benefits of the rule but an outline of alternative approaches that might achieve the proposed regulatory goal at lower cost with an exploration of the reasons why such alternatives could not be adopted. The Order recognized that not all benefits (or costs) could be quantified in monetary terms and called for non-quantifiable benefits to be described. The Order also called for the identification of the losers and gainers from the regulation.

The scrutiny process was placed under the control of the Office of Management and Budget (OMB) which was given a discretion to designate any rule as major. The OMB was also given the responsibility for determining the adequacy of the RIA.

Order 12291 was followed by the OMB's Interim Regulatory Impact Analysis Guidance (Interim Guidance, OMB, 1981) which gave instructions on RIA preparation and was followed by Final Guidance in 1989. These documents strongly favoured quantification in monetary terms and argued for the use of 'most likely assumptions' where uncertainties were encountered.

Using such guidance, the OMB scrutinized with zeal from the inception of the system. In 1981 ninety-five regulations were either withdrawn or reconsidered as a result of scrutiny and a similar rejection and withdrawal rate continued throughout the eighties. In 1988, eighty-five regulations were withdrawn or rejected. McGarity has commented: 'This represented only 3 to 4 per cent of all the rules that OMB reviewed but . . . OMB has had a very significant impact on the relatively small universe of regulations that really matter.'[8]

The RIA system continued to operate through the Bush administration. George Bush, when Vice-President, chaired President Reagan's Task Force on Regulatory Relief which fielded disputes between OMB and the Executive and, as President, Bush retained his predecessor's appraisal system.

(ii) Appraisals in Britain

In Britain the origins of general regulatory appraisal can be traced to Lord Young's work in the Cabinet Office in the mid-1980s where the 'Enterprise Unit' was set up to work on a

[8] McGarity, *Reinventing Rationality*, 22.

variety of regulatory issues. In 1985 Lord Young moved to the Department of Employment (DE) taking with him the Enterprise Unit and its dozen or so staff. The DE had taken over responsibility for small businesses from the Department of Trade and Industry (DTI) and the renamed Enterprise and Deregulation Unit (EDU) was concerned to reduce regulatory burdens on such businesses in accordance with proposals set out in the DTI paper *Burdens on Business*.[9] Notably, steps were taken to establish a central task force to scrutinize departmental regulations and to assess the compliance costs imposed by new controls. The procedures introduced were influenced by practice at the OMB, indeed, the head of the EDU visited Washington for a period to study the operation of Executive Order 12291. Thus departments were instructed to establish their own deregulation units so as to carry out compliance cost assessments (CCAs) of 'all proposed regulations which could affect business' for which they had responsibility. These CCAs were to be submitted to the EDU for scrutiny.

The British system thus differed from that used in the USA by placing emphasis on quantifying compliance costs rather than effecting a balancing of costs and benefits. Moreover, when the White Paper *Building Business, Not Barriers*[10] was produced in May 1986 it was clear that the EDU had been created to represent not the public but a narrower set of interests: 'The EDU acts in some sense as a proxy for the voice of business within Whitehall and considers departments' proposals from the viewpoint of business.'[11]

The current British appraisal system is operated from within the DTI by the (renamed) Deregulation Unit (DU). There is a minister responsible for deregulation in each regulatory department and fifteen Departmental Deregulation Units (DDUs) have been established. The work of the DU is steered by an advisory panel of business persons.

The DTI produced guides to compliance cost assessment in 1990 and 1992.[12] These make it clear that the objectives of

[9] DTI, *Burdens on Business* (1985). [10] Cmnd 9794 (1986). [11] Ibid.
[12] DTI, *Counting the Cost to Business* (1990), and DTI, *Checking the Cost to Business: A Guide to Compliance Cost Assessment* (1992).

the CCA strategy are to inform ministers before decisions are taken of the costs to business of complying with new regulations and to encourage business to produce accurate estimates of compliance costs. All papers for Cabinet and Cabinet committees now have to spell out compliance costs under highly inclusive conditions set out in the 1988 White Paper *Releasing Enterprise*[13] which states: 'Departments are to compile CCAs for every proposed regulation that could affect business.'

Responsibility for initiating a CCA rests with the originator of a proposal and the guidelines call for draft CCAs at the stage when draft proposals are circulated for discussion. Such draft CCAs are to be discussed with the business community during consultations, and departmental economists and accountants are to be involved in drawing up CCAs at the earliest stages. The DDU is to be given the opportunity to comment on draft CCAs up to the point when they are submitted to ministers.

The CCAs themselves must outline the purposes and expected benefits of the measure; list the business sectors involved; summarize total estimated compliance costs for all affected sectors; summarize total estimated compliance costs for a 'typical' business in the sectors principally concerned; describe how resultant costs may affect the competitive position of UK enterprises; show sources used and consultations conducted in the CCA; set out how compliance costs will be monitored and reviewed; and explain why any different approach capable of achieving the relevant objectives at lower cost was rejected. The CCA, however, was not intended to become a CBA. The 1992 Guide to CCAs states that benefits are to be described *briefly* (the Guide's emphasis) and points out that the case for the proposed measure will be more fully argued in other documents.

Compliance-cost assessments apart, CBAs have been used extensively in British departments for some time, especially in the areas of transport, urban development, education, defence, and health.[14] Thus the Department of Transport routinely

[13] Cm 512 (1988).

[14] See G. H. Peters, *Cost-Benefit Analysis and Public Expenditure* (1973).

carries out CBAs of proposed road safety regulations.[15] There are few published CBA studies, however, of systems of British regulation,[16] although the field of health and safety at work provides an exception on this front. The Robens Committee of 1972 published the first serious attempt to cost accidents, and subjecting all proposed health and safety requirements to economic assessment has for some time been standard practice in the HSE.[17]

2. Appraisals Appraised

Subjecting proposed rules to economic appraisal may involve a variety of techniques ranging from the use of full-scale CBAs to costings of compliance. (For the purposes of clarity in the following discussion it will be assumed that appraisals involve CBAs, but in drawing conclusions at the end of the chapter the variety of potential appraisal techniques will be returned to.) The proponents of economic appraisals put forward a series of claims which can be summarized under the Chapter 3 headings in the following terms.[18]

The Legislative Mandate. Appraisals enhance the pursuit of articulated policy goals by measuring regulatory alternatives against such goals.

Accountability. Appraisals subject rule-makers to an objective eye; they identify costs borne by society; they reveal policy judgements that might otherwise be hidden beneath a veneer of technical expertise and they avoid the pursuit of hidden agendas within a bureaucracy.

Due Process. Appraisals keep the rule-making process open so that a wide variety of options and arguments can be considered; they encourage access to those arguing for alternative regulatory options; they avoid the premature adoption of

[15] See A. B. Saunders and D. A. Benson, *The Practical Application of Social Costing in Road Safety Policy Making* (1975).

[16] But see e.g. K. Hartley and A. Maynard, *The Costs and Benefits of Regulating New Developments in the UK Pharmaceutical Industry* (1982).

[17] Health and Safety Executive, *Plan of Work 1981–2* (1980).

[18] See J. F. Foster, 'An Advocate Role Model for Policy Analysis' (1980) 8 PSJ 958, 959; McGarity, *Reinventing Rationality*, 112–21.

particular solutions,[19] and they guide towards rational decision-making rather than political partisanship.

Expertise. Appraisals highlight the need to review goals; they draw attention to informational and research gaps; and they encourage experts to clarify their justifications for rules.

Efficiency. Appraisals make for more effective rule-making processes by insisting that policy-makers identify fresh options and search for alternatives that may impose fewer burdens on industry;[20] they encourage rational and effective rule-making by demanding that information on the advantages and disadvantages of policies be used in a coherent and systematic fashion; and they identify 'correct' decisions on an efficiency basis.

In responding to such claims it is clear that, when appraisals are operated within legal and practical constraints, a correspondingly extensive series of difficulties is encountered. The first of these concerns the compatibility of appraisals with rule-makers' legal mandates.

(i) The Legislative Mandate: Analysis and the Law

Where regulators are instructed by statute to pursue certain objectives they may, when rule-making, be prohibited by the law from sacrificing those objectives in pursuit of ends dictated by economic efficiency. The tension between statutory objectives and the dictates of a CBA will be greatest where the statute is strongly redistributive or promotes ends other than efficiency.

On this point Sunstein has argued that US regulatory statutes fall into three groups.[21] In the first are those that aim to promote efficiency, such as anti-trust statutes and those protecting against an 'unreasonable risk' to health and safety. Order 12291 procedures, he states, can clearly be applied to rules made in pursuit of such aims. The second group comprises statutes that do not aim at economic efficiency, for

[19] See G. Edwards and I. Sharkansky, *The Policy Predicament* (1981), 118; C. J. Diver, 'Policy-making Paradigms in Administrative Law' (1981) 95 Harv.LR 414, 415.

[20] A. Meltsner, *Policy Analysts in the Bureaucracy* (1976), 132–3. G. Eads, 'Harnessing Regulation: The Evolutionary Role of White House Oversight' (1981) *Regulation* 18.

[21] C. R. Sunstein, 'Cost Benefit and the Separation of Power' (1981) 23, Arizona LR 1267–82.

example civil rights legislation and laws to protect the environment notwithstanding the cost. Rules made under such statutes do not submit easily to economic analysis.[22] In the third group are statutes with mixed aims, as commonly found in the pollution field. CBA testing of subsequent rules depends on whether it can be argued that the statutory purpose has been subverted in making rules in pursuit of efficiency.

Under British law the unfettered statutory discretion should present few problems for proponents of CBA, but more complex issues arise with statutes that permit rules to be made to achieve specified ends where 'reasonably practicable'. Does this allow the passing of regulatory rules so as to maximize efficiency? *Edwards* v. *National Coal Board*[23] indicates that such a provision allows risks to be balanced against avoidance costs, but the case also suggests that the British courts are not inclined to allow issues to turn wholly on a CBA or to translate all relevant issues into economic terms. Such a judicial approach may be encouraged by two factors: the reluctance of lawyers fully to set out costs and benefits before judges; and a judicial inclination to decide issues according to legalistic criteria, applied through the language of distributional rights and justice rather than by reference to economic factors. Where a statute refers to efficiency or economic considerations, an important factor again is judicial reluctance to venture into economics. Thus in *Bromley LBC* v. *Greater London Council*[24] the 'Fare's Fair' case involving the GLC's proposal for reduced London public transport fares, the judges of the Court of Appeal and House of Lords showed little desire to examine the economic underpinnings of terms such as 'economic' or 'cost-effective'.

Finally, in the case of statutes giving power to be exercised in order to achieve certain objectives, irrespective of efficiency, real danger attends the use of subsequent rules on the basis of a CBA. Halsbury's *Laws of England* (4th edn., vol. 1, para. 60) states the position succinctly: 'If the purposes for which the

[22] See the Supreme Court's decision *American Textile Manufacturers Institute* v. *Donovan* 452 US 490 (1981). On scrutiny of the analysis see *Small Refiner Lead Phase-Down Task Force* v. *EPA* 705 F. 2d 506 (DC Cir. 1983).

[23] [1949] IKB 704; see also *Associated Dairies* v. *Hartley* [1979] IRLR 171.

[24] [1983] 1 AC 768.

power can legitimately be exercised are specified by statute, and those powers are construed as being exhaustive, an exercise of that power in order to achieve a different and collateral object will be pronounced invalid.'

Thus if a statute openly rules out economic factors ('rules shall be made to ensure the safety of passengers, regardless of cost'), exercising a rule-making power on the basis of a CBA would breach the principle summarized. Where a statute is silent on economic matters ('the safety of passengers shall be ensured') cases are liable to turn on the rule-maker's success in arguing either that the statute's objectives were not inconsistent with economic analysis or that the analysis had taken account of those objectives.

Proponents of regulatory analysis might argue that the purpose of such analysis is not to substitute efficiency ends for statutory objectives but to assess the costs and benefits associated with different objectives so that the most efficient routes to those objectives can be pursued. Such a response, however, presupposes that attributing emphasis to different objectives is a value-free exercise. As noted above, this cannot be assumed and the values analysts bring to bear may not be those that the legislature has chosen to pursue in a particular statute. If, moreover, a cynical view is taken and the process of analysis is seen as a means simply to reduce the flow of regulatory rules, there is more clearly a conflict between statutory ends and the purposes of such a process.

(ii) The Politics of Appraisal: Accountability, Due Process, and Expertise

Full-blown regulatory analysis tends to stress economic factors and those that are quantifiable to the detriment of 'softer' policy components. It can be argued, moreover, that the process of analysis obscures central policy issues in a web of economic technicalities and an arcane language. Thus Peter Self criticized the Roskill Commission's £1m. CBA of potential London airport sites:

> The main effect of the exercise was to translate policy issues into complicated technical analysis without thereby elucidating or resolving

those issues. The main use of cost-benefit analysis appears to be as a supporting argument for particular organizational or policy viewpoints.[25]

The process of analysis may thus mask policy-making and come between rule-makers and those being consulted. It may accordingly reduce accountability and the ability of affected parties to participate in the rule-making process. Decision-makers may use analyses as screens behind which to avoid public accountability and may use CBAs to rationalize policies arrived at on the basis of unarticulated grounds.

The notion that regulatory analysts operate in a value-free manner is fanciful. Analysts approach tasks with their own values, preconceptions, and favoured approaches to problems. They incline towards efficiency, wealth maximization, and the satisfaction of private preferences rather than distributional objectives or the values associated with procedural rights and collective or public goals. They are in a position to skew the rule-making process in the direction demanded by such a focus (e.g. by manipulating assumptions under a guise of objectivity) and the prevalence of imponderables in most regulatory rule-making endeavours makes it easy for analysts to narrow policy agendas or even to introduce and operate according to policies that are hidden and involve minimal levels of accountability.[26]

A diffusion of accountability may be another effect of analysis and this may weaken channels of oversight. Thus Bryner has argued in relation to political oversight in the United States: '[It] often obscures responsibility and reduces democratic accountability. It is not clear who will ultimately be responsible for agency decisions—OMB officials, federal judges, subcommittee staff members or agency officials'.[27] Where the overseeing body operates (as with OMB) largely by informal pressure and avoids commenting on rules in writing it is

[25] P. Self, *Administrative Theories*, 212. See also Bryner, *Bureaucratic Discretion*, 58–64; M. Green 'Cost-Benefit Analysis as a Mirage', in T. Clark, M. Kesten, and J. Miller (eds.), *Reforming Regulation* (1980).

[26] McGarity, *Reinventing Rationality*, 157–8.

[27] Bryner, *Bureaucratic Discretion*, 81.

especially difficult to determine respective responsibilities and so to hold to account.[28]

On the question of due process, one danger of analysis is that rights of fair participation will be devalued in so far as analysis offers privileged access into the policy-making or review processes to certain groups—notably to industry. The OMB has been criticized on this front[29] and, as noted above, the DTI's *Guide to Compliance Cost Assessment* makes it clear that CCAs are designed to provide just this—privileged business access. Such preferential treatment operates to the detriment of participation by other parties interested in regulatory rules—for instance those potential regulatory beneficiaries for whose protection regulation may have been introduced.

As for expertise, here again regulatory analysis may operate as a restraint. An accusation made of the OMB review is that it has employed analysis not so much as a means of objective rational scrutiny but in order to exert control over the substantive policies of regulators—as a method, for example, of giving preference to undisclosed goals or to one 'legitimate' regulatory objective rather than another.[30] Such a process, it can be argued, not merely detracts from the pursuit of the legislative mandate and diminishes accountability but also undermines the application of regulatory expertise.[31] The regulator may question the point of developing balanced regulatory rules only to see those rules reoriented through the analysis process.

(iii) Efficiency.

Will appraisals make for more efficient and effective rules? At first glance the cost-benefit testing of rules involves a sensible balancing of social costs and social benefits so as to choose the

[28] Bryner, *Bureaucratic Discretion*, 84; US General Accounting Office Report: *Improved Quality, Adequate Resources and Consistent Oversight Needed if Regulatory Analysis is to Help Control Costs of Regulation* (1982), 4.

[29] Bryner, *Bureaucratic Discretion*, 285–6.

[30] Ibid.

[31] It has been argued that oversight has 'undermined the Occupational Safety and Health Administration's autonomy and its ability to make rational health and safety policy . . . OSHA could not do the things it had to do if it was to establish itself as an effective, expert agency', see Noble, *Liberalism at Work*, 175.

policy that maximizes net social benefits.[32] It employs the measuring-rod of money and offers a precise, quantitative approach to regulatory decision-making—provided that each cost and benefit can be calculated in monetary terms. Unfortunately, however, economists differ on which costs and benefits are properly to be taken into account in CBAs and they diverge in their approaches to evaluation. Such differences affect calculations on the relative desirability of regulatory strategies and rules. CBAs, accordingly, do not hold out the prospect of clear-cut conclusions to regulatory problems. Difficulties concerning assumptions, valuations, and predictions are unavoidable[33] and such difficulties will tend to be greatest in the sphere of social regulation where effects are particularly uncertain and valuations (e.g. of life) are subject to dispute. A series of further problems is also encountered.

Distributional Impacts. CBAs are concerned with the efficient allocation of resources, not the distribution of resources. They look to maximize wealth, not divide it out in a particular or fair fashion. Regulatory decisions, however, do have winners and losers, their impacts affect different groups in varying ways. Distributional concerns may, indeed, provide the primary rationale for regulatory programmes such as price controls or those dealing with transportation and the environment. On such matters, however, CBAs offer little help. They tend to assume that a dollar or pound gain is of equal weight to whomsoever it accrues; that the present distribution of wealth is acceptable and that regulation or deregulation has an insignificant distributional effect. In reality, however, the way that people attribute value is a product, at least in part, of their wealth and to ignore this biases the CBA in favour of those who already possess economic power. There is, moreover, a contradiction involved in such use of CBAs—if regulation is justly needed this implies that the existing distribution of wealth is skewed and so it cannot at the same time be

[32] See generally D. W. Pearce, *Cost Benefit Analysis* (2nd edn. 1983); E. J. Mishan, *Cost Benefit Analysis* (2nd edn. 1982) and R. Layard and S. Glaister (eds.), *Cost-Benefit Analysis* (2nd edn. 1994).

[33] See Baldwin and Veljanovski, 'Regulation by Cost-Benefit Analysis', 54.

contended that the existing distribution is satisfactory for the purposes of a CBA. Regulation may, indeed, be chosen explicitly or implicitly as a means of redistributing wealth—a choice inconsistent with using CBA as a bench-mark for regulatory rules.

Data Constraints and Measurement. The problem of measurement is central to the CBA strategy. Identifying the impact of a rule is a difficult task. It is likely to involve predictions concerning the adaptive responses of those affected by a rule. Thus a rule demanding that workers be supplied with protective equipment (e.g. hard hats) may reduce certain kinds of accidents (e.g. head injuries) for a period but workers may adapt their working methods in a way that displaces hazards and results in an increase in other types of injury. Protection on one front may lead to recklessness on another and these effects may be difficult to anticipate and quantify.[34] CBA studies seldom take on board such adaptive responses and data on the effects of past legislation is rarely available and difficult to draw lessons from.

The impact of a rule will of course be affected by the procedures and strategies used in enforcing that rule. CBAs must accordingly make assumptions concerning enforcement activity, levels of compliance, and patterns of compliance. In reality CBAs tend to assume that compliance is full or is evenly spread across different sectors. Studies, however, show enforcement to be a complex and highly selective process that produces uneven patterns of compliance.[35] Economists, moreover, have made few attempts to model this process. If it is not known, for example, which sectors of industry will be most affected by a rule (the sectors that impose costs on society or those that do not) or whether accidents will be reduced by 10 per cent or 40 per cent then CBA testing will not be possible with any degree of precision.

[34] See e.g. S. Peltzman 'The Effects of Automobile Regulation' (1975) 83 JPE 677; W. K. Viscusi, 'The Impact of Occupational Safety and Health Regulation' (1979) 10 BJE 117.

[35] See e.g. K. Hawkins, *Environment and Enforcement: Regulation and the Social Definition of Pollution* (1984); B. Hutter, *The Reasonable Arm of the Law*; G. Richardson *et al.*, *Policing Pollution* (1980).

Quantifying the costs of rule-making, of enforcement, and of achieving compliance is a process beset with other difficulties. In the first place, problematic assumptions have to be made about what would happen in the absence of regulation (or under a method of implementing the rule other than that proposed). Compliance costing again involves variables relating to enforcement practices, compliance rates, shifted compliance costs, and double counting. The effects on industry may involve 'hidden' costs such as reductions in productivity and incentives, expenditure on responding to regulators (or on avoiding or evading regulation), and distortions in investment and production.

Not only the availability but the quality of data on compliance costs is problematic. McGarity thus comments on US experience:

> By far the most frequently cited impediment to regulatory analysis is the lack of adequate information. Because agency regulatory analysts rarely have sufficient time and resources to undertake original research, they are perforce limited to using existing off-the-shelf studies that are rarely up to the task . . . The net result is an analysis that is beset with guesswork and plagued by large uncertainties.[36]

Such data, moreover, is usually in the hands of industry, or has been commissioned by industry, and there are, accordingly, strong incentives to distort the figures. There is a political dimension to the problem since the stronger the lobbying power of an industrial group, the more it will tend to be favoured in the costing process. Not only that, but such a process tends to focus on those most directly affected, organized, and vocal. The interests of, and costs borne by, large numbers of unorganized or ill-represented individuals may be inadequately considered and, as a result, total social costs may be considerably underestimated. One response to this problem is to provide public funding for interest groups, as has been proposed in Canada,[37] but cost-cutting governments (those

[36] McGarity, *Reinventing Rationality*, 126–7; see also pp. 43, 72, 85, 87–8, 108, 126–32.

[37] Economic Council of Canada, *Interim Report: Responsible Regulation* (1979).

most likely to apply CBAs or compliance costing to rules) are unlikely to be inclined towards such funding.

Measuring benefits is also problematic, particularly in the sphere of social regulation, because of the absence of market-based data on the value of cleaner rivers or safer cars. Such benefits, accordingly, are readily the subject of speculation or manipulation. In valuing such benefits as human life, economists may differ by several orders of magnitude and figures may be selected either to pass or fail a CBA test. In the USA, arguments on the valuation of life have involved proposed figures ranging from $300,000 to $3.5m.[38] Even assuming economists can agree on valuations for certain benefits, it is arguable that a level of arbitrariness is involved in putting figures on such matters as life, the right to children, peace and quiet, good health, and other intangibles. Techniques exist that allow figures to be produced—for example it can be asked what people would be willing to pay to enjoy a lower risk of death—but it is questionable whether economic valuations should lead, rather than merely supplement, the policy choices implicit in rule-making.

In attempting to apply CBA tests, many intangibles will defy pricing because relevant data is unavailable. Order 12291 recognizes this by requiring non-quantifiable benefits to be described, but qualitative effects still have to be balanced against quantitative ones. The danger of the CBA process is that in purporting to offer quantitative guidelines it emphasizes 'hard' figures to the detriment of 'soft' factors. As has been noted elsewhere, this suggests that CBA will be weakest where the need for rational and effective regulation is greatest.[39]

Administering Appraisals. If proposed regulatory rules are to be scrutinized with any degree of rigour, a layer of government is required above the level of the agency or department promulgating the rule. Will this merely increase the weight of government bureaucracy being 'carried' by industry or will it help to

[38] McGarity, *Reinventing Rationality*, 275. On varying assumptions and policymaking in the US health and safety field see C. Noble, *Liberalism at Work* (1986), 112–15.

[39] See Baldwin and Veljanovski, 'Regulation by Cost-Benefit Analysis', 56.

streamline and render more effective the rule-making and regulatory processes?

As practised at present in the USA and in Britain, economic appraisals are operated by modest numbers of staff. The US Office of Management and Budget's Office of Information and Regulatory Affairs (OIRA) employs about forty professionals, the DTI's Deregulation Unit operates with about twenty specialists. (In addition there are the agency and departmental staff responsible for CBAs or compliance-cost assessments). The burdens of the scrutiny process are, however, also borne within the rule-making departments who have to prepare analyses for scrutiny. On the one hand, scrutiny can be expected to deter the making of clearly inefficient rules, on the other, it can be expected to increase the resource requirements for making a regulatory rule.

Analysis, moreover, is not cheap—an estimate has put the cost of the average US Regulatory Impact Analysis (RIA) at $100,000.[40] Where extra resources are not committed to departments or agencies for the purpose of conducting analyses (and they have not been in the USA),[41] there is a diversion of funds out of regulation into analysis. The problem for the administrator is that a cut in the resources available for regulation may be effected by this method and without reasoned justification. This leads to the criticism that analysis is better seen as a means of reducing regulatory activity, and burdens on industry, than as a way of improving the regulatory process.[42] The primary effect of analysis in the United States has thus been said to be a slowing down in the process of issuing new regulations.[43]

Thus, the claim that regulatory analysis allows a wide range of options to be considered in the rule-making process must itself be scrutinized. In so far as CBA testing resembles a

[40] US General Accounting Office, *Improved Quality, Adequate Resources and Consistent Oversight Needed if Regulatory Analysis is to Help Control Costs of Regulations* (1982).

[41] McGarity, *Reinventing Rationality*, 139.

[42] See Bryner, *Bureaucratic Discretion*, 83–4.

[43] See A. B. Morrison, 'OMB Interference with Agency Rulemaking: The Wrong Way to Write a Regulation', (1986) 99 Harv.LR 1059; C. De Muth and D. Ginsberg, 'White House Review of Agency Rulemaking', (1986) 99 Harv.LR 1075.

'comprehensively rational' approach to policy-making (which ideally lists all of the alternative strategies, determines all of the consequences attending these, and compares the array of consequences[44]), it is liable to questioning by those who doubt the feasibility of a comprehensive approach and incline more to a strategy of 'muddling through' or 'marginal incrementalism'.[45] Braybrooke and Lindblom thus note that the rational comprehensive model is deficient in eight respects in so far as it is insufficiently adapted to the following: man's limited problem-solving capacities; inadequacies of information; the costliness of analysis; failures in constructing a satisfactory evaluative method; the closeness of fact and value in policy-making; the openness of variables; the need for strategic sequences of analytical moves; the diverse forms in which the policy problems actually arise.[46]

Proponents of regulatory analysis may hold that their method allows a wide range of options to be explored before a solution is settled upon, but there are limits to a bureaucracy's capacity to investigate alternatives.[47] Such investigations may prejudice deadlines, they may be resisted by policy-makers inclined towards certain solutions, and top decision-makers have a limited capacity to consider widely-ranging options.[48] By the time a CBA is put in train options may have been narrowed by policy-makers and analysts may lack the special expertise required to make apparent to them the full range of regulatory possibilities. They may tend to adopt the route of least resistance by focusing their attention on appraising options already identified.

The accuracy of past appraisals is also difficult to establish.

[44] See H. Simon, *Administrative Behaviour*, 3rd edn. (1976), chs. 4 and 5. On CBA and rationality see P. Self, *Administrative Theories*, 34.

[45] C. E. Lindblom, 'The Science of Muddling Through' (1959) 19 PAR 24.

[46] D. Braybrooke and C. E. Lindblom, *A Strategy of Decision* (1963); see also C. Ham and M. Hill, *The Policy Process in the Modern State* (1984), ch. 5, esp. p. 80; C. Diver, 'Policymaking Paradigms in Administrative Law' (1981) 95 Harv.LR 393; Y. Dror, 'Muddling Through: "Science" or "Inertia"' (1964) 24 PAR 153; G. Smith and D. May, 'The Artificial Debate between Rationalist and Incrementalist Models of Decision-Making' (1980) PP 147.

[47] R. C. Crampton and R. K. Berg, 'On Leading a Horse to Water: NEPA and the Federal Bureaucracy' (1973) 71 Mich.LR 511, 531.

[48] McGarity, *Reinventing Rationality*, 126.

Feedback on previous CBAs is rare. McGarity notes that of the major US agencies he studied, only one undertook routine retrospective analysis of the predictions it made in relation to past rule-making endeavours.[49] The pressures of new work and current budgets, and a perception that measuring past performance might not enhance career prospects, are factors that hardly encourage the institution of such reviews. Nor does the lack of readily available information. Firms may be willing to go to some lengths to calculate compliance costs if there is a prospect of reducing the regulatory burdens they may face as a result of a proposed rule—they are less likely to commit resources merely to help evaluate the past performance of appraisers.

Delay is a particular administrative problem occasioned by CBA scrutinizing. Some regulatory actions have to be taken in response to problems or crises that call for a rapid response. This may rule out significant analysis. Any decision-maker, moreover, has to reconcile the needs for timely action and for quality of analysis. Such tensions are made more acute when resources are highly limited.

The single greatest administrative impediment to the effective analysis of rules has been said to be the resistance offered by the rule-making department or agency.[50] This may be due to a number of factors, for example: distrust of regulatory analysis and its techniques; commitment to established ways of responding to problems; or a perception that such analyses impede the compromises and bargains that have to be struck in bureaucratic and political life.

Departmental and agency staff, moreover, have their own interests and policy aims which may not always be seen in pure efficiency terms. These may be the products, *inter alia*, of statutory requirements, organizational traditions, personal objectives, or managerial interests. The danger is that where CBAs have to be satisfied, officials will treat such exercises as merely hurdles to be overcome by dressing up a proposed regulatory rule in pseudo-economic terms. Forces within the

[49] Ibid. 137. [50] Ibid., 160.

governmental process may accordingly thwart the CBA approach. A significant problem in the British context may be the British Civil Service with its emphasis on the generalist as policy-maker. In spite of the Fulton Committee's recommendations,[51] the administrative class has successfully resisted specialization and the teasing apart of economic and policy questions. Administrators making policy, especially at the higher levels, might be expected to resist demands that policy matters be handed over to professional economists to be translated into the language of CBA so that something passing for a 'correct' solution can be produced. Such administrators may fear, apart from anything else, that appraisals may produce both results that are politically difficult to handle and a form of policy argument that is foreign to their accustomed *modus operandi.*

Conclusions

How, then, does the economic appraisal technique score according to the bench-marks of legal mandate, accountability, due process, expertise, and efficiency?

Claims under the legislative mandate rationale are fraught. As has been seen, economic appraisals may not merely obscure the nature of the legislative mandate but may create a real conflict between the dictates of economic efficiency and the distributive concerns of statutes. Where such conflicts occur, issues of legality may arise. These issues can perhaps be overcome by using appraisals in a subsidiary role for evaluating statutorily-defined objectives and as guides to choosing the lowest cost means of securing objectives. What appraisals cannot do in a convincing manner is make distributional choices or selections between different statutory ends. These points apply as much to CCAs as CBAs.

Claims that economic analyses increase accountability are, we have seen, weakened by charges that they render issues less accessible and intelligible to potential scrutiny and they allow analysts to pursue hidden agendas in an unaccountable fashion.

[51] *Report of the Committee on the Civil Service* Cmnd 3638, (1968); see also P. Hennessy, *Whitehall* (1989), 190–208. Current Civil Service reforms may yet bear on this issue, however.

Although steps might be taken to open analysis processes up to public scrutiny, the feasibility of taking such steps has to be judged against time and resource constraints. In any event, new procedures to allow greater openness are unlikely to increase the accessibility of arguments that are couched in highly technical economic language. The British system of compliance-cost assessment operates as an internal review procedure, it offers little opportunity for external assessment of CCAs and, in its present form, can make only the weakest of claims under the accountability heading.

On due process and the fair treatment of those affected by rules, full-scale CBA testing again makes claims that are suspect. As we have seen, it provides participatory access in a highly selective manner and favours the opponents of regulatory rules. The British compliance-cost system is at least honest in this respect—it purports to be nothing more than a means of preferential access for those business interests who may suffer from the imposition of compliance costs. Were claims for support to be made on the basis that CCAs contribute to the fairness of processes for consulting those liable to be affected by rules, one might be sceptical indeed.

The expertise brought to bear on the rule-making process may also be prejudiced by analysis. It might be argued that costs, benefits, and alternative strategies stand to be dealt with more thoroughly under a system of economic appraisals, but in so far as appraisal diverts both resources and arguments away from statutorily-defined ends, substitutes economic for specialist or technical discussion, and operates as a mere impediment to rule-making, it detracts from the application of expertise. A compliance-cost assessment system may be more liable to criticism than a CBA scheme on this count since it pays less attention to estimations of benefits.

On the issue of efficiency, the testing of potential rules by use of CBAs might be expected to bring a gain in one respect—it is likely to increase the attention that rule-makers pay to the dictates of wealth maximization. If, however, efficiency is given a broader meaning and it is asked whether rules of a higher quality are likely to be produced by resort to analysis, there are a number of problems with the device. As we have seen, there are severe data constraints to be faced. Difficult judgements have to be made on enforcement, adaptive responses, 'hidden' regulatory costs, and the position that would have obtained in the absence of regulation. The quality of data available to appraisers is questionable as is the freedom of such data from bias. The assumptions made in placing figures on benefits are dubious as are those made in relation to the acceptability of the existing distribution of wealth. Whether CBAs can be administered efficiently is also a significant issue. A degree of bureaucratic resistance has to be anticipated, the limited feasibility of appraising alternatives has to be taken on board as do the costs to the administration of complying with the requirements of appraisers. Steps can be taken to improve information gathering and use (e.g. by consulting more broadly in the course of conducting analyses), but the problems noted are unlikely to disappear.

Does the British compliance-cost system offer a less problematic route to appraisal than the full-blown CBA method? Unfortunately it may yield the worst of two worlds. It attempts to quantify costs rather than benefits (assuming, as noted, that these will be argued out 'more fully in other documents'[52]). In doing so it does not avoid all the difficulties of cost quantification outlined above but it offers no means of balancing these against the benefits derived. It attempts to assess the price of the goods but offers no estimation of the value of the goods being paid for. On the one hand, such an approach might be seen as the policy-making equivalent of buying a pig in a poke, on the other it might be justified as a sensible attempt to cost proposals, one that avoids the pitfalls of benefit quantification. The latter justification may bravely be presented but a technique that describes each side of an equation according to a different method may be indulging in a practice that is (to use Dylan Thomas's phrase) 'like comparing Milton with Stilton'.

To return to the questions posed at the start of the chapter: is there a case for economic appraisals of rules? Is this so in spite of arguments for satisfying values other than efficiency?

[52] DTI Guide to Compliance Cost Assessment, item 1(3).

The combined answer must be that there is a role for appraisals to play in rule-making but that this must be a highly constrained one because of the need to satisfy non-efficiency values such as those associated with accountability, fairness, expertise, and the terms of statutory mandates. To give appraisals a central role in rule-making is to court the danger of pursuing efficiency to the exclusion of the other values noted. What can be done, however, is to use assessments of costs and benefits, not as part of a special review programme designed to impede regulation (as an end in itself) or in order to give industry's protests a special emphasis, but as an integral part of the policy-making process within the department or agency. To this end, the role of appraisals might be limited, and other values served, by adopting the following approaches:

- Appraisals should focus on questions set by policy-makers not by the appraisers themselves.
- Appraisals should look to the costs and benefits of 'live' proposals for rules. They should briefly note alternative methods of achieving set objectives but should not purport to offer a comprehensive review of options with a 'correct' solution.
- Appraisals should avoid spurious elaboration and levels of technicality that impede policy discussions.
- Assumptions on imponderables should be spelled out as should those on enforcement and adaptive responses.
- Particular groups or individuals should not be given preferential access to appraisal processes.
- Appraisals, and the information upon which they are based, should be openly disclosed as part of the rule-making process. Such documents should be available to the public and to the scrutinizing agents and committees of Parliament.
- The limitations of appraisals, in general, and of the particular appraisal, should be openly disclosed.
- The courts should continue to ensure that appraisals do not loom so large in the rule-making process as to constitute a resort to irrelevant considerations, or indeed do not themselves take into account irrelevant considerations.[53]

[53] See the test in *Wednesbury* [1948] 1 KB 223.

The key to using appraisals in rule-making is thus an acknowledgement of their limited potential and objectivity. In the real world, the legitimacy of the rule-making process can best be enhanced when the appraisers are clearly allocated a subsidiary rather than a supervisory role.

PART III

The European Dimension

8 Rules and the European Union

Using rules for the purposes of domestic government gives rise to a host of difficult issues, as has been seen in previous chapters. A further set of questions is posed by governing at the European level. There is an array of rule-types that can be employed in pursuit of Union[1] objectives and choosing between different kinds of rule requires that a number of judgements be made by European rule-makers and domestic officials. Such choices, in turn, give rise to questions of legitimacy.

This chapter looks at the variety of Community rules and their legal effects. It considers issues of rule selection and enforcement in the Community and assesses the legitimacy of Community rules when judged according to the bench-marks discussed in Chapter 3.

I: THE ARRAY OF EUROPEAN RULES

As with domestic governmental rules, it is possible to divide Community rules into those of primary, secondary, and tertiary type and attention here will again focus on secondary and tertiary rules.[2]

[1] The European Communities (Amendment) Act 1993 gives effect to the Maastricht Treaty—the Treaty on European Union (TEU)—in domestic legislation. This chapter accordingly follows present convention by referring to the 'Union' when speaking in the most general terms but to the 'Community' or 'EC' in the context of the legal system, legal provisions, rules and institutions other than the Council. On the 1993 Act see P. Beaumont, *European Communities (Amendment) Act 1993* (1993).

[2] See generally e.g. D. Lasok and J. Bridge, *Law and Institutions of the European Union*, 6th edn. (1994), ch. 5; S. Weatherill, *Cases and Materials on EEC Law* (1992), chs. 1–3, 16. This chapter is concerned with Community enacted law and accordingly does not discuss non-enacted Community law or international agreements as sources of Community law. Non-enacted Community law is made up of the 'general principles of law' or the 'common law' of the Community which has been adopted by the European Court. International agreements have been said to be an 'integral part of Community Law' in Case 181/73, *Haegeman* v. *Belgium* [1974] ECR 449; but the issues they raise go beyond the scope of this discussion.

1. Primary Rules

The founding Treaties with their Annexes, Protocols, and supplementing Treaties (e.g. the Single European Act 1986 and the Treaty on European Union 1992) form the basis of the Community legal order. From the United Kingdom viewpoint, a notion of delegation has been said best to describe the force of the Treaties: they apply because the European Communities Act 1972 and the European Communities (Amendment) Act 1993 incorporate them by reference so that powers were delegated to the Community to legislate for the United Kingdom.[3]

This perspective, of course, contrasts with that of the European Court of Justice (ECJ) which sees Community institutions as endowed with sovereign rights and Member States as having limited their sovereign rights.[4] What is plain is that Treaty provisions may confer enforceable rights upon individuals or Member States—that is they may be directly effective provided that they are clear and unambiguous, unconditional, and do not depend on further action by Community or Member State authorities.[5]

2. Secondary Rules

Second to Treaty provisions rank the law-making acts of the Community institutions. These acts derive their authority from the provisions of the Founding Treaties and their validity can be assessed by making reference to the Treaties. Three forms of obligatory act are provided for in Article 189 of the Treaty of Rome 1957 (as amended): Regulations, Directives, and Decisions.

(i) Regulations

Within the terms of Article 189 EC, Regulations are 'binding in their entirety' and are directly applicable in all Member

[3] See T. C. Hartley, *The Foundations of European Community Law*, 3rd edn. (1994), pt. III.
[4] Case 26/62, *Van Gend ën Loos* (1963) ECR 1.
[5] See e.g. A. Dashwood, 'The Principle of Direct Effect in European Community Law', (1978) 16 JCMS 229.

States. They thus create rights enforceable in court directly at national or Community level and have uniform effects across Member States, but they must derive authority from a specific Treaty provision.[6] Thus Regulations, like other measures, contain in their preambles references to relevant Treaty provisions and statements of objectives to be achieved.[7] Regulations that are defective either in substance or because an essential procedural requirement has been infringed may be declared invalid by the ECJ but they are presumed valid and effective until that point. Publication of Regulations is mandatory and the Official Journal of the Community is the vehicle provided. Whether or not an act is a Regulation is, however, not determined by the publicity or the form adopted. The ECJ has ruled that it is the content and nature rather than the form of the act that indicates its legal status.[8]

Regulations have automatic effect: they bind Member States and have legal force without the need for further domestic provisions. Indeed, employing domestic implementing measures runs counter to the Treaty where such measures jeopardize the simultaneity and uniformity of Regulations.[9] It follows that Member States are not free to implement Regulations in an incomplete or selective manner.[10] Regulations may be challenged directly before the ECJ by Member States, the Council, or the Commission under Article 173(1) EC and by individuals if of direct and individual concern to them (Article 173(2) EC).

Both the Council and the Commission may make Regulations, but they do so in carrying out different functions, and the validity of Regulations stands to be judged in accordance with the Treaty provisions governing the powers and functions of the two institutions.

[6] See Case 45/86, *EC Commission* v. *EC Council* [1987] ECR 1493.

[7] See e.g. Lasok and Bridge, *Law and Institutions of the EU*, ch. 5.

[8] See e.g. Case 250/81, *Greek Canners Assoc.* v. *EC Commission* [1982] ECR 3535.

[9] Case 39/72, *EC Commission* v. *Italy* [1973] ECR 101. A Regulation may, however, expressly require the Member State to take implementing action—see Case 231/78, EC *Commission* v. *UK* [1979] ECR 419.

[10] Case 231/78, *EC Commission* v. *UK* [1979] ECR 419.

(ii) Directives

Whereas a Regulation is 'binding in its entirety and is directly applicable' in Member States, a Directive is only binding 'as to the result to be achieved' and leaves to the Member State 'the choice of form and methods' (Article 189 EC). The Directive was thus intended by the framers of the Treaty to lay down objectives and it is arguable that there was no intention to make Directives directly effective.[11] The Directive can thus be seen not so much as a means of making uniform laws across Member States as of achieving the approximation, or harmonization, of laws in pursuit of common objectives.

As with Regulations, Directives have to be based on specific Treaty provisions to which they are subordinate and their validity will be judged by the ECJ. Directives are addressed to Member States, not individuals, and Member States are obliged legally to implement them by binding Acts—rather than by advisory circulars or mere administrative practices.[12] The Commission may enforce the duty to implement by resort to Article 169 EC; Member States can use Article 170 EC to enforce against each other, but private parties are given no such express power in the Treaty. Directives may emanate from either the Council or the Commission and it is usual for a time-limit for implementation to be imposed on Member States.

In the case of both Regulations and Directives, important

[11] See e.g. Hartley, *Foundations of European Community Law*, 210.

[12] See Case 160/82, *EC Commission* v. *Netherlands* [1984] 1 CMLR 230; EC *Commission* v. *Netherlands, Re Groundwater Directive* (1989) 1 CMLR 479. On the case for allowing implementation through collective agreements see A. Adinolfi, 'The Implementation of Social Policy Directives through Collective Agreements' (1988) 25 CMLR 291. Agreements are envisaged by Article 118b EC which states that the Commission shall endeavour to develop the dialogue between management and labour at the European level, which could 'lead to relations based on agreement'. This Article represents the product of the United Kingdom's veto of a more ambitious base for social policy measures—see E. Szyszczak, 'L'Espace Sociale Européen: Reality, Dreams, or Nightmare?' (1991) GYIL 284, 287. The Treaty on Political Union 1992, Social Policy Protocol, Articles 3 and 4, bolsters Article 118b in allowing the social dialogue to lead to contractual relations. See R. Nielsen and E. Szyszczak, *The Social Dimension of the European Community*, 2nd edn. (1993), ch. 7. On implementation by means of self-regulatory measures see E. Steyger, 'European Community Law and the Self-Regulatory Capacity of Society' (1993) 31 JCMS 171.

issues may arise concerning the particular Article that is the legal basis upon which the provision is presented.[13] Choice of legal basis may, *inter alia*, determine the role of the European Parliament in rule-making. The issue has arisen most notably in the field of environmental protection and has been considered by the ECJ in the *Titanium Dioxide Case*.[14] This case followed the Council's adopting a Directive on managing waste in the titanium oxide industry[15]. The Commission had proposed Article 100A EEC as the legal basis for the Directive on the ground that its objective was establishing the internal market. The Council changed the basis to Article 130S EEC, which was concerned with environmental protection. The significance for the European Parliament was clear: Article 100A EEC allowed the Council to act by qualified majority, but only when acting on a proposal produced by the Commission in co-operation with the European Parliament. Article 130S required unanimity in Council, but the Commission only had to consult the European Parliament.

In the *Titanium Dioxide Case* the Commission, supported by the Parliament, fought to avoid being sidelined by tactical choice of legal basis and sought the annulment of the Directive on the grounds that its true basis was Article 100A EEC. The ECJ ruled that choice of legal basis was a matter of law for it to decide, that Article 100A EEC was indeed the correct basis, and that the annulment would be ordered. In doing so, the ECJ indicated *inter alia* that (at least in finely balanced cases) it would favour the basis giving greater democratic input through strengthened parliamentary influence and that it would give

[13] See e.g. Bradley, 'The European Court and the Legal Basis of Community Legislation' (1988) 13 ELR 379; A. McGee and S. Weatherill, 'The Evolution of the Single Market: Harmonisation or Liberalisation?' (1990) 53 MLR 578; S. Crosby, 'The Single Market and the Rule of Law' (1991) 16 ELR 451; the chapter by J. Usher, in White and Smythe (eds.), *Current Issues in European and International Law* (1990); H. Sevenster, 'The Titanium Dioxide Case' (1991) 2 Utilities Law Revised 133; S. Weatherill, 'Regulating the Internal Market: Result Orientation in the House of Lords' (1992) 17 ELR 299.

[14] Case C-300/89 *Commission* v. *Council* [1992] ECR I-2867. See Sevenster, 'The Titanium Dioxide Case', and Somsen, 'Case C-300/69, *Commission* v. *Council (Titanium Dioxide)*' (1992) 29 CMLR 140. The issue also arose in 1993 in relation to the Working Hours Directive with the UK contesting its base.

[15] Directive 89/428, OJ 1989 L201/56.

priority to market-completing rather than to other policies. Some commentators may have sympathized with the ECJ's approach, but the need to clarify issues of basis has been expressed as have doubts concerning the conceptual framework used to discern whether measures are market-completing or environment-protecting.[16]

Although direct effect for Directives cannot be taken to have been intended by the Treaty's authors, the ECJ has ruled that after expiry of the time-limit for implementation, a Directive is capable of direct effect if sufficiently clear, unambiguous, and unconditional.[17] Thus individuals may rely on Directives to enforce rights based on Community law or to defend themselves against a State law that is at variance with the Directive. Directives can, accordingly, be used vertically by an individual against the State or institutions providing public services and exercising special powers under State control[18] but the ECJ has stated that they cannot be directly enforced horizontally, i.e. against private parties.[19] In *Marshall*[20] the ECJ ruled that Directives could only be directly enforced by an individual against the State or an organ of the State. The implications of State liability may, nevertheless, be considerable. The *Francovich*[21] ruling indicates that where an individual suffers damage through a Member State's failure to implement

[16] See e.g. Weatherill, 'Regulating the Internal Market', 311–13. for a view less sympathetic to the extended application of Article 100A EC see Crosby, 'The Single Market'.

[17] Case 41/74, *Van Duyn* v. *Home Office* (No.2) [1975] ECR 1337. On the direct effect of Directives see P. Morris, 'The Direct Effect of Directives: Some Recent Developments—The European Court' (1989) JBL 233; S. Prechel, 'Remedies after *Marshall*' (1990) 27 CMLR 451; J. Steiner 'Coming to Terms with EEC Directives' (1992) 55 MLR 215. E. Szyszczak, 'Sovereignty: Crisis, Compliance, Confusion, Complacency?' (1990) 15 ELR 480; S. Weatherill, *Cases and Materials*, ch. 3; G. Howells, 'European Directives: The Emerging Dilemmas' (1991) 54 MLR 456; G. de Burca, 'Giving Effect to European Community Directives' (1992) 55 MLR 215.

[18] See *Foster* v. *British Gas plc* [1991] 1 QB 405, 428 (ECJ); see also [1991] 2 AC 306.

[19] Though see the argument *infra* that *Marleasing* opens the prospect of horizontal direct effect for Directives.

[20] Case 152/84, *Marshall* v. *Southampton and South West Hampshire Area Health Authority (Teaching)* [1986] ECR 723; see de Burca, 'Giving Effect to EC Directives'; J. Coppel, 'Rights, Duties and the End of *Marshall*' (1994) 57 MLR 859.

[21] See Joined Cases C-6/90 and C-9/90, *Francovich* v. *Italian State* and *Bonifaci* v. *Italian State* [1992] IRLR 84. Discussed in A. Barav, 'Damages Against the State for Failure to Implement EC Directives' (1991) NLJ 1584. E. Szyszczak, 'European Community Law: New Remedies, New Directions' (1992) 55 MLR 690.

Community obligations, then an action in damages may avail against the State if the objective sought by the Directive involves the creation of individual rights, if the content of such rights is ascertainable from the Directive itself, and if the individual's losses and the State's breach of duty are causally linked.[22]

Directives also have indirect effects. The ECJ has held[23] that national courts must interpret national law in the light of the wording and purposes of Directives and has even indicated that this obligation arises as soon as the Directive has been adopted at Community level rather than on the expiry of any time-limit.[24] UK courts for some time restricted this interpretative obligation where the domestic measures were not specifically designed to implement EC law[25] but in *Marleasing* v. *La Commercial Internacional de Alimentacion SA*[26] the ECJ reasserted the obligation in the strongest terms. As de Burca has put it: '*Marleasing* appears as a rule requiring domestic courts to give effect to the provisions of Directives in actions between private parties, regardless of the terms of the national legislation which is being interpreted.'[27] As has been pointed out,[28] this may constitute an attempt by the ECJ to give horizontal direct effect to Directives.

(iii) Decisions

Under Article 189 EC, a Decision can be made by the Council or the Commission and is 'binding in its entirety upon those to whom it is addressed'. It thus differs from a Directive

[22] See Szyszczak, 'EC Law' 695. The ECJ has also ruled that where a limitation period on remedies is imposed by a Member State, that period will be scrutinized and will not start to run until proper implementation of the Directive: see Case C-208/90, *Emott* v. *Minister for State and Social Welfare* [1991] CMLR 894.

[23] Case 14/83, *Von Colson* v. *Land Nordrhein—Westfalen* [1984] ECR 1891.

[24] Case 80/86, *Officer Van Justitie* v. *Kolpinghuis Nijmegen* [1987] ECR 3969.

[25] See e.g. *Duke* v. *Reliance* [1988] AC 618; *Marshall* v. *Southampton and South West Hampshire Health Authority* (1991) ICR 136; *Finnegan* v. *Clowney Youth Training Programme Ltd* [1990] 2 AC 407. In *Webb* v. *Emo Air Cargo (UK) Ltd* [1993] 1 WLR 49 the House of Lords abandoned the *Duke* limitation and accepted *Marleasing*.

[26] Case C-106/89, unreported, 13 Nov. 1990.

[27] de Burca, 'Giving Effect to EC Directives', 233. For an expression of caution on *Marleasing*'s impact see N. Maltby, '*Marleasing*: What is All the Fuss About?' (1993) 109 LQR 301.

[28] Ibid. 231–4.

in leaving no discretion as to the manner of its implementation. It may be addressed to Member States, individuals, or corporations and has to be notified to the addressee whereupon it takes effect. As with Regulations and Directives, Decisions must be 'substantiated' with reference to a Treaty provision and, again, it is content and object rather than form that determines whether an act is a Decision as opposed to a Regulation or Directive.[29]

Decisions may be enforced by the Commission under Article 169 EC and, within the terms of Article 173 EC, may be judicially reviewed at the instance of Member States, the Council, the Commission, or individuals to whom the Decision is addressed or who have a direct and individual concern in a Decision. Not all Decisions are, however, legally binding. Binding Decisions are formal Acts made under Article 189 EC and complying with relevant procedural requirements. Non-binding Decisions are not formal acts of the institutions, they do not comply with Treaty requirements and are not liable to judicial control by the ECJ. They can be seen as executive, administrative, or political rather than as legal acts.[30]

3. Tertiary Rules

The tertiary rules, or 'soft laws' of the EC are increasingly important and are encountered in a number of guises.[31] Such rules may have legal as well as political effects. Prime examples of soft law are Recommendations and Opinions. These are dealt with in Article 189 EC's list of the powers of the Council and the Commission. Recommendations and Opinions are said to possess 'no binding force'. They can be seen as having a persuasive and constructive role in the formulation and execution of the policies of the Union. They cannot be cited as

[29] Cases 16–17/62, *Confédération Nationale des Producteurs de Fruits et Légumes* v. *EC Council* [1962] ECR 471.

[30] See e.g. Case 114/86 *UK* v. *EC Commission (re Lome 11 Service Contracts)* [1989] 1 CMLR 32.

[31] See e.g. K. C. Wellens and G. M. Borchardt, 'Soft Law in European Community Law' (1989) 14 ELR 267; F. Snyder, 'The Effectiveness of European Community Law: Institutions, Processes, Tools and Techniques' (1993) 56 MLR 19, 31–6.

sources of Community law but can be regarded as 'auxiliary elements of the law-making process of the Community',[32] or even as 'part of an evolution towards hard law'.[33]

Soft law provisions may not be directly effective but they can give rise to indirect legal effects. Thus in *Grimaldi* v. *Fond des Maladies Professionelles*[34] the ECJ ruled that a Commission Recommendation, although not binding, had to be taken into account when interpreting national law.

In addition to the non-binding Acts noted in Article 189 a number of other instruments may be used by Community institutions and Member States. Classifying by form[35] implies the inclusion of:

- Resolutions of the institutions or the Member States (or both) often drafted in the shape of binding acts.
- Declarations of the institutions or the Member States (or both) or of individual Member States.
- Programmes which indicate a future policy to be pursued by the institutions or Member States.
- Communiqués and conclusions of the institutions or of the Member States in which the result of a meeting is laid down.
- Decisions of the Representatives of the Member States governments meeting in Council.
- Deliberations, memoranda, guidelines, and other non-Treaty acts that result from Community processes.

Resolutions often indicate how a subject will be developed and these may have the nature of programmes. They may produce legally binding effects. Thus the Hague Resolution of 3 November 1986 was adopted by the Council and dealt with common fisheries policy. Annex VI required that Member States should seek Commission approval for proposed fish preservation measures and should consult the Commission at all stages. The European Court of Justice (ECJ) found that the

[32] See Lasok and Bridge, *Law and Institutions of the EU* ch. 5.

[33] Wellens and Borchardt, 'Soft Law in EC Law', 292.

[34] Case C-322/88 [1988] II ECR 4407. See Nielsen and Szyszczak, *The Social Dimension of the European Community* 163, 260.

[35] See Wellens and Borchardt, 'Soft Law in EC Law', 301.

UK was obliged not to take unilateral measures inconsistent with that Resolution[36] and that, like a Directive, the Resolution could found a defence for an individual charged with violating the UK legislation that had been passed in contravention of the resolution.[37]

In dealing with the Hague Resolution the ECJ referred to Article 5 EC which bears on the status of much soft law. This Article sets out the general principle that Member States must act co-operatively so as to fulfil not merely obligations that arise from the EC Treaty but also those arising from actions taken by the institutions. A Resolution (like any item of soft law) cannot be used to modify primary or secondary Community rules[38] but, as with the Hague Resolution, it may, when read with Article 5 EC, produce legal effects. Judging whether a Resolution will create legal effects may be problematic.

In contrast with its ruling on the Hague Resolution, the ECJ has treated certain Resolutions as mere expressions of political intention by Member States which could not be accompanied by legal effects.[39] More consistently with the approach taken to the Hague Resolution, however, some Resolutions of the European Parliament have been attributed with legal consequences.[40] As with domestic tertiary rules, it is necessary to refer to a number of factors and principles in attempting to predict such legal consequences. For its part, the ECJ will consider such matters as: the relevance of Treaty provisions in the area; the mode of publication of the instrument; the Community's competence in the area (as compared with that of the Member State); and the principles of legal certainty and legitimate expectations.

Even where soft law lacks legal effects, items such as Resolutions and Recommendations can make a subject a mat-

[36] Case 141/78, *France* v. *UK* [1979] ECR 2923.

[37] Case 269/75, *R* v. *Tymen* [1981] ECR 3079.

[38] Case 59/75, *Manqhera* [1976] ECR 91; Case 43/75, *Defrenne* [1976] ECR 455.

[39] See Case 90, 91/63, *Commission* v. *Luxembourg and Belgium* [1964] ECR 625; Case 9/73, *Schlüter* (1973) ECR 1135; Case 59/75, *Manghera* [1976] ECR 91.

[40] Case 230/81, *Luxembourg* v. *Parliament* [1983] ECR 255; Case 294/83, *Les Verts* (1986) ECR 1339; Case 34/86, EC *Council* v. *European Parliament* [1986] ECR 2155.

ter of Community concern and hence may remove it from the domestic jurisdiction of Member States.[41] Soft law can, furthermore, serve as a basis for national legislation. Thus, Article 3, paragraph 3, of the Act of Accession, United Kingdom, Denmark, and Ireland states that the new Member States shall observe the principles and guidelines deriving from Declarations, Resolutions, or other positions and shall take measures 'as may be necessary to ensure their implementation'. This Article does not turn soft law into hard law,[42] but it suggests that the ECJ will consider the Community character of each soft law item and it does not rule out the imposition of obligations through soft law.

Joint Declarations of the Institutions or of Member States are not treated as binding by the ECJ when determining the individual's legal position,[43] but they may be used to reinforce an interpretation of a legal text.[44] Where, however, the Declaration is unilateral or unpublished, the ECJ will not use it as a guide to interpretation.[45] The most celebrated Declaration is the Social Charter which was adopted as a 'Solemn Declaration' at the Strasbourg Summit of 1989 with the UK the only one of the twelve Member States refusing to endorse it.[46] From the UK Government's point of view, the Social Charter may be seen merely as a non-binding political statement of very limited legal significance. The ECJ might be expected to take a different approach, however, and treat it as a form of indirectly effective soft law that provides interpretative assistance in dealing with social policy legislation.

As with Resolutions and Declarations, the legal effects of programmes, deliberations, communiqués, decisions of Council and other memoranda, such as White Papers[47] and guidelines,

[41] See Case 22/70, *EC Commission* v. *EC Council* [1971] ECR 263 (the ERTA case).

[42] Case 44/84, *Hurd* v. *Jones* [1986] 46 CMLR 2/42.

[43] Case 342/82, *Commission* v. *Belgium* [1985] ECR 1861.

[44] See Wellens and Borchardt, 'Soft Law in EC Law', 307.

[45] Case 143/83, *Commission* v. *Denmark* [1986] 46 CMLR 1, 44.

[46] See Nielsen and Szyszczak, *Social Dimension of the EC*, 26–9, R. Hepple, 'The Implementation of the Community Charter of Fundamental Social Rights' (1990) 53 MLR 643; E. Vogel-Polsky, 'What Future is there for a Social Europe following the Strasbourg Summit?' (1990) 19 ILJ 65; P. Watson, 'The Community Social Charter' (1991) 28 CMLR 37.

[47] e. g. the White Paper, *Completing the Internal Market*, COM (85) 310 Final.

are by no means certain. Nor is the form of the soft law rule a reliable guide to its effects. The ECJ has made it clear that it will look to the contents and context of the rule in assessing it, rather than accept form at face value. What can be said of soft laws is that if, in spite of their nomenclature, they satisfy Treaty criteria for binding Community acts then they may both have legal effects and be liable to ECJ review. Thus the ECJ has ruled that binding acts must involve 'the exercise, upon the conclusion of an internal procedure laid down by law, of a power provided for by law which is intended to produce legal effects of such a nature as to affect adversely the interest of the applicant by modifying its legal position'.[48]

II: SELECTING RULES: ISSUES OF FORM AND DESIGN

Secondary and tertiary EC rules are made by the institutions of the EC/EU under Treaty authority and, in considering the tactics of rule-choice it is, therefore, the approach of those institutions rather than of Member States that is the focus here. An assessment of legislative tactics should also bear in mind two general distinctions to be seen in Community motivations. The first is between negative and positive legislative approaches.[49] Thus much Community law is aimed at suppressing behaviour inconsistent with Treaty objectives—it is negative or 'red light'[50] in nature and is amplified by rules forbidding the imposition of trade barriers or restrictions on free movement.[51] Another legal thrust is, however, positive ('green light') and echoes Article 2 EC's objective of *promoting* a harmonious development of economic activities. It is exemplified in rules designed to enable and encourage the development of a Single European Market.[52] The second broad distinction is between measures that are aimed principally at creating such a

[48] Case 22/70, *EC Commission* v. *EC Council. Re European Road Transport Agreement* [1971] ECR 263.

[49] See Weatherill, *Cases and Materials*, ch. 16, and Articles 2 and 3 EC.

[50] C. Harlow and R. Rawlings, *Law and Administration* (1984), chs. 1 and 2.

[51] See e.g. Articles 12, 30, 48, and 95 EC.

[52] See the discussion of the 'New Approach' *infra*, pp. 233–8.

Single European Market—that are based on a 'market-integrating' rationale, and measures whose primary focus lies on improving standards of protection for those living or working in the market. The latter can be termed the 'social protection' rationale.

Thinking on rule-choices is by no means static in the Community. An examination of approaches to rule-making reveals nothing more clearly than a process of development on the part of policy-makers and legislators. Nor are the issues faced by Community rule-makers necessarily confined to selecting the appropriate form or design of a measure. The question of legal base may give rise to at least three issues or choices: whether a market-integrating or social protection rationale is to be presented;[53] whether action is to require unanimity or a qualified majority in Council;[54] and whether the European Parliament is to be consulted on a proposal by the Commission or involved in a co-operative or conciliation and veto process.[55] As indicated above,[56] the ECJ treats issues of legal base as matters for it to decide and, accordingly, the makers of potential rules may feel some pressure to decide such question with an eye to legal as well as tactical considerations.

1. Secondary Rules

The main debates on form and design in Community secondary rule-making now centre on the use of Directives. It is on Directives, therefore, that this section will focus after noting the tactical issues associated with Regulations and Decisions. These two forms of act have in common their fully binding nature. Decisions are binding only upon those to whom they are addressed. They may, however, be addressed either to Member States, individuals, or corporations, and are thus of special utility when an individualized but legally binding action has to be taken. Regulations, in contrast, are of 'general

[53] Contrast, say, Articles 100A and 118A EC.

[54] Contrast, say, Articles 110S and 118A EC.

[55] Contrast, say, Articles 118A, and 100A EC.

[56] *Supra* p. 233, and Case C-300/89, *Commission* v. *Council* Judgment of 11 June 1991.

application' and 'directly applicable in all Member States' (Article 189). They are the most strongly integrating form of Community secondary legislation.[57] Where, therefore, the objective of the legislation is to impose a uniform rule, equally binding across Member States, the Regulation may be deemed appropriate. The advantages of Regulations over Directives are that Member State action is not called for, or a time-limit involved, before Regulations are enforceable; enforcement is more readily available to (and between) individuals since Regulations are horizontally as well as vertically effective; and Regulations supposedly give a higher level of integration since they do not rely on implementation by means of Member State legislation as is the case with Directives.

The last of these advantages is capable of overstatement. Although Regulations are in formal terms directly applicable, it may in fact only be possible to apply them after Member States have adopted the legislative, regulatory, administrative, and financial measures that are necessary to ensure their effective application. Such Member State action can be rendered necessary by imperfect drafting and one way to respond to the problem is for Council Regulations to delegate power to the Commission to make implementing Regulations. Where Member State action is required, however, practical uniformity is by no means assured. As Gaja *et al.* comment: 'The need for legislation on the part of Member States may arise although it has not been anticipated. In this case some Member States' courts or even certain public authorities may do their utmost to give the Regulation all its effects, while other courts or authorities may refrain from doing so.'[58]

Where action on the part of Member States is anticipated, either in the form of legislation or measures necessary for practical implementation, then the measure designed for this purpose is the Directive rather than the Regulation. The strongest case for using Regulations is based on the needs for uniformity and immediate binding effect, needs best met by Regulations

[57] See G. Gaja, P. Hay, and R. Rotunda, 'Legal Techniques for Integration', in M. Cappelletti *et al.* (eds.), *Integration Through Law* (1986), vol. 1, bk. 2.
[58] Ibid. 124.

that are sufficiently clear and precise as to require no further action or elucidation by Member States. In so far as Member States may, to Community advantage, play a positive role in implementing legislation and in so far as flexibility is required as to the means used by the Member States, then the case for Regulations diminishes and that for Directives grows.

The broad strength of Directives is, as indicated, that they are binding as to results yet Member States are given discretion to choose the form and method of enforcement. If a Community rule has to be applied through a number of different regulatory systems, organizations, and cultures (as in a field such as health and safety at work) the Directive device allows a degree of harmonization to take place while avoiding the unrealistic assumption that such national variations can be put to one side.

The extent to which Directives can be implemented evenly and effectively in Member States is perhaps the core problem facing those governing through Community secondary legislation.[59] Effective use of Directives demands not only that legal implementation occurs but also that practical implementation takes place. Evenness of implementation on both these fronts is necessary if distortions of competition are not to result from unequal regulation. Directives, moreover, generally seek to harmonize Member State actions yet tensions occur because harmonizing measures tend to a lesser or greater extent to involve dual aims: to integrate the market by freeing trade from restraints and to improve protections for those involved in or affected by the market.

(i) The New Approach to Directives

The Community has sought to manage such tensions by adjusting its use of Directives. The most significant development has been the move from the 'traditional' towards the 'new' approach to technical Directives.[60] The 'traditional'

[59] Ibid. 128. See also G. Ciavarini-Azzi, *The Implementation of EC Law by the Member States* (1985).

[60] See e.g. J. Pelkmans, 'The New Approach to Technical Harmonisation and Standardisation' (1986–7) 25 JCMS 249.

approach to harmonization prevailed in the Community until the mid-1980s. This strategy assumed that the problems arising from the existence of different regulatory systems in the Member States could only be tackled by harmonization in the form of uniform rules imposed by means of Directives.[61] Such harmonization has been said to have been marked by three main points.[62] First, harmonization was attempted only where necessary to counter such Member State rules as prejudiced the functioning of the Common Market. Second, unanimity in the Council was required. Third, Community law was not substituted for national law (as with a Regulation) but Directives made under Article 100 were used to dictate results whilst leaving form and means to Member State discretion.

Over the first two and a half decades of the Community's existence, legislators devoted attention to the production of a very limited number of Directives focusing on specific technical aspects of products. A serious problem, however, was that the output of national regulations vastly exceeded the output of 'aspect Directives' at Community level and the effect was not so much to reduce trade barriers as to slow down the rate of their increase.[63] Pelkmans has summarized the drawbacks of the traditional approach with the following list of points:[64]

(i) Time-consuming and cumbersome procedures were employed.
(ii) Excessive uniformity of rules was involved.
(iii) Unanimity was required by Article 100 EC so that Member States enjoyed a veto and action was difficult in sensitive areas.
(iv) There was a failure, except rarely, to develop a linkage between the harmonization of technical regulations and European standardization, which lead to wasteful duplication, useless inconsistencies, and lost time.

[61] See R. Dehousse, '1992 and Beyond: The Institutional Dimension of the Internal Market Programme' (1989) 1 LIEI 109.

[62] See D. Vignes, 'The Harmonisation of National Legislation and the EEC' (1990) 15 ELR 358.

[63] Pelkmans, 'New Approach', 251.

[64] Ibid.

(v) European harmonization and standardization procedures were slow relative to national regulation and standardization.
(vi) There was a neglect of the problems of certification and testing.
(vii) There was an incapacity to solve the 'third country problem'.[65]
(viii) Implementation problems were encountered in Member States.
(ix) There was a lack of political interest in harmonizing measures on the part of ministers.

These factors produced, by the early 1980s, what were said to be 'profound feelings of frustration and disappointment'.[66]

It was through the notion of mutual recognition that a response to such problems was to be devised. The catalyst was the decision in the *Cassis de Dijon*[67] case. The ECJ therein ruled that Member States might not prohibit for sale in their territory goods lawfully produced and marketed in another Member State even if the technical requirements applied to the products in question differed from those applicable to domestically produced goods. National regulations could take precedence over the principle of free movement only if necessary to satisfy 'mandatory requirements' such as effectiveness of fiscal supervision, protection of public health, fairness of commercial transactions, and protection of the consumer.

The principles established in *Cassis de Dijon* suggested that the traditional notion of harmonization was not the only way to remove trade barriers and, in its 1985 White Paper, the Commission argued that since the objectives of national legislation on protective issues were 'more often than not identical', the rules and controls developed to achieve such objectives should be recognized in all Member States.[68] That White

[65] The problem of providing for the free movement of goods in the Community while avoiding the risk that goods entering one Member State from a third country (a non-Member State) might pass to another Member State and subvert the system of controls operating in that Member State. See Articles 9, 10, and 115 EC; Weatherill and Beaumont, *EC Law*, 425–7.

[66] Ibid.

[67] Case 120/78, [1979] ECR 649; (1979) 3 CMLR 494.

[68] Commission of the EC, *Completing the Internal Market* COM (85) 310 Final.

Paper closely followed a Council Resolution approving a 'New Approach' to technical harmonization and standards which was based on the following four principles:[69]

(i) Legislative harmonization should be limited to adopting, by means of Directives based on Article 100 EC, essential safety requirements to which products should conform.

(ii) The task of drawing up technical specifications conforming to the essential requirements of the Directive should be entrusted to organizations competent in the relevant area.

(iii) These technical specifications should be voluntary, not mandatory.

(iv) National authorities should be obliged to recognize the presumptive conformity to essential requirements of products complying with harmonized standards.

The New Approach was thus intended to halt the proliferation of excessively technical, separate Directives for each product and to give producers the option of either producing in accordance with harmonized standards or demonstrating by another means that their products conformed with the essential requirements of the Directive. Directives under the New Approach were thus aimed at setting out broad performance standards rather than laying down detailed specifications.

The Commission's 1985 White Paper stressed that barriers created by different national product regulations and standards had a double-edged effect: 'they not only add extra costs, but they also distort production patterns, increase unit costs, increase stock holding costs, discourage business co-operation and fundamentally frustrate the creation of a common market'[70]

The White Paper went on to argue that a genuine common market could not be realized by 1992 if the traditional approach based on Article 100 EC, with its unanimity require-

[69] Council Resolution of 7 May 1985, A New Approach to Technical Harmonisation and Standards (1985) OJC 136/1. See especially Annex, 'Guidelines for a New Approach to Technical Harmonisation and Standards'. Repr. in Weatherill, *Cases and Materials*, 425.

[70] Ibid., para. 60.

ment, was adhered to. On the one hand, a strategy based totally on harmonization would be over-regulatory, time-consuming to implement, inflexible, and stifling of innovation; on the other hand, a strategy based on mutual recognition alone might produce a common trading market but might not encourage an expansion of the market reflecting the competitiveness that a continental-scale market could generate. The New Approach to harmonization would seek to realize the advantages of both systems by distinguishing areas where it was essential to harmonize from those capable of being left to mutual recognition and by adapting the four principles set out in the Council Resolution of 7 May 1985.

A number of advantages deriving from the New Approach have thus been anticipated.[71] The time consumed by rule-making stands to be reduced under the New Approach since the task of technical specification is delegated to standard-setting bodies. The excessive uniformity of rules is likely to be ameliorated by using Directives to combine uniformity of objectives with flexibility as to means. The unanimity requirement of the traditional approach has been amended with Article 100A (introduced by the Single European Act of 1986) which provides for qualified majority voting in the Council and constitutes a significant step in overcoming the resistance potentially forthcoming from a single country. Harmonization under the New Approach is linked directly to standardization, thus reducing duplication and inconsistencies. An increase in the tempo of European standardization relative to national standardization also stands to be expected of the New Approach because of the delegation of standard-setting.

As for international competitiveness, the New Approach may offer an advance in so far as it encourages the penetration of international markets by means of high quality standards. As Pelkmans has argued: 'Because specialization is becoming ever more refined, and scale effects in many cases form an important determinant of the export position, the quality approach offers a much better perspective, not only for industry and the consumer, but also for the economy as a whole.'[72]

[71] See Pelkmans, 'New Approach'. [72] Ibid. 260.

Standardization may thus encourage the growth of markets and make such markets possible. The New Approach may also reduce the workload on the Commission as highly detailed regulations become less necessary. Increased attention may then be paid to other trade-inhibiting problems.

At this point it should be noted that the New Approach has been developed primarily in relation to Articles 100 and 100A EC, measures that are directed at market integration. In relation to Directives based on the social protection rationale, there has been a separate but parallel strand of development, one that, again, moves away from wholesale reliance on highly detailed Directives. In this area, the major development has been the Framework Directive, a device whose operation can best be examined by looking at an example. One is readily provided in the field of health and safety regulation under Article 118A EC.

Article 118A instructed Member States to pay particular attention to encouraging improvements in the working environment as regards the health and safety of workers and to set as their objective 'the harmonization of conditions in this area, while maintaining the improvements made' (Article 118A (1)). In order to help achieve this objective, the Council was instructed to act by qualified majority on proposals from the Commission in co-operation with the European Parliament to 'adopt, by means of Directives, minimum requirements for gradual implementation having regard to the conditions and technical rules obtaining in each of the Member States' (Article 118A (2)).

The Commission issued a Third Action Programme on health and safety in 1987[73] and this was approved by the Council in December of that year.[74] A major advance in this programme came in June 1989 with the adoption of a Framework Directive for the Introduction of Measures to Encourage Improvements in Safety and Heath of Workers.[75]

[73] COM (87) Final.

[74] Council Resolution on Safety, Hygiene and Health at Work, 21 Dec. 1987 OJC 28/88.

[75] (89/91/EEC) OJL 183/89.

This has been described as a 'most radical measure',[76] the significance of which is noted by Nielsen and Szyszczak in the following terms :

> The adoption of this Directive marks a change in method on the part of the Community from adopting Directives concerning specific risks or specific sectors to adopting an overall Directive which is to apply alongside a number of individual Directives giving more details about the health and safety requirements concerning specific risks or sectors.[77]

The Framework Directive has now been followed by a series of more detailed 'daughter Directives' on specific risks.[78] The 'framework' approach adopted in this area also incorporates two further noteworthy features: it offers requirements for gradual implementation and it imposes 'minimum requirements' so that Member States are left free to improve on these standards with national measures offering better protection for workers. A Framework Directive was used in health and safety regulation because the Commission recognized the difficulties of harmonizing in a field where national laws and regulatory systems were highly divergent.[79] In strategy the Framework Directive resembles the Health and Safety at Work Act 1974 in so far as it lays down a set of broad duties for employers and employees while leaving detailed coverage of specific risks to other rules. Use of such a device echoes the New Approach to technical harmonization in that detailed Directives are not methods of first resort but are tools for selective use only.

The Framework Directive is thus an example of differentiated and flexible integration in so far as its terms do not

[76] See A. C. Neal, 'The European Framework Directive on the Health and Safety of Workers: Challenges for the United Kingdom' (1990) 6 IJCLLIR 80–117.

[77] Nielsen and Szyszczak, *Social Dimension of the EC*, 237. On health and safety regulation in Europe see R. Baldwin and T. C. Daintith, *Harmonization and Hazard: Regulating Workplace Health and Safety in the European Community* (1992).

[78] On e.g. use of machines and equipment, display screen loads and carcinogens and biological agents, see the Directives 89/654 EEC OJL 393/89; 89/655 EEC OJL 393/89; 89/656/EEC OJL 393/89; 90/269 EEC OJL 156/89; 90/270 EEC OJL 156/90; 90/394 EEC OJL 196/90; 90/679 EEC OJL 374/90.

[79] See Commission proposal for a Council Directive on the Introduction of Measures to Encourage Improvements in the Safety and Health of Workers at the Workplace' COM (88) 73 Final, p. 3.

assume uniformity, they allow implementation to be phased, and countenance stricter rules at the national level. Such flexibility is a conscious response to the problems of regulating disparate regimes (problems likely to grow as EC membership enlarges) but it is not one free from difficulty.[80] First, there is the problem of the level playing field and the need to have some commensurability of practical implementation (discussed below in dealing with enforcement). Second, the prospect of a 'two- (or more) speed Europe' may be of concern and arguments may turn on the obligation of those countries making advances most rapidly to help slower countries, for example with regional assistance. Such a prospect may, of course, not always be greeted negatively, as Harrop has indicated:

> A more variegated pattern of integration enables the more dynamic countries to press on ahead, acting as catalysts to new policy areas and providing a way of breaking the soul-destroying deadlock and paralysis of the EC . . . Perhaps the Single European Act with more use of majority voting will help to lay to rest a damaging split into two groups in the Community.[81]

Third, the technique of minimum harmonization is not uncontentious. On the one hand, it can be seen as an 'honourable means of reconciling' the needs of market integration with the protection of interests;[82] on the other, it may be viewed as a sign of the decreasing integrative force of Member States and 'an easy way to evade the inconvenient necessity of finding an agreement'.[83]

Both the New Approach to market-integrating Directives and the framework approach to protective Directives thus constitute attempts to effect difficult balances between the requirements of the free market and the needs of workers and

[80] See e.g. J Harrop, *The Political Economy of Integration in the EC* (1989) ECLJ 2; Weatherill, *Cases and Materials*, 436–40.
[81] Ibid. 189.
[82] K. Mortelmans, 'Minimum Harmonisation and Consumer Law' [1988] ECLJ 2, 5.
[83] K. Taschner, in L. Kramer, *EEC Consumer Law* (1986), para. 86, quoted in Weatherill, *Cases and Materials*, 440. See also J. Currall, 'Some Aspects of the Relation between Articles 30–36 and Article 100 of the EEC Treaty with a Closer Look at Optional Harmonisation' (1984) 4 YEL 169.

consumers. Too rigorous or uniform an approach to harmonization may adversely affect both competition within the market and the competitiveness of the market; too much flexibility can create resentment and threaten the level playing field of Europe; too much attention to freedom in the market may reduce standards to the level attainable by the poorest performer.[84] It remains to be seen whether the various models of Directive will produce regulatory regimes that can implement democratically-established mandates effectively and accountably, that are even-handed and respectful of due process rights, and that are amenable to the exercise of expertise.

(ii) Directives, Scope, and Subsidiarity

Success on the above fronts may turn to some extent on the Community's decisions as to the scope or inclusiveness of the regulatory regimes that it establishes. On this point, McGee and Weatherill[85] distinguish three Community strategies which involve respectively 'exhaustive regulation', 'partial regulation', and 'no regulation'. Exhaustive regulation employs Community legislation covering the entire field in question and excludes Member State competence. This does not mean, however, that an inflexible system of rules has to be created. The New Approach to technical harmonization establishes Community-wide performance standards and is exhaustive in depriving Member States of the ability to establish inconsistent rules, but because the content of essential requirements is left inexplicit, this avoids having a single rule set in stone. This is the approach covering such areas as toy safety, construction products, and machine safety.[86]

The New Approach can be seen as deregulatory, first, because it substitutes a single Community rule for large numbers of national rules and so reduces trade barriers, and second, because it permits a choice of methods capable of reflecting national approaches and preferences. On an optimistic view, it

[84] See O. Brouwer, 'Free Movement of Foodstuffs and Quality Requirements: Has the Commission got it Wrong?' (1988) 25 CMLR 237.

[85] A. McGee and S. Weatherill, 'The Evolution of the Single Market: Harmonisation or Liberalisation?' (1990) 53 MLR 578.

[86] Directives 88/378, 89/106, and 89/392.

is exhaustive regulation without undue restraint. Whether this involves an undue sacrifice of social protection to the needs of market integration is a residual concern.

Partial regulation does not demand that all Member States achieve the same results, it allows the adoption of different performance standards. Thus the Directive on Product Liability allows Member States to choose whether to include certain defences against liability in their legislation. The cause of such partiality is usually the opposition of some Member States to certain rules. The effect is that the Single Market principle is not fully realized. The case for partial regulation is that some limited progress is made towards market integration or social protection where exhaustive regulation would not be possible. A significant concern is that partial regulation sets a compromise in a legal mould and it may be difficult to move beyond that position at a later date.[87]

'No regulation' may take place at the European level where, as for example in the field of taxation, unanimous consent is required before action can take place and where political sensitivity on the topic is high in the Member States. European policy-makers may, however, take a decision not to regulate in an area in accordance with the principle of subsidiarity. It is the principle of subsidiarity, indeed, that has been held out by the British Prime Minister, John Major, as the key means of ensuring the acceptability of Community rules, most notably by preventing the encroachment of Community rules on the province of the British Parliament.[88] Thus, in the November 1992 Maastricht debate in the House of Commons,[89] Mr Major stated:

[87] McGee and Weatherill, 'The Evolution of the Single Market', 590–1.

[88] On subsidiarity see N. Emiliou, 'Subsidiarity: An Effective Barrier Against the Enterprises of Ambition?' (1992) 55 ELR 383; editorial comment (1990) , 27 CMLR 181; M. Wilke and H. Wallace, 'Subsidiarity: Approaches to Power-sharing in the European Community', RIIA Discussion Paper no. 27 (1990); cited in Weatherill, *Cases and Materials*, 449–52; D. Lasok, 'Subsidiarity and the Occupied Field' (1992) 142 NLJ 1228; A. G. Toth, 'The Principle of Subsidiarity in the Maastricht Treaty' (1992) 29 CMLR 1079; D. Z. Cass, 'The Word that Saves Maastricht?' (1992) 29 CMLR 1107; S. Weatherill, 'Subsidiarity and Responsibility' (1992) 6 University of Nottingham Research Papers in Law.

[89] HC Debs., vol. 213, cols. 283–376, 4 Nov.1992.

On subsidiarity, we secured the principle in the Maastrict treaty, and it is justiciable. In Lisbon we made progress and agreed that subsidiarity should be integrated in the work of the Community as a legally binding rule. In Birmingham we agreed a framework for specific decisions in Edinburgh. That framework provides for a clearer understanding of what Member States should do and what needs to be done by the Community. It provides for action by the Community only where Member States have given it the power to do so in the Treaties, and only where proper and necessary. It also provides for the lightest possible form of legislation, with maximum freedom for Member States on how best to achieve the Community's objectives.[90]

Can the subsidiarity principle deliver on these promises? Much depends on the meaning of subsidiarity, its scope and its enforceability. As to meaning, the notion of subsidiarity may incorporate a number of tests to determine when Community action is called for.

The 'effectiveness' test is encountered in Article 12 (2) of the European Parliament's 1984 Draft Treaty on European Union and states that the Union of Member States 'shall only act to carry out those tasks which may be undertaken more effectively in common than by the Member States action separately'.[91] This phrasing contrasts with the 'better attainment' test of Article 130 r(4) EC (introduced by the SEA and applying only to the area of environmental protection) which states that the Community shall act 'to the extent to which the objectives [assigned to it] can be attained better at Community level'.

A third test is based on the concept of a 'spillover'. Thus Article 12(2) of the draft Treaty on European Union noted the particular need for Community action in the case of tasks 'whose execution requires action by the Union because their dimensions or effects extend beyond national frontiers'. A fourth approach invokes a presumption in favour of performing junctions at the small-scale individual/private/local level

[90] HC Debs., vol. 213, col. 286, 4 Nov. 1992.
[91] Draft European Union Treaty of the European Parliament 1984 OJC 77/83.

rather than at the higher governmental level.[92] Finally, the 'absolute necessity' test calls for action at the Community level only if the required result can *only* be attained at Community level.[93]

The above tests make different assumptions concerning the values prioritized. The 'effectiveness' model applies what seems a pure efficiency test but the 'better attainment' wording is consistent with reference to such values as fairness and democratic accountability. The 'spillover' test looks to fairness between nations as well as effectiveness, and the presumptive and absolute necessity tests place faith in the democratic value of small-scale or minimal government.

The Maastrict Treaty provides that in creating an 'ever-closer union among the people of Europe' decisions are to be taken 'as closely as possible to the citizens[94]'. The objectives of the Union are to be achieved while respecting the principle of subsidiarity, which calls for Community action 'only if and in so far as the objectives of the proposed action cannot be sufficiently achieved by the Member State and can therefore, by reason of the scale or effects of the proposed action, be better achieved by the Community. Any action by the Community shall not go beyond what is necessary to achieve the objectives of this Treaty.'[95]

The tests to be applied are thus multiple. The better attainment test is combined with an absolute necessity criterion, reference is made to spillovers in looking to 'scale' considerations, and the issue of effectiveness is also taken on board.

The scope of the test is, however, modest. It applies, per

[92] See editorial note (1990) CMLR 182–3.

[93] See Emiliou, 'Subsidiarity', 401. The Report to the EEC Commission by the High-Level Group on the Operation of the Internal Market, *The Internal Market After 1992: Meeting the Challenge* (1992), Chairman Peter Sutherland, advocated (p. 23) a 'common-sense' approach to subsidiarity based on five criteria: *need* (Community action should only be taken when demonstrably better than national solutions); *effectiveness* (the most effective form of action should be chosen); *proportionality* (Community solutions should go no further than is necessary); *consistency* (confusion should be avoided); and *communication* (the merits of measures should be readily explicable to citizens and consumers).

[94] See Articles A(2) and B of the Treaty on European Union and Article 3(b) EC introduced by the TEU.

[95] Article 3(b) EC.

Article 3(b) EC, only to areas of concurrent competence. This means that where the Treaty gives the Community exclusive competence the subsidiarity principle will have no effect. John Major has argued that the subsidiarity principle will play an important political role in allocating competencies,[96] but others have viewed it as operating with only marginal effect. As far as rule-choice is concerned, subsidiarity may, nevertheless, be seen as influential even by those who doubt its value in allocating competence. Thus Peter Shore has said:

> subsidiarity is a fig leaf. It does not deal with the return of powers or the prevention of powers leaving the United Kingdom. It refers only to the methods by which the European State can implement its policies in the Member States—perhaps in a slightly more agreeable way. Perhaps the Regulations, to take an obvious example, might become Directives. Perhaps we could find some even looser form of Directive than has yet been legally defined. As long as the nation state does what the Community wants, then the forms that it adopts to do so can be a matter for subsidiarity.[97]

On enforceability, Mr Major has portrayed the principle of subsidiarity as 'justiciable'.[98] It might thus be though that a potent means of curtailing what Mr Major calls the 'creeping competence'[99] of the Community has been produced by establishing a principle that can be read with the Maastricht principle that the Community will have only the powers assigned to it by Treaty (with Member States holding residual powers). The Community will still possess implied powers,[100] however, and the intrinsic justiciability of the subsidiarity principle has been doubted. The House of Lords Select Committee on the European Communities has stated that it 'does not believe that subsidiarity can be used as a precise measure against which to judge legislation'.[101] The Select Committee on Foreign Affairs

[96] HC Debs., vol. 213, col. 286, 4 Nov. 1992. The Delors Report, *Economic and Monetary Union in the Economic Community* OOPEC Luxembourg (1989), made reference to subsidiarily in attributing competencies (para. 20).

[97] HC Debs., vol. 213, col. 334, 4 Nov. 1992.

[98] See Nigel Spearing MP, ibid., col. 364.

[99] HC Debs., vol. 213, col. 290, 4 Nov. 1992.

[100] See Emiliou, 'Subsidiarity', 400.

[101] Report on Economic and Monetary Union and Political Union, HL Session 1989/90, 27th Report (1990), p. 55.

has been advised by a series of lawyers that subsidiarity 'is not a precise legal concept'[102] and the Counsel to the Speaker has submitted to the Scrutiny Committee that subsidiarity is a principle of policy which is far too imprecise to have any clear legal effect.[103]

Even if subsidiarity is a matter upon which the ECJ is drawn to make rulings, it should not be assumed that the principle will operate to defend Member States' areas of competence from Community intrusion. Weatherill has argued that the 'defensive' view of subsidiarity expressed by some British politicians since Maastricht is unlikely to find favour with the ECJ which is liable to be mindful of an array of provisions establishing Community regulatory capacity; to Member States' duties under Article 5 EC to co-operate in the integration and regulation of the Community market; and to its own emphasis on the responsibilities of national authorities to develop the Community legal structure.[104] It is inevitable, argues Weatherill, that the ECJ will be called upon to rule on the compatibility of Community acts with Article 3(b) EC, but it is highly unlikely that the ECJ will annul a Community measure for violation of Article 3(b) EC. So deep is the impact of the Community law of market integration and regulation that presently evolving institutional and constitutional processes are unlikely to be suddenly halted, still less reversed, by the ECJ according to some 'defensive' model of subsidiarity. Weatherill concludes of subsidiarity: 'it will not be used to demarcate national and Community competencies, for in very

[102] HC Debs., vol. 213, col. 331, 4 Nov. 1992 (David Howell). See also Wilke and Wallace, 'Subsidiarity'; House of Commons Foreign Affairs Committee, *The Operation of the Single European Act: Minutes of Evidence*, 17 Jan. 1990; the House of Lords Select Committee on the European Communities in its 17th Report: *Political Union: Law-Making Powers and Procedures*, Session 1990/1 (HL Paper 80), para. 57, stated that of all its witnesses, *only* the Foreign and Commonwealth Office favoured ECJ review on the basis of subsidiarity and the Select Committee concluded (paras. 90–1): 'to open up the possibility of annulment or revision of legislation by the European Court on such subjective grounds (as subsidiarity) would lead to immense confusion and uncertainty in Community law . . . we believe that it would be undesirable to give the European Court a power of such a sensitive political nature and of such uncertain effect.'

[103] Ibid. Emiliou suggests that where the ECJ cannot avoid dealing with subsidiarity, it should restrict itself to 'marginal review': 'Subsidiarity', 405.

[104] Weatherill, 'Subsidiarity and Responsibility'. For a Commission view see 'The Principle of Subsidiarity', Com. Doc. SEC (92) 1990, 27 Oct. 1992.

many areas of regulatory activity the Community's structure has gone far beyond such rigid division. Community membership confines States' capacity to pursue independent policies; Article 5 is a vivid expression of this general proposition.'[105]

The Edinburgh summit of December 1992 produced an agreement that dealt *inter alia* with subsidiarity but did little to render the concept precise. The summit emphasized three concepts as relevant in interpreting clauses of the Maastricht Treaty dealing with subsidiarity. First, that the Community can only act where given the power to do so by the Member States—'implying that national power is the rule and Community power the exception'. Second, that Community action should only take place 'where an objective can better be attained at the level of the Community', and, third, that Community actions should be the minimum necessary and the means chosen to enforce rulings at Community level 'should be proportional to the objective pursued'.[106] What Edinburgh accomplished can perhaps best be described as a *political* reaffirmation of the Community's preference for decision-making at national level where there is not a strong case for Community action.

As for enforcing subsidiarity principles in the ECJ, that court *may* be drawn into decisions on subsidiarity but some commentators have expressed severe doubts as to the ECJ's willingness[107] or suitability to rule on breaches of the subsidiarity principle.[108] Stress has been laid on the political nature of such issues; the potential threats to legal certainty of both Community and national legislation; the delays, occasioned by needless legal disputes, that might ensue; and the extent to which the ECJ would become involved in the day-to-day running of the Community.

[105] Ibid. 15; also Hartley, *Foundations of EC Law*, 162.

[106] *Guardian*, 14 Dec. 1992.

[107] In evidence to the House of Lords Select Committee on the European Communities, Professor John Usher has argued that the ECJ is likely to treat the subsidiarity principle as a political principle and non-justiciable—see House of Lords Select Committee on the European Communities, 17th Report, Q15.

[108] See Emilou, 'Subsidiarity', 402–3; House of Lords Select Committee on the European Communities, 17th Report, paras. 53, 122.

To some, the realistic view of subsidiarity is as 'a socio-political term, rather than a legal or constitutional principle'.[109] On this view, making subsidiarity work may, accordingly, depend not on its judicial enforcement, but on its being established and applied as an agreed political convention within the Community. As David Howell has argued,[110] new procedures may have to be established to ensure that Member State parliaments can monitor and police the observance of such a convention and this may demand that Member State parliaments have a say on proposals before they reach the legislative stage.

In summary, what does subsidiarity have to offer as a way of ensuring the acceptability of Community rules? If Weatherill is right, the potentially 'defensive' role of the principle may not be realized through ECJ decisions. Alternatively, subsidiarity may, if observed as a political convention, help to reduce the use of Community rules in circumstances where domestic rules would be more effective. It may instil a bias in favour of local rather than central controls and hence in favour of more accountable regulatory regimes. Against such sanguinity have to be balanced the problems of defining subsidiarity, of assessing its scope, and of enforcement. Additionally, there is the danger that subsidiarity may come to be seen in efficiency terms. This would mean that in allocating competencies, and in dealing with concurrent competencies, factors such as accountability and fairness might be neglected in the rush for effective forms of central control. What may, however console domestic rule-makers is that subsidiarity could encourage the use of forms of central regulation that allow Member States flexibility on choices of implementing rules.

2. Tertiary Rules

The rules of Community 'soft' law offer a less formal alternative to Regulations, Directives, and Decisions and may prove particularly attractive where there is resistance to secondary

[109] Wilke and Wallace, 'Subsidiarity', 4; House of Lords Select Committee on the European Communities, 17th Report, paras. 92, 122.

[110] HC Debs., vol. 213, col. 331, 4 Nov. 1992.

legislation. It may, indeed, be the case that informal Community action proves feasible where secondary legislation would be politically impossible. Thus the Social Charter was able be given the indeterminate legal status of a 'Solemn Declaration' in spite of the UK's refusing to endorse it.[111] On some topics the need for soft law to play such a role is reduced in so far as the Single European Act introduced qualified majority voting in the Council with such measures on Articles 100A EC and 118A EC. There may, however, still be a case for using soft law in order to offer Member States a higher level of flexibility on implementation than would be offered even by a Directive.

An area where such reasoning might apply is that of industrial relations. In some Member States the prevalent policy in the industrial relations area is to have recourse to collective agreements rather than to statute law. If collective agreements are deemed not to constitute adequate measures for implementing Directives (as appears the case)[112] then considerable resistance to the introduction of Directives may be encountered. Adinolfi thus argues that one of the main reasons for the opposition of some Member States (including the UK) to the Community proposal on introducing information and consultation procedures at the workplace (the 'Vredeling proposal'[113]) lay in the fact that its implementation would require the adoption of legislative provisions in the labour relations field.[114] One possible solution to such problems is to adopt, in place of a Directive, a Recommendation—indeed this was the solution favoured by the UK in relation to the Vredeling proposal.[115]

Soft laws serve a number of broad purposes for Community policy-makers.[116] First, soft laws, laid down in recommendatory texts, may, as noted, have the effect of removing a subject

[111] On the Social Charter as soft law see Nielsen and Szyszczak; *Social Dimension of the EC*, 26–9.

[112] See A. Adinolfi, 'Implementation of Social Policy Directives'. On implementing Directives by means of self-regulatory rules see E. Steyger, 'European Community Law and the Self-Regulatory Capacity of Society' (1993) 31 JCMS 171.

[113] On the proposal see OJC 297/3 (1980); OJC 217/3 (1983).

[114] Adinolfi, 'Implementation of Social Policy Directives', 293.

[115] Ibid. 294 n. 6.

[116] See Wellens and Borchardt, 'Soft Law in EC Law', 281–2, 309–20; D Matthews and D. G. Mayes, *The Role of Soft Law in the Evolution of Rules for a Single European Market: The Case of Retailing* (1994).

area from the domestic jurisdiction of Member States and of making that area a matter for Community concern. Thus, in the ERTA case, the European Court indicated that this consequence occurred 'each time the Community, with a view to implementing a common policy envisaged by the Treaty, lays down common rules whatever form these may take'.[117] For Community legislators and policy-makers such a strategy may have the useful effect of 'chilling' work on new national regulatory rules and of rendering the national legislative frameworks static. It thus provides space within which Community measures can be devised.

Second, soft law can provide a justification for state conduct or a basis for national legislation. Thus, Article 3, paragraph 3 of the Act of Accession, United Kingdom, Denmark, and Ireland provides that the new Member States will observe the principles and guidelines deriving from declarations, resolutions, or other positions taken up and will take 'such measures as may be necessary to ensure their implementation'. Although the ECJ has indicated that this last sentence does not attach 'any additional legal effects' to such acts,[118] the legal consequences of items of soft law are left subject to examination on their particular merits. Member States, moreover, may take steps in implementation of 'soft law'. Wellens and Borchardt note the measures taken by Germany and the Netherlands, such as the making of a formal request to their business communities, in furtherance of the *Community Code of Conduct for Enterprises Having Affiliates, Subsidiaries or Agencies in South Africa.*[119]

Third, soft law may provide a framework for negotiation between Member States and may establish a programme for further action. Thus, in the health and safety field, three action programmes have been the subject of Council resolutions in 1978, 1984, and 1987[120] and these programmes have been used by the Commission to declare its intention to propose sets

[117] *Commission* v. *Council* (1971) ECR 263, Para 17, quoted in Wellens and Borchardt, 'Soft Law in EC Law', 310.

[118] Case 44/84, *Hurd* v. *Jones* [1986] 46 CMLR 2, 42.

[119] 20 Sept. 1977, EC Bulletin (1977), no. 9, p. 51.

[120] See Council Resolutions 29 June 1978 OJC 165 of 11 July 1978, p. 1; 27 Feb. 1984, OJC 67 of 8 Mar. 1984; 21 Dec. 1987, OJC 28 of 3 Feb. 1988.

of further rules in the form of Directives, Recommendations, and other measures.[121] A further notable example is provided by the Resolution of the Council and Representatives of Governments of Member States on the Realization of the Economic and Monetary Union of 1971.[122]

Fourth, soft law can create expectations that the conduct of states, organizations, and individuals will conform to its pronouncements. It has been argued,[123] for instance, that decisions of Community Summits, or Resolutions of the Council, can create legal effects through the notion of legitimate expectations. Fifth, during the process of promulgating secondary, or hard, legislation, soft law can give 'legitimacy, prohibitive or prescriptive effect'[124] to state conduct before the stage of full legality is reached. Thus, for some time after the taking of the 1971 Decision of the Council and the Representatives of Member States Governments on Realizing the Economical and Monetary Union, a Directive was not employed but soft law initiatives were jointly taken by Member States in partial realization of the 1971 Decision. Those actions would in Community law be considered legitimate as interim measures before full legal implementation of the Decision. Examples exist, moreover, of highly specific programmes being financed by Community sources and carried out on the basis of resolutions.[125]

Finally, soft law produced by an international organization may possess the character of binding or hard law within the internal system of the organization. Thus, declarations by the Community institutions as to such matters as fundamental rights[126] may, within the limits of the institutions' respective functions, have legally binding effects provided that they are intended as more than merely political commitments.[127]

To summarize, the devices constituting the soft law of the

[121] See Nielsen and Szyszczak, *Social Dimension of the EC*, 236.

[122] OJ 1971, C-28/1.

[123] See Wellens and Borchardt, 'Soft Law in EC Law', 313–14.

[124] Ibid.

[125] See the e.g. of the action programme for education cited ibid. 314.

[126] See the Joint Declaration of the European Parliament, Council and Commission on Fundamental Rights, 5 Apr. 1977, OJ 1977, C-103.

[127] See Cases 90–91/63, *Commission* v. *Luxembourg and Belgium* [1964] ECR 625; Case 9/73, *Schlüter* (1973) ECR 1135; Case 59/75, *Manghera* [1976] ECR 91.

Community are clearly treated by the institutions as having considerable utility, not least as a means of supplementing secondary legislation. They do produce legal effects in varying degrees and one of the difficulties associated with Community soft law (as with domestic soft law) is that of predicting such legal effects in the absence of rigorous guiding principles. Whether soft law, as a collective device, satisfies the broad range of desiderata discussed in Chapter 3 will be assessed in the final section of this chapter.

III. ENFORCING RULES IN THE EUROPEAN COMMUNITY

Community rules are intended, within the terms of the Treaties, to be both legally and practically implemented by Member States. Thus, Article 5 EC instructs Member States to take 'all appropriate measures, whether general or particular, to ensure fulfilment of the obligations arising out of this Treaty or resulting from action taken by the institutions of the Community. They shall facilitate the achievement of the Community's tasks.'[128] Nor is enforcement on the ground a peripheral issue. As a study by the European Institute of Public Administration (EIPA) put it :

> implementation of Community Law is not yet completed by elaborating, in whatever form, a national legal or administrative act in order to comply with the obligation to integrate Community acts into binding national legal measures. The actual application of Community Law by the national administrations determines the efficiency of this law and the degree of legal harmonization.[129]

Devising and selecting rules that can produce results effectively is difficult enough domestically[130] but the European Community context adds a further problem: that of producing

[128] Article 189 also makes Directives binding 'as to the result to be achieved'.

[129] H. Siedentopf and J. Ziller (eds.), *Making European Policies Work: The Implementation of Community Legislation in the Member States* (1988), i. 2; see also R. Dehousse, C. Joerges, G. Majone, F. Snyder, and M. Everson, *Europe after 1992: New Regulatory Strategies*, European University Institute Working Paper no. 92/31 (1992).

[130] See ch. 6 *supra.*; on rules and harmonization see Baldwin and Daintith, *Harmonization and Hazard.*

regulatory regimes that are even-handed across Member States as well as effective. There are clear tensions between evenness and effectiveness, particularly in the social sphere. Thus, as noted above, a desire to ensure *even* regulation might in practice lead to application of the standards that the poorest performers can meet. On the other hand, a scheme aiming to achieve the highest cumulative levels of protection might countenance the use of differential standards. Trade-offs between evenness and effectiveness have to be made. What is clear, moreover, is that unevenness in the playing field may not merely create resentment, it may also affect levels of governmental compliance-seeking and, in turn, compliance itself. The EIPA study noted that German entrepreneurs were significantly prejudiced due to uneven enforcement of social regulation on drivers' hours:[131] 'They feel abused and disadvantaged by the exercise of regulations that were intended to guarantee harmonization.'[132] Similarly, in the UK the regulations on drivers' hours were perceived to be more strictly enforced than elsewhere: 'The UK is said to be the only Member State which imprisons people for breaches of 543/69 and 1463/70 . . . in addition drivers can and do lose their licence for such breaches. It is strongly felt that there is no point in having common regulation throughout the EC unless there are also common enforcement policies and common penalties.'[133] The EIPA conclusion, based on its review of road transport regulation, was that, far from harmonizing competitive conditions across Member States, a very uneven effect had resulted *inter alia* from different enforcement practices and variations in penalties : 'This unequal treatment of offences is a source of friction between operators and enforcement agencies and a disincentive to enforce the regulations generally.'[134]

Nor did the EIPA study judge that such fears were ill-founded. It noted the existence of strong evidence that national governments were implementing Community Regulations in a manner that suited their domestic traditions and that they had exploited technical ambiguities and weaknesses in Commission

[131] Siedentopf and Ziller, *Making European Policies Work*, ii. 216.
[132] Ibid. ii. 228. [133] Ibid. ii. 700. [134] Ibid. ii. 114.

monitoring wherever possible.[135] Not only that but little reassurance could be derived from scrutiny of the Commission's general approach to enforcement: 'the Commission for the most part gives very little impression of wanting to check up on how exactly Community Directives are being applied and to what effect.'[136]

What, then, can be done to improve the evenness and effectiveness with which rules are applied in disparate regimes? What can be done to make clear the trade-offs that are made between evenness and efficiency?

An examination of Union-wide regulation in one particular sector, again that of health and safety at work, may provide some answers to these questions. This is a particularly useful area to examine since it involves Directives based on both market integrating and social protection rationales and it constitutes an attempt to regulate across a set of highly disparate regimes. This part of the chapter will accordingly outline in brief the development of rules for regulating health and safety at work in Europe; indicate the disparities encountered in Member States' schemes for regulating health and safety at work; consider how evenness and effectiveness of regulation can be assessed in Europe; and examine how the evenness and effectiveness of rule implementation can be improved.

1. The Development of Health and Safety Regulation in Europe[137]

As noted, the European Community has taken an interest in health and safety issues from both the social protection and market-integrating perspectives. Community social protection interest in the area began in the 1960s and a major develop-

[135] Siedentopf and Ziller, *Making European Policies Work*, i. 99.
[136] Ibid. ii. 665.
[137] This section owes much to work with Professor Terence Daintith under the auspices of the Institute for Advanced Legal Studies of London University, work reported in detail in Baldwin and Daintith *Harmonization and Hazard.* On developments in regulating health and safety in Europe see R. F. Eberlie, 'The New Health and Safety Legislation of the European Community' (1990) 19 ILJ 81; A. Neal, 'The European Framework Directive'; E. Szyszczak, '1992 and the Working Environment' (1991) IJSWFL 3; Nielsen and Szyszczak, *Social Dimension of the EC* ch. 6.

ment was the creation of a Community Advisory Committee on Safety, Hygiene and Health Protection at Work in 1974. This Committee played a major role in drawing up the Community's First Action Programme on safety and health at work which was adopted by Council Resolution in 1978.[138] The Commission initiated a programme with the agreement of both sides of industry and investigated such matters as the causes of occupational accidents and diseases. A Second Action Programme followed in 1984[139] and a series of Directives was produced dealing, in the main, with particular hazards. The Single European Act of 1986 came into force in 1987 and introduced Article 118A EC into the EC Treaty. This was significant in allowing the Council to act on a qualified majority on Commission health and safety at work proposals developed in co-operation with the European Parliament. Article 118A EC instructed Member States to encourage improvements especially in the working environment, as regards the health and safety of workers, and to 'set as their objective the harmonization of conditions in this area, while maintaining the improvements made'.[140] The Council was to act by passing Directives imposing 'minimum requirements for gradual implementation' having regard to the conditions in the Member States.

Subsequent actions followed closely. The Third Action Programme was produced in 1987[141] and in 1989 a Framework Directive was adopted.[142] The significance of the latter was its marking a change from the use of Directives on specific risks to the combination of an overall Directive laying down general duties with a number of daughter Directives concerning specific risks or sectors. The most noteworthy provision of the Framework Directive is Article 5(1) which imposes on employers an obligation to ensure the health and safety of workers in every respect related to work. The phrasing of this

[138] OJ 1978, C-165.

[139] OJ 1984, C-67.

[140] On the legal definition of the 'working environment' (or lack of this) see Szyszczak, 'L'Espace Sociale', 3–6.

[141] COM 87 (520) Final.

[142] Directive 89/391, OJ 1989 L183. See Nielsen and Szyszczak, *Social Dimension of the EC*, 237–42.

duty in absolute terms contrasts with the incorporation of reasonableness tests into the general duties of the UK Health and Safety at Work etc. Act 1974. By 1991 nine daughter Directives had been adopted on such topics as personal protective equipment, visual display screen units, and biological agents.[143] Such is the influence of the Community in this area that it has now become the main force in developing new legislation on health and safety at work—a fact recognized at Community and domestic levels.[144]

Community steps to complete the internal market have, as indicated, made their main impact on health and safety matters in so far as product standards have been regulated. Until the mid-1980s, technical requirements were largely harmonized by detailed Directives. The New Approach, as noted, is more selective, and distinguishes areas requiring harmonization from those where reliance can be placed on Member States' mutual recognition of national regulations and standards. Harmonization, nevertheless, is called for in the case of 'essential health and safety requirements'.[145] Product standards under the approach are developed by private European standard-setting organizations and these standards yield technical specifications giving manufacturers of products a presumptive conformity to essential requirements in Directives.

Article 100A EC is the legal base for a number of Directives relevant to health and safety and, like Article 118A EC, this endorses Council action by qualified majority. So far, topics such as toy safety, pressure vessels, machinery safety, and telecommunications terminal equipment have been made the subject of Article 100A EC New Approach Directives. Although the primary intention of Article 100A EC is to remove trade barriers, that Article states that Commission proposals on *inter alia* health and safety at work will 'take as a base a high level of protection'. Article 100A EC Directives may,

[143] See Directives 89/654, OJ 1989 L393; 89/655 OJ 1989 L393; 89/656 OJ 1989 L393; 90/269 OJ 1990 L156; 90/270, OJ 1990 L156 90/394 OJ 1990 L196; 90/679 OJ 1990 L374.

[144] See OJ 1978, 1. 165; Commission of the European Communities, *Social Europe* Vol. 2/90; HSC/E *Annual Report 1989–90*, p. vii.

[145] COM. 85 (310) Final, pp. 64, 68.

moreover, produce a degree of homogeneity of standards across Member States. Thus, for example, the machinery Directive of 1989 demands, as a precondition of free product movement, that machinery avoids producing dangerous gases, liquids, dust, vapours, or wastes. The effect of such a provision (at least where a manufacturer envisages exporting the machinery) is to 'design hazards out' of processes and to do so consistently throughout the Community.

2. Regulating Disparate Regimes

The combining of Article 118A EC with a Framework Directive and a series of daughter Directives was a conscious attempt to apply rules across hugely varying regulatory regimes.[146] An examination of six 'sample' Member States (UK, France, Italy, West Germany, Spain, and the Netherlands) indicates the nature of the regulatory differences confronting EC legislators.[147] These differences mainly concern governmental and legal systems; sanctions; legal standards and modes of proof; and enforcement processes.

Taking governmental and legal systems first, the Member States vary greatly concerning their placement of health and safety in the array of governmental responsibilities. Some states, such as the UK, Netherlands, Spain, and Italy, treat enforcement principally as a criminal matter and separate this from social insurance considerations. In contrast, inspecting functions are also entrusted to insurance authorities in Germany and France. The degree to which the social insurance system bears the costs of industrial accidents and diseases also varies. Similarly, injured parties may pursue civil actions independently of the social insurance or criminal law systems

[146] See EC Commission, 'Proposal for a Council Directive on the Introduction of Measures to Encourage Improvements in the Safety and Health of Workers at the Workplace' COM (88) 73 Final, 7 Mar. 1988. See also the Commission's 'Communication on its Programme concerning Safety, Hygiene and Health at Work' COM (87) 520 Final.

[147] See Baldwin and Daintith, *Harmonization and Hazard*. For other accounts see S. Campbell, *Labour Inspection in the European Community* (1986); D. Clubley, *Handbook of Labour Inspection in the European Community* (1990); HSE, *Workplace Health and Safety in Europe* (1991).

in a number of Member States but in Spain, civil and criminal liabilities are linked, and in Germany social security law rules out civil actions for personal injuries between employers and employees.

European rules on health and safety have to link into very different legal systems in the Union. Thus there exist common law and codified systems, those with and without written constitutions, those whose systems give international treaties higher status than ordinary domestic law and those which do not. As indicated above, the area of law covering health and safety may be the ordinary criminal law (as in the UK) but it may involve a complex combination of criminal, civil, labour, administrative, social security, and revenue law (as in Germany). Similarly, the use of the ordinary criminal courts in the UK contrasts with resort to a range of courts and tribunals in Germany. In other countries, such as France, the combination is almost as complex as in Germany.

The area of law covering health and safety is of special significance in assessing and comparing regulatory rigour since if civil actions loom large in the regulatory structure, access to civil justice affects rigour strongly. If, on the other hand, criminal law is central, the practices of public enforcers assume importance. The very institutions of enforcement are, however, dissimilar across the Community. In the UK a central agency has primary responsibility with local authority officers enforcing in particular sectors. In the Netherlands and Spain central ministry officials enforce, but in Italy local health authorities are given this function. German enforcement, in turn, is highly diffused, involving the police, state labour inspectorates, and the social security and insurance institutions. France differs again in placing special emphasis on the trade unions who have power to institute criminal proceedings.

The sanctions and remedies used in enforcement also range widely. Criminal sanctions are common across Member States, but civil actions vary more markedly in their role. As noted, some countries (e.g. Germany) rule out civil actions in favour of compensation provisions, some (e.g. Italy and Spain) link civil and criminal cases and some (e.g. the UK) offer no direct linkage. Civil actions generally play a small part in enforcement but administrative remedies are heavily employed in some countries (e.g. UK, Netherlands, Spain, and Germany) and less so in France where, as in Spain, employers may face legally endorsed withdrawals of labour on safety and health grounds.

Turning to legal standards and modes of proof, certain Member States, such as the UK and the Netherlands, rely on a mixture of broad principles of liability together with more detailed rules in specified areas. A contrasting emphasis on more precise rules is found in Germany. In the UK and in the Netherlands the general duties imposed on employers call on them to take such actions as are reasonable (bearing in mind costs and benefits) but there is no equivalent of reasonableness testing in Spain, Italy, Germany, and France. The last three Member States mentioned do, however, tend to read apparently absolute duties in context so that some degree of qualification is involved.

Proving liability again involves disparity of processes and standards. A first contrast is between the adversarial mode of proof seen in UK criminal cases and the inquisitorial processes of Continental systems. Second, health and safety issues are affected by a number of assumptions peculiar to particular Member States. In the UK, breach of an Approved Code of Practice (ACOP) will be taken as evidence of the relevant statutory breach unless statutory compliance is demonstrated. In Dutch and Italian civil cases, the plaintiff merely has to prove that an injury was caused by work in order to place the onus on the employer to show reasonableness. In Spain, inspectorate certifications of violation are presumed to be true. In Germany there is variation according to the relevant area of law, as in France.

As much as by the above factors, regulatory rigour is affected by the organization of enforcement processes in the Member States. Since, as seen above, very different organizations are involved in enforcement in the Community and since these possess very different philosophies, strategies, administrative arrangements, and resourcing levels, it is difficult to draw even crude comparisons of regulatory rigour. Effective regulation may be said to require, *inter alia*, appropriate levels of information, expertise, commitment and executive capability.[148] This list takes on board such factors as staff competence, organizational and legal effectiveness, vitality, soundness of strategy, clarity of objectives, managerial skill, political support, and resources. On all of these points, variations across Member States are not only likely to occur but will be almost impossible to quantify.

To summarize, any attempt to compare the rigour with which Member States ensure practical implementation of Community rules is fraught with difficulty even if it is assumed (perhaps rashly) that equivalence of *legal* implementation has occurred. To compare regimes by measuring the efforts, or inputs, of regulators is to analyse on the basis of a large number of imponderables.

3. Assessing Evenness and Effectiveness: The Problem of Measurement

Within the terms of the Treaty of Rome, 'evenness' of regulation means regulation that does not distort competition in the EC market.[149] Effectiveness in terms of Article 118A EC means improving safety and health conditions at work. How, though, should performance on these fundamental aims be measured across Member States?

Three general approaches to measurement can be considered: one focuses on regulatory inputs; a second scrutinizes likely compliance costs to industry; and a third compares outputs. The first of these can be dealt with quickly because the problems involved have already been discussed in looking at the multiplicity of variables that affect regulatory rigour. As noted, to seek to evaluate respective regulatory systems by

[148] See Ch. 6 *supra*, and e.g. Van Meter and Van Horn, 'The Policy Implementation Process: A Conceptual Framework' (1975) Administration and Society 445; P. Sabatier and D. Mazmanian, 'The Conditions of Effective Implementation' (1979) PA 481.

[149] See Article 3 EC.

comparing what their regulators do is to embark on a very suspect enterprise.

Comparing compliance costs in different countries might be effected by selecting a series of enterprises across Member States and assessing whether, for example, manufacturers of similar descriptions face similar regulatory costs in particular sectors and so compete on a level playing field.

Such an approach is, however, highly problematic for two main reasons. First, enterprises in different Member States may occupy different starting-points on the scale of health and safety protection. Some enterprises may have spent on hazard avoidance over a number of years and may have reached high levels of protection; others may not have done so. To compare compliance costs in present years thus prejudices Member States with higher existing performance levels. Second, assumptions have to be made concerning the equivalence, not merely of the standards of compliance being demanded by regulators, but also of the probabilities of those standards being applied. The difficulties associated with input measurement are accordingly likely to be encountered.

A version of the compliance costs approach may, however, facilitate measurement. This involves the imposition of a charge or fine for each injury—a charge that is fixed evenly across the Community. Such a device thus depends on creating equal incentives to protect. The attractiveness of the method is that whatever the Member State or sector, the employer has to pay a fixed charge for each category of injury. Employers who have attained high performance levels will thus be rewarded for past investment as accident rates will be lower in their workplaces. The regulator, moreover, does not have to calculate what constitutes a 'reasonable' standard or an appropriate incidence of accidents because all accidents will be charged. All the regulator needs to do is fix the marginal social cost for each class of injury or disease.

Such a system proves on second glance, however, to be problematic. Failures to avoid accidents would only be punished equally if charges were imposed with equal rigour throughout the Community (and input measurement problems arise again). Nor should it be assumed that the marginal social cost of each injury could be established without a great deal of debate. This process would assume contentiously, for instance, the existence of uniformities across the Community on such items as health care costs. The acceptability, moreover, of allowing the incidence of accidents to turn on levels of profitability, is also highly questionable both morally and in Community terms. The Community takes the view that certain standards and levels of protection are entitlements that should be protected rather than commodities for sale in the market. The Community's commitment to standards is clear from Article 118A which instructs the Council to adopt 'minimum requirements' on health and safety matters.

The third strategy noted, that of measuring outputs, is more hopeful, though still not without difficulties. This would look to levels of protection as realized in the place of work and to levels of injury and disease in 'equivalent' enterprises. Measuring levels of protection would involve scrutinizing 'sample' employers in different Member States and the making of judgements concerning levels of protection encountered. Selecting 'sample' employers would give rise to difficulties, as might the processes of comparing inspection levels, but these do not seem insuperable.

Comparing injury and disease statistics is more problematic. The Health and Safety Executive carried out such a comparison involving the UK, France, West Germany, Italy and Spain in 1991[150] and described this as a 'complex and difficult' task,[151] made more so by differences in employment structure and the way that Member States define and record accidents and diseases. The HSE report also makes it clear that a series of social and economic (rather than regulatory) influences bears upon the frequency of accidents and diseases, notably: the level of production and pace of work (e.g. amount of overtime); the capacity being made use of; the rate of economic growth; the size of the 'black economy' and its competitive effect on employers; the level of mechanization and level of

[150] HSE, *Workplace Health and Safety in Europe* (1991); see also OECD *Employment Outlook* (1989).

[151] HSE, *Workplace Health and Safety*, 7.

training in safe use of equipment; general training levels; managerial priorities (profit or safety?); the turnover rate of staff; the cost of replacing sick staff; and the social and political emphasis upon safety. Disentangling such factors so as to judge levels of regulatory rigour with reference to accident and disease statistics clearly demands significant expertise and resources. Which of the above factors should be included or excluded in assessing regulatory rigour is, furthermore, a matter liable to give rise to dispute.

Summarizing then, there are a number of ways in which the evenness and effectiveness of rule implementation can be measured in the Union. These means of measurement are, however, all beset with difficulties although the greatest potential for convincing analysis in the health and safety sector appears to be offered by a focus on outputs—perhaps combining scrutinies of levels of protection offered on the ground together with analyses of accident and disease rates.

4. Improving The Evenness And Effectiveness of Implementation

Devising a means of measuring evenness and effectiveness in rule implementation is necessary but not sufficient to secure that evenness and effectiveness is achieved. Practical steps have to also be taken. What, then, can be done to make harmonizing legislation work more effectively?[152]

A first condition of success is selection of the appropriate form of legislative rule. On this front we have seen that highly specific Regulations have generally given way to more flexible Directives for the reasons given in the Commission's 1985 White Paper.[153] The rationale behind the Framework Directive of 1989 was the need to underpin more detailed provisions by instructing Member States to impose broad duties on employers. This strategy has gained flexibility but, as seen,

[152] See F. Snyder, 'The Effectiveness of European Community Law: Institutions, Processes, Tools and Techniques' (1993) 56 MLR 19; Dehousse *et al.*, *Europe after 1992.*

[153] See also Council Resolution on a New Approach to Technical Harmonisation and Standards.

issues of commensurability loom large when such devices are used in regulation. Given disparities in Member State systems, such flexibility can be seen as unavoidable and consideration should thus turn to how implementation can best be managed on the ground within such a flexible system.

One way to aim for even and effective application is to opt for strong *central* control over practical implementation. At present, however, the central Community institutions are notable for their weakness on this front. This was a point made strongly in the report of the Florence Project which stressed the Community's lack of central enforcement agencies and its reliance on Member State organs for executive action.[154] Dehousse and co-authors have more recently referred to the 'regulatory deficit' within the Community and have pointed to the lack of such administrative competence and power at Community level as would allow direct enforcement of Decisions.[155]

Article 169 EC does give the Commission power to bring infringement proceedings in the European Court of Justice if a Member State fails to fulfil a Treaty obligation and has not complied with a Commission reasoned opinion. Although the Commission has intensified infringement actions in recent years,[156] there are limits to the potential of such strategies to secure effective and even rule implementation. The resources of the Commission and the ECJ are finite and the informational demands are severe. To monitor legal implementation is highly demanding; to scrutinize practical implementation on a routine basis would be well beyond the capacity of the Community central institutions.[157] Those institutions, moreover, have not shown themselves to be quick to look at effects on the ground. The Florence Project commented:

[154] See M. Cappelletti, M. Seccombe, and J. Weiler (eds.), *Integration Through Law* (1986) vol. i, book 2, pp. 60, 68, 86, 87, 307; R. Dehousse, 'Integration v. Regulation? On the Dynamics of Regulation in the European Community' (1992) 30 JCMS 383, 389–93.

[155] Dehousse *et al.*, *Europe after 1992*.

[156] Siendentopf and Ziller, *Making European Policies Work*, i. 146–7; Snyder, 'EC Law', 28–31.

[157] See Cappelletti *et al.*, *Integration Through Law*, i. ii. 67; Dehousse *et al. Europe after 1992*, 18.

The Commission and the Court appear to follow a rather formalistic course. The Commission has insisted that there should be some general Member State provisions implementing the Directive, and has not given weight to practice—possibly also in view of the difficulties in ascertaining practices. The Court has shared the Commission's attitude. The Court's case law appears to encourage Member States which may desire not to implement a Directive, to adopt some inadequate legislation and then to decline to take the additional measures which may be necessary in order to put it into practice.[158]

Snyder also has noted that the ECJ's primary aim has been limited in scope to enforcing the correct transposition of Directives into national law.[159]

Even if the Commission relies upon reasoned opinions and reports rather than on full-scale court actions, there are still informational difficulties, particularly if the regulatory inputs approach to measurement is adopted. The original Community Social Regulations required Member States to send implementation reports to the Commission for collation and onward reporting to the Council of Ministers—as does the Framework Directive, Article 18 (3). This system, however, has proved difficult to put to effective use in other areas.[160]

Member States cannot always be relied upon to supply full data on enforcement inputs or outputs and a lag of a number of years bedevils the use of such information. Added to this is the problem of putting this information into standardized form and of expending resources to cope with misleading, unintelligible, or incomplete information.[161] Such difficulties reduce the effect of Article 169 as a device for securing evenness of implementation. Article 170 provides that Member States may take other Member States to the Court of Justice for failure to fulfil Treaty obligations, but the matter must be brought before the Commission first for a reasoned opinion and thus the same

[158] Cappelletti *et al.*, *Integration Through Law*, i. II. 129; see also p. 86.

[159] Snyder, 'Effectiveness of EC Law', 50.

[160] For example, in relation to the implementation of road transport social legislation see Commission of the European Communities, Fourteenth Report on the Implementation of Council Regulation (EEC) no. 543/69 of 25 Mar. 1969, COM (87) 389 of 11 Sept. 1987.

[161] Siedentopf and Ziller, *Making European Policies Work*, 100–1 (A. Butt Philip).

problems that affect Article 169 are likely to apply to actions under Article 170.

In addition to resourcing and informational problems, other difficulties also impose limits on central enforcement of implementation by resort to Articles 169 and 170. Thus Paul Craig has pointed out that there is a potential conflict of interest involved in Commission enforcement actions.[162] The Commission may desire to enforce but it may also be motivated not to offend a Member State that is capable of responding to such enforcement activity by opposing Commission legislation in Council. A second point is that remedies are limited. Article 171 EC instructs errant Member States to comply with the decisions of the ECJ but if such a Member State continues to fail to implement Community law then there may be little further that can be done. Finally, central enforcement involves a potential public relations problem. Vigorous enforcement by the Commission may sit uneasily next to Community claims to be moving towards a closer social and political union. To rely on strong central enforcement based on Articles 169 and 170 may thus be to fly in the face of practicalities.

Operating without formal resort to law, the Commission might act to strengthen central control of practical implementation by co-ordinating levels of penalties and procedures for checks and inspections; establishing enforcement guidelines and criteria; consulting more widely and directly with enforcement agencies about implementation; assisting in the training (or even funding) of enforcers across Europe; acting as a source of information exchange and guidance for enforcers; and by auditing enforcement practices.[163] The Commission has argued that since consistency in the application of Community laws is important, and a function of administrative practices rather than legal rules, it is necessary to work towards consistency by 'exchanges of experience'. This, the Commission said was the approach adopted by the Matthews programme in the

[162] P. P. Craig 'Once Upon a Time in the West: Direct Effect and the Federalisation of EEC Law' (1992) 12 OJLS 453.

[163] Siedentopf and Ziller, *Making European Policies Work*, 189; Cappelletti *et al.*, *Integration Through Law*, iii. 225.

customs field and the Commission proposed to extend this into other areas covered by a body of Community rules.[164] The Sutherland Report of 1992 went further in dealing with the internal market and recommended that Member States should, as a matter of standard practice, draw up enforcement guidelines for groups of Directives with the Commission then co-ordinate these with overall guidance on such topics as working procedures for enforcement.[165]

Such co-ordinating functions might be given to specialized agencies.[166] In the opinion of some commentators[167] the time has come to extend the use of specialized regulatory agencies within Europe. Such bodies might prove useful in a number of respects by providing expertise in preparing, executing, evaluating, and co-ordinating Community policies; linking national administrations; informing decision-makers; supporting Member States with scarce administrative resources; monitoring implementation; organizing exchanges of experience; and helping to develop innovative responses. Agency structures might, moreover, offer greater stability and more systematic action than is possible when relying on Commission action and might, additionally, encourage public discourse on regulatory matters. Objections to the use of such agencies might, however, be made. Member States would be likely to resist with vigour the delegation to autonomous agencies of broad law-making and enforcement powers—the intrusion on Member State competence would be highly provocative. Nothing in the EC treaties, moreover, provides for such structures.

Agencies with relatively modest roles might, however, prove more acceptable. These might act as information-gatherers and co-ordinators of national regulatory actions rather than substitutes for this and would serve a limited role in encouraging consistent approaches to practical enforcement across the Union. A European Environment Agency commenced

[164] See Commission of the European Communities, Seventh Annual Report to the European Parliament on Commission Monitoring of the Application of Community Law—1989, OJ 1990, C-232/1 at C-232/7, quoted in Snyder, 'Effectiveness of EC Law', 39.

[165] Sutherland Report (1992), 18, 19, 57–9.

[166] See Dehousee *et al.*, *Europe after 1992*, 42, 47, 50–2.

[167] Ibid.

operations in late 1993 and a European Agency for Safety and Health at Work was established by Council Regulation in July 1994.[168] The latter agency, was set up mainly to collect and disseminate technical, scientific, and economic information in the Member States in order to pass this on to Community bodies, Member States, and interested parties and to promote exchanges of information in the field of safety and health at work. The Council declined to give the European Agency for Safety and Health at Work direct responsibility for monitoring practical enforcement or even for training national enforcement officials.[169]

An alternative to the agency is the Standing Committee of Experts as is established in the field of discrimination[170] and as Hepple has recommended for supervising implementation of the Community Charter of Fundamental Social Rights of Workers.[171] Such a Committee might carry out complaints, monitoring and reporting functions, but it would require substantial administrative support in order to monitor practical implementation properly—the kind of resourcing that would justify the establishment a free-standing agency.[172]

For its part, the Council is able to take initiatives on implementation. Thus it can adopt Resolutions calling on Member States to give full effect to legislative measures. An example is the Council Resolution on the Action Programme on the Environment of 1987[173] which stressed the need for action in particular priority areas. Resolutions can also be useful in setting down performance objectives, as seen in the energy field

[168] See OJ No L120/1, 7 May 1990 (establishing the European Environment Agency) and OJ No L216/1, 18 July 1994 (establishing the European Agency for Safety and Health at Work).

[169] For a full statement on the role of the agency see OJ No L216/1, 18 July 1994 Article 3. Some commentators do see the data collecting role of agencies as a first step in the direction of fully fledged regulatory agencies: see G. Majone, 'The European Community Between Social Policy and Social Regulation' (1993) 31 JCMS 153, 166.

[170] See M. Verwilghen, *Equality in Law Between Men and Women in the European Community* (1986), vols. i and ii.

[171] B. Hepple, 'The Implementation of the Community Charter of Fundamental Social Rights' (1990) 53 MLR 643.

[172] One danger is that a Standing Committee of Experts might simply duplicate the Commission's role; see Szyszczak, 'L'Espace Sociale', 305.

[173] See OJ 1987 C-289/3 and the Action Programmes on health and safety described *supra* p. 255.

where targets for energy saving and reducing dependence on specified fuels have been established. Thus Council Resolutions might set targets for reducing injuries and diseases. These might be combined with Commission or agency monitoring and the publication of results and recommendations.

A centralized approach to control poses general problems of resourcing which a decentralized system may be thought to avoid. Thus it has been argued[174] that the Community might rely on the direct applicability of Community law by placing more emphasis on Regulations rather than Directives and by facilitating enforcement proceedings before national courts by individuals, Member States or Community institutions—with resort, where necessary, to preliminary rulings of the ECJ under Article 177.[175] Such a strategy has, indeed, been emphasized by the Commission in relation to the Single Market programme, with Communications being used both to indicate the Commission view of the law and to encourage participants in the market to insist on their community rights.[176] *Francovich*, moreover, exemplifies the ECJ's increasing willingness to view individuals as potential enforcers of community legal rights.[177] A further reform argued for is to give interest groups powers to compel the Commission publicly to consider and give reasons for not pursuing infringement actions.[178] This step might be combined with appropriate increases in Commission funding and the granting to interest groups of more generous standing to challenge legislation under Article 173 EC and Commission refusals to act under Article 175 EC.

[174] See Siedentopf and Ziller, *Making European Policies Work*, i. 148; P. P. Craig, 'Once Upon a Time in the West: Direct Effect and the Federalisation of EEC Law' (1992) 12 OJLS 453.

[175] The Sutherland Report (*supra*, note 93) proposed that Directives might be used to harmonize national laws in the first instance, but that after a satisfactory degree of approximation had been achieved, such Directives might be converted into directly applicable Regulations (see pp. 12, 34).

[176] See generally J. Schwarze *et al.*, *The 1992 Challenge at National Level: Reports and Conference Proceedings 1990* (1990), which discusses the use of such Communications. The Sutherland Report recommends (p. 41) that, in giving advice the Commission and Member States should stress the advantages of taking disputes before national courts.

[177] Joined Cases C-6/90 and C-9/90, *Francovich and Bonfaci* v. *Italy* [1992] IRLR 84. See Szyszczak, 'EC Law'.

[178] See Nielsen and Szyszczak, *Social Dimension of the EC*, 269.

Such monitoring arrangements, involving resort to court actions, may seem to be a way to reduce resource problems for central institutions, but the ECJ's restricting itself in the main to matters of failure to transpose into law remains a problem and resourcing problems at the centre may not be reduced where the essence of the strategy employed is to instigate action by Community central institutions. In addition, resource constraints affecting individuals, pressure-groups, and enterprises may detract from such techniques.[179] There are considerable difficulties of information-gathering and expertise involved in mounting challenges to the enforcement practices of Member States other than one's own, and reliance on interest group actions may not fully overcome these difficulties. There is, in any event, a question whether the effectiveness of Community law can be adequately ensured by a system triggered by *ad hoc* claims by individuals or groups.[180]

As noted above, enforcing rules in the Union involves a number of difficulties that are also encountered at the Member State level. At both levels of government rule-makers have a propensity to legislate speculatively in the hope that rules will, in some mechanical way, change the world.[181] In response to this problem it could be argued that Europeans should demonstrate a healthy disrespect for programmes which are not linked to specific executory commitments and to adequate institutional arrangements and that policy-makers and Member States should establish arrangements for monitoring and co-ordinating enforcement *before* legislating.[182] It might be replied that when a Member State discusses the introduction of a Directive it does exactly this in considering its own obligation to adapt to EC rules. The problem, however, is that individual

[179] See Szyszczak, 'L'Espace Sociale', 303–7.

[180] See Snyder, 'Effectiveness of EC Law', 51–3, who also argued that there are limits to the ECJ's ability to rely on Article 5 to imply and impose practical duties on Member States. Further extension, says Snyder, may jeopardize the ECJ's own legitimacy without achieving social or political results, since adjudication cannot, beyond a point, substitute for political processes and tools without becoming counter-productive.

[181] See *supra* Ch. 6.

[182] R. Bieber, R. Dehousse, J. Pinder, and J. Weiler, 'Back to the Future: Policy Strategy and Tactics of the White Paper on the Creation of a Single European Market,' in R. Bieber *et al.*, (eds.), *92: One European Market* (1988).

Member States tend to focus on internal problems and their own needs to adapt[183] rather than on attending to issues of commensurability and effectiveness. The Community institutions, furthermore, are orientated towards making rules rather than enforcing them and tend to be slow to link the two processes. This tendency may be a product of pressures within the Community to sustain levels of rule production—to legislate and move on. It may also be encouraged by the division of responsibilities within the Community. As has been argued: 'The quantitative explosion of Community measures may be in part the consequence of a system in which the central legislative authority is not fully responsible for the execution of its own policies.'[184]

The harmonization of regulatory rules requires not only that a conceptual apparatus be developed for measuring the evenness and effectiveness of practical implementation but also the development of institutions and techniques for monitoring and co-ordinating such implementation. A review of experience with Community health and safety legislation indicates that much work needs to be done on both of these fronts. There is little reason, moreover, to think that Community rule-making in other spheres is exempt from such difficulties.

IV: ASSESSING EUROPEAN RULES

How, then, can European rules be attributed legitimacy according to the bench-marks set out in Chapter 3? In answering this question particular issues may be raised by certain kinds of rule but a number of general points should be made concerning Community secondary and tertiary rules.

1. The Legislative Mandate

Is it the case that Community secondary and tertiary rules can be justified by making reference to the primary legislation of a

[183] See J. Lodge (ed.), *The European Community and the Challenge of the Future* (1989), 303–12.

[184] Cappelletti *et al.*, *Integration Through Law*, i. II. 68.

democratically legitimate body? Such justificatory claims, we saw in Chapter 3, were difficult enough to make within a single state. In Europe the linkage is far more problematic. It may be argued, from the UK point of view, that the European Communities Act 1972 and the European Communities (Amendment) Act 1993 give effect to the Community Treaties as amended and thus lend legitimacy to rules made under Treaty authority. Such a process can, however, be viewed as an example of the broadest form of delegation of legislative power, so broad as to undermine claims that particular rules are endorsed as to their substance by the UK Parliament. The linkage, furthermore, between a Treaty term and, the content of, say, a Directive is often so loose as in itself to render claims weak. The Treaty term will often authorize action in an area (see e.g. Article 118A) but is likely to take the form of an extremely general instruction rather than that of a detailed blueprint for particular actions. In the normal course of Community legislative delegation it is the step from Treaty provision to secondary or tertiary rule that involves the major injection of substantive content. This step, however, is taken by the unelected Community institutions, the Council and the Commission, with the elected organ, the Parliament, playing a limited role. Thus Craig's comments on Community decision-making apply equally to Community rule-making: '[It] is imbued with less democratic legitimacy . . . as this phrase is normally understood, than in any other nation state which is governed by some species of democratic ordering.'[185]

The strands of democratic legitimation remain weak in relation to most secondary and tertiary Community rules.[186]

[185] P. P. Craig, *Public Law and Democracy in the United Kingdom and the United States of America* (1990), 228; see also Snyder, 'Effectiveness of EC Law', 24.

[186] On the democratic deficit in the Community generally see the section following and S. Williams, 'Sovereignty and Accountability in the European Community' (1990) 61 Pol.Q. 299; C. Harlow, 'A Community of Interests? Making the Most of European Law' (1992) 55 MLR 331; J. H. Kaiser, 'Limits to European Community Legislation', in J. Schwarze (ed.), *Legislation for Europe 1992* (1989). L. Hancher, '1992 and Accountability Gaps: The Transnuclear Scandal' (1990) 53 MLR 669, 678. K. Neunreither, 'The Democratic Deficit of the European Union: Towards Closer Cooperation between the European Parliament and the National Parliaments' (1994) 29 G&O 299; K. Featherstone, 'Jean Monnet and the "Democratic Deficit" in the European Union' (1994) 32 JCMS 149.

Where, as with legislation under the New Approach, extensive reference is made to standards made by private bodies, the lines of democratic authority are weaker still.

A truly legislating European Parliament might go some way to legitimate Community rules but, as has been pointed out, a number of real difficulties would be encountered were this route to be followed. First, the role of the Commission would have to be made subsidiary to that of an administration, perhaps one reflecting the political orientation of the group controlling Parliament. (It is doubtful whether a truly empowered legislature, directly elected, might coexist with a government formed from non-elected, nationally appointed individuals.)[187]

Second, tensions would arise between the aims and political positions of the Commission, the Council, and the newly empowered Parliament. Third, such a Parliament might become overloaded in attempting to devise, administer, and monitor complex legislation to be applied across a number of Member States with different social, cultural, and legal traditions. A particular problem should be noted in the case of tertiary rules and claims under the legislative mandate. The very indeterminacy surrounding the status and legal effects of these measures prejudices such claims.

2. Accountability and Control

The accountability/control rationale urges that rule-makers should be supported because they are strongly controlled or held to account by legitimate bodies. It might thus be argued that the European Parliament (EP) perhaps does not lay down mandates for rule-makers but it does offer a means of holding rule-makers to account.[188] The EP's committees shadow the major areas of Community activity; the chairs of EP committees sometimes participate in Council meetings; Council members and Commissioners are questioned by the EP; and there are regular question times in the EP. The Single European Act and the

[187] Craig, *Public Law and Democracy*, 232.

[188] See generally House of Lords Select Committee on the European Communities, 17th Report; J. Lodge, *The European Community*, ch. 3.

Treaty on European Union have also given the EP some legislative teeth. The Single European Act reduced the area of the Council veto, expanded areas in which the EP had to be consulted, and introduced the co-operation procedure into a number of sectors.[189] The Treaty on European Union most notably established the conciliation and veto procedure and created for the first time a veto for the EP on Community legislation.[190]

Against the view that the EP is a strong legitimating force, however, it has been contended, notably by Shirley Williams, that there is a democratic deficit within the Community constituted by 'the gap between the powers transferred to the Community level and the control of the elected Parliament over them'.[191] On the reasons for the democratic deficit, Williams stresses the following points:

- The EP's lack of authority to raise revenues.
- The marginal input of the EP on the initiation of proposals, which mainly emerge from the Commission in consultation with committees of experts.
- The role of civil servants, consultative committees, and COREPER, the Committee of Permanent Member States Representatives, in advising on the progress of a proposal to the Council and 'the importance of this bureaucratic structure in enhancing the influence of national governments and weakening that of the Commission and of Parliament itself'.[192]
- The failure of European parliamentarians and parties to develop resources and forms comparable to those of national bureaucrats and governmental politicians.

Juliet Lodge has pointed out that except on specific areas of budgetary control, EP Committees do not exercise oversight powers over the executive and she has stressed the essential difference between Community and domestic policy-making:

[189] Co-operation procedure enhances EP influence: *inter alia* it gives the EP more time to scrutinize by introducing a Second Reading and it provides that where the EP rejects a common position, unanimity rather than qualified majority is required in Council—a factor increasing EP leverage in the legislative process: see Weatherill and Beaumont, *EC Law*, 97–102.

[190] For matters covered by conciliation and veto procedure see Weatherill and Beaumont, *EC Law*, 103.

[191] Williams, 'Sovereignty and Accountability', 306.

[192] Ibid. 305.

'EC policy-making processes are largely dominated by bureaucracies and governments that provide little scope for parliamentary institutions (whether national parliaments or the EP) to intervene and to exercise roles traditionally believed to be the hallmarks of legislatures in liberal democratic politics.'[193]

More optimistically, a number of factors can be cited as evidence of greater democratic influence with the community. Thus Williams (who, in the article discussed, wrote in advance of the Treaty on European Union) does concede that the EP has learned to maximize its potential influence over Community decision-making processes (for example by using the threat of rejecting a common opinion at second reading, so as to gain pledges that the EP's amendments will be accepted).[194] Lodge has argued that the EP's legislative role has steadily strengthened since co-operation procedure was introduced by the Single European Act[195] and the Treaty on European Union has boosted the EP further. Deficiencies remain—the EP does not even have to be consulted on some topics but the new conciliation and veto procedure does, on certain issues (including Article 100a EC measures for establishing the internal market), give the last word to the EP. The Edinburgh summit of December 1992 also moved in the direction of greater openness in the Community with agreements: that there should be a greater onus not only on the Commission but also on national ministers and on Euro-MPs to demonstrate that action at Community level is required in order to respond to real needs in Member States; that some meetings of the Council of Ministers will be televised and voting records will be published; and that the EP and national parliaments will be encouraged to collaborate more in controlling decision-makers at both national and community level.[196]

193 Lodge, *The European Community*, 30.

194 Williams, 'Sovereignty and Accountability', 308; see also Lodge, *The European Community*, 58.

195 Lodge, *The European Community*, 76. See also Harlow, 'A Community of Interests', 334.

196 *Guardian*, 14 Dec. 1992: 'Leaders hope "transparency" will clear fears over Union', by John Palmer. These openings of process may prove undramatic: the Edinburgh agreement does not commit the Council to hold public debates on specific legislative proposals without a unanimous vote: see Weatherill and Beaumont, *EC Law*, 783–4.

It can be contended, also, that the EP is not the only source of democratic accountability within the Community. Thus Carol Harlow argues:

Implicit in the reasoning of Lodge and Williams is a view of Parliaments as the most legitimate, perhaps even the only truly democratic, representative institution. But this is to reduce citizenship . . . to the cross on a voting slip every five years. It leaves little space for regional and local politics.[197]

Harlow looks to non-parliamentary avenues of participation and argues that EC institutions are highly permeable to public opinion; that interest-representation in the Community is 'beginning to be both well understood and well organized'.[198] She points to the growth of lobbying within the Community; the escalating activities of cause and interest groups; the breadth of participation allowed through the Community committee structures; and to the influence exerted by the Green movement and by women's movements. For Carol Harlow the conclusion to be drawn is that Community patterns of interest-representation 'replicate national patterns with which we seem broadly comfortable'.[199]

She would not agree with Williams's statement that the Community languishes without citizen participation or that 'the man and woman in the European street feels uninvolved',[200] but Harlow does concede that: 'one of the strongest arguments for strengthening the input of the European Parliament into the lawmaking process is the heightened status and legitimacy which would ensue.'[201]

Perhaps, therefore, Harlow and Williams might be at one in urging that a good deal could be done to strengthen legitimation

[197] Harlow, 'A Community of Interests', 334.

[198] Ibid. 332; see also S. Mazey and J. J. Richardson, 'Interest Groups in the European Community', in J. J. Richardson (ed.), *Pressure Groups* (1993); *Lobbying in the European Community* (1993).

[199] 'Community of Interests', 350. Mazey and Richardson, 'Interest Groups', cite the opportunities for access that European policymaking offers to interest groups but caution that certain factors may make inputs difficult, e.g. uncertainties as to the scheduling of the policy agenda; competition between Member States as to the content of this agenda; and problems of locating the real source of policy decisions.

[200] Williams, 'Sovereignty and Accountability', 313.

[201] Harlow, 'Community of Interests', 350.

through accountability at the Community level. Although the Edinburgh summit emphasized the need for greater transparency in Community decision-making and promised more daylight on Council debates, commentators have already warned that Ministers are so reluctant to embarrass any of their Council colleagues that such steps as publishing the records of formal votes are unlikely to make the defence of national or vested interests more visible.[202] The absence of these or similar reforms emphasizes the democratic deficit that remains in the Community.

To some extent, of course, any weakness in legitimation at the Community level might be compensated for by strong accountability to Member State democratic institutions—notably to national parliaments. Here again, though, there are problems, notably the following:[203]

- National parliaments have little or no input into Commission proposals whereas governmental input through bureaucratic structures is considerable.
- Commission proposals are not within the jurisdiction of national parliaments and Council proceedings are closed. It is, therefore, very difficult for a parliament to exert influence over its own government's policies. Community involvement thus shifts power away from parliaments to governments.
- Parliaments can generally only criticize after the event and decisions cannot be reopened.
- In the UK no senior Minister in the House of Commons bears specific responsibility for Community affairs.
- Qualified majority voting has produced a real loss of control for national parliaments since a minister can be outvoted in the Council.

National parliaments, indeed, have no explicit role in the Community legislative process. Ministers in the Council are

[202] David Gardner, 'Bonfire of Brussels Laws fails to Catch Light', *Financial Times* 14 Dec. 1992.

[203] Williams, 'Sovereignty and Accountability', 302–3; J. Usher, evidence to House of Lords 17th Report, QQ6–7 (see also evidence of Sir Christopher Prout, MEP, at Q121). On cooperation between the European Parliament and national parliaments see Neunreither, 'The Democratic Deficit of the European Union'.

empowered to make decisions in their own right without any necessary prior consultation of national parliaments, and ministers have generally been reluctant to indicate the positions they have adopted in Council negotiations. It is, nevertheless, the case in the UK that, by virtue of a House of Commons resolution of 24 October 1990, a minister will not without special reasons consent to a Community legislative proposal in the Council until a debate on the issue has taken place on the floor of the House of Commons or in Standing Committee.[204]

The quality of UK scrutiny of European legislation by elected representatives depends largely on the activities of the House of Commons Select Committee on European Legislation and the two European Standing Committees of the House of Commons.[205] The Select Committee on European Legislation (SCEL) scrutinizes draft European legislation and draws the attention of the House of Commons to issues of importance.'[206] The rigour of SCEL review is a product, to some degree, of the information it receives from government departments and this has not always been full or timely. In June 1990 the SCEL noted the Government's acceptance that

[204] See HC Debs., col. 399, 24 Oct. 1990 (the undertaking has also been given in the House of Lords). The Government has accepted that where ministers invoke special reasons and agree to a proposal before a debate can be held, the debate shall be held within a sitting month of the agreement being given or the Select Committee on European Legislation's recommendation being made—see the Government's response to the 4th Report from the Select Committee on Procedure, Session 1988–9 (HC 622–1, 1988/9), Cm 1081, para. 38.

[205] The House of Lords European Communities Committee (ECC) contributes to parliamentary scrutiny by reporting on the more significant proposals emanating from the Community (28 reports were made in 1989–90). Around half of ECC reports are debated in the House of Lords; the remainder are for information. The ECC will also write to appropriate ministers on specific issues. The Report from the Select Committee on the Committee Work of the House—the Jellicoe Committee (House of Lords Paper 35–1, 1991/2)—stressed the value of the ECC's work, doubted the feasibility of the ECC considering draft proposals before these were sent to Council, said that the ECC could not extend its role to consider the practical implementation of Community legislation, and urged a more selective approach to scrutiny.

[206] In 1989 the Select Committee on Procedure examined the Scrutiny of European Legislation: see 4th Report from the Select Committee on Procedure, Session 1988/89, (HC 622–1, 1988–9). On scrutiny of Community legislation see T. St John N. Bates, 'The Scrutiny of European Secondary Legislation at Westminster' [1976] ELR 27; D. Coombes, 'Parliament and the European Community' in Walkland and Ryle (eds.), *The Commons Today* (1981); M. Kolinsky, 'Parliamentary Scrutiny of European Legislation' [1975] 10 G & O 46; see also HC Select Committee on European Legislation.

the House should be involved at an earlier stage in the Community legislative process.[207] The Government has accepted that general debates on Community developments should precede each twice yearly Heads of Government meeting but has been slow to respond to the proposal[208] that, in anticipation of such debates, lists of principal items on the summit agenda (with short statements on implications for the UK) should be laid before the House and its Committees.

The problem of gaining and processing sufficient information on complex Community issues, and of doing so to short parliamentary deadlines, is one that also affects the two European Standing Committees of the Commons. These Committees (ESCs) were set up in October 1990 and were the 'centrepiece' products of the Procedure Committee's Report on the Scrutiny of European Legislation of November 1989.[209] The purposes of establishing the ESCs and a new scrutiny procedure were threefold: to shift away from the pattern of late-night debates of Community legislation on the floor of the House towards consideration in Committee at a 'more civilized and productive' time of day; to allow more effective questioning of ministers on Community documents; and to create a body of expertise in the ESCs by appointing members for complete sessions.

The ESCs have lifted the main Community work off the floor of the house. Thus, in 1989, out of fifty-two scrutiny debates, thirty-seven were on the floor of the House, but by 1991 out of a total of thirty-seven, seven were on the floor and

[207] See 1st Special Report of the Select Committee on European Legislation: The Scrutiny of European Legislation, Session 1989/90, (HC 512, 1989–90), para. 7. On the need for early parliamentary input into the Community legislative process see Hansard Society, *Making the Law : The Report of the Hansard Society Commission on the Legislative Process* (1992), paras. 539–46.

[208] See 4th Report from the Select Committee on Procedure, Session 1988/9, (HC 622–1, 1988–9), and 1st Special Report of the Select Committee on European Legislation: The Scrutiny of European Legislation, Session 1989/90 (HC 512, 1989–90), para. 9.

[209] See 4th Report, (HC 622–1, 1988–9), cited above n. 208.

thirty in the ESCs. These Committees have provided useful opportunities for questioning ministers and, according to the Select Committee on Procedure: 'There is general agreement that the Committees have provided a more efficient forum both for sustained questioning and subsequent debate . . . the marked shift away from sterile late-night debates in the chamber represents a much more productive use of the House's time.'[210]

In spite of such general endorsement, however, concerns have been expressed on a number of fronts. A major issue is whether the ESCs can come fully to grips with Community legislative proposals without specialist advice, briefing, and assistance. The provision of such assistance has not been recommended by the Procedure Committee or the Government.[211] The reasoning is that the ESCs are extensions of the House of Commons *legislative* functions rather than Committees mimicking the *enquiry* functions of Select Committees.[212] A number of ESC members have, nevertheless, pointed to what one has called a 'dire need for specialist support'[213] and have argued that such support, either through provision of a secretariat of specialist clerks, specialist advisers, permanent researchers able to brief the ESCs, or other forms of 'staff capacity', are vital if members are to 'measure up to the task of dealing with the massive range of business coming from Brussels'.[214]

One proposed solution to the questions of Committee expertise and of overlaps between the ESCs and the Select Committees has been the suggestion that each departmentally related Select Committee should be empowered to establish a sub-committee to deal with European business.[215] The

[210] Select Committee on Procedure, 1st Report. Review of European Standing Committees, Session 1991/2, (HC 31, 1991–2), para. 52. This conclusion is echoed in the Government's response to the Procedure Committee's Review of European Standing Committees (HC 331, 1991–2), appendix.

[211] Ibid., paras. 23 and (v) respectively. [212] Ibid., (HC 31, 1991–2), para. 23.

[213] Ibid., appendix 5, Mrs Gwyneth Dinwoody, MP. See also appendices 1, 6, 9, 12, 24.

[214] Ibid., appendix 24, Dr Jack Cunningham.

[215] See Rt. Hon. Terence Higgins, MP, appendix 19 of Procedure Committee, 4th Report (1988–9) HC 622–1; also Alistair Burt, MP, appendix 3 of Procedure Committee, 1st Report (HC 31, 1991–2), para. 31.

Government has rejected such a notion and this leaves residual problems in relation to both issues.

Some difficulties have been encountered by ESC members in obtaining documents on time, but generally each member receives: a copy of the Community document under scrutiny; a copy of the relevant department's explanatory memorandum; a copy of the Scrutiny Committee's report on the relevant document; and a copy of any government supplementary memorandum. The workload of the two Committees is heavy and militates against comprehensive scrutiny of documentation. On this front it is noteworthy that the Procedure Committee recommended in 1989 that there be five ESCs with ten members each but the Government has established only two such ESCs, citing as a reason the low number of MPs available to serve. The range of subject areas covered by the two Committees is, as a result, extremely broad and there is evidence that ESC members feel that this makes it difficult for them to be properly briefed or to acquire the kind of expertise which they believe would make their scrutiny of European documents more effective.[216]

A final difficulty concerns the results of ESC scrutiny. The Procedure Committee recommended in 1991 that, on leaving the ESC, the motion for consideration on the floor of the House should the same as the resolution agreed by the ESC.[217] The Government rejected this view, stating that the motion on the floor should be in the name of the Government, in a form it could agree.[218] The Procedure Committee restated its 'flat disagreement' with the Government, arguing: 'If . . . the ESC's views can simply be cast aside, as is implicit in the Government's position, we believe that many ESC members will begin, quite understandably, to question whether their time and effort can continue to be justified.'[219]

In summary, the Select Committee on European Legislation and the ESCs offer valuable contributions to the scrutiny

[216] Ibid., (HC 31, 1991–2), appendix 11. [217] Ibid.

[218] Select Committee on Procedure, 3rd Report, Session 1991–2 (HC 331, 1991–2), Appendix, para. x.

[219] Ibid., para. 6.

process, but a number of procedural improvements, it seems, could still be made.[220] The perennial problem will remain that of dealing with a wide range of highly complex information to a tight schedule and with limited resources. The issue of specialist advice and assistance for the ESCs may well call for reconsideration in future years, as may the Government's ideas on the respective roles of the ESCs and the Select Committees.

What, though, does such scrutiny amount to? It involves the UK Parliament in a degree of oversight, it provides opportunities for questioning and for more informed debate, but nowhere in the Union can Member State parliaments amend Community legislation and, as indicated above, the approval of such Member State parliaments is not necessary for the promulgation of such legislation. It can hardly, therefore, be claimed by Community legislators that they are in any realistic sense controlled by national parliaments.

Legal control is exercised in the Union by the ECJ which can judicially review the legality of Regulations, Directives, and Decisions which are binding. It cannot formally assess the legality of non-binding measures such as Recommendations and Opinions, but, as was seen above, it will take decisions on whether to attribute legal effects to soft law measures (though a degree of uncertainty attends such attributions).[221] The ECJ does explain and interpret the Treaties and subordinate Community legislation. This allows the Court to lay down and define Community law but, resources apart, judicial review has limited potential to legitimate secondary and tertiary legislation. This is, first, because the Court focuses on the *legality* rather than the merits or substance of the rules; second, because its interventions are sporadic and dependent on actions by other institutions, Member States or individuals (who are subject to restrictions as to *locus standi*); and, third, because the breadth of legal discretion given to the Community institutions by the Treaty limits their liability to judicial review.

It is difficult to argue that accountability to the broad public

[220] Select Committee on Procedure, 3rd Report, Session 1991, 2 *loc.cit.*, para. 1.
[221] See Wellens and Borchardt, 'Soft Law in EC Law'.

by means of open government effectively compensates for the low level of Community legislators' accountability on the fronts discussed.[222] Thus the Hansard Society has pointed to a lack of openness in Community law-making and called for greater access and transparency—recommending, for example, that there should be available in all reference libraries in major cities, and on request from HMSO, 'a complete update of legislation emanating from Brussels both in draft forms and in that recently adopted'.[223] Similarly, in 1992, the Sutherland Report stressed that the Commission needed to introduce better procedures for making citizens aware of proposed legislation at an early stage; for disclosing background information; for discussing issues of subsidiarity; for ensuring transparency in the Community legislative process; and for achieving wide and effective consultation on Commission proposals.[224] Increasing the openness of Community legislative processes and making relevant materials more easily available might enhance accountability, but there are countervailing pressures operating within the Community. Thus, for instance, the Single European Act's introduction of action by qualified majority into new areas is a factor that increases the pace of Community legislation. This may allow the institutions to take actions more effectively but it does not enhance accountability.

3. Due Process

The third kind of claim that might be made on behalf of Community secondary and tertiary rules stresses that legislators pay heed to due process rights. This claim demands support on the basis that those affected by a rule have been treated fairly. In a Community of twelve Member States, fairness of treatment is a concern of special importance. As has been indicated in this chapter, however, the question of evenness in the legal and practical implementation of Community legislation is

[222] For calls for greater transparency in Community government see Snyder, 'Effectiveness of EC Law', 53–4; and the Sutherland Report, 11–12, 28–30.

[223] See Hansard Society Report, paras. 570–1.

[224] Sutherland Report, 28–30.

highly fraught. On this issue legitimacy claims cannot be founded with conviction.

Fairness to affected parties demands not merely that rules be applied evenly but that those parties have reasonable input into rule-making processes. As was noted in Chapter 3, however, a difficulty is deciding whose interests ought to be considered and the extent of such interests and consideration. The makers of Community secondary and tertiary rules engage in broadly based consultations and might seek to justify their activities accordingly.[225] As noted, however, the openness of Community law-making is subject to question and the post-Single European Act increase in legislative tempo will not strengthen claims to openness. The New Approach to technical harmonization poses, furthermore, some new problems of fairness:

> The difficulty lies in the privatization of the standards making process which supports the New Approach. For financial reasons it is likely that business will capture the standardization process within CEN.[226] Consumer organizations lack the resources to participate fully in CEN committee work; in any event, consumer representation is ill-organized and haphazard in several Member States. Enforcement authorities should have an input, but in the UK the parlous state of local authority funding makes this a vain hope. If standards making becomes the province of business alone, the balance between consumer protection and free trade will be distorted, prejudicing overall public confidence in the Community.[227]

To a lesser extent, such problems of differential access affect Community secondary rule-making more generally.[228] In the case of tertiary rules (soft law) the problems are more serious since consultative procedures are less rigorously adopted and structured in relation to rules whose binding nature is uncertain. It has been suggested[229] that the Community might usefully draw on the precedent of the US Administrative

[225] See Harlow, 'Community of Interests', on consultation and lobbying.
[226] The two major Europe-wide standards bodies referred to in the New Approach are CEN (Comité Européen de Normalisation) and CENELEC (Comité Européen de Normalisation Electro-technique).
[227] McGee and Weatherill, 'Evolution of the Single Market', 585.
[228] See Hansard Society Report, para. 543.
[229] See Dehousse *et al.*, *Europe after 1992*, 29–31.

Procedure Act 1946 and lay down a single set of rules governing such matters as access to legislative or regulatory processes and the availability of judicial review. It has also been proposed[230] that rights to request public hearings on important regulatory decisions should be considered for the European Parliament and for regions particularly affected by Community decisions. Such potential developments involve difficulties—a Community APA would, for instance, give rise to all of the problems encountered with domestic APAs[231] and delay might be a particularly acute issue. Imaginative steps, nevertheless, have to be considered with some urgency if the legitimation of Community secondary and tertiary rules is to be enhanced rather than allowed to decline further.

4. Expertise

Community legislators might claim that their rules offer a distillation of expert knowledge as encountered across the Member States and that the limitations of their own claims under the legislative mandate, accountability/control, and due process headings are understandable, given the need to apply expert judgements. Such judgements, it might be argued, are not compatible with the constraints implied by the above three kinds of claim.

In making this argument a potential problem for Community legislators is that it is difficult convincingly to claim that, say, devising a rule to govern an aspect of health and safety at work, involves so arcane a set of judgements that the process and its results cannot be explained or accounted for. A second difficulty arises from any implied assumption that collecting the views of national experts during the process of rule-making produces a cumulative expertise. It may well be the case that on consulting a variety of experts a collection of contradictory advice is amassed. Resolving such contradictions may not always be possible nor may such a resolution, where it does prove possible, produce an expert judgement. Critics

[230] Ibid. 27. [231] See *supra*, pp. 76–80.

may argue that a 'paralysis of analysis' rather than a cumulative expertise is likely to be achieved by such processes. It may be countered that Community legislators bring their own expertise to bear on problems rather than simply gather together expert judgements on topics. Again, however, there is likely to be a problem in claiming expert action since consultative processes are liable to produce numbers of 'expert' judgements that differ from those of Commission staff. Claiming expertise in such circumstances is speculative.

Such problems might be responded to by setting up administrative agencies at the European level. These bodies, it has been suggested,[232] might both 'Europeanize' expertise and open up the system of government to non-governmental actors. They might co-operate with communities of experts in Member States, enhance expert discourse, and accordingly increase legitimation on an expertise rationale. As already indicated,[233] however, Member States are likely to resist the use of bodies that both intrude on their competencies and present new problems of accountability.[234] To expand the use of agencies with limited roles as *coordinators* of expertise might, nevertheless, prove politically acceptable. Such bodies would not automatically overcome the usual problems associated with expertise claims, such as those posed by divergence between experts, but they would offer a way of feeding higher levels of expertise into Community lawmaking processes—and of doing so with a greater degree of openness than present arrangements offer.

5. Efficiency and Effectiveness

Finally, Community legislators may argue that secondary and tertiary rules are *effective*—that they deserve support as procedural devices because they produce results. Certain rules and rule-types have however been criticized for their lack of effec-

[232] See Dehousse *et al.*, *Europe after 1992*, 17–19, 50–2.

[233] See *supra* p. 267.

[234] On the general problems of accountability posed by governmental agencies see R. Baldwin and C. McCrudden, *Regulation and Public Law* (1987).

tiveness (as in the 1985 White Paper) and we have seen in a major portion of this chapter that, even leaving aside problems of defining the legislative mandate, there are severe difficulties encountered in measuring regulatory effectiveness and in achieving practical implementation. As with domestic rules, furthermore, there is the unavoidable question of whether the governmental objectives sought to be achieved might have been pursued more effectively by employing strategies that differ from those actually used and which place different emphases on rules or even make resort to processes other than rules, such as negotiations, *ad hoc* incentives, or market-induced pressures.[235]

Conclusions

Governing at the European Community level gives rise to a host of particular difficulties of rule selection and use. The array of rule-types available is wide and in the area of tertiary rules the nature and effect of certain measures is highly problematic. The Community has made considerable progress in devising new means of producing legislation but this progress has not been free from negative aspects. The most severe problems encountered are perhaps those attending the issue of practical implementation. The unavoidable tension between effectiveness and evenness makes this more than a legal or technical question and one of political concern to Member States. We have seen that present procedures for measuring and ensuring the effective and even application of Community secondary and tertiary rules leave a great deal to be desired. Community secondary and tertiary rules, indeed, tend to score badly across all five legitimating rationales. This fact does much to explain why in recent years and in the Maastricht debates, so much controversy has attended discussions on both Community rule-making and the subsidiarity issue. For

[235] See e.g. Gaja, Hay, and Rotunda in Cappelletti *et al.*, *Integration Through Law*. For a more general statement of the advantages to be gained from an internal market free from barriers and restrictions, see P. Cecchini, *The European Challenge: 1992, The Benefits of a Single Market* (1988).

Europeans the future challenge will be to take every opportunity to improve methods of legitimating Community rules and to avoid using Community rules on issues or in ways that preclude effective legitimation.

PART IV

Rules and Alternatives

9 Processes and Governmental Strategies

Governmental processes are generally linked to various broad strategies of government. Such broad strategies may involve, for example, providing for agency regulation in an area; or giving the sector over to operation by a public corporation; or imposing a system of monitored self-regulation; or delegating a public function to a private provider; or allowing the market to operate within a system of governmentally-imposed fiscal incentives. The processes that can be used are also various. Thus, for example, resort may be made to rules of different kinds but, alternatively, an array of adjudicative processes may be adopted; decisions may be made managerially; policies, actions, or decisions may be negotiated; formal or informal arbitrations may be conducted; particularized contractual arrangements may be employed; or inquiries of various kinds may be instituted. The linkage of process to strategy is, however, inevitably close, and it is accordingly difficult to claim legitimacy for a process if the overall strategy is not to be deemed worthy of support. To give an example: the maker of prescriptive regulatory rules on, say, pollution standards may rely heavily on the efficiency and due process rationales in claiming support for the processes adopted, but that support is unlikely to be forthcoming if critics are able to argue convincingly that the pollution could be controlled more efficiently and fairly by abandoning the strategy of regulating by prescriptive standard-setting and turning to another strategy—for instance one allowing market forces to govern the issue through processes of negotiation.

For a process to be legitimate, it should be possible to make a convincing claim that it is the appropriate process combined with the appropriate strategy. Just as it should not be assumed that rules are the automatic way to implement strategies or programmes, it should not be taken for granted that the strategies involved are optimal. Renate Mayntz describes the potential pitfall thus:

To a certain extent it is a methodological requirement of implementation research to treat the programme as given in order to have a baseline for defining what perfect or faulty implementation consists of in the particular case. But this methodological device can surreptitiously become an implicit assumption, i.e. that all is well if only the programme gets implemented as designed.[1]

Processes have thus to be seen in context and, where a governmental task is under consideration, it is appropriate to ask three questions: first, whether government should undertake the task at all (rather than, for example, allow the market to dictate); second, whether the proposed strategy for achieving the task is optimal; and, third, whether the most acceptable process for giving effect to that strategy involves certain types of rule.

Both of the first two questions may be answered by considering how different strategies are likely to perform according to the Chapter 3 criteria. There are a number of potential strategies in the governmental tool-box and these may or may not call for rules as implementing devices.

The tool-box metaphor is borrowed from Christopher Hood:[2]

Government administration is about social control, not carpentry or gardening. But there is a tool kit for that, just like anything else. What government does to us is to try to shape our lives by applying a set of administrative tools, in many different combinations and contexts, to suit a variety of purposes.

Hood argues that there are four basic kinds of governmental resource, which can be employed by means of a series of devices or tools for either *detecting* (taking in information) or *effecting* (making an impact on the world outside). These four resources are nodality, treasure, authority, and organization.

[1] 'The Conditions of Effective Public Policy' (1983) 11 PP 123, 124. On the need to consider alternative governmental strategies see C. Hood, *The Tools of Government* (1983), 115. Not only may other strategies prove more satisfactory, there is the perennial problem of creative compliance—see Ch. 6 *supra.*

[2] Hood, *Tools of Government*, 2; for an analysis of forms of law used for implementing economic policy, see T. C. Daintith, 'Law as a Policy Instrument: Comparative Perspectives' in id. (ed.), *Law as an Instrument of Economic Policy: Comparative and Critical Approaches* (1988).

'Nodality' denotes a government's being in the centre of an information or social network. 'Treasure' refers to the possession of a stock of moneys or valuables (this may be taken to include items of 'new property' or largesse).[3] 'Authority' denotes the possession of legal or official power 'officially to demand, forbid, guarantee, or adjudicate';[4] and 'organization' refers to the possession of a body of skilled persons. Each resource gives a government certain capabilities. Nodality allows information to be traded and dispensed, treasure gives economic power, authority provides an ability to make legal determinations, and organization gives a physical capability to influence or act directly.

Following Hood's analysis, particular governmental strategies can be arranged to correspond to the above resources and capabilities. Focusing on strategies for effecting government ('effectors') the following breakdown of tools emerges:[5] by means of nodality, information can be distributed selectively (or suppressed), it may be broadcast generally (e.g. a public hygiene announcement); it may serve as propaganda; 'bespoke messages' can be targeted at individuals; queries can be responded to; or group-targeted messages can be issued.

Resorting to 'treasure', administrations may indulge in 'cheque-book government'.[6] This is what Terence Daintith would term the use of *dominium* as distinct from *imperium*: 'I use the term *imperium* to describe the government's use of the command of law in aid of its policy objectives, and the term *dominium* to describe the employment of the wealth of government for this purpose.'[7]

Governmental wealth can be used to offer customized payments as inducements; to issue contracts, grants, loans, or subsidies (with or without attendant conditions) and to encourage a system of government by incentive, bargaining, or

[3] See C. Reich, 'The New Property' (1964) 73 Yale LJ 778.

[4] Hood, *Tools of Government*, 5.

[5] Ibid., chs. 2–5.

[6] Ibid., ch. 3.

[7] T. C. Daintith, 'The Techniques of Government', in J. Jowell and D. Oliver (eds.), *The Changing Constitution*, 3rd edn. (1994). See also id., 'Legal Analysis of Economic Policy (1982) 9 JLSoc. 191; id., 'Law as a Policy Instrument:'.

negotiation.[8] Authority, or *imperium*, may be manifest in such tools as laws that order, prohibit, command, and permit. These 'tokens of authority'[9] are not necessarily general in nature; thus 'directed' (as opposed to 'blanketed') tokens may relate to specific individuals, places, organizations, or objects (for example when operators' licences are issued). The constraints offered by such strategies may range from low-constraint approvals or recommendations to high-constraint orders and prohibitions. Thus regulatory strategies based on *dominium* or *imperium* may, at one end of the scale, offer non-restrictive incentives (as in tax inducements) and at the other may involve highly restrictive and interventionist 'command and control' systems (where, for example, a regulatory agency mandates standards and becomes involved in managerial and operational matters within the industry). Along the scale is a series of regulatory strategies of differing degrees of restrictiveness, involving, for example, liability rules, prohibitions, permits, standards, concessions, price controls, and restraints on trade practices and market structures.[10]

The organization inherent in government allows it to act physically and directly either in relation to individuals (as where a facility is offered to a particular person), with respect to groups or 'at large'.[11] An example of the latter would be the provision of a disinfecting footbath placed at the entry of a public swimming pool.

As indicated above, what constitutes the most appropriate tool or strategy for a particular governmental task is liable to involve a contentious assessment of potential legitimacy ratings and such an assessment will have to take into consideration the processes used to implement the strategy.

Certain governmental strategies and circumstances would

[8] See Daintith, 'Legal Analysis of Economic Policy'.

[9] Hood, *Tools of Government*, ch. 4.

[10] On choices of regulatory strategy see S. Breyer, *Regulation and Its Reform* (1982); id., 'Analysing Regulatory Failure: Mismatches, Less Restrictive Alternatives and Reform' (1979) 92 *Harv.LR* 549. For a review of regulatory strategies based on the use of financial incentives rather than command and control approaches see A. I. Ogus, *Regulation: Legal Form and Economic Theory* (1994), ch. 11. Ogus, ch. 12, also points to the regulatory use that can be made of changes in private law.

[11] Hood, *Tools of Government*, ch. 5.

appear to demand the use of rules, but no necessary relationship exists between particular strategies and particular processes. *Imperium* might be expected to be exercised through rules but it may be used in a particularized fashion (as with a 'directed token'). *Dominium*, or economic power, is often used in a particularized fashion (as where grants, constraints or loans are applied to specific persons), but it is also frequently associated with broad rules (for example where it is stated that government contracts will not be allocated to employers whose workforces do not contain designated percentages of disabled persons). Informationally and organizationally-based devices of government are no less capable of either particular or general application.

Hood offers guidelines concerning the circumstances in which generalized strategies are likely to produce governmentally desired ends. He points to a series of factors to be considered, notably: the size of the population addressed by a device (if small, a particularized device may be efficient); the degree of voluntary attention and receptiveness likely to attend the issue (if the population will self-inform and self-regulate on the topic, a particularized, and expensive, approach may not be necessary); and the degree of social consensus on the matter (which if high may conduce to a more generalized strategy).[12]

It is the *de facto* association of some governmental strategies with highly inclusive and restrictive administrative rules that causes some critics to look for alternative tools for achieving designated purposes. Richard Stewart has, indeed, posited a 'crisis of legalisation' in United States regulation:[13]

> This dual crisis of legalisation ultimately stems from the heavy use, in the US regulatory welfare state of command strategies of law, as contrasted with constitutive strategies. Constitutive strategies are procedural and structured: they create a framework within which interests recognised as legally empowered determine substantive outcomes through their individual decisions and through joint decisions

[12] Hood, *Tools of Government*, 35, 51, 68, 84.

[13] R. B. Stewart, 'Regulation and the Crisis of Legalisation in the United States', in T. C. Daintith (ed.), *Law as an Instrument of Economic Policy*, 108–9.

reached through specified transaction rules—such as rules for voting or contracting . . .

Administrative regulation, by contrast, is unabashedly command-oriented and instrumental; it coercively specifies conduct in order to achieve particular substantive ends. As centralized regulation has increasingly displaced constitutive strategies of law, the problems of overload, erosion of normativity and cumulative substantive irrationality and ineffectiveness become more and more apparent.

The solution, for Stewart, is thus to shift towards 'constitutive' regulatory strategies or what have been called 'less restrictive' or 'incentive-based' regulatory methods.[14] These alternatives include: creating competitive markets structured by antitrust laws; using economic incentives such as taxes, subsidies, and government contracts rather than commands to influence behaviour; resorting to government ownership or franchising systems; using information and persuasion techniques; relying on private law liability rules enforced by private litigants; and employing negotiations and informal bargaining processes. Thus, for instance, in the pollution field Stewart has suggested[15] that the 'malaise of regulatory legalism', that has been caused by social regulation and the expansion of standing rights to seek judicial review, can be responded to by replacing legalistic controls with market incentives so that, for instance, marketable rights to pollute are used instead of the 'command and control' regulation of polluters.[16]

It may, of course, be possible to exaggerate the extent to which US problems of legalization flow from command and control regulation itself rather than from, for example, a particular set of approaches to judicial review; from the existence of certain conditions leading to litigiousness; or from the operation of particular rule-making processes. The extent to which

[14] On incentive-based systems of regulation see Ogus, *Regulation*, ch. 11; Breyer, *Regulation and its Reform*; R. B. Stewart, 'The Discontents of Legalism: Interest Group Relations in Administrative Regulation (1985) *Wis.LR* 685; R. B. Stewart, 'Regulation and the Crisis of Legalisation'.

[15] 'The Discontents of Legalism'.

[16] For a European view of the crisis in regulatory law and the limits of command law, see G. Teubner, 'After Legal Instrumentalism? Strategic Models of Post-Regulatory Law', E.U.I. Working Paper No. 100 (1984); id., 'Juridification: Concepts, Aspects, Limits, Solutions', in G. Teubner (ed.), *Juridification of Social Spheres* (1987).

'less restrictive' regulatory methods will escape the need for rules and the dangers of legalism may also be prone to overstatement. Methods such as anti-trust laws are not noted for their freedom from complex rules and other 'less restrictive' methods of control usually have to be structured by means of rules of one kind or another.[17] Most importantly, such controls usually have to be set within a scheme of enforcement that is rule-based.[18] Thus, when franchising systems are used, regulators frequently face the problem of ensuring that franchise holders adhere to the rules of the game as established by the terms of the franchise bid and the resultant allocation.[19] Similarly, when marketable rights to pollute are employed, quite complex systems of rules may have to be policed by bureaucracies so as to ensure that the market in such rights is not distorted; that non-holders of rights do not pollute; and that holders of rights keep within the terms of their permits.[20] Alternatives to classical modes of command and control regulation may have a tendency to develop into schemes bearing an unnerving resemblance to the regimes that they have replaced or been preferred to.

Incentive-based schemes may possess their own limitations[21] but the discussion prompted by Stewart does demonstrate the close linkage between assessments of processes and evaluations of governmental strategies. The reforms Stewart offers are not

[17] See e.g. R. S. Markovits, 'Antitrust: Alternatives to Delegalisation', in Teubner (ed.), *Juridification of Social Spheres.*

[18] On the problems of applying mandatory disclosure and taxation schemes see E. Bardach and R. A. Kagan, *Going by the Book* (1982), 267–70, 294.

[19] See R. Baldwin, M. Cave, and T. Jones, 'The Regulation of Independent Local Radio and Its Reform' (1987) 7 International Review of Law and Economics 177; O. Williamson, *The Economic Institutions of Capitalism* (1987), ch. 13; S. Domberger, 'Economic Regulation through Franchise Contracts' in J. Kay, C. Mayer, and D. Thompson (eds.), *Privatisation and Regulation: The UK Experience* (1986).

[20] See Bardach and Kagan, *Going by the Book*, 295–7.

[21] A point not escaping press atttention: one editorial recently cautioned, 'The fashionable right-wing view is that market mechanisms are more efficient regulators than laws. Impose taxes on companies that pollute; they are more flexible and do not require policing. But even if this were true (the record of company tax evasion is not encouraging) it is hard to see that the principle can have more than a limited application' (*Independent on Sunday*, 21 Nov. 1993). See also Ogus, *Regulation*, 250–6 and Breyer, *Regulation and its Reform*, 278–80. On the general limitations of alternatives to 'command and control' regulation see Bardach and Kagan, *Going by the Book*, chs. 8, 9, and 10.

mere attempts to improve the legitimacy of command-oriented rules. His argument is that command *strategies* lead up a blind alley and that it is necessary to change to different strategies and to different kinds of rule. Similarly we saw in Chapter 3 that the British movement towards 'new public management' reflected a desire to change both strategies and processes of government. A series of Conservative administrations had been dissatisfied with the performance of public bureaucracies controlled by statutory means and had desired to shift focus towards a contractually-framed system of securing public services. The new control mechanisms were the markets and consumer power, the new rules were quasi-contractual rather than derived from statute. The 'new public management' can, like 'less restrictive' regulatory proposals, be assessed with reference to the Chapter 3 bench-marks, but attention should be paid to both the overall strategy and the chosen implementing processes.

Conclusions

If, in relation to a proposed governmental strategy, there is a choice of potential implementing processes, how can choices be made between kinds of process—between, say, rules, adjudicative techniques, managerial styles of decision-making, negotiations, arbitrations, and inquiries?

It is possible to make some general statements concerning the respective virtues of different procedural devices. Thus, in his well-known article comparing rule-making with adjudication in the development of administrative policy[22] David Shapiro, *inter alia*, makes the points:

[22] D. Shapiro, 'The Choice of Rulemaking or Adjudication in the Development of Administrative Policy' (1965) 78 Harv.LR 921. See also G. Robinson, 'The Making of Administrative Policy: Another Look at Rulemaking and Adjudication and Administrative Procedure Reform' (1970) 118 UPa.LR 485; editorial, 'Rethinking Regulation: Negotiation as an Alternative to Traditional Rulemaking' (1981) 94 Harv.LR 1871; L. Fuller, 'The Forms and Limits of Adjudication' (1978) 92 Harv.LR 353; id., 'Collective Bargaining and the Arbitrator' (1963), Wis.LR. 3; id., 'Mediation: Its Forms and Functions' (1971) 44 S.Cal.R.Rev. 305; J. Jowell, 'The Limits of the Public Hearing as a Tool of Public Planning' (1978) 21 Ad.LR 123.

- Rule-making yields advantages of participation and accountability over adjudication in so far as greater provision is made for notice and comment. This also increases the level of expertise involved in policy formulation.
- Rule-making is more conducive to advanced planning than adjudication.
- Retroactivity is minimized by rule-making.
- Uniformity of standards developed through rule-making promotes both fairness and accountability.
- Rule-making procedures tend to be more flexible than adjudicatory processes and hence there is less risk of distorting broad policies during their formulation.
- Rules tend to be more accessible and clearer than the results of adjudications, this implies greater accountability.
- Rule-making promotes greater fidelity to statutory standards than does adjudication and the courts find it easier to police such fidelity in the case of rulemaking.

Comparisons, such as those made by Shapiro, are, however, of limited utility if particular contexts and associated strategies are not considered. Nor should it be forgotten that the boundaries between different processes can be blurred. (Many adjudications decide particular issues but also lay down rules and policies of a generalizable nature.) It is impossible to deal *ex ante* with all possible combinations of context and strategy, but some understanding of the potential of different processes can, perhaps, be gained by looking at each of the various governmental processes in the way that has been attempted in this book in relation to rules.[23] Against such a background, the appropriateness of using the various process-forms in relation to different strategies and circumstances can be gauged. At the end of the day, the anticipated context has to be analysed and an attempt made to find the combination of strategy and process that is likely to merit the highest overall legitimacy rating.

[23] Mashaw's *Buraucratic Justice* (1983) is noteworthy as an extended analysis of adjudicatory processes.

10 Conclusions

In employing rules so as to contribute to good government difficult decisions have to be made concerning each of the various aspects of rules, and the alternatives to rules have always to be borne in mind. A starting-point in analysing rules is an awareness of the different dimensions that rules possess and it is equally important to separate the technical advantages from the political motives for rule-use.

It is argued here that choosing processes for governing involves more than selecting a particular balance between rules and discretions. Using rules is only one way of exerting control or executing functions within government and discretions can be created or constrained by devices and processes other than rules.

The first important issue in selecting governmental processes is to establish bench-marks according to which evaluations can be made. This is done in Chapter 3 by considering how various rationales for justifying powers and processes have been dealt with in the period since Davis brought the notion of discretion to public awareness. It is argued in Chapter 3 that governmental processes can best be evaluated by making reference to a language of justification and to five rationales for claiming support. These rationales are all in themselves contentious but there is said to be nothing fatal in contention. Indeed, it is stressed that contention lies at the heart of seeking legitimation.

In applying such rationales to the body of secondary and tertiary rules encountered in British government it is remarkable how weak many potential claims to legitimacy are. Secondary legislation, for example, often lacks clear authorization, it is subject to weak systems of accountability and control, and the participatory rights of affected parties are often ill protected. These problems are all the more severe in relation to tertiary rules and where secondary or tertiary rules are employed to implement European Community Directives, or in pursuance of policies emanating from the European Union, or within the contractual frameworks of government, special problems of legitimation are encountered. On the positive side, however, secondary and tertiary rules have an important role to play in defining and clarifying statutory mandates and in producing expertise and efficiency gains. The conclusion to be drawn is that, if such rules are to be used, all possible steps should be taken to improve the legitimacy claims to be made on behalf of them—notably by increasing obligations to disclose rules; by linking tertiary and secondary rules more clearly to statutory provisions, and by making the status and force of such rules more clear. It is cautioned in Chapter 4, nevertheless, that since the legitimacy of secondary and tertiary rules rests to a great extent upon the effectiveness of their contribution to government, issues of enforceability and the relation between compliance and effectiveness in securing the right results are of first importance.

In pursuance of these issues Part II draws on a case study of regulatory rules in the health and safety sector. Chapter 5 examines how a particular approach to rules flowed from the Robens Report of 1972 and how this has left a lasting imprint on regulatory operations. The Robens legacy demonstrates quite graphically how distortions and mistaken assumptions can be build into a regulatory structure and how difficult it is, even decades later, to reform regulation so as to make it more effective and legitimate. The analysis of Chapter 5 shows, furthermore, how decisions on resources and staff levels can dictate potential strategies on rule-making and enforcement (The appropriate styles of rule-making and compliance-seeking may, indeed, differ for each level of resourcing).

Chapter 6 picks up the question of how rules can be made to work and introduces broader themes. Achieving compliance with the rules is said to be necessary for effective rule use but it is not sufficient—compliance with rules has to produce the right results. On the issue of compliance-seeking it is argued that rules are operated through enforcement strategies, which in turn have, if appropriate, to be attuned to variations in the regulatees and the mischiefs involved. A 'compliance-oriented' approach to regulatory rule-making is put forward suggesting that rule-makers analyse the relevant mischiefs and mischief-creators before proceeding to ask which enforcement strategies will best influence the mischief-creators and which types of rule will best complement those strategies. As to why rulemakers tend to respond inadequately to matters of compliance-seeking, there appear to be three major reasons: their mistaken adherence to a 'top-down' approach to rules and policies; their tendency to underestimate the problems and distortions that attend rule-making processes; and their vulnerability to internal and external political pressures. The response called for in Chapter 6 is a greater awareness of the above tendencies; a close attendance to issues of enforcement; an avoidance of administrative structures that exacerbate the top-down problem; a realism concerning matters of process; and a disinclination to solve political problems of the present by fudging rules and laying down difficulties for future enforcers.

How can compliance-seeking be linked with the achievement of desired results? In Section II of Chapter 6 it is pointed out that, for a number of reasons, compliance may result in a lack of effectiveness in securing such results. Rules, notably, may fail through inappropriateness in the kinds or levels of the standards they employ and rules may prove over- or under-inclusive. Dealing with these problems demands an awareness of the compliance-seeking strategies to be employed in relation to particular rules and the compliance-seeking effects of steps taken to respond to such issues as inclusiveness. It is cautioned that certain tensions will not evaporate and that trade-offs may have to be made between, for example, achieving greater accuracy in dealing with inclusiveness and enhancing compliance-seeking. Ways can be found to respond to these difficulties—for example, problems of inclusiveness can be addressed by allowing field enforcers to exercise discretion and enforce selectively. Again, however, there is a trade-off to be made, this time between the dictates of effectiveness and of accountability.

A further difficulty is discussed in Chapter 6, the problem of creative compliance and the tendency of regulatees to avoid complying with the spirit of the law by sidestepping the letter of the law. This problem is aggravated by the existence of a series of factors that pressures regulators to employ formalistic types of rule—the very kinds of rule most susceptible of avoidance by creative compliance. The appropriate rule-makers' response is to adopt a compliance-oriented approach but to bear in mind the ability of the regulatee in any given situation to take him or herself beyond the scope of the rules. In extreme cases of creative compliance the rule-maker may have to take courage, face up to critics who call for precision and certainty in rules, and opt for non-formalistic rules of a vague and goal-oriented nature.

An extended discussion of effectiveness in rule-making and rule-use should not, however, detract from consideration of the other key process values examined in Chapter 3—notably accountability, fairness, and expertise. Chapter 6 concludes by reasserting the relevance of these desiderata and throughout the discussion of effectiveness in Chapter 6 the need to trade off increases in effectiveness against other goals is repeatedly stressed.

The case for applying more formal tests of efficiency to regulatory rules is explored in Chapter 7, and evaluations are made according to the Chapter 3 bench-marks. Economic appraisal techniques are beset with a number of problems as far as their claims to efficiency are concerned—notably informational and administrative difficulties. The claims that appraisals increase accountability and fairness are again problematic—due principally to limitation of openness and to potential biases in access. Nor, since appraisals divert resources from regulatory processes, can strong claims be made on the expertise front. As for the mandate argument, appraisals may set up real conflicts between the dictates of efficiency and the prescriptions of statutes. In spite of such difficulties it is, nevertheless, concluded that, within the numerous constraints set out in Chapter 7, a limited and subsidiary rule for appraisals does exist within the policy-making process.

At the European level, we see that governing with rules

poses particular and severe problems of selection and mode of use—not least because claims to legitimacy tend generally to be weaker at this level of government. The array of rule-types and dimensions is as wide as is encountered domestically and special problems attend the issue of practical implementation. The European Union has yet to come to grips with the need to measure and ensure the effective and even application of secondary and tertiary rules. Such rules tend to score badly across all five legitimating rationales and to some extent this explains widespread concerns across Member States at the balance between the respective legislative and enforcement competences of the Member States and the Community.

The alternatives to rules are outlined in Chapter 9 and it is cautioned that rules should not be assumed to be a first option in the tool-box of governmental processes. The importance, moreover, of choices of broad governmental strategies is stressed and it is pointed out that claiming legitimacy for a process involves, by implication, claiming a degree of support for the governmental strategy within which the process operates. (The reputation of a rule may depend on its associates). As for choosing between different processes or tools for implementing any given governmental strategy, it is possible, as has been attempted here, to point to the generic strengths and weaknesses of a procedural device, but particular contexts have to be examined and a selection made of the process that combines with the governmental strategy so as to create the system most deserving of legitimacy.

It is not being suggested that potential rule-makers should adopt a comprehensively rational approach to their task so that, before a rule can be made, all possible processes, enforcement methods and governmental strategies have to be reviewed in all possible combinations. That would be a recipe for inaction. What is suggested is that, within practical, political, economic, and legal constraints, rules should be seen in their broad governmental context and assessed with reference to the full range of legitimating values. Finally, it should be repeated at the end of a book devoted to rules that an interest in rules should not become an obsession that blinds to alternative processes. A more informed view of rules may assist in the pursuit of good government but it will only do so if it broadens perspectives rather than blinkers them.

Appendix

Primary, Secondary and Tertiary Rules in Britain: Notes on Potential Legitimacy Claims

	PRIMARY
Legislative Mandate	1. Direct authority from Parliament but: • Parliament's intention may be vague or contentious. • Only broad principles may be apparent. • May rely on secondary or tertiary rules for substance.
Accountability	1. Direct to Parliament but: • Government may control, not Parliament. • Deficiencies of parliamentary process, e.g. lack of time, information, guillotine. 2. Statute may be framework only, leaving substance to governmental rules. 3. Judicial review expensive, difficult to obtain, limited in scope to European issues.
Fairness/ Due process	1. Consultation by Government and through Members of Parliament but Government may legislate swiftly or on ideological grounds with poor consultation of those potentially affected—and may hold its mandate to justify this.
Expertise	1. Limits on parliamentary time, expertise, specialist knowledge, continuity of interest in the topic.
Efficiency	1. Low responsiveness and adaptability, expensive to produce. 2. High level of authority and symbolic impact may be be advantageous. 3. Legalistic framing may make application and self-regulation difficult.

SECONDARY	TERTIARY
1. Some authority from Parliament but nature of this can be uncertain and mandate often vague. 2. Extent to which usurps role of primary legislation can be contentious. 3. Haphazard collection of forms, lack of standardization gives impression of irrationality.	1. Mandate lacking. 2. Status unclear. 3. Legal force uncertain. 4. May conflict with primary and secondary rules. 5. Executive may be seen as usurping roles of legislature and judiciary. 6. Whether relevant statute authorized rulemaking often unclear.
1. Low parliamentary scrutiny. 2. Statutory standards often broad and vague. Purposes for which authorization given are often vague. 3. Variety of procedures for promulgating. 4. Parliamentary debates rare. 5. Judicial review expensive, difficult to obtain, limited in scope. 6. Legal force of rules uncertain; this issue often not clarified by parent statute.	1. Parliamentary scrutiny lacking. 2. Statutory standards absent (and not feasible to introduce these). 3. Judicial control only on very limited grounds.
1. Consultation sporadic—duty depends on particular statute. No general 'notice and comment' procedure. 2. Problems of who is consulted and to what extent. 3. Although no fixed procedures for all such rules, voluntary consultation *may* be more extensive and selective than is possible in relation to primary legislation.	1. No general procedure for consultation which may be lacking. 2. No judicially-imposed duty to consult or disclose rule being applied. 3. Voluntary consultation may be selective, extensive, and specialist. 4. Disclosure of rule encourages openness.
1. Greater attention to detail possible them with primary rules. Department/agency may have more time, expertise, specialist knowledge, and continuity of interest than Parliament. 2. Technical issues more successfully dealt with than in primary legislation.	1. All advantages of secondary rules plus greater informality and flexibility. 2. Cumulative expertise can be distilled into rules and staff allowed to operate at high levels with low training.
1. Greater responsiveness and adaptability than primary rules, cheaper to produce. 2. Higher levels of expertise and specialist knowledge incorporated than primary rules—may assist application. 3. May be formalistic and inaccessible which may detract from application.	1. Responsiveness and adaptability high. 2. Cheap, easy to produce. 3. Encourages consistency but can be flexible. 4. Non-formalistic language eases application; accessibility versatile. 5. Versatile: can be used to persuade, inform, encourage, compromise, set out broad policies, play evidential role.

Bibliography

Abrams, N., 'Internal Policy: Guiding the Exercise of Prosecutorial Discretion' (1971) 19 UCLA LR 1.

Ackerman, B., *Social Justice in the Liberal State* (New Haven, Conn., 1980).

Adinolfi, A., 'The Implementation of Social Policy Directives Through Collective Agreements' (1988) 25 CMLR 291.

Adler, M., and Asquith, S. (eds.), *Discretion and Welfare* (London, 1981).

Albrow, M., *Bureaucracy* (London, 1970).

Allen, C. K., *Law and Orders*, 3rd edn. (London, 1965).

Anthony, R. A., 'Interpretative Rules, Policy Statements, Guidances, Manuals and the Like: Should Federal Agencies Use them to Bind the Public?' (1992) 41 Duke LJ 1463.

Ashford, N. A., *Crisis in the Workplace: Occupational Disease and Injury* (Cambridge, Mass., 1976).

Asimow, M., 'Delegated Legislation: United States and United Kingdom' (1983) OJLS 253.

—— 'Non-legislative Rulemaking and Regulatory Reform' (1985) Duke LJ 381.

Ayres, I., and Braithwaite, J., *Responsive Regulation* (Oxford, 1992).

Baldwin, R., *Regulating the Airlines* (Oxford, 1985).

—— 'Health and Safety at Work: Consensus and Self-Regulation', in R. Baldwin and C. McCrudden, *Regulation and Public Law* (London, 1987).

—— 'The Next Steps: Ministerial Responsibility and Government by Agency' (1988) 51 MLR 622.

—— 'Why Rules Don't Work' (1990) 53 MLR 321.

—— and Daintith, T. C., *Harmonization and Hazard: Regulating Workplace Health and Safety in the European Community* (London, 1992).

—— and Hawkins, K., 'Discretionary Justice: Davis Reconsidered' [1984] PL 570.

—— and Horne, D., 'Expectations in a Joyless Landscape' (1986) 49 MLR 685.

—— and Houghton, J., 'Circular Arguments: The Status and Legitimacy of Administrative Rules' [1986] PL 239.

—— and McCrudden, C., *Regulation and Public Law* (London, 1987).

—— and Veljanovski, C. G., 'Regulation by Cost-Benefit Analysis' (1984) 62 Public Administration 51.

—— Cave, M., and Jones, T., 'The Regulation of Independent Local Radio and its Reform' (1987) 7 International Review of Law and Economics 177.

Bankowski, Z., and Nelken, D., 'Discretion as a Social Problem', in M. Adler and S. Asquith (eds.), *Discretion and Welfare* (London, 1981).

Barav, A., 'Damages Against the State for Failure to Implement EC Directives' (1991) NLJ 1584.

Bardach, E., *The Implementation Game* (Cambridge, Mass., 1977).

—— and Kagan, R., *Going by the Book: The Problem of Regulatory Unreasonableness* (Philadelphia, Pa., 1982).

Barker, R., 'Legitimacy, Obedience and the State', in C. Harlow (ed.), *Public Law and Politics* (London, 1986).

—— *Political Legitimacy and the State* (Oxford, 1990).

Barrett, S., and Fudge, C. (eds.), *Policy and Action* (London, 1981).

Barron, A., and Scott, C., 'The Citizen's Charter Programme' (1992) 55 MLR 526.

Barry, B., *Political Argument* (Hemel Hempstead, 1990).

Bartrip, P., and Fenn, P., 'The Administration of Safety: The Enforcement Policy of the Early Factory Inspectorate 1844–1864' (1980) 58 Pub. Admin. 87.

Bates, T. St J. N., 'The Scrutiny of European Secondary Legislation at Westminster' [1976] ELR 27.

—— 'Scrutiny of the Administration', in Ryle and Richards (eds.), *The Commons under Scrutiny*, 3rd edn. (London, 1988).

Baumgartner, M. P., 'The Myth of Discretion' in K. Hawkins (ed.), *The Uses of Discretion* (Oxford, 1992).

BBC, *Extending Choice: The BBC's Role in the New Broadcasting Age* (London, 1992).

Beatson, J., 'Legislative Control of Administrative Rule-making: Lessons from the British Experience?' (1979) 12 CILJ 199.

—— 'A British View of *Vermont Yankee*' (1980) 55 Tulane LR 435.

—— 'Public and Private in English Administrative Law' [1987] PL 34.

Beaumont, P., *European Communities (Amendment) Act 1993* (London, 1993).

Beetham, D., *The Legitimation of Power* (London, 1991).

Beloff, N., *The General Says No* (London, 1963).

Bennion, F., *Statutory Interpretation*, 2nd edn. (London, 1992).

Bieber, R., Dehousse, R., Pinder, J., and Weiler, J., 'Back to the Future: Policy Strategy and Tactics of the White Paper on the Creation of a Single European Market', in Bieber *et al.* (eds.), *92: One European Market* (Baden Baden, 1988).

Birkinshaw, P., *Freedom of Information* (London, 1988).

—— Harden, I., and Lewis, N., *Government by Moonlight: The Hybrid Parts of the State* (London, 1990).

Bradley, A. W., 'Research and Reform in Administrative Law' (1974) 13 JSPTL 35.

—— 'The European Court and the Legal Basis of Community Legislation' (1988) 13 ELR 379.

—— 'Tell Us Why', *Solicitors' Journal*, 4 Feb. 1994, 88–9.

—— and Ewing, K. D., *Constitutional and Administrative Law*, 11th edn. (London, 1993).

Bradshaw, J., 'From Discretion to Rules: The Experience of the Family Fund', in M. Alder and S. Asquith (eds.), *Discretion and Welfare* (1981).

Braithwaite, J., 'Enforced Self-Regulation: A New Strategy for Corporate Crime Control' (1980) 28 Public Policy 257.

—— *To Punish or Persuade: Enforcement of Coal Mine Safety* (Albany, NY, 1985).

—— and Grabosky, P., *Occupational Health and Safety Enforcement in Australia* (Canberra, 1985).

Braybrooke, D., and Lindblom, C., *A Strategy of Decision* (New York, 1963).

Breyer, S., 'Analysing Regulatory Failure: Mismatches, Less Restrictive Alternatives and Reform' (1979) Harv.LR 549.

—— *Regulation and Its Reform* (Cambridge, Mass., 1982).

—— and Stewart, R. B., *Administrative Law and Regulatory Policy*, 3rd edn. (Boston, Mass., 1992).

Brouwer, O., 'Free Movement of Foodstuffs and Quality Requirements: Has the Commission Got it Wrong?' (1988) 25 CMLR 237.

Bryden, P., Public Interest Intervention in the Courts', 66 Can.BR 490.

Bryner, G., *Bureaucratic Discretion* (New York, 1987).

Bull, D., The Anti-Discretion Movement in Britain: Fact or Phantom? (1980) JSWL 65.

Campbell, S., *Labour Inspection in the European Community* (London, 1986).

Cane, P., 'Public Law and Private Law', in J. Eckelaar and J. Bell (eds.), *Oxford Essays in Jurisprudence*, 3rd ser. (1989).

—— 'Statutes, Standing and Representation' [1990] PL 307.

Cappelletti, M., Seccombe, M., and Weiler, J. (eds.), *Integration Through Law* (Berlin, 1986).

Carr, C. T. *Delegated Legislation: Three Lectures* (Cambridge, 1921).

Carson, W. G., 'Some Sociological Aspects of Strict Liability and the Enforcement of Factory Legislation' (1970) 33 MLR 396–412.

—— 'The Conventionalisation of Early Factory Crime' (1979) 7 IJSL 37–69.

Cass, D. Z., 'The Word that Saves Maastricht?' (1992) 29 CMLR 1107.

Ceccini, P., *The European Challenge: 1992, the Benefits of a Single Market* (Aldershot, 1988).

Cheit, R. E., *Setting Safety Standards: Regulation in the Public and Private Sectors* (Berkeley, Ca., 1990).

Ciavarini-Azzi, G., *The Implementation of EC Law by the Member States* (Florence, 1985).

Clark, T. B., Kesten, M. H., and Miller, J. C. III (eds.), *Reforming Regulation* (Washington, DC, 1980).

Clubley, D., *Handbook of Labour Inspection in the European Community* (London, 1990).

Comaroff, J. L., and Roberts, S., *Rules and Processes* (Chicago, Ill., 1981).

Commission of the European Communities, *Social Europe* Vol. 2/90 (Luxembourg, 1990).

Commission for Racial Equality, *Second Review of the Race Relations Act 1976* (1992).

Connolly, W. (ed.), *Legitimacy and the State* (Oxford, 1984).

Coombes, D., 'Parliament and the European Community', in Walkland and Ryle (eds.), *The Commons Today* (London, 1981).

Craig, P. P., *Public Law and Democracy in the United Kingdom and the United States of America* (Oxford, 1990).

—— *Administrative Law* 3rd edn. (London, 1994).

—— 'Dicey: Unitary, Self-correcting Democracy and Public Law' (1990) 106 LQR 105.

—— 'Once Upon a Time in the West: Direct Effect and the Federalisation of EEC Law' (1992) 12 OJLS 453.

—— 'Legitimate Expectation: A Conceptual Analysis' (1992) 108 LQR 79.

Crampton, R. C., and Berg, R. K., 'On Leading a Horse to Water: NEPA and the Federal Bureaucracy' (1973) 71 Mich.LR 511.

Cranston, R., *Law, Government and Public Policy* (Melbourne, 1987).

Creighton, B., and Gunningham, N. (eds.), *The Industrial Relations of Occupational Health and Safety* (Sydney, 1985).

Crosby. S., 'The Single Market and the Rule of Law' (1991) 16 ELR 451.

Currall, J., 'Some Aspects of the Relation between Articles 30–36 and Article 100 of the EEC Treaty with a Closer Look at Optional Harmonisation' (1984) 4 YEL 169.

Daintith, T. C., 'Legal Analysis of Economic Policy' (1982) 9 JLSoc. 191.

—— (ed.), *Law as an Instrument of Economic Policy: Comparative and Critical Approaches* (Berlin, 1988).

—— 'The Techniques of Government', in J. Jowell and D. Oliver (eds.), *The Changing Constitution*, 3rd edn. (London, 1994).

Dashwood, A., 'The Principle of Direct Effect in European Community Law'; (1978) 16 JCMS 229.

Davis, K. C., *Discretionary Justice* (Chicago, Ill., 1971).

—— 'An Approach to Legal Control of the Police' (1974) 52 Tex.LR 703.

Dawson, S., Willman, P., Bamford, M., and Clinton, A., *Safety at Work: The Limits of Self-Regulation* (Cambridge, 1988).

de Burca, G., 'Giving Effect to European Community Directives' (1992) 55 MLR 215.

de Gier, E., *Implementation of EC Directives on Working Conditions and Product Safety: Possibilities and Limitations* (Amsterdam, 1991).

De Muth, C., and Ginsberg, D., 'White House Review of Agency Rulemaking' (1986) 99 Harv.LR 1075.

De Smith, S. A. and Brazier, R., *Constitutional and Administrative Law*, 7th edn. (London, 1994).

Dehousse, R., '1992 and Beyond: The Institutional Dimension of the Internal Market Programme' (1989) 1 LIEI 109.

—— 'Integration v. Regulation? On the Dynamics of Regulation in the European Community' (1992) 30 JCMS 383.

——Joerges, C., Majone, G., Snyder, F., and Everson, M. *Europe after 1992: New Regulatory Strategies*, E.U.I. Working Paper 92/31 (Florence, 1992).

Department of Trade and Industry, *Burdens on Business* (London, 1985).
Dickens, L., 'The Advisory Conciliation and Arbitration Service: Regulation and Voluntarism in Industrial Relations' in Baldwin and McCrudden (1987).
Dickinson, J., *Administrative Justice and the Supremacy of Law in the United States* (1927).
Diver, C. S., 'Policymaking Paradigms in Administrative Law' (1981) 95 *Harv.LR* 393.
—— 'The Optimal Precision of Administrative Rules' (1983) 93 *Yale LJ* 65.
Domberger, S., 'Economic Regulation through Franchise Contracts' in J. Kay, C. Mayer and D. Thompson (eds.), *Privatisation and Regulation: The UK Experience* (Oxford, 1986).
Downs, A., *Inside Bureaucracy* (Boston, Mass. 1967).
Drake, C. D. and Wright, F. B., *The Law of Health and Safety at Work: A New Approach*, (London, 1982).
Drewry, G., 'Forward from FMI: "The Next Steps" ' [1988] PL 505.
—— 'Mr Major's Charter: Empowering the Consumer' [1993] PL 248.
Dror, Y., 'Muddling Through: "Science" or "Inertia"?' (1964) 24 PAR 153.
—— *Public Policymaking Re-examined* (Scranton, Penn., 1973).
Dunleavy, P., and O'Leary, B., *Theories of the State: The Politics of Liberal Democracy* (London, 1987).
Dunsire, A., *Control in a Bureaucracy* (Oxford, 1978).
—— *Implementation in a Bureaucracy* (Oxford, 1979).
Dworkin, R., *Taking Rights Seriously* (Cambridge, Mass., 1977).
—— *A Matter of Principle* (Cambridge, Mass., 1985).
—— *Law's Empire* (London, 1986).
Eads, G., 'Harnessing Regulation: The Evolutionary Role of White House Oversight' (1981) *Regulation* 18.
—— and Fix, M., 'Regulatory Policy', in J. Palmer and I. Jawhill (eds.), *The Reagan Experiment* (Washington DC, 1982).
Eberlie, R. F., 'The New Health and Safety Legislation of the European Community (1990) 19 ILJ 81.
Economic Council of Canada, *Interim Report: Responsible Regulation* (1979).
Edley, C., *Administrative Law: Rethinking Judicial Control of Bureaucracy* (New Haven, Conn., 1990).
Edwards, G., and Sharkansky, I., *The Policy Predicament* (San Francisco, Ca., 1981).
Edwards, J., and Batley, R., *The Politics of Positive Discrimination* (London, 1978).
Ehrlich, I., and Posner, R., 'An Economic Analysis of Legal Rulemaking' (1974) 4 JLS 257.
Elias, P., 'Closing in the Closed Shop' (1980) 9 ILJ 201.
—— 'Legitimate Expectation and Judicial Review', in J. Jowell and D. Oliver (eds.), *New Directions in Judicial Review* (1988).
Ely, J., *Democracy and Distrust* (Cambridge, Mass., 1980).

Emiliou, N., 'Subsidiarity: An Effective Barrier Against the Enterprises of Ambition?' (1992) 55 ELR 383.

Evans, J. M., 'The Duty to Act Fairly' (1973) 36 MLR 93.

Featherstone, K., 'Jean Monnet and the "Democratic Deficit" in the European Union' (1994) 32 JCMS 149.

Fenn, P., and Veljanovski, C. G., 'A Positive Economic Theory of Regulatory Enforcement' (1988) 98 *Economic Journal* 1055.

Foster, J. F., 'An Advocate Role Model for Policy Analysis' (1980) 8 PSJ 958.

Foulkes, D., *Administrative Law*, 7th edn. (London, 1990).

Freedman, J., *Crisis and Legitimacy* (Cambridge, 1978).

Freidland, M. L. (ed.), *Securing Compliance* (Toronto, 1990).

Friendly, H. J., 'Judicial Control of Administrative Action' (1970) 23 JLE 63.

Frug, G. E., 'Why Neutrality?' (1983) 92 Yale LJ 1591.

—— 'The Ideology of Bureaucracy in American Law' (1984) 97 Harv. LR 1277.

Fuller, L., 'Collective Bargaining and the Arbitrator' (1963) Wis.LR 3.

—— *The Morality of Law* (New Haven, Conn., 1964).

—— 'Mediation: Its Forms and Functions' (1971) 44 South California Rights Review 305.

—— 'The Forms and Limits of Adjudication' (1978) 92 Harv.LR 353.

Gaja, G., Hay, P., and Rotunda, R., 'Legal Techniques for Integration', in Cappelletti *et al.* (eds), *Integration Through Law*, vol. 1, bk. 2 (Berlin, 1986).

Galligan, D. J., 'The Nature and Function of Policies within Discretionary Power' [1976] PL 332.

—— *Discretionary Powers* (Oxford, 1986).

Ganz, G., 'Legitimate Expectation', in C. Harlow (ed.), *Public Law and Politics* (London, 1986).

—— *Quasi-Legislation: Recent Developments in Secondary Legislation* (London, 1987).

Garner, J. F., 'Consultation in Subordinate Legislation' [1964] PL 105.

Genn, H., 'Great Expectations: The Robens Legacy and Employer Self-Regulation', Centre for Socio-Legal Studies, mimeo (Oxford, 1987).

Gerth, H., and Mills, C. W. (eds.), *From Max Weber: Essays in Sociology* (London, 1958).

Gifford, D. J., 'Decisions, Decisional Referents and Administrative Justice' (1972) 37 LCP 3.

Goodin, R. E., 'Welfare, Rights and Discretions' (1986) OJLS 232.

Grabosky, P., and Braithwaite, J., *Of Manners Gentle: Enforcement Strategies of Australian Business Regulatory Agencies* (Melbourne, 1986).

Green, M., 'Cost-Benefit Analysis as a Mirage', in T. Clark, M. Kosten, and J. Miller (eds.), *Reforming Regulation* (1980) 382.

Griffith, J., and Street, H., *Principles of Administrative Law*, 5th edn. (London, 1973).

Gunningham, N., *Pollution, Social Interest and the Law* (London, 1974).

—— *Safeguarding the Worker* (Sydney, 1984).

Habermas, J., *Legitimation Crisis*, trans. T. McCarthy (London, 1976).

Ham, C., *Policy-Making in the NHS* (London, 1981).

—— and Hill, M., *The Policy Process in the Modern Capitalist State* (Brighton, 1984).

Hamilton, R. W., 'Procedures for the Adoption of Rules of General Applicability: The Need for Procedural Innovation in Administrative Rule-making' (1972) 60 Cal.LR 1976.

Hancher, L., '1992 and Accountability Gaps: The Transnuklear Scandal' (1990) 53 MLR 669.

Hansard Society, *Making the Law: The Report of the Hansard Society Commission on The Legislative Process* (London, 1992).

Harden, I., *The Contracting State* (Buckingham, 1992).

—— and Lewis, N., *The Noble Lie: The Rule of Law and The British Constitution* (London, 1986).

Harlow, C. (ed.), *Public Law and Politics* (London, 1986).

—— 'A Community of Interests? Making the Most of European Law' (1992) 55 MLR 331.

—— and Rawlings, R., *Law and Administration* (London, 1984).

—— —— *Pressure Through Law* (London, 1992).

Harrop, J., *The Political Economy of Integration in the EC* (Aldershot, 1989).

Hart, H. L. A., *The Concept of Law* (Oxford, 1961).

Hart Ely, John, *Democracy and Distrust* (Cambridge, Mass., 1980).

Hartley, K., and Maynard, A., *The Costs and Benefits of Regulating New Developments in the UK Pharmaceutical Industry* (London, 1982).

Hartley, T. C., *The Foundations of European Community Law*, 3rd edn. (Oxford, 1994).

Hawkins, K., 'Bargain and Bluff: Compliance Strategy and Deterrence in the Enforcement of Regulation' (1983) 5 LPQ 35–73.

—— *Environment and Enforcement: Regulation and the Social Definition of Pollution* (Oxford, 1984).

—— 'The Prosecution Process', unpublished MS on file at Centre for Socio-Legal Studies, Oxford (1987).

—— 'FATCATS and Prosecution in a Regulatory Agency' (1989) 3 LP 370.

—— 'On Legal Decisionmaking' (1989) 4 *Washington and Lee Law Review* 1161.

—— 'Rule and Discretion in Comparative Perspective: The Case of Social Regulation', (1989) 50 OSLJ.

—— 'Compliance Strategy, Prosecution Policy and Aunt Sally' (1990) 30 BJCrim. 444.

—— 'The Use of Legal Discretion: Perspectives from Law and Social Science', in K. Hawkins (ed.), *The Uses of Discretion* (Oxford, 1992).

—— (ed.), *The Uses of Discretion* (Oxford, 1992).

—— and Hutter, B. M., 'The Response of Business to Social Regulation in England and Wales: An Enforcement Perspective' (1993) 15 LP 199.

—— and Thomas, J. (eds.), *Enforcing Regulation* (Boston, Mass., 1984).

—— —— (eds.), *Making Regulatory Policy* (Pittsburgh, Pen., 1989).

Hayek, F. A., *The Constitution of Liberty* (London, 1960).

Hayhurst, J. D., and Wallington, P., 'The Parliamentary Scrutiny of Delegated Legislation' [1988] PL 547.

Health and Safety Executive, *Plan of Work 1981–2* (London, 1980).

—— *Workplace Health and Safety in Europe* (London, 1991).

Held, D., *Models of Democracy* (Oxford, 1987).

Henkel, M., 'The New Evaluative State' (1991) 69 Pub. Admin. 121.

Hennessey, P., *Whitehall* (London, 1989).

Hepple, B. A., Review of *Discretionary Justice* [1969] CLJ 313.

—— 'The Implementation of the Community Charter of Fundamental Social Rights' (1990) 53 MLR 643.

Hewart, Lord, *The New Despotism* (London, 1929).

Hill, M., 'Some Implications of Legal Approaches to Welfare Rights' (1974) 4 BJSW 189.

—— 'The Policy–Implementation Distinction: A Quest for Rational Control?', in S. Barrett and C. Fudge (eds.), *Policy and Action* (London, 1981).

Hood, C., *The Limits of Administration* (London, 1976).

—— *The Tools of Government* (London, 1983).

—— *Administrative Analysis: An Introduction to Rules, Enforcement and Organisations* (Brighton, 1986).

—— 'A Public Management for All Seasons' (1991) 69 Pub. Admin. 3.

—— and Jackson, M., *Administrative Argument* (Aldershot, 1991).

Howarth, W., 'Poisonous, Noxious or Polluting: Contrasting Approaches to Environmental Regulation' (1993) 56 MLR 171.

Howells, G., 'European Directives: The Emerging Dilemmas' (1991) 54 MLR 456.

Howells, L., 'Worker Participation in Safety' (1974) 3 Ind.LJ 87.

Hutter, B. M., *The Reasonable Arm of the Law?* (Oxford, 1988).

—— 'Regulating Employers and Employees: Health and Safety in the Workplace' (1993) 20 JLS 452.

Jacob, J., 'Lawyers go to Hospital' [1991] PL 255.

Jenkins, K., *et al.*, 'Improving Management in Government: The Next Steps' (HMSO, London, 1988).

Jenkins, W. I., *Policy Analysis: A Political and Organisational Perspective* (London, 1978).

Jergesen, A. D., 'The Legal Requirement of Consultation' [1978] PL 290.

Jones, B. L., *Garner's Administrative Law*, 7th edn. (London, 1989).

Jowell, J. L., 'The Legal Control of Administrative Discretion' [1973] PL 179.

—— *Law and Bureaucracy* (Port Washington, New York, 1975).

—— 'The Limits of the Public Hearing as a Tool of Public Planning' (1978) 21 Ad.LR 123.

—— 'Implementation and Enforcement of Law', in L. Lipson and S. Wheeler (eds.), *Law and the Social Sciences* (New York, 1986).

—— 'The Rule of Law Today', in J. L. Jowell and D. Oliver (eds.), *The Changing Constitution*, 3rd edn. (Oxford, 1994).

—— and Lester, A., 'Beyond Wednesbury: Substantive Principles of Administrative Law' [1987] PL 368.

—— and Oliver, D. (eds.), *The Changing Constitution*, 3rd edn. (Oxford, 1994).

Kagan, R., Regulatory Justice: Implementing a Wage-Price Freeze (New York, 1978).

—— 'Understanding Regulatory Enforcement' (1989) 11 LP 89.

—— and Scholz, J., 'The "Criminology of the Corporation" and Regulatory Enforcement Strategies', in K. Hawkins and J. Thomas (eds.), *Enforcing Regulation* (Boston, Mass., 1984).

Kaiser, J. H., 'Limits to European Community Legislation', in J. Schwarze (ed.), *Legislation for Europe 1992* (1989).

Kelman, S., *Regulating America, Regulating Sweden: A Comparative Study of Occupational Safety and Health Policy* (Cambridge, Mass., 1981).

Kinnersly, P., *The Hazards of Work: How to Fight Them* (London, 1973).

Knoepfel, P., and Weidner, H., 'Formulation and Implementation of Air Quality Control Programmes' (1982) 10 PP 85.

Kolinsky, M., 'Parliamentary Scrutiny of European Legislation' [1975] 10 G & O 46.

Lacey, N., 'The Jurisprudence of Discretion: Escaping the Legal Paradigm', in K. Hawkins (ed.), *The Uses of Discretion* (Oxford, 1992).

—— 'Government as Manager, Citizen as Consumer: The Case of the Criminal Justice Act 1991' (1994) 57 MLR 534.

Landis, J. M., *The Administrative Process* (New Haven, Conn., 1938).

Lasok, D., and Bridge, J., *Law and Institutions of the European Union*, 6th edn. (London, 1994).

—— 'Subsidiarity and the Occupied Field' (1992) 142 NLJ 1228.

Law Commission, 'Administrative Law: Judicial Review and Statutory Appeals (London, 1993).

Layard, R. and Glaister, S. (eds.), *Cost-Benefit Analysis*, 2nd edn. (Cambridge, 1994).

Levitt, R., *Implementing Public Policy* (London, 1980).

Lewis, N., 'The Citizen's Charter and Next Steps: A New Way of Governing' (1993) Pol.Q.316.

—— *How to Reinvent British Government* (London, 1993).

—— 'Regulating Non-Governmental Bodies: Privatisation, Accountability, and the Public–Private Divide', in Jowell and Oliver (eds.), *The Changing Constitution* 2nd edn. (Oxford, 1989).

Lewis, R., 'Codes of Practice on Picketing and Closed Shop Agreements and Arrangements' (1981) 44 MLR 198.

Liebman, L., and Stewart, R., 'Bureaucratic Vision' (1983) 96 Harv.LR 1952.

Lindblom, C. E., 'The Science of Muddling Through' (1959) 19 PAR 79.

Lipset, S. M., *Political Man* (London, 1963).

Lodge, J. (ed.), *The European Community and the Challenge of the Future* (London, 1989).

Long, S. B., 'Social Control: The Civil Law: The Case of Income Tax Enforcement', in H. L. Ross (ed.), *Law and Deviance* (1981).

Loughlin, M., 'Procedural Fairness: A Study of the Crisis in Administrative Law Theory' (1978) 28 University of Toronto LJ 215.

—— *Public Law and Political Theory* (Oxford, 1992).

Lowi, T., *The End of Liberalism* (New York, 1969).

Luhmann, N., *The Differentiation of Society* (New York, 1982).

McAuslan, P., 'Administrative Law, Collective Consumption and Judicial Policy' (1983) 46 MLR 1.

—— and McEldowney, J. (eds.), *Law, Legitimacy and the Constitution* (London, 1985).

McBarnet, D., 'Law and Capital: The Role of Legal Form and Legal Actors' (1984) 12 IJSL 233.

—— 'Law, Policy and Legal Avoidance' (1988) JLS 113.

—— It's Not What You Do, But the Way That You Do It: Tax Evasion, Tax Avoidance and the Boundaries of Deviance', in D. Downes (ed.), *Unravelling Criminal Justice* (London, 1991).

—— and Whelan, C., 'The Elusive Spirit of the Law: Formalism and the Struggle for Legal Control' (1991) 54 MLR 848.

—— —— 'Beyond Control: Law, Management and Corporate Governance', in J. McCaherty, S. Picciotto, and C. Scott (eds.), *Corporate Control and Accountability* (Oxford, 1993).

McCaherty, J., Picciotto, S., and Scott, C. (eds.), *Corporate Control and Accountability* (Oxford, 1993).

MacCormick, D. N., *Legal Reasoning and Legal Theory* (Oxford, 1978).

McCrudden, C., 'The Commission for Racial Equality: Formal Investigations in the Shadow of Judicial Review', in R. Baldwin and C. McCrudden, *Regulation and Public Law* (London, 1987).

—— 'Codes in a Cold Climate: Administrative Rulemaking by the Commission for Racial Equality' (1988) 51 MLR 409.

—— 'The Northern Ireland Fair Employment White Paper: A Critical Assessment' (1988) 17 ILJ 162.

McEldowney, J., 'Contract Compliance and Public Audit as Regulatory Strategies in the Public Sector', paper to Citizen's Charter Conference, University of Warwick, 23 Sept. 1993.

McGarity, T. O., *Reinventing Rationality: The Role of Regulatory Analysis in the Federal Bureaucracy* (Cambridge, 1991).

—— 'Some Thoughts on Deossifying the Rulemaking Process' (1992) 41 Duke LJ 1385.

—— and Shapiro, S., *Workers at Risk: The Failed Promise of the Occupational Safety and Health Administration* (Westport, Conn., 1993).

McGee, A., and Weatherill, S., 'The Evolution of the Single Market: Harmonisation or Liberalisation?' (1990) 53 MLR 578.

Macpherson, C. B., *The Life and Times of Liberal Democracy* (Oxford, 1977).
Majone, G., *Evidence, Argument and Persuasion in the Policy Process* (New Haven, Conn., 1989).
—— 'The European Community Between Social Policy and Social Regulation' (1993) 31 JCMS 153.
Maltby, N., '*Marleasing*: What is all the Fuss About?' (1993) 109 LQR 301.
Markovits, R., 'Antitrust: Alternatives to Delegalisation', in G. Teubner (ed.), *Juridification of Social Spheres* (Berlin, 1987).
Mashaw, J., 'Administrative Due Process: The Quest for a Dignitary Theory' (1981) 61 BULR 885.
—— *Bureaucratic Justice* (New Haven, Conn., 1983).
Matthews, D. and Mayes, D. G., *The Role of Soft Law in the Evolution of Rules for a Single European Market: The Case of Retailing*, National Institute of Economic and Social Research, Discussion Paper No. 61 (London, 1994).
Mayne, J., 'Public Power Outside Government' (1993) 64 Pol.Q. 327.
Mayntz, R., 'The Conditions of Effective Public Policy' (1983) 11 PP 123.
Mazey, S., and Richardson, J. J., 'Interest Groups in the European Community', in J. J. Richardson (ed.), *Pressure Groups* (London, 1993).
—— —— 'British Pressure Groups in the European Community' (1992) Parliamentary Affairs 92.
—— —— *Lobbying in the European Community* (Oxford, 1993).
Megarry, R. E., 'Administrative Quasi-Legislation' (1944) 60 LQR 125.
Meltsner, A., *Policy Analysts in the Bureaucracy* (Berkeley, Ca., 1976).
Mendeloff, J., *Regulating Safety* (Cambridge, Mass., 1979).
Miers, D., and Page, A., *Legislation*, 2nd edn. (London, 1990).
Miller, J., and Yandle, B., *Benefit-Cost Analysis of Social Regulation* (Washington, DC, 1979).
Mishan, E. J., *Cost Benefit Analysis*, 2nd edn. (London, 1982).
Mitnick, B. M., *The Political Economy of Regulation* (New York, 1980).
Molot, H., 'The Self-Created Rule of Policy and Other Ways of Exercising Administrative Discretion' (1972) 18 McGill LJ 310.
Morris, P., 'The Direct Effect of Directives: Some Recent Developments: The European Court' (1989) JBL 233.
Morrison, A. B., 'OMB Interference with Agency Rulemaking: The Wrong Way to Write a Regulation' (1986) 99 Harv.LR 1059.
Morrison, H., *Socialisation and Transport* (London, 1933).
Mortelmans, K., 'Minimum Harmonisation and Consumer Law' [1988] ECLJ 2.
Neal, A. C., 'The European Framework Directive on the Health and Safety of Workers: Challenges for the United Kingdom (1990) 6 IJCLLIR 80.
Neunreither, K., 'The Democratic Deficit of the European Union: Towards Closer Cooperation between the European Parliament and the National Parliaments' (1994) 29 *Government and Opposition* 299.
Nichols, T., and Armstrong, P., *Safety or Profits: Industrial Accidents and the Conventional Wisdom* (Bristol, 1973).

Nielsen, R., and Szyszczak, E., *The Social Dimension of the European Community*, 2nd edn. (Copenhagen, 1993).

Noble, C., *Liberalism at Work* (Philadelphia, Pa., 1986).

Nozick, R., *Anarchy, State and Utopia* (Oxford, 1974).

Ogus, A. I., *Regulation: Legal Form and Economic Theory* (Oxford, 1994).

Organization for Economic Co-operation and Development (OECD) *Employment Outlook* (Paris, 1989).

Palmer, J., and Jawhill, I. (eds.), *The Reagan Experiment* (Washington, DC, 1982).

Pateman, C., *Participation and Democratic Theory* (Cambridge, 1970).

—— *The Problem of Political Obligation* (Cambridge, 1985).

Pearce, D. W., *Cost Benefit Analysis*, 2nd edn. (London, 1983).

Pearce, F., and Tombs, S., 'Ideology, Hegemony and Empiricism' (1990) 30 BJCrim. 423.

Pelkmans, J., 'The New Approach to Technical Harmonisation and Standardisation' (1986–7) 25 JCMS 249.

Peltzman, S., 'The Effects of Automobile Regulation' (1975) 83 JPE 677.

Peters, G. H., *Cost-Benefit Analysis and Public Expenditure* (London, 1973).

Polanyi, M., *The Logic of Liberty* (London, 1951).

Pollard, D., and Hughes, D., *Constitutional and Administrative Law*, (London, 1990).

Poulantzas, N., *State, Power, Socialism* (London, 1980).

Pound, R., *Jurisprudence* (St. Paul, Minn., 1959).

Powell, P., *et al.*, *2000 Accidents*, National Institute of Industrial Psychology (UK) Report 21 (London, 1971).

Prechel, S., 'Remedies after *Marshall*' (1990) 27 CMLR 451.

Pressman, J., and Wildavsky, A., *Implementation* (Berkeley, Ca., 1973).

Prosser, T., 'The Politics of Discretion' in M. Adler and S. Asquith (eds.), *Discretion and Welfare* (London, 1981).

Purnell, C., 'The Impact of the COSHH Regulations on the Working Environment' (1992) 1 *International Journal of Regulatory Law and Policy* 205.

Quirk, P. J., *Industry Influence in Federal Regulatory Agencies* (Princetown, NJ, 1981).

Rawlings, R., 'Continuity and Evolution: From Donoughmore to *Justice* via Franks', in M. Citi (ed.), *Il Controllo Giurisdizionale dell' Attivita Amministrativa in Inghilterra* (Milan, 1982).

Rawls, J., *A Theory of Justice* (Oxford, 1971).

Raz, J., *Practical Reason and Norms* (London, 1975).

Reich, C., 'The New Property' (1964) 73 Yale LJ 778.

—— 'Individual Rights and Social Welfare: The Emerging Legal Issues' (1965) 74 Yale LJ 1245.

Reiner, R., *The Politics of the Police*, 2nd edn. (Brighton, 1992).

Reiss, A., and Biderman, A., *Data Sources on White-Collar Law Breaking* (1980).

Reiss, A., Jr., review of *Discretionary Justice* (1970) 69 Mich.LR 792.

Richardson, G., Ogus, A., and Burrows, P., *Policing Pollution* (Oxford, 1983).

Richardson, J. J. (ed.), *Pressure Groups* (Oxford, 1993).
—— and Jordan, A. G., *Governing Under Pressure* (Oxford, 1979).
Robinson, G., 'The Making of Administrative Policy: Another Look at Rulemaking and Adjudication and Administrative Procedure Reform' (1970) 118 UPa.LR 485.
Robson, W. A., 'The Committee on Ministers' Powers' (1932) 3 Pol.Q. 346.
Rubin, E. L., 'Law and Legislation in the Administrative State' (1989) Col.LR 369.
Ryle, M., and Richards, P. G., The Commons under Scrutiny, 3rd edn. (London, 1988).
Sabatier, P., and Mazmanian, D., 'The Conditions of Effective Implementation: A Guide to Accomplishing Policy Objectives' (1979) Policy Analysis 481.
Saphire, R. B., 'Specifying Due Process Values: Towards a More Responsive Approach to Procedural Protection' (1978) 127 UPa.LR 111.
Saunders, A. B., and Benson, D. A., *The Practical Application of Social Costing in Road Safety Policy Making* (1975).
Schauer, F., *Playing By The Rules* (Oxford, 1991).
Schneider, C. E., 'Discretion and Rules: A Lawyer's View', in K. Hawkins (ed.), *The Uses of Discretion* (Oxford, 1992).
Schuck, P. H., 'Regulation, Non-Market Values and the Administrative State: A Comment on Professor Stewart' (1983) 92 Yale LJ 1602.
Schwartz, B., and Wade, H. W. R., *Legal Control of Government* (Oxford, 1992).
Schwarze, J. (ed.), *Legislation for Europe 1992* (1989).
—— *et al.*, *The 1992 Challenge at National Level: Reports and Conference Proceedings* (Baden-Baden, 1990).
Scott, C., 'Rules versus Discretion in the New Public Sector', paper to Citizen's Charter Conference, University of Warwick, 23 Sept. 1993.
Seidenfeld, M. 'A Civic Republican Justification for the Bureaucratic State (1992) 105 Harv.LR 1512.
Self, P., *Administrative Theories and Politics*, 2nd edn. (London, 1978).
Selznick, P., *TVA and the Grass Roots* (1949).
Sevenster, H., 'The Titanium Dioxide Case' (1991) 2 *Utilities Law Review* 133.
Shapiro, D. L., 'The Choice of Rulemaking or Adjudication in the Development of Agency Policy' (1965) 78 Harv.LR 921.
Shapiro, M., 'Administrative Discretion: The Next Stage' (1983) 92 Yale LJ 1487.
Sharfman, I. L., *The Interstate Commerce Commission* (New York, 1931).
Shavell, S., 'Liability for Harm Versus Regulation of Safety' (1984) 13 JLS 357.
—— 'A Model for the Optimal Use of Liability and Safety Regulation' (1984) 15 Rand Journal of Economics 271.
—— 'The Optimal Structure of Law Enforcement' (1993) Journal of Law and Economics 255.
Shiffrin, S., 'Liberalism, Radicalism and Legal Scholarship' (1983) 30 UCLA Law Review 1103.

Siedentopf, H., and Ziller, J. (eds.), *Making European Policies Work: The Implementation of Community Legislation in the Member States* (London, 1988).

Simon, H., *Administrative Behaviour*, 3rd edn. (New York, 1976).

Smith, G., 'Discretionary Decisionmaking in Social Work', in M. Adler and S. Asquith (eds.), *Discretion and Welfare* (London, 1981).

—— and May, D., 'The Artificial Debate between Rationalist and Incrementalist Models of Decision Making' (1980) 8 PP 147.

Snyder, F., 'The Effectiveness of European Community Law: Institutions, Processes, Tools and Techniques' (1993) 56 MLR 19.

Somsen, H., 'Case C-300/69, *Commission* v. *Council (Titanium Dioxide)*' (1992) 29 CMLR 140.

Steiner, J., 'Coming to Terms with EEC Directives' (1992) 55 MLR 215.

Stettmen, J. M., and Daum, S. M., *Work is Dangerous to your Health* (1973).

Stewart, R., 'Regulation in a Liberal State: The Role of Non-Commodity Values', (1983) 92 *Yale LJ* 1357.

Stewart, R., 'The Discontents of Legalism: Interest Group Relations in Administrative Regulation' (1985) Wis.LR 685.

Stewart, R. B., 'Regulation and the Crisis of Legalisation in the United States', in T. C. Daintith (ed.), *Law as an Instrument of Economic Policy: Comparative and Critical Approaches* (Berlin, 1988).

—— 'The Reformation of American Administrative Law' (1975) 88 *Harv.LR* 1667.

Steyger, E., 'European Community Law and the Self-Regulatory Capacity of Society' (1993) 31 JCMS 171.

Strauss, A. L., *Negotiations* (San Francisco, 1978).

Strauss, P. L., 'Some Comments on Rubin' (1989) 89 *Col.LR* 427.

Sunstein, C. R., 'Cost Benefit and the Separation of Power' (1981) 23 *Arizona LR* 1267.

Surry, J., *Industrial Accident Research: A Human Engineering Appraisal* (Toronto, 1969).

Sutherland, P. *et al.*, *The Internal Market After 1992: Meeting the Challenge*, Report to the EEC Commission by the High Level Group on the Operation of the Internal Market ('The Sutherland Report') (Brussels, 1992).

Szyszczak, E., 'Sovereignty: Crisis, Compliance, Confusion, Complacency?' (1990) 15 ELR 480.

—— 'L'Espace Sociale Européen: Reality, Dreams or Nightmare?' (1991) GYIL 284.

—— 'European Community Law: New Remedies, New Directions' (1992) 55 MLR 690.

—— '1992 and the Working Environment' (1992) 1 IJSWFL 3.

Tettenborn, A. M., 'Prisoners' Rights' [1980] PL 74.

Teubner, G., ' "After Legal Instrumentalism": Strategic Models of Post-Regulatory Law', EUI Working Paper no. 100 (Florence, 1984).

—— 'Juridification—Concepts, Aspects, Limits, Solutions' in id. (ed.), *Juridification of Social Spheres* (Berlin, 1987).

—— *Juridification of Social Spheres* (Berlin, 1987).

Titmuss, R. M., 'Welfare "Rights" Law and Discretion' (1971) 42 Pol.Q. 113.

Toth, A. G., 'The Principle of Subsidiarity in the Maastricht Treaty' (1992) 29 CMLR 1079.

Tribe, L., 'Structural Due Process' (1975) 10 Harv.LR 269.

Tucker, E., *Administering Danger in the Workplace* (Toronto, 1990).

Twining, W., and Miers, D., *How to Do Things With Rules*, 3rd edn. (London, 1991).

Unger, R., *Knowledge and Politics* (New York, 1975).

—— *Law in Modern Society* (New York, 1976).

United States General Accounting Office, *Improved Quality, Adequate Resources and Consistent Oversight Needed if Regulatory Analysis is to Help Control Costs of Regulations* (Washington, DC, 1982).

Van Meter, D. S., and Van Horn, C. E., 'The Policy Implementation Process: A Conceptual Framework' (1975) *Administration and Society* 445.

Veljanovski, C. G., 'Regulatory Enforcement: An Economic Study of the British Factory Inspectorate' (1983) 5 LPQ 75.

—— 'The Economics of Regulatory Enforcement', in K. Hawkins and J. Thomas (eds.), *Enforcing Regulation* (Boston, Mass., 1984).

Verwilghen, M., *Equality in Law Between Men and Women in the European Community* (Louvain-la-Neuve, 1986).

Vignes, D., 'The Harmonisation of National Legislation and the EEC' (1990) 15 ELR 358.

Viscusi, W. K., 'The Impact of Occupational Safety and Health Regulation' (1979) 10 BJE 117.

Vogel, D., *National Styles of Regulation: Environmental Policy in Great Britain and the United States* (Ithaca, 1986).

Vogel-Polsky, E., 'What Future Is There for a Social Europe Following the Strasbourg Summit?' (1990) 19 ILJ 65.

Wade, H. W. R., *Administrative Law*, 6th edn. (Oxford, 1988).

Walkland, S., and Ryle, M. (eds.), *The Commons Today* (London, 1981).

Watson, P., 'The Community Social Charter' (1991) 28 CMLR 37.

Weatherill, S., *Cases and Materials on EEC Law* (London, 1992).

—— 'Regulating the Internal Market: Result Orientation in the House of Lords' (1992) 17 ELR 299.

—— 'Subsidiarity and Responsibility' (1992) 6 University of Nottingham Research Papers in Law.

—— and Beaumont, P., *EC Law* (London, 1993).

Weber, M., *Economy and Society* (New York, 1968).

Weekly, H. L., *Organisational Intelligence* (1967).

Weiler, P., 'Two Models of Judicial Decision-making' (1968) 46 Can.BR 406.

Wellens, K. C., and Borchardt, G. M., 'Soft Law in European Community Law' (1989) 14 ELR 267.

White, L. J., *Reforming Regulation-Process and Problems* (Englewood Cliffs, 1981)

Whittaker, A. M. 'Legal Technique in City Regulation' (1990) Current Legal Problems 35.

Wilke, M., and Wallace, H., 'Subsidiarity: Approaches to Power-sharing in the European Community', RIIA Discussion Paper no. 27 (1990).

Williams, D. W., 'Extra-Statutory Concessions' (1979) 3 BTR 137.

Williams, S., 'Sovereignty and Accountability in the European Community' (1990) 61 Pol.Q. 299.

Williamson, O., *The Economic Institutions of Capitalism* (London, 1988).

Wilson, G. K., *The Politics of Safety and Health* (Oxford, 1985).

Woolf, A. D., 'Robens Report: The Wrong Approach?' (1973) 2 Ind.LJ 88.

Woolf, H., 'Public Law, Private Law: Why the Divide? A Personal View' [1986] PL 220.

—— 'A Possible Programme for Reform' [1992] PL 221.

Young, K., ' "Values" in the Policy Process' (1977) 5 PP 1.

—— and Mills, L., *Public Policy Research: A Review of Qualitative Methods* (London, 1980).

Zander, M., *The Law-Making Process*, 4th edn. (London, 1994).

—— *The Police and Criminal Evidence Act 1984*, 2nd edn. (London, 1990).

Zellick, G., 'The Prison Rules and the Courts' [1981] Crim.LR 602.

—— 'The Prison Rules and the Courts: A Postscript' [1982] Crim.LR 589.

Index

Accessibility, 10–11
Accountability claims, 43
  in Europe, 273–83
  secondary legislation, and, 65–74
  tertiary rules, and, 107–11
Administrative law
  Richard Stewart on, 33–6
Administrative Procedure Act 1946, 77–80
Allen, C.K., 91
Ambient standards, 175
Asimow, M., 112

Bardach, Eugene, and Kagan, Robert
  over-regulation, on, 29, 182–4
Barrett, S. and Fudge, C., 164–5
Bench-marks
  establishment of, 300
Braybrooke, D., and Lindblom, C.E., 210
By-laws, 62

California Adult Authority, 26
Capital Markets, 32
Citizens Charter, 30, 34, 119
Codes of practice, 105–6
Commendatory rules, 83
Compliance, 143–74
  across the board regulation, 162
  administrative notices, and, 146–7
  advice, and, 152–3
  anti-formalistic approach, 187
  creative, 185–9
  devolution of discretion, 184
  ease of prosecution, 160–1
  education, and, 153
  enforcement costs, 170
  Factory Inspectorate, 143–57
  formalism, 188
  Health and Safety Executive, 143–57
  inclusiveness, problems of, 175–85
  information, and, 154–6
  intelligibility of packages, 161
  key hazards, and, 157–8
  level of performance, 176
  misformulation, and, 175–85
  negotiation, and, 148–52
  pattern of ideologies, 169–70
  penalty systems, and, 184–5
  persuasion, and, 148–52
  policy-making, and, 164–7
  political constraints, 169–74
  precision of rules, 179–81
  prerequisites for effective agency implementation, 171–2
  process, problem of, 167–9
  promoting, and, 154–6
  prosecution and, 146–7, 178
  regulatory ratchet, 183
  rule-types, 143–57
  securing, 143–74
  securing results, 174–89
  seeking, 143–57
  self-assessment, 162–4
  self-regulation, 162–4
  size of packages, 161
  standards based on reasonableness, 160
  steps to encourage rules conducive to, 173–4
  targeting of enforcement priorities, 158–9
  tax and accountancy fields, 188
  top-down approach, 164–7
Compliance Cost Assessments, 196–9, 204, 207
Compliance-oriented approach to rules, 157–9
Compliance-seeking
  achieving results, and, 302–3
Compliance-seeking strategies, 12
Contract, government by, 110–11
Contracting state, 111
Cost-Benefit Analysis, 193–216
Courts
  secondary legislation, and, 72–4
Craig, Paul
  democratic theory, 49
  European decision-making, 272
Criminal Injuries Compensation Board, 95–6

Daintith, Terence
  dominium and *imperium*, on, 293
Davis, Kenneth Culp
  concept of justice, 21–2

Davis, Kenneth Culp (*cont.*):
discretion, on, 5, 19–24
'legalistic' case for rule-making, 19–24
openness in government, on, 22
Decision-making, nature of, 24–6
arbitrary, 25
capricious, 25
'discrete' notion of decisions, 26
parole, 25
Democratic theory
legitimacy, and, 49–57
Denning, Lord
Immigration Rules, on, 90
Local Review Committee Rules 1967, on, 88–9
Deregulation Units, 197–8
Design standards, 175
Developing rules, 117–18
Dimensions of rules, 7–11
Directives, 61, 222–25
Disclosure of rules, 114–17
Discretion, 16–58
Kenneth Culp Davis on, 19–24
meaning, 16–17
Dispensing power, 11–12
Diver, Colin
precision of rules, on, 179–81, 190
Donoughmore Committee, 60, 62
Due process
claims 44
in Europe 233–85
secondary legislation, and, 74–80
tertiary rules, and, 111–19

Eclectic liberalism, 52–54
Economic appraisals, 193–216
accountability, 199, 202–4
accuracy, 210–11
administering, 208
appraisal of, 199–212
assessment of, 212–16
Britain, in, 196–9
British method, 214
case for, 214–16
compliance cost assessments, 197–8
cost, 209
cost-benefit analysis, 194
data constraints and measurement, 206–8
benefits, 208
intangibles, 208
procedures and strategies, 206–7
quality of data, 207
delay, 211
Deregulation Unit, 197–8
development of strategy, 193–9
diffusion of accountability, and, 203–4
distributional impacts, 205–6
due process, 199–200, 202–4
efficiency, 200, 204–12
Enterprise Unit, 196–7
expertise, 200, 202–4
impact statements, 194–5
legislative mandate, 199, 200–2
London public transport, 201–2
Office of Management and Budget, 196
politics of, 202–4
regulatory analysis, and, 201–2
Regulatory Impact Analysis, 195–6
resistance to, 211–12
staff, 209
USA experience, 193–6
Efficiency claims, 46
in Europe, 287
secondarly legislation, and, 62–4
tertiary rules, and, 85–6
Ehrlich, Isaac, and Posner, Richard
economic analysis of legal rule-making, 177–9
Emission standards, 175
Employer-types, 151–2
Enabling rules, 11
Enforcement *see* Compliance
Enterprise Unit, 196–7
Ethical liberalism, 50
European Community *see* European Union
European Union, 219–8
accountability, 273–83
administrative agencies, 286
array of rules, 219–30
assessing rules, 271–87
central control over implementation, 264
centralized approach to control, 269
compliance costs approach, 260–2
consistency in application of law, 266–7
control, 273–83
co-ordinating functions, 267
Decisions, 225–6
enforcement, 226
tactical issues, 231–2
Declarations, 229
democratic influence, 275
democratic legitimation, 272–3
development of health and safety regulation, 254–7

Action Programmes, 255–6
civil justice, and, 258–9
enforcement processes, 259–60
governmental and legal systems, 257–8
internal market, and, 256–7
legal implementation, 260
legal standards, 259
modes of proof, 259
regulatory disparate regimes, 257–60
remedies, 258–9
sanctions, 258–9
differential access, 284–5
Directives, 222–5
'aspect Directives', 234–5
direct effect, 224–5
form and design, 231–48
harmonization, and, 235–6
health and safety, 238–40
indirect effect, 225
international competitiveness, and, 237–8
legal basis, 223
minimum harmonization, 240
mutual recognition, and, 235
New Approach to, 233–41
scope, 241–8
subsidiarity, 241–8
Titanium Dioxide case, 223–4
due process, 283–5
effectiveness, 287
effectiveness of regulation, 260–3
'effectiveness' test, 243
efficiency, 287
enforcing rules, 252–71
enforcement actions, 266
European Parliament, 273–7
European Standing Committees, 279–80
even-handed regimes, 253
evenness of regulation, 260–3
expertise, 285–6
fairness to affected parties, 284–5
founding Treaties, 220
Framework Directives, 238–40
implementation, 252–71
improving evenness and effectiveness of implementation, 263–71
informational difficulties, 265
initiatives on implementations, 268–9
injury and disease statistics, 262–3
issues of form and design, 230–52
joint declarations, 229
legal control, 282–3
legislative mandate, 271–3
measurement of compliance, 260–3
monitoring arrangements, 269–70
Maastricht Treaty, 244
'no regulation', 242
obtaining documents, 281
parliaments, of Member States, role of, 278
partial regulation, 242
primary rules, 220
recommendations, 228–9
Regulations, 220–1
tactical issues, 231–2
Resolutions, 227–8
results of ESC scrutiny, 281–2
rule-choices, 231–52
secondary rules, 220–6
selecting rules, 230–52
selection of form of rule, 263–4
'soft laws', 226–30, 248–52
speculative legislation, 270–1
'spillover' concept, 243–4
Standing Committee of Experts, 268
subsidiarity, 242–48
enforcement of principles, 247
socio-political term, as, 248
tertiary rules, 226–30, 248–52
domestic jurisdiction, and, 250
expectation of conformity to, 251
framework for negotiation, as, 250
industrial relations, 249
internal organizations, and, 251
state conduct, and, 250
UK scrutiny of legislation, 278–9
weakness in legitimation, 277
Evaluating governmental processes, 33–57
democracy, and, 38–9
legitimacy of administrative process, 39–40
nominalist thesis, 36–7
process values, search for, 33–41
Evidential rules, 82–3, 103–6
Expertise claims, 45
in Europe, 285–7
secondary legislation, and, 62–4
tertiary rules, and, 85–6

Factory Inspectorate, 143–57
advice, 152–3
education, 153–4
informing, 154–7
negotiation, 148–52
notices, 146–7
persuasion, 148–52

Factory Inspectorate (*cont.*):
- powers of inspectors, 144–6
- promoting, 154–7
- prosecutions, 146–7

Freedom of information
- tertiary rules, and, 109–10

Frug, Gerald
- democratic theory, 51
- justifying bureaucracy, 42

Galligan, Denis, 191
- *Discretionary Powers*, 37–9

Ganz, Gabriele, 11, 59
- legal form, on, 8

Gifford, Daniel,
- repetition of decisions, on, 24

Governmental strategies, 291–9
- authority, 293
- incentive-based schemes, 297–8
- modality, 293
- organization, 293
- respective virtues of different procedural devices, 298–9
- rules, and, 294–5
- treasure, 293

Guidelines for rule-makers, 189–91
- effectiveness, 189–91

Gunningham, N.
- health and safety at work, on, 135–8

Hansard Society, 120
- secondary legislation, on, 71

Hard-look review, 80

Harlow, Carol
- European Parliament, on, 276–7

Hawkins, Keith
- discretion, on, 16–17

Hayhurst, J.D., 59

Health and safety at work, 125–41
- Act of 1974, 128–9
- administrative sanctioning, 130–1
- advice and assistance, 129
- agency rule-making, 139–40
- appraisal of Robens design, 133–8
- Approved Code of Practice, 131–3
- competitive industries, and, 135
- costs, and, 136
- demands for reform, 126
- enforcement, 130
- European dimension, 254–60
- European Agency for Safety and Health at Work, 268
- evolution of regulatory system, 125–41
- guidance note, 133
- health hazards, 136
- identity of interest between employers and employees, 133–4
- ill-intentioned ill-informed employer, 149
- incentives to avoid accidents, 134–5
- legacy of Robens Report, 139–40
- minor hazards, 149–50
- nature of employers, and, 137
- origins of regulation, 125–6
- problematic employer, 149
- regulations, 131, 132
- Robens, Report, 126–8
  - implementation, 128–9
  - institutional arrangements, 127
  - overall regulatory strategy, 127–8
  - rules, and, 129–33
  - self-regulation, 127
- role of criminal law, 130–1
- serious or major hazards, 150
- tripartism, 139–40
- voluntary codes, 129–30
- well–intentioned ill–informed employer, 149
- well–intentioned well–informed employer, 148–9

Health and Safety at Work Act 1974, 9

Health and Safety Commission, 128–9

Health and Safety Executive, 128–9, 143–57
- advice, 152–3
- education, 153–4
- hierarchy of rule-types, 144–5
- informing, 154–7
- making rules for others, 172
- negotiation, 148–52
- notices, 146–7
- persuasion, 148–52
- powers of inspectors, 144–6
- promoting, 154–7
- prosecutions, 146–7
- support for, 172

'Henry VIII' clauses, 64–5

Hepple, B., 268

Highway Code, 9, 82–3, 103–4

Hill, Michael
- policy-implementation distinction, on, 169

Hood, Christopher
- New Public Management, on, 31
- tools of government, on, 292–5

Hood, Christopher, and Jackson, Michael
- *Administrative Argument*, 39–40

Immigration Rules, 87, 89–90
Inclusiveness, 11, 175–85
Informal rules
  legal effects, 9
Instructions to officials, 82
Intelligibility, 10–11
Interpretative guides, 81

Joint Committee on Statutory Instruments, 67–70
Jowell, Jeffrey
  rule of law, on, 18–19
  rules as shields, 27
Judicial review,
  secondary legislation, and, 72–4
Justice, concept of, 21
  pursuit of, 22–4

Kinnersly, Patrick
  health and safety at work, on, 133–4

Lacey, Nicola
  rule of law, on, 17–18
Landis, James M.,
  expertise model, on, 35
Laying procedures, 66–8
Legal force or effect, 9
Legal form
  labels, 8
Legalistic case for rules, 19–33
Legislative mandate claims, 43
  in Europe, 271–3
  secondary legislation, and, 64–5
  tertiary rules, and, 86–106
Legitimacy
  democratic theory, and, 49–57
Legitimacy claims, 41–9
  accountability, 43–4
  assessment of merits, 55
  control, 43–4
  due process, 44
  efficiency, 46
  expertise, 45–6
  five rationales for, 41–6
  language of legitimacy, 48
  mandate, 43
  nature of, 47–9
  trade-off between two or more types, 55–6
Legitimate expectations, 98–101
Local Authority Orders, 62
Lodge, Juliet, 274–5
Long, Susan
  analysis of US tax laws, 23
Loughlin, M., 7
Luhmann, Niklas
  legitimacy claims, on, 54

Maastricht Treaty, 244
McBarnet, Doreen
  creative compliance, on, 185–9
McGarity, T.O.
  economic appraisals, on, 193–4
Making rules work, 142–92
Mashaw, Jerry
  Bureaucratic Justice, 40
  professional treatment, on, 45
Mayntz, Renate
  processes, on, 291–2
Merits Committee, 70–1

Natural Justice
  tertiary rules, and, 101–2
Next Steps programme, 30, 31, 82
New Deal, 35
New Public Management, 29–31
Notice and comment procedures, 77–80

Open government, 110, 118–19
Orders, 61
Orders in Council, 61

Parole
  decision-making, 25
Pelkmans, J., 234–5, 237
Picketing code, 83, 104–5
Police and Criminal Evidence Act 1984, 9
Political constraints
  compliance, and, 169–74
Posner, R., 177
Precision, 10
Prescription, 10
Prescriptive rules, 82
Primary rules
  potential legitimacy claims, 306–8
Prison Rules, 93–4
Privatization
  tertiary rules, and, 110–11
Procedural rules, 81
Process values, 33–41
Processes, 291–9

Regulation, its reform, 295–8
Reiss, Albert J. Jr.,
  failure of rules, on, 23
Rights and rules, 26–7
Rimington, J., 146–7

Robens Report, 126–141
Rule
  duty to adhere to, 98–101
  meaning, 7
Rule of law, 17–19
Rule-makers, why they fail, 159–174
Rules, uses of, 11–15
  as shields, 27
  process problems, 167
  political constraints, and, 169–73
  precision of, 179–81
  misformulations of, 175–85
Rules, discretion and legitimacy, 16–58
    see also Discretion; legitimacy
Rules made by governments, 59–121
Rules of practice, 84–5
Rules, rights and protections, 26–8
Rule-types
  compliance, and, 143–57
  Government, and, 7–15
Rules versus discretion approach, 17–33
  legal paradigm, 17–19
  'new public management', 29–31
  polycentric issues, 29
  procedural justice, 27
  rule of law, 17–19
  rules, rights and protections, 26–8
  service delivery, and, 30–31
  structuring, feasibility of, 28–33

Sabatier, P. and Mazmanian, D., 171
Sanction, 10
Scope, 11
Secondary legislation, 60–80
  accountability, 65–74
  basic procedure, 76–7
  by-laws, 62
  consultation, and, 74–6
  control, 65–74
  courts, and, 72–4
  directives, 61
  due process, 74–80
  efficiency, 62–4
  expertise, 62–4
  Hansard Society on, 71
  history, 60–1
  Joint Committee on Statutory
    Instruments, 67–70
  judicial review, and, 72–4
  justifications for, 62–80
  laying procedures, 66–8
  legislating by reference, 69
  legislative mandate, 64–5
  Local Authority Orders, 62
  meaning, 59–60
  Merits Committee, 70–1
  nomenclature, 62
  notice and comment procedures, 77–8
  orders, 61
  Orders In Council, 61
  regulations, 61
  Special Procedure Orders, 61–2
  will of Parliament, and, 64–5
Secondary rules, 4
  European Union, 220–6
  potential legitimacy claims, 306–8
Securing compliance, 143–74 *see also*
    Compliance
Self-assessments, 162–4
Self, Peter
  politics of participation, 167–8
Self-regulation, 161–4
Shapiro, David, 298–9
Sharfman, I.L.,
  Interstate Commerce Commission, on,
    24
Shiffrin, S.
  ethical liberalism, on, 50, 52, 53
Shore, Peter
  subsidiarity, on, 245
'Soft law', 226–30, 248–52
Specification standards, 175
Specificity, 10
Special Procedure Orders, 61–2
Standards, types of, 175–6
Statutory Instruments, 8–9, 61
Stewart, Richard
  administrative law, on, 33–6
  crisis of legislation, on, 295–6
Structuring, 28–33
Subsidiarity, 242–8
Sunstein, C., 200

Targeting, 158–9
Technical advantages of rules, 12–14
Tertiary rules, 4, 80–121
  accountability, 107–11
  codes of practice, 105–6
  commendatory rules, 83
  compulsory rule-making, 118–19
  contracts between public bodies and
    service providers, 101
  control, 107–11
  Criminal Injuries Compensation
    Scheme, 95–6
  degree of precision, 88–9
  differing roles, 90–1
  disclosure of relevant policy, 116

due process, 111–19
duty to adhere to, 98–101
duty to develop, 117–19
duty to publish, 114–17
efficiency, 85–6
European Union, 248–52
evidential role, 103–6
evidential rules, 82–3
expectations, 91–8
expertise, 85–6
fairness, 99–100
freedom of information, and, 109–10
Highway Code, 103–4
Immigration Rules, 87, 89–90
implied legitimate expectations, 92–3
instructions to officials, 82
interpretative guides, 81
judicial scrutiny, 109
justifications for, 85–119
language of, 89
legal force, 86–106
legislative mandate, 86–106
natural justice, and, 101–2
parliamentary scrutiny, 107–8
Picketing Code, 104
positive role of, 119–20
post-adoption procedure, 113–14
potential legitimacy claims, 306–8
prescriptive rules, 82
Prison Rules, 93–4
privatization, and, 110–11
procedural, 101–3
procedural rules, 81
reasonableness, 91–8
reasonableness tests, 97–8
rules of practice, 84–5
statutory duty to consult, and, 112–13
statutory standards for control, 108
unfair non-disclosure, 114–17
vires, 91–8
voluntary codes, 83–4
voluntary governmental action, and, 118–19
Titmuss, R.M., 27
Top-down approach, 164–7
Tripartism, 139–40

Unger, Robert
formal notion of justice, on, 28–9
Uses of Rules, 11–12

Van Meter, D.S. and Van Horn, C.E., 171
Voluntary codes, 83–4, 129–30

Weatherill, S., 246–8
Wellens, K.C. and Borchardt, G.M., 250
Whelan, Christopher, 186, 188
White paper on Open Government July 1993, 118–19
Williams, Shirley
European Parliament, on, 274–5
Woolf, A.D.,
Robens Report, on, 138

Zellick, Graham
Prison Rules, on, 94–5

F

Factual conditionals, 115
  meaning of (C 5.4A), 117
  verb tenses for (C 5.4B), 118
Feedback, partner, 190
few, limiting generic nouns with, 82*n*.5
Focus, 187
Fragments
  Chart 2.1A, 28
  Editing Guide for, 152
  editing sentences with (A 2.3), 31
  editing writing for (A 2.4, 2.5, 2.12), 32, 42
  finding/fixing (C 2.1B), 29
  identifying (A 2.2), 30
  and joining words (C 5.1B), 101
Freewriting, 188
Full clauses, for reporting (C 3.3A), 61
Future, the
  expressions/time clauses linked to,
    (C 1.3A, C 1.3B, C 1.3C), 15
Future tense, 33
  active (RC 1.7), 168
  in conditional sentences (C 5.4B), 118
  for reporting (C 4.3), 87
  use of (C 2.3A), 38

G

Generalizations
  analyzing/editing writing for (A 3.3), 56
  analyzing tenses in (A 3.1), 55
  and degree of certainty (A 3.4), 58
  Editing Guide for, 153
  editing writing for (A 3.10, 3.11), 66
  grammar problems/tips for (C 3.1D), 54
  reducing certainty of, (C 3.2) 57–59
  rewriting, for certainty (A 3.5), 59
  tenses for stating, (C 3.1A), 50–56, 52
  writing (A 3.6), 59
Generating ideas
  general questions for, 187
  and ideas from others (A C.1), 189
Generic nouns, 79–84
  Editing Guide for, 155
  editing writing for (A 4.8), 84
  recognizing (A 4.7), 84
  sentences using (A 4.6), 83
  in technology writing (C 4.2B), 82–83
Gerunds, 141, 144*n*.8. *See also* Complements
"*get*" passive, forming (C 4.1), 76
Grammar basics, 1–22. *See also specific topics*
  parts of speech, 5–11
  phrases vs. clauses, 11–13
  subjects, 11–13
  time expressions and verbs, 14–16
  verbs, 11–13
  word forms, 16–21
Grammar Reference Cards, 149
Grammar Reference Charts, 159–184
  basic parts of speech, 159–160
  definite article *the*, 165–166
  determiners, 162
  forms of modal + verb (active), 168
  forms of verb tenses (active), 168
  irregular verbs, 169
  joining words, 183
  noncount nouns, 163–164
  passive forms, 180
  passive uses/special cases, 181–182
  phrases, 170
  prepositions, 173–174
  pronouns, 161
  punctuation of direct quotations, 177
  reduced relative clauses, 184
  reporting verbs, 178–179
  subject-verb agreement, 175–176
  verb forms, 167
  word endings, 171
  word partnerships, 172

H

hardly ever, and generalizations (C 3.2), 58
however, 99
Hypothetical conditionals, 115
  meaning of (C 5.4A), 117
  sentences using past (A 5.14), 119–120
  verb tenses for (C 5.4B), 118

I

Ideas
  generating, 187
  from others (A C.1), 189
if, 115, 119
in contrast, 99
Indefinite pronouns (RC 1.2), 161
Independent clauses, 27–32
  Chart 2.1A, 28
  identifying (A 2.2), 30
  joined (C 5.2), 108
Infinitive phrases (RC 1.10), 170
Infinitives, 141. *See also* Complements
  joined (C 5.2), 108
  passive form of (RC 4.1), 180
  and subject-verb agreement (C 2.2), 34
  verb forms (RC 1.6), 167
Information, adding (A 5.10), 111
-ing words or phrases, 111
  joined (C 5.2), 108
  and subject-verb agreement (C 2.2), 34
Irregular verbs (RC 1.9), 169

J

Joined clauses/phrases/words, 106–111
  parallel structure in (C 5.2), 108
Joining words, 99–111
  analyzing reading for (A 5.1), 103
  choosing (A 5.2), 103
  Editing Guide for, 155–156
  editing sentences with (A 5.5), 105–106
  editing writing for (A 5.11, 5.18), 111, 122
  errors with (A 5.6), 106
  examples/meanings of (C 5.1C), 102
  expanding use of (A 5.4), 105
  function and punctuation of, 99–106
  information about (C 5.1A), 100
  parallel structure for, 106–111
  problems with (C 5.1B), 101
  Reference Chart 5.1, 183
  sentences using (A 5.3), 104

L

little, for limiting generic nouns, 82*n*.5
Looping, 188

M

many
  and generalizations (C 3.2), 58
  for limiting generic nouns, 82*n*.5
Mapping, 187
Markers, complement, 145
may, and generalizations (C 3.2), 57
might, and generalizations (C 3.2), 57
Modals, 168*n*.11
  active (RC 1.8), 168
  be with, 34*n*.4
  and generalizations (C 3.2), 57
  passive (RC 4.1), 180
  Reference Chart 1.1, 160
Modifiers, dangling, 113
most
  and generalizations (C 3.2), 58
  for limiting generic nouns, 82*n*.5
much, for limiting generic nouns, 82*n*.5

N

Noncount nouns, 6
  articles with (C 1.1B), 7
  as determiners (RC 1.3), 162
  Editing Guide for, 155
  generic (A 4.2A), 82
  problems with forms of (C 1.4A), 18
  Reference Chart 1.4, 163–164
  and subject-verb agreement (C 2.2), 34
  in technology writing (C 4.2B), 82–83
Non-finite clauses, 102*n*.8
Nonrestrictive relative clauses, 130
Noun complements
  Chart 6.2B, 143–144
  Editing Guide for, 157
  errors with (A 6.12), 146–147
  writing sentences with (A 6.11), 146
Noun phrases
  joined (C 5.2), 108
  Reference Chart 1.10, 170
  for reporting (C 3.3A), 62
Nouns, 6
  article + noun patterns (A 4.2A), 81–82
  categories of, 6
  and generalizations (C 3.2), 57
  editing for problems with (A 1.4, 1.10),
    10–11, 21
  Editing Guide for, 151, 155
  editing writing for (A 2.12, 4.14, 4.8), 42,
    84, 92
  generic (A 4.6, 4.7), 79–84
  identifying/editing (A 1.5), 11, (A 1.9), 21
  in interview reports (A 4.11), 89
  joined (C 5.2), 108
  prepositions with (RC 2.2), 174
  problems areas for (C 1.1C), 8
  problems with forms of (C 1.4A), 18
  Reference Chart 1.1, 159
  reference for (A 1.1), 9
  specific, 80
  word endings for (RC 1.11), 171
  in technology writing (C 4.2B), 82–83
Numerals, as determiners (RC 1.3), 162

O

often, and generalizations (C 3.2), 58
one of, subject-verb agreement (C 2.2), 34
or, 106

P

Parallel structure, 106–111
  analyzing writing for (A 5.7), 109
  completing sentences with (A 5.9), 110
  Editing Guide for, 156
  editing sentences with (A 5.8), 109–110